MID-MICHIGAN MODERN

MID-MICHIGAN MODERN

FROM FRANK LLOYD WRIGHT TO GOOGIE

SUSAN J. BANDES

EXPANDED EDITION

Michigan State University Press | East Lansing

⊗ The paper used in this publication meets the minimum requirements of ANSI/NISO Z39.48-1992 (R 1997) (Permanence of Paper).

MICHIGAN STATE UNIVERSITY PRESS
East Lansing, Michigan 48823-5245

LIBRARY OF CONGRESS CATALOGING-IN-PUBLICATION DATA
Names: Bandes, Susan J., author.
Title: Mid-Michigan modern : from Frank Lloyd Wright to Googie / Susan J. Bandes.
Description: Expanded Edition. | East Lansing : Michigan State University Press, [2021] | Includes bibliographical references and index.
Identifiers: LCCN 2021001048 | ISBN 9781611862171 (paperback)
Subjects: LCSH: Midcentury modern (Architecture)—Michigan. | Architecture and society—Michigan—History—20th century.
Classification: LCC NA730.M52 M533 2021 | DDC 720.977409/04—dc23
LC record available at https://lccn.loc.gov/2021001048

Book design by Charlie Sharp, Sharp Des!gns, East Lansing, MI
Cover design by Kelly Salchow MacArthur

Michigan State University Press is a member of the Green Press Initiative and is committed to developing and encouraging ecologically responsible publishing practices. For more information about the Green Press Initiative and the use of recycled paper in book publishing, please visit *www.greenpressinitiative.org*.

Visit Michigan State University Press at *www.msupress.org*

Contents

Preface

A casual meeting for coffee in the spring of 2012 started me on the path towards discovering the mid-century architectural legacy in mid-Michigan. At that meeting with staff of the State Historic Preservation Office, I learned about the Michigan Modern project they had begun and the exhibition at the Cranbrook Art Museum planned for two years hence. Their enthusiasm was contagious, and I found myself wondering afterwards how I could contribute to the project. As a first step, I decided to teach an upper-level art history class at Michigan State University in which we would inventory the mid-century architectural legacy of East Lansing. As I prepared for the course, I discovered that usual research resources were nonexistent. There was no central repository for materials; the architectural firms that were active then had closed or merged, and their papers had disappeared. Digging around, I found important information in the Library of Michigan, Archives of Michigan, the Lansing Public Library and regional branches, the City of East Lansing, and various county registers of deeds. The most helpful of all, however, were the people who had stories to tell. After the course, I realized there was much more to uncover and that the task was timely. Many of those involved with architectural projects in the 1950s were getting on in years, and my task was to record information and call attention to this architectural legacy before it was lost.

In spring 2013, I curated an exhibition on East Lansing Modern at the Michigan State University Museum, which opened in May. At the same time, I wrote a biking and driving tour of sixteen buildings in the area, which is downloadable from the Michigan Modern website. As word about the project got out, people contacted me with information as well as suggestions of buildings to include, and interest developed.

Having unearthed so much information and so many significant buildings as well as contextual information, the next logical step was to write a book, but to expand to a larger geographical area in order to include Frank Lloyd Wright's homes in Okemos and buildings in the National Register of Historic Places in Lansing's downtown. This decision opened the floodgates and created the realization that a book like this cannot be comprehensive—as I keep on finding more buildings that could have been included, or pockets of modernist houses that deserve further consideration. But I hope that it inspires the reader to appreciate this period of our architectural history and to look anew at our built environment. Mid-Michigan, in effect, is used as a case study. The discussions of individual projects and the reasons why a client chose a modernist design are specific and individual yet have parallels in many other mid-sized cities. The issues, concerns, and insights will resonate with people across the country.

I have many to thank for their help and encouragement. A large list is included here while others are mentioned in the text. In helping me get started, I thank the SHPO staff (Brian Conway, Laura Ashley, Amy Arnold, and especially Todd Walsh, who was my liaison). Local archivists, librarians, and preservationists Whitney Miller, Jill Abood, David Votta, Heidi Butler, and Ron Springer aided my quest for primary resources, as did Diane Sowash. Numerous people opened their homes to me, trusted me with their blueprints and drawings, allowed me to traipse around with my photographers, and provided invaluable information about their homes. Among them are Pauline Adams, Marcia Aldrich and Richard Isomaki, Joel and Marilyn Aronoff, Peter Berg and Lisa Fine, Roger and Mary Bresnahan, Christine Canfield and Jon Hansen, Kirk Domer, Jim Gibbs, the late Betty Hagberg, the late Addiann Hines, William Jacoby and Sandy Schneider, Jim Perkins, Norm and Nancy Pollack, Audrey and Dan Seidman, Bill and Jan Simpson, Pauline and the late Ted Sondag, Emily Tabuteau, and Bill and Chris Triola. My work in various church archives was facilitated by Reverend David Dressler, Reverend Margie Osborn, and Msgr. George C. Michalek. Additionally, I thank Bill and Linda Demmer for graciously hosting my research trip to Taliesin West.

The large number of color plates and figures illustrating the text required a publication subvention. I am grateful to Michigan State University, Office of the Vice President for Research, for awarding me a HARP Production grant (Humanities and Arts Research Program) that paid for new photography and reproduction images. I was able to hire Kim Kauffman, Ed Bonnen, and Natasha Crljenica, who spent hours with me photographing buildings.

Additional generous funding was provided by many local enthusiasts of modernism: Lori and Harold Emmons, Linda and Bill Demmer, Joe and Kerry Chartkoff, Judith and Jeffrey Kastin, Janet Kreger, Jan and Ron Fedewa, Jane Veith, Jack and Sue Davis, Pauline Adams, Jackie and Seamus Shinners, and the Department of Art, Art History, and Design at Michigan State University.

Alex Nichols was the expert digitizer of old photographs and plans. Amy Lazet and Katelyn Lewis, my able student assistants, took on the daunting task of reading the *Lansing State Journal* on microfiche.

Thanks to my dear friends who were my editors and commentators, Ilene Schechter and Jenny Banks, and Elinor Holbrook, who shares an abiding interest in mid-Michigan modern.

Finally, I thank all of those who patiently listened to stories of my project and whom I infected with the mid-century bug.

As I predicted, after the initial publication of this book, I learned about houses I had not been aware of before. When the MSU Press decided to bring the book out in paperback, I eagerly jumped at the chance to explore more. During the initial research years ago, several students and I read the *Lansing State Journal* on microfilm, which was time-consuming and tedious but necessary as the primary source of information on local architecture. Since then, the historical issues of the journal have been digitized and are searchable. In the time of COVID, when libraries have been closed, this digitalization made research for the new chapter feasible. Early on, I found Virginia Redfern's 1964 article about a pontoon ride on the Grand River in which she described the houses she passed. By coincidence, homeowners of two of them had contacted me, so I decided to use "on the water" as the organizing theme for the chapter. A second criterion was being able to identify the architect of the design. Unfortunately, this is not typically obvious. In real estate ads, builders are often listed as their reputations were better known to people than local architects, with the exception of Frank Lloyd Wright. By putting the puzzle pieces together, I discovered not only architects who were new to me but also architectural designers. The American Institute of Architects (AIA) registered architects have been added to "Appendix 2: Biographies of Architects and Landscape Architects." Another goal was to uncover and include other examples by these architects and designers to better understand their style and to make connections to their clients.

In all of my research, it became obvious that I had not come across any female architects. While this is not surprising, since architecture remains a field dominated by men, I decided to find out if there were any women practicing in mid-Michigan between 1940 and 1970. *The AIA Historical Directory of American Architects* for 1956 lists thirty-one architects in the Lansing area including two women, Anna R. Peters and Florence Dyer Baldwin. The 1962 directory lists forty-five architects: six in East Lansing, four in Okemos, and thirty-five in Lansing; Peters is the lone woman since Baldwin had retired. By 1970, fifty-three architects are listed: forty-two in Lansing, eight in East Lansing, two in Okemos, one in Haslett; again Peters is the only woman. Unfortunately, I have not yet identified examples of their work. Information on both has been added to appendix 2 together with Jane L. Smith, one of the very few practicing landscape architects in the area.

Again, I am grateful to those who enthusiastically shared their homes and knowledge with me for the new chapter in this paperback edition: Yvonne Caamal Canul and Victor Caamal Canul, Bruce Bower and Christine Altese, Barbara Stynes, Birgit Puschner and Charles Laub, Barbara Coey, Gary Scheuren and Hans Schwab, Pia and Wolfgang Banzhaf, Ana Luisa Cardona, Drs. Fedon and Elizabeth Mavromatis, Andrew and Sarah Finley, Erica Murdock and Michael Smokevitch, and Lisa and Jamie Beardslee. Many others including Meegan Holland, Laurie Sommers, Ilene Schechter, Todd Walsh, and especially Elinor Holbrook eagerly aided me. Also, I am very appreciative of the financial support from the Department of Art, Art History and Design, MSU, for Kim Kauffman's new photography and copyright permission costs.

Despite having the opportunity to add many houses in the new chapter, there remains much more to be discovered. My geographical focus remains consistent in the book, but there are pockets of modernist buildings beyond Lansing, East Lansing, and Okemos. Spectacular houses from the period have come to my attention in Grand Ledge and Eagle, for example, and my hope is that these, too, will be the subject of research in the future.

Introduction

There is growing interest around the world in understanding the mid-century modern architecture movement, which evolved during the period of the 1940s through the 1960s. Many architects, such as Charles and Ray Eames and George Nelson, have been admired all along while others are being rediscovered. Recent publications and exhibitions have helped to expand our knowledge of particular geographic areas, architects, and projects. Just a few examples are *Long Island Modernism*, *California Design*, and *Michigan Modern: Design That Shaped America*.[1] This study, which focuses on mid-Michigan, seeks to contribute to the dialogue by considering both world-renowned architects and lesser-known local practitioners. Among these are Frank Lloyd Wright, Minoru Yamasaki, Keck & Keck, and William Kessler. It explores how modernism was received in the area by looking at the motivation behind various commissions and design decisions; the impetus by individuals and families to choose contemporary design over familiar and comfortable houses; the impression or identity businesses and government intended to convey through the use of modernist architecture; and the messages religious institutions sought to project in ecclesiastical structures. This study also calls attention to a wide array of buildings, and records the information unearthed from numerous people and sources so that future researchers can continue the story.

The geographical parameters are closely confined to the center of the state, and specifically to the cities of Lansing and East Lansing and the surrounding suburbs. These restrictions, however, provide ample opportunity to explore innovations in a Midwestern urban area that were likely replicated in other cities of the same size. Yet the specific economics of the region contributed to the reception of modernism. Oldsmobile was headquartered in Lansing, which is also the seat of state government, and East Lansing is home to Michigan State University. In each of these large sectors, there were architects, designers, engineers, artists, and others who embraced modernism.

The reception of "modern" and "modernist" architecture is at the heart of the following discussion. Modern design was defined locally as the use of modern construction techniques such as radiant heat, prefabricated components, and large Thermopane windows. An open plan for the kitchen, living, and dining areas; a one-story ranch design; and the connections between the inside and outside became commonplace in the 1950s and 1960s. Although modern design rarely meant totally embracing the glass and steel aesthetic of Mies van der Rohe or Walter Gropius and the International style, their influence is seen in several examples, such as Lansing City Hall and the retail store designed by George Nelson. However, mid-Michigan did fully embrace Frank Lloyd Wright's ideas of organic architecture and adapted a modified Prairie style for homes as well as small offices. Numerous planar brick banks and office buildings still dot the landscape. Modernist architecture went further than this, though. Houses were often characterized by shed or flat roofs, dynamic plays of open and closed spaces, new uses of the new construction techniques, intentional passive solar heating, and particular attention paid to organic architecture in terms of how the building relates to the site. Although Wright, Nelson, Minoru Yamasaki, Hugh Stubbins Jr., and Keck & Keck, architects of national and international stature, left their mark here, local architectural firms were more frequently hired, and their particular mid-Michigan "lean towards modernism" is what typified the built heritage.

In 1974, fifteen local mid-Michigan architecture firms were asked by a *Lansing State Journal* writer, "Is architecture in Greater Lansing worth boasting about? And as an individual architect, which single building in Lansing turns you on most of all?" Some made disparaging comments such as "architect-designed buildings are mediocre, but improving," or "conservatively bland . . . languishing in the afterbirth of the trend-setters on both coasts." Yet others did find buildings to enthuse about: the Michigan State Medical Society Building (MSMS) by Minoru Yamasaki; the Goetsch-Winckler House by Frank Lloyd Wright; Liebermann's by George Nelson; the Auto-Owners Insurance Building, Lansing City Hall, and the Lansing Public Library by Lee and Kenneth C. Black; and the Michigan Education Association by Warren Holmes Company.[2] Yamasaki and Wright are obvious choices, but who are Kenneth Black and Warren Holmes?[3]

Digging around in various research resources, one can discover that they each headed major architectural firms at mid-century that produced significant buildings that are now landmarks of the area.

The case of Kenneth C. Black (1901–1991) is telling. For much of the twentieth century, he was one of the area's most highly regarded practitioners. After training at the University of Michigan with Eliel Saarinen, he received the prestigious George G. Booth Traveling Fellowship to spend a year studying architecture in Europe, and was headquartered at the American Academy in Rome. He worked in New York from 1926 until 1930, when he returned to Lansing to join his father's architecture practice. Upon his father's retirement, the practice became Kenneth C. Black Associates. In 1973 it merged with the Warren Holmes Company, which subsequently merged with Mayotte, D'Haene and Associates in 1986. This scenario of mergers as well as closures has had the effect of fading memories of the original firms and the roles they played.

In 1947, the *New York Times* reported Kenneth Black's comments in "Calls for Change in Urban Planning," in which he urged the nation's architects to be more attentive to "the elusive quality of humanness and [to] weave it into the physical framework of our cities" by doing away with the artificial grid of streets, unwarranted restrictions and antiquated building codes, and the profit motive. He urged his colleagues to "create an atmosphere of intimacy with human life."[4]

This same architect used the hometown newspaper, the *Lansing State Journal*, to address the community on January 1, 1951, and gently encourage it to embrace modernist architecture.[5] After a brief history of architectural styles in America, he emphasized that as new technologies came along, such as electric lights or furnaces that replaced fireplaces, they had been embraced by all.

> Following the first World War, American architects in increasing numbers began asking themselves, "Isn't it silly to keep on copying historic styles of architecture, when the type of life we live in the United States today bears no resemblance whatever to the life of the people of the Middle Ages? Why not develop a new architecture which will make it possible to use modern materials and equipment as efficiently as possible? . . .
>
> Architects began to seek new solutions to problems in planning and design . . . new types of buildings began to appear, types in which appearance was dictated by a more intelligent use of materials and by a more realistic approach to the needs of modern life . . . The new buildings were actually more pleasant places in which to live and work than the old, even though their appearance bore no resemblance whatever to historic styles of architecture.

> The public flocked to trade in stores and to eat in restaurants where that "modern atmosphere" gave them a feeling of being a part of our dynamic and progressive contemporary life. . . . We can now look forward to the day, in the not too distant future, when contemporary design will be accepted by all classes of people and for all types of buildings. We are . . . marching forward with confidence. The future is a challenge to our creative ability.

Black's buildings in the Lansing area, such as the 1956 International-style City Hall complex that was compared locally to Lever House in New York, and his own 1964 elegant ranch, which exhibits a more decorative trend of modernism, reveal him to be a sophisticated practitioner and steadfast spokesman for modernism in mid-Michigan. While his name may be forgotten, the buildings he designed contribute significantly to the livability and comfortable scale of Lansing's built environment. The case is similar with other mid-century buildings that are part and parcel of the city's personality and appearance. Examples by the other thriving mid-century firms such as Warren Holmes Company; Manson, Jackson & Carver; and Laitala and Nuechterlein will be discussed here.

Lansing's growth spurt was in the years from 1910 to 1930, when demand for automobiles increased and the city became a manufacturing hub for Oldsmobile, General Motors, and affiliated businesses that supported the automobile industry. As the seat of state government, Lansing attracted politicians, lawyers, professional associations, and their staff, who moved to the center of the action, also adding to the city's population. East Lansing's expansion occurred after World War II, due to the presence of Michigan State College, which attracted large numbers of returning veterans funded by the G.I. Bill. They inundated the college, necessitating the quick growth of the faculty and the East Lansing campus, and all required housing. This expansion of the college caused shortages locally in construction materials and temporarily raised construction costs. Nationally the booming population of the 1950s spurred the use of prefabricated materials and the building of thousands of small, clientless designs built on speculation in new subdivisions. Modernist houses, designed by architects for individual clients, were far from the norm, and this remains the case across the country.[6] In the 1940s and early 1950s, they were often sandwiched into small lots within the city limits. With the optimism of the postwar years, greater prosperity and spending, and dependence upon the automobile, however, people moved out to the suburbs and purchased larger lots and built more expansive houses, sometimes with the help of architects.

The increasing interest in and awareness of Michigan's mid-century modernist legacy is due to the critical role played by the State Historic Preservation Office (SHPO), whose Michigan Modern project has done a great service in calling attention to the topic. The Michigan Modern website together with two museum exhibitions and two symposia in 2013 and 2014 have helped to clarify for the record the role Michigan designers played in the movement. The SHPO staff also spearheaded the daunting task of inventorying the state's modernist heritage and has been responsible for researching and nominating to the National Register of Historic Places many significant examples.[7] One goal of this focused project is to contribute to SHPO's initiative.

This book considers architects and typologies. The first half is about residential architecture; the second is about public, commercial, educational, and religious structures. Chapter 1 considers Frank Lloyd Wright's legacy in mid-Michigan, including those homes that were built and those that were planned only. Significantly, this includes the Usonia 2 project for Michigan State College faculty that would have been Wright's first manifestation of a moderate-cost housing development. The Goetsch-Winckler House, the only one of these designs that was built, is one of the purest examples of Usonian architecture. Together with three additional local Wright-designed houses, they span his entire career. Three more were designed but not constructed. Correspondence preserved in the Frank Lloyd Wright Archives reveals the interesting and often contentious relationships between the clients and the architect. Chapter 2 treats Michigan's architect laureate, Alden B. Dow, who designed five houses (four of which were built) and one church, again spanning his career. The innovative Chicago architects Keck & Keck are the subject of chapter 3. They designed two houses that used their unique ventilation system and passive solar heating; one was built.

The majority of houses, however, were designed by Michigan firms, and most of those were local. The homes they designed for themselves are the topic of chapter 4. Those they designed for others are explored in chapter 5, which includes examples by Ralph Rapson, William Kessler, and Kenneth C. Black. Chapter 6 is about Lantern Hill, the Home-Sites, Inc., project that is the second instance where Michigan State College faculty got together, purchased land, and hired an architect—this time, Hugh Stubbins Jr. from Massachusetts. Chapter 7 discusses the "Trade Secrets" House of 1953. Although built with one of many readily available plans, the goal here was not to build as inexpensively as possible, but to provide an economical way to take advantage of the building trades' latest innovations.

The second half of the book considers public structures. Chapter 8 explores governmental buildings, professional association headquarters, smaller commercial structures, banks, a supermarket, and examples of Googie architecture. It starts with City Hall, Lansing's prime example of the International style, and ends with exuberant vernacular roadside attractions as well as geodesic domes. Chapter 9 looks at academic buildings on the Michigan State University campus, one elementary school, and three contemporary public libraries. The latter comparison gives a snapshot of the myriad styles of modernism, from the steel and glass of the International style to a more ornamented variation that followed. The last chapter presents sacred structures, primarily Christian churches. Four projects are explored in depth as a way to understand the complex negotiations between architect, the building committee, and the congregation. Each is also placed in the context of contemporary church architecture of the 1950s and 1960s, changing liturgical requirements, and the inevitable conflicts between what congregations desired and what they could afford. It concludes with a discussion of the synagogue built for the Shaarey Zedek congregation in the 1960s.

Appendix 1 includes illustrations and brief descriptions of seventy-one modernist structures in mid-Michigan, organized chronologically. This year-by-year survey allows certain trends to emerge. For example, the two earliest houses are by Frank Lloyd Wright and Alden B. Dow. Clearly the people who commissioned them were pioneer modernist thinkers themselves. Homes built by architects for themselves in the years right after the war are borderline modernist. In fact, 1951 emerges as one of the most active years for new architectural designs, followed by 1958, 1961, 1964, and 1967.

Another characteristic that becomes obvious in studying the illustrations is that the most interesting and exciting designs are those that are sensitive to context and local site conditions. Many of the homes seem modest on their street side but expansive at the back. Many were sited on the highest spot of the property, often with views of a river flowing behind. Since mid-Michigan is not known for topographic variation, these unusual lots were important to find, especially for those architects who espoused organic design. Brief biographies of the architects discussed in the text are included in appendix 2.

There is no central repository of information on the subject, and much of the primary source material has already been lost. The records of the architectural firms that no longer exist are gone, as are many of those who worked with these firms or commissioned the buildings. Scholarly treatments of mid-Michigan architecture are scarce. Only one local building is the subject of a monograph—Frank Lloyd Wright's Goetsch-Winckler House and the Usonia 2 project.[8] The Michigan State University campus as a whole is discussed in Stanford and Dewhurst's 2002 study.[9] Also, the State Historic Preservation Office unearthed valuable information for the National Trust Register of Historic Places' nominations of Lansing's downtown historic district, the Goetsch-Winckler House, and Minoru Yamasaki's Michigan State Medical Society building. For the rest of the area's built environment, however, finding material is a challenging treasure hunt. Church archives do tend to have rich documentation of their buildings. The Frank Lloyd Wright Archives, Alden B. Dow Archives, and Keck & Keck papers contain drawings and correspondence that facilitate reconstruction of their projects. Homeowners sometimes know about the history of their homes, and occasionally they have the blueprints. However, for commercial structures that have changed hands and functions, such as banks and offices, the history is often missing.

The *Lansing State Journal* is the most fruitful source of information to flesh out the picture of how the community reacted to modernism, and to that end, it is used and quoted extensively in this book. For several decades, and when the area was much smaller than it is today, the *Lansing State Journal* discussed homes, churches, and office buildings as they were completed. Warren Brintnall (1922–1998), a reporter and editor for the paper for forty-five years, is the unsung hero whose writing gently swayed the readership toward modern design. He wrote about comfortable Colonials as well as shed roofs and floor-to-ceiling glazing, often quoting the homeowners and architects' comments about their goals.[10] The *Lansing State Journal* also is an important source for statistical information on building projects as well as trends in the area and nationally.

The discussions of buildings included here are far from comprehensive, and they are limited to Lansing, East Lansing, and Okemos. There are many pockets of mid-Michigan modernist architecture still to be researched, more stories to be recorded, additional buildings to be carefully analyzed in their contexts, and architects to be rediscovered. This book is a start at reclaiming that history and bringing awareness to the mid-century mid-Michigan built environment.

Chapter 11 is new in the expanded paperback edition of this book. It explores residences along the water designed by some architects who have already been discussed, as well as several newly introduced architects and a few architectural designers. Worthy of their special sites along rivers, creeks, and man-made lakes, these residences were often large houses for wealthy clients. To further adumbrate their designers' approaches, inland comparisons by several are included. Stories begun earlier, specifically related to Wright and Lantern Hill, are continued. The biographical section has been enlarged as have the descriptions of sixteen new plates inserted in the appropriate chronological sequence.

Frank Lloyd Wright in Mid-Michigan

Frank Lloyd Wright's legacy in mid-Michigan spans nearly three decades and varies from a small Usonian home of 1,350 square feet to a larger Prairie version over 3,700 square feet. While four of his designs were built, eight others were stopped at various stages in the process. The history and significance of the Goetsch-Winckler, the earliest of these houses, and the communal project later known as Usonia 2 were explored in depth in the fiftieth anniversary exhibition celebration of the Goetsch-Winckler at the Kresge Art Museum, Michigan State University, in 1990, and in the subsequent publication, *Affordable Dreams: The Goetsch-Winckler House and Frank Lloyd Wright* (1991).[1] The history of the other mid-Michigan houses, whether completed or not, is presented here for the first time. Research at the Frank Lloyd Wright Archives has yielded a trove of new information about the mid-Michigan clients as well as Wright's evolving experiments with design and materials.

Usonia 2 and the Goetsch-Winckler House

For Usonia 2, a group of Michigan State College (MSC) faculty got together, purchased land north of Mount Hope Road close to the campus, and divided it into seven plots. They were eight faculty members and their families. Sidney H. Newman, a professor of philosophy and psychology, was in charge. Four were art professionals: Alma Goetsch and Kathrine Winckler were professors of art education; Jesse J. Garrison taught art history; and Erling Brauner was a professor of painting. Clarence D. Hause taught physics; Clarence R. Van Dusen was in the Department of Speech and Dramatics; and Alexis Panshin, the last to join the group, was a professor of forestry.[2] They formed a cooperative and planned to build at the same time in order to save costs on construction by contracting as a group with an architect, builders, and other tradespeople. The homes were to be affordable for the young members, who would share the communal farm at the center of the property.

Several of those in the initiative knew about Frank Lloyd Wright's latest thinking regarding Broadacre City and enthusiastically persuaded the others that he was the right architect for their project. Wright had begun to work on moderate-cost houses in the second half of the 1930s, and the first Usonian, the Jacobs house, was built in 1936 in Madison, Wisconsin. Members of the MSC group visited that house, as well as Wright himself at Taliesin East. By 1938, they decided to engage him as their architect.

Wright presented an overall ground plan dated September 1, 1939, plus two separate drawings that show preliminary designs for six of the houses.[3] Each family had written letters to Wright explaining their physical requirements, financial constraints, and likes and dislikes. He responded with a variety of plans: a hexagonal core for the Panshins, an L-shape for the Garrisons, a third design with an entrance at the center and on the short end for another. The number of bedrooms also differed depending upon the requirements of the clients. In addition, Brauner wanted a painting studio, Garrison required numerous bookshelves, Panshin asked for a shop and darkroom. Documents in the Frank Lloyd Wright Archives reveal each family's relationship with Wright, the evolution of their designs, and ultimately, the demise of the project by summer 1940.[4] As the designs grew to meet the needs of each family unit, the costs increased. Neither local banks nor the Federal Housing Authority in Washington, DC, would provide mortgages due to Wright's new construction techniques, such as prefabricated walls, gravity heat, and flat roofs. The slab foundation, lack of separation between the kitchen and other spaces, and the ceilings that were less than eight feet high were also enumerated.[5] As a result, the project faltered. Of the original project members, Alma Goetsch and Kathrine Winckler went ahead with their home on a different site, and the Brauners built another Wright design after the war at a new location. Other members of the group independently built on their original plots, left the college, or purchased houses elsewhere.

The situation with the Panshins is of interest as one example of their initial excitement compared with the reality of working with Wright. According to correspondence, Alexis first became interested in Wright's architecture when he was working at Forest Products Laboratory in Madison, Wisconsin, in 1934–35.[6] When the Panshins arrived at MSC, they were pleased to find the group who were equally interested

▶ **FIGURE 1.** Goetsch-Winckler House, Frank Lloyd Wright, carport, Okemos. Photograph © 2014 Kim Kauffman.

► **FIGURE 2.** Goetsch-Winckler House, Frank Lloyd Wright, interior, Okemos. Photograph © 2014 Kim Kauffman.

in Wright's architecture and who had already hired him to design their homes. On July 7, 1939, the Panshins told Wright that they had $6,000 to spend, somewhat less than others in the group,[7] yet the house Wright designed for them was the most elaborate. Its central feature was a hexagonal room with a workspace/kitchen, ample living room, a study, and a shop. The bedroom wing, with three bedrooms and two baths, was down a long gallery that projected diagonally to one side.[8] On the other side were a carport and a toolshed.

At first the Panshins were excited about the design, but soon became worried about the proposed materials. "Untreated wood does check and disintegrate under pressure." Further, Alexis was concerned about "the use of contrasting woods for the outside where they lose their individuality through weathering, as is happening in the Jacobs' house, where in places the redwood has bleached and the pine darkened until there is no contrast. I am convinced that cheaper and better results could be obtained through use of inexpensive wood protected in the conventional way."[9] Panshin also rejected Wright's horizontal bands of contrasting wood paneling on the interior and questioned whether the houses would have enough insulation to keep them warm.[10] They withdrew on August 12,[11] then signed on again,[12] but eventually left the project altogether. After the war, they purchased land adjacent to the Brauners and across the street from the Edwardses, each of whom was building a Wright-designed house. The Panshins, however, hired the Keck & Keck architecture firm from Chicago to design theirs (see plate 11).

Alma Goetsch and Kathrine Winckler persisted in their dream of a Wright home (plate 3). Both were from Wisconsin and were familiar with Wright's architecture and philosophy. Plus, they had two salaries to support their $6,600 project, a combined income of $4,500. Their house on Hulett Road, which is now listed in the National Register of Historic Places, stands today as built in 1939–1940 as a pure statement of Usonian architecture. The house seems to hug the land and is evidence of Wright's approach to organic architecture. The flat roof, cantilevered carport, in-line plan, horizontal lines, gravity heat, slab construction, and redwood board-and-batten prefabricated walls are all Usonian characteristics. The carport is at the narrow end turned to Hulett Road, which was then a dirt road and sparsely populated (figure 1). This was rural suburbia.

To enter the house, one looks hard to distinguish which of the floor-to-ceiling glazed units is the actual door. These glazed doors are also used throughout the house. In the living space and bedrooms, they open to the enclosed lanai and make the rooms feel large. The lanai was a nod to Alma Goetsch's desire to feel safe in the countryside.[13]

Inside the house, the ceiling at the entrance is low and the space is compressed, only to open up in the living/studio area as the ceiling rises and clerestory glazing lets light in (figure 2). Across the room a wall of windows overlooks the landscape that drops precipitously to a ravine. The treehouse effect intentionally melds the exterior and interior. The open hearth of red common brick provides a focal point in this space, which closes up again at the eastern alcove with a built-in sofa and bookshelves above. A small kitchen "workspace" is on the back side of the hearth wall. The bedroom wing is on the other side of the living space. At 1,350 square feet, the house is small, and one of the bedrooms is miniscule; the other is only slightly larger, but the public spaces have an expansiveness that belies the square footage. Wright used a four-by-four-foot module to organize all of the components, and the shape is repeated in the cement floor and the plywood on the ceilings; it also guided the placement of windows and doors.

The house quickly proved too small for the two women, who asked Wright for an addition in 1942.[14] Although designed, it could not be built because it brought the house too close to the property line on the west. They asked Wright again for another bedroom in 1947 and then decided to build a completely new house. Plans were started in 1948 and completed in July 1949. This time Wright designed a large red brick house with a pitched roof and two-car carport, replete with a landscape plan showing a fountain and a long driveway with one lane in and a parallel road out, separated by a green median.[15] The bedroom/studio wing was set at a 120-degree angle to the rest of the house. There were two fireplaces, ample storage for paintings, and many built-in seats. Some of these amenities were removed to save costs, and cement block replaced the brick. Nevertheless, after finally finding a builder in 1953 who was willing to tackle the building, the two women realized that the costs were still beyond their means, and Goetsch-Winckler II remained on the drawing board.[16] Had it been realized, it would have been built on a flat plot on North Okemos Road in Okemos. Instead the women left for Fayetteville, Arkansas, which was another university town with a local architect. They hired E. Fay Jones to design Goetsch-Winckler III, their retirement home.[17] The story of these prescient women as clients of two of the most significant American architects of the twentieth century is recounted in *Affordable Dreams*.

The Goetsch-Winckler house was well known in the local community and nationally. Many children came for art lessons with the two women, and many visiting dignitaries at the university enjoyed the women's legendary social events. As a result of experiencing the house, several friends and colleagues who were enamored of it sought out Wright to design for them, including the Muehlbergers and the O'Donnells, who received designs but did not construct their houses, and the Schabergs, who built the last Wright home in the area.

The Erling and Katherine Brauner House

After abandoning the Usonia 2 project in 1940, Katherine and Erling Brauner still hoped to build a home designed by Wright (plate 14). In November 1946 they purchased five acres, of which one and a half were usable, on a cul-de-sac in Okemos. On November 17, they wrote to Wright asking for a $10,000 house with three bedrooms, one bath, living space, and utility and work space for them and their three children.[18] In response, Wright pointed out that the original design would need to be revised and that costs were now double those from 1939, and he offered a concrete-block solution.[19] Hoping to spur Wright on, the Brauners wrote approximately once a month starting in the spring of 1947 asking for plans, explaining that costs were dropping, that brick was plentiful.[20] Throughout 1948, the Brauners wrote to Wright, cajoling, begging, and flattering him, urging him to send the designs. When the drawings finally arrived at the end of the summer, the house looked much larger than what they could afford. They visited Wright in early September and significant changes were made. Finally new drawings arrived in October, but the costs were now $20,000.[21] Brauner reminded Wright that the agreed-upon budget was half that amount.[22] Wright's response on November 22nd was curt: "Don't hope to build that house for under $15,000 . . . no such thing as a $10,000 house; think of future earnings and needs."[23]

As the specifics were worked out and cost-cutting substitutions were found, Wright agreed to lower his fee—but Brauner was not to tell anyone.[24] Once the designs were finalized and ground was broken on April 28, 1949, construction moved along quickly. The family moved in on September 18. The final cost was $16,000 plus a lot of hard labor by Mr. Brauner, who did all of the electrical and cabinetry work and the trim carpentry. Brauner wrote in 1967 that "For one reason or another I enjoyed Mr. Wright's confidence to the extent that he encouraged me to proceed as my own contractor without the necessity of an apprentice supervisor."[25]

Among the distinguishing features of the Brauner house is the use of perforated concrete blocks with glass inserted between the two parts of the mold. These are aligned in three horizontal rows on the upper portion of the north façade and allow light to enter into the otherwise dark gallery space behind. Concrete blocks without glass enclose the carport area and entrance to the house. Another unique feature is the long, dramatic pitch of the roof that shelters the

▶ **FIGURE 3.** Brauner House, Frank Lloyd Wright, exterior, Okemos. Photograph © 2014 Kim Kauffman.

carport and shields the entrance from view. Long, deep eaves continue around the rest of the house to protect it from the elements (figure 3). The interior space centers around the fireplace/kitchen core. The light, open living and dining spaces have large windows that look out towards the marsh below. The bedroom wing is set apart, up several steps from the public space of the house. The house is beautifully sited on the rise of the land to take advantage of varied contours of the lot.

The James and Dolores Edwards House

This cul-de-sac on Arrowhead Road was the scene of a lot of activity in the late 1940s. In addition to the Brauners, the Panshins were constructing their Keck & Keck home on the adjacent lot to the east, having given up on working with Wright after Usonia 2 was disbanded. Across the street, James and Dolores Edwards were building their brick-and-cedar Wright design, which was completed in 1949 (plate 16). Additionally, a few blocks away, John F. A. Taylor, a philosophy professor, and Elizabeth, his wife, had built a Streamline Moderne two-story house in 1946 (plate 6). A decade later, he would be a driving force in the embrace of modernism at Edgewood United Church (see plate 44).

The Edwardses approached Wright at the urging of Miss Goetsch. As James explained in his initial letter to Wright on August 2, 1948, he did not want to follow "dull plans and methods of home construction."[26]

> Some of the dissatisfaction with orthodox building comes from my work. I am the manufacturing engineer for Olds. Our assignment is to develop new and better ways of making things—without complete regard to conventional production practices. We usually find that when we get back to the basic facts—better methods are not difficult to develop.
>
> Our thinking on home building follows the same line. We would like to forget the usual house construction and start with the theory that our home can play with us and work with us if we let it—if we can get your help. . . .
>
> We are three, wife, age 30, son, 7—I am age 34. Annual income $9–10,000. Informal entertaining limited to a few friends once or twice a month. We have overnight guests not more than three times a year. When relatives visit, usually two weeks—no more than two people at once.
>
> Two cars. My son and I should have a work area. The hammer and saw sort of thing. My wife enjoys dress making.
>
> We fish some, golf some, picnic some. Our family group is pretty sacred to us, and our ideals and goals are being together and enjoying being home together.

> We are not nomadic, we like the feeling of having our roots down.[27]

He then gives the budget: $15,000–16,000 inclusive of land. When Wright asked him to summarize his thinking about the house, he responded with a detailed letter about space and material requirements that fit well with Wright's ideas, except for the kitchen.[28] These included rough wood with a deep, rich brown stain; glass and light, but designed for privacy; low overhanging eaves; ground-hugging; a little pitch to the roof; "ceiling height in the living dining area to give the effect of spaciousness that might drop down in one section to have a feeling of coziness, security and comfort, . . . a generously sized kitchen."

In response to Edwards's request "not to exceed $16,000," Wright nonchalantly answered, "Who knows except that every house we are building on costs predicted three years ago [is] now costing twice as much plus 10% or more. So you should set your stakes at $20,000 to get a $10,000 house."[29] The final costs were closer to $23,000 plus the architect's 10 percent fee.[30]

Although he expressly wrote, "we prefer to live inside the city limits," in November 1948 the Edwardses ended up choosing an undeveloped, large suburban plot with a rural feel on which to build. Having learned that the land was once the site of an old Chippewa Indian trading site and campground, under the supervision of Chief Okemos—hence the name of the subdivision, "Indian Hills"—Edwards asked for Wright's comments on naming the house Arrowhead and using the arrowhead in an abstract design on a wall.[31] In fact, Arrowhead was the name of this road.

Work got underway in March 1950; the family moved in by July 1951. The Edwardses' seven-room, L-shaped house with red brick and cedar trim is planned on a four-by-four foot module. Oriented from southwest to northeast on the property, it is set well into the plot. Seen from the road below (to the south), it appears to rise up from the sloping terrain, asserting itself over the landscape. From the east, however, the house seems to nestle into the hillside. The entrance is on this upper level on the side of the house away from the road. From the carport, one proceeds into a small entry and down four steps into the spacious triangular living space with windows on three sides. Several steps up lead to the terrace, with its broad, overhanging eave. The workspace/kitchen, which also accesses the terrace, is separated from the dining area by an accordion plywood door. From above, clerestory windows admit daylight into the kitchen, dining room, and hallway that extends to the bedroom wing to the south. In 1968, Jack Howe of Taliesin Associates provided a 16 by 42 foot addition to this end.

Shortly after moving in, Mrs. Edwards wrote a letter of appreciation to Wright on July 25, 1951:

> Mr. Wright, you once told me that Jim and I would find ourselves in this new home and find we are capable of many things we were not aware of. I have thought of that many times—this is not just a new home for us but a new and better way of life. We are so very fortunate and appreciative of what you have given us.[32]

Unfortunately, they were able to enjoy their home for only a short time. In mid-1952, Mr. Edwards was transferred to Texas to help develop a GM aircraft and auto plant. His hope of engaging Wright to make a larger version of their Michigan home, and to leave the Dallas–Fort Worth area enriched by it, came to nothing.

The Donald and Mary Lou Schaberg House

The fourth and latest Wright-designed house in the area was built for Donald and Mary Lou Schaberg in 1958, following nearly ten years of planning (plate 45). In his first letter to Wright in 1949, Schaberg explained that

> Every Sunday afternoon throughout our high school days, three of us fellows making our usual tour or drive would visit the Goetsch-Winckler home, even if we just were to pull in and back out again. We love it. And after ten years of reading about you, Mr. Wright, and scanning through books with your many illustrations of Usonian homes, I wonder if your time would permit drawing a home of that type for my wife and myself.
>
> Your clients, Jim and Dolores Edwards, our apartment neighbors in East Lansing, and we have repeatedly studied your sketch of their home many times and have continued to praise it highly on each occasion.[33]

He went on to explain that he and his wife were newly married and expected children in the future; he was in wholesale lumber and could obtain some building materials at distributor's costs; and his father owned a hardware store. He concluded by asking for a home for around $14,000. Having been taken on by Wright as a client, the Schabergs secured property in the River Forest subdivision on the west side of Lansing and sent Wright the survey of their two lots. Anxious months passed, and Don's letters were initially polite but pleading, asking for plans so they could start to build in September 1950.[34] Begging and cajoling followed, as did their first son, and in May 1950, Don referred to these "sketchless days [that] linger on," and the letter was signed, "the trying to wait patiently Don Schaberg."[35] Wright's reply was "Your patience has its reward this side of heaven."[36] Nonetheless, more months passed. Finally, in late August, the preliminary plans arrived for the $18,000 house. Although some revisions were made, construction did not begin. A *Lansing State Journal* article on Sunday, June 17, 1951, "Local Homes Reflect Frank Lloyd Wright's Touch," reported that "Plans have been set aside temporarily for what would have been the fourth Frank Lloyd Wright home in the Lansing area. Mr. and Mrs. Donald Schaberg . . . have begun construction of a different house on the site of 2301 Cumberland. The plans are being kept for possible use at another location sometime in the future." Instead, the Schabergs commissioned Conway C. Hamilton, a local architect, to build a 1,565-square-foot ranch home on their land.[37]

Indeed, Schaberg never gave up his dream of a Wright home. By January 1954, he was back in touch with the architect, asking for a larger home to accommodate their growing family (a third child had been born) and an increased budget of $40,000. Almost exactly a year later, Schaberg wrote that while they waited for revised plans, a Detroit mass builder moved in and purchased 125 acres one half-block away from their site, rendering the site "unsuitable for a Frank Lloyd Wright home."[38] They then purchased a new lot in Okemos. In April, Schaberg asked Wright for a partial basement: "In having such an exclusive and expensive home we feel these additions would not increase costs any appreciable amount. In building a house of this nature, which we love, we feel it only fair to ourselves that it have our requirements. In five years our house still remains the best one for us but time has meant a larger home. . . . Is it possible to sell our plans and start over again?"[39]

On January 4, 1956, Schaberg wrote to Wright, "We are the Schabergs—the changing family from Lansing," explaining that the contractor received a set of figures, the bank approved a loan, but the dilemma was that they needed a larger living and dining area, larger bedroom, and bath adjoining the master bedroom.[40] It took several more months of polite pleading to obtain the revisions, which finally arrived in mid-April. By the time they were ready to build in March 1957, they had six children. Following changes from poured concrete to tan brick, and after detailed discussions of carpeting, built-in furniture, and designs for individual seating, the family finally moved into their home in March 1958.

The house is a single story with an attached two-car carport set on flat land. Bricks were used on the interior and exterior, as well as mahogany plywood and cypress for the trim, and hand-split cedar shakes on the roof. The carport has large brick pylons dividing the stalls (figure 4). On the opposite side of the entrance area, there is a large, integrated raised-brick planter, and while the plan has no symmetry, it does have balance (figure 5). Inside, the brick fireplace rises to the height of the open gable of the living room ceiling. The dining space faces the terrace outside, sharing the wall with the small kitchen space. There are three bedrooms,

► **FIGURE 4.** Schaberg House, Frank Lloyd Wright, exterior, carport, Okemos. Photograph © 2014 Kim Kauffman.

two bathrooms, a master bedroom and bath, and a study off the gallery hallway. Throughout, the low pitch of the gable is reflected in the ceiling height, and the line continues on the exterior to form broad eaves.[41] In 1966 Jack Howe of Taliesin Associates provided a 1,200-square-foot addition consisting of a family room, bedroom, gallery, and fish pond, and changing the house from an "L" to a "U" shape. The pool was designed by Wes Peters in 1980.

Schaberg built on a twenty-five-acre site in Okemos, which he had purchased with several friends. They subdivided it into large lots, and the houses that were eventually built form a distinguished group by some of the area's most important architects. Designs include Alden B. Dow's home for his son Michael and daughter-in-law Rhea (see plate 81), and three by John Crouse of Mayotte-Webb (plates 73, 74, and 80). A second Wright design for the Hartmans was to be built here as well. "Wrightwind" was the name chosen for the newly platted road in honor of the architect.

The Stanley and Monna Lee Hartman House

Stanley and Monna Lee Hartman, whose five acres adjoined the Schabergs' property, hoped to build at the same time as the Schabergs to save on construction costs. He was president of Hartman Gravel Company. In a letter dated August 24, 1955, they asked Wright for a "minimum house of wood and brick consisting of a large living room containing a dining area, kitchen, three bedrooms, 1½ baths and a double carport."[42] They had two sons, and another bedroom could be added later if needed. "The view faces south where we would like a terrace accessible from the living room and master bedroom." Unlike the Schabergs' experience of long delays, the Hartmans' plans were ready very quickly, by October 1955 (figure 6). Upon receiving them, Mr. Hartman wrote:

> There just aren't words to describe how thrilled we are with the plans. We like the way the oak tree has become an integral part of the whole. The lanai seems especially appropriate here because it gives a feeling of unity with the outdoors and protection at the same time. Both the Schabergs and we are looking forward to building our homes together soon. They are as excited as we are over the drawings.[43]

It took the Hartmans several months to consider the drawings, and even after a face-to-face meeting with Wright in May 1956, they took some time to get back to him. Their letter dated December 19, 1956, contained a long list of changes and desires, from minor details to major ones, such as changing the access to and size of the basement, enlarging the boys'

◀ **FIGURE 5.** Schaberg House, Frank Lloyd Wright, exterior, rear and side, Okemos. Photograph © 2014 Kim Kauffman.

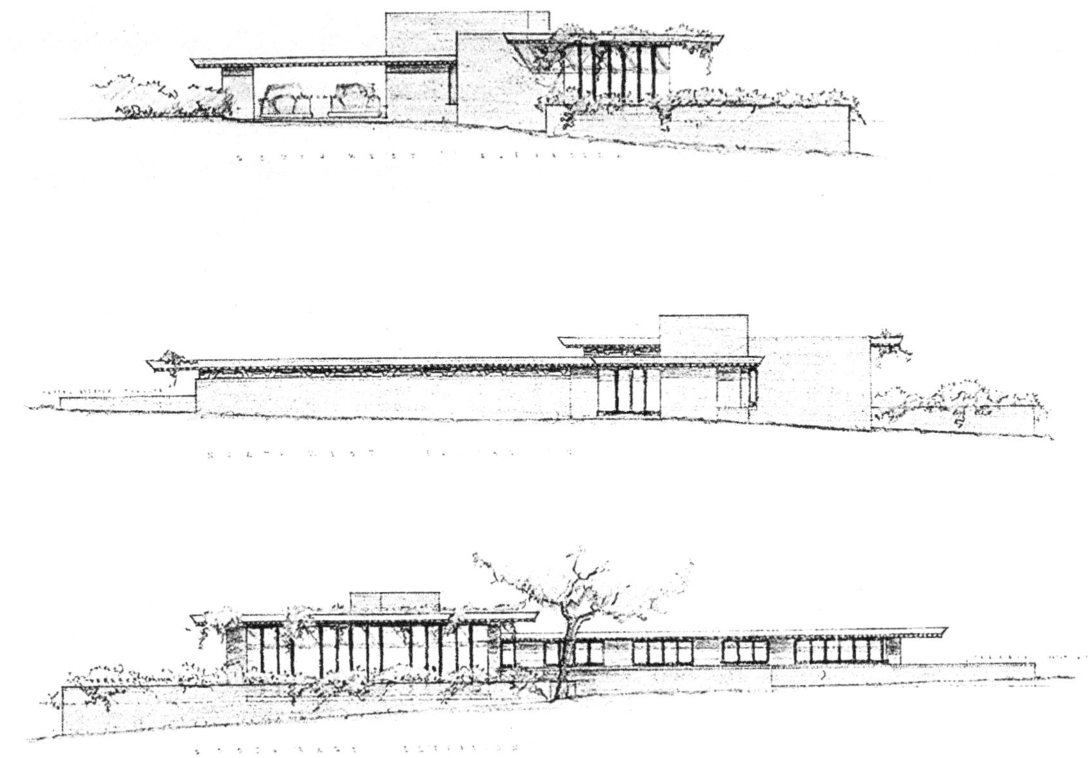

▲ **FIGURE 6.** Hartman House, Frank Lloyd Wright, elevations, unbuilt. The Frank Lloyd Wright Foundation Archives (The Museum of Modern Art | Avery Architectural & Fine Arts Library, Columbia University, New York). All rights reserved.

▶ **FIGURE 7.** Hartman House, Frank Lloyd Wright, plan, unbuilt. The Frank Lloyd Wright Foundation Archives (The Museum of Modern Art | Avery Architectural & Fine Arts Library, Columbia University, New York). All rights reserved.

bedrooms and the kitchen as well as the toolshed.[44] After this, things slowed considerably. In January 1957, the Hartmans asked for blueprints.[45] In February, after explaining that the last of the utility poles were being brought in and placed in a hollow out of sight, they asked for "at least some part of our plans so that this work can move ahead."[46] The plot plan arrived promptly on March 17, and the house was quickly staked on the property.[47] Hartman thanked Wright for attending to some of his suggested changes, while reiterating others that had been ignored. On June 26, 1957, he reported that the Schabergs had started to build and he, too, hoped to start as soon as completed plans were received.[48] In August 1958, the Hartmans were still adjusting the plan—shortening some rooms, adding a den, and reorganizing the boys' rooms, master bath, and closets.[49]

Wright's ideas for the house are preserved in several drawings in the Frank Lloyd Wright Archives (figures 6, 7; plate 36). He provided a long, low-slung building, oriented with the long axis running from southwest to northeast. The carport is at a right angle, placed slightly off-center to the south. The living room rises higher than the bedroom wing and has long windows on three sides. On the back side of the house, there is abundant fenestration, while the closed long side of the bedroom wing is relieved by the placement of narrow windows and perforated boards under the eave. Wright responded to their request for a terrace by providing one that wraps around the living room and another at the end of the bedroom wing. With the lanai and flat line of the roof, the design resembles a stretched-out version of the Goetsch-Winckler house.

One significant issue the Hartmans had was the height of the ceiling, a complaint that Wright had already heard from other clients including the Newmans of Usonia 2. "The ceiling at 6′8″ would not be high enough because we are all rather tall people. Would it be possible to raise the ceiling to between 7′3″ and 7′6″? This might be accomplished by reducing the difference between the floor levels of the living room and bedroom wing to somewhat less than the one foot now specified."[50] The letter ends, "Although we have had to delay our building plans temporarily, we still hope to start in the very near future." But after that, the correspondence ends and the Wright-designed house went unbuilt. As their daughter Pat explained, a number of unexpected life events occurred that changed the family's situation—among them, the death of Mrs. Hartman's mother and the birth of Pat, their daughter, in 1957. The latter made a three-bedroom house no longer feasible. Plus persistent issues of low ceiling heights contributed to the decision not to build.[51]

Eventually the Hartmans contracted the local firm of Mayotte-Webb to design their home at 1185

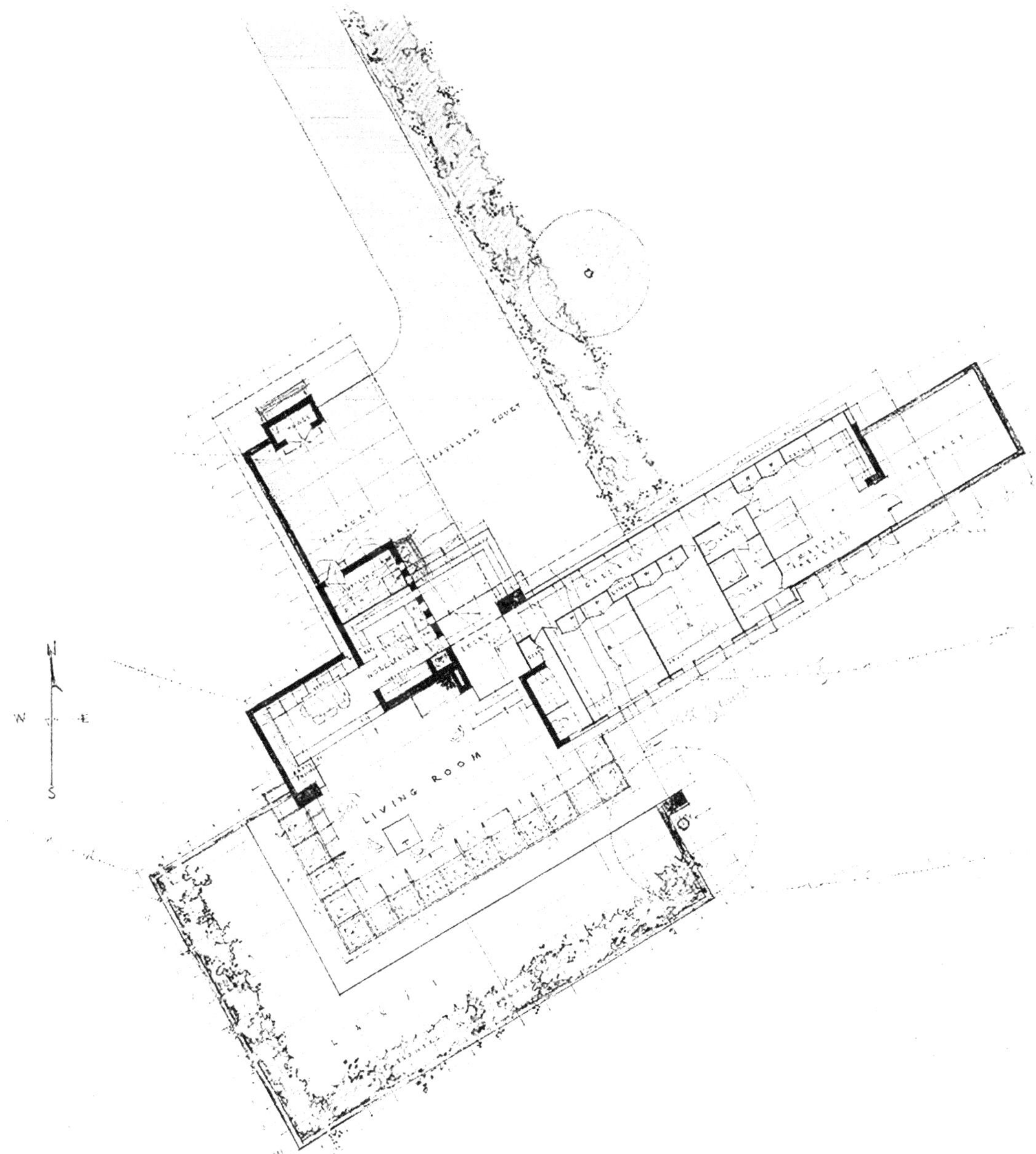

Wrightwind Drive, which was completed in 1965 (plate 74). John Crouse, who was responsible for several houses on Wrightwind Drive and the adjoining White Oaks Drive, used Wright's design as a starting point. As built, the house exhibits Wright's original look and its essential relation to the surroundings. It exemplifies both architects' ideas of organic architecture.

The Dale and Beatrice O'Donnell House

Another house designed by Wright for mid-Michigan clients met the same fate despite the enthusiasm and efforts of both parties. Dale and Beatrice O'Donnell purchased land on North Okemos Road adjoining that which Alma Goetsch and Kathrine Winckler had purchased for Goetsch-Winckler II, the new house designed by Wright in 1948–49. The O'Donnells' initial contact with Wright was in December 1948. In August 1949 they added comments to their original information, such as that the costs should be between $15,000 and $20,000; their acreage was wooded, with undergrowth along the entire front of the property that they hoped to keep; they were both forty-eight years old with no children; and they were each employed.[52] Dale worked for New York Life Insurance, with offices in Detroit and Lansing, and handled estate planning; Beatrice was a professor of home economics at Michigan State College. She was appointed in 1944 and promoted to assistant professor in August 1948.[53]

They entertained and wanted a living room large enough for twenty-five to thirty people, an office for two with an adjoining bath, a combination (or adjoining) kitchen and utility room, and a carport for two or three cars. As to special needs, they foresaw that Beatrice could use the house for group conferences:

> It would be worth a real contribution if young home economic women at MSC could have more experience with organic architecture. . . . [They both] love our home and enjoy those activities that lift life above the everyday happenings. Beauty in our home raises our spirits.

Their more intimate needs were also explained:

> We like to read . . . and to have books throughout the house. . . . We enjoy privacy . . . and the opportunity to relax. . . . We have found unexpected pleasures in taking care of a few large plants which we have watched grow and unfold. We enjoy leisurely meals served in different parts of the house.[54]

In the New Year (1950), the O'Donnells wrote to Wright urging him to send plans: "1st of January, mild, spring like in Michigan. Walked our wooded acres . . . seem beautiful . . . dream of possible Frank Lloyd Wright home. Talked with Goetsch and Winckler. Both they and we are eager to build this spring. Have temporary housing through July 15."[55] They received a typical Wrightian response: "If your patience will match our persistence all will be well."[56]

When the preliminary studies finally arrived in September for a house budgeted at $25,000, the O'Donnells were very excited and, as in many similar letters to Wright from clients, expressed how they dreamed of living in it (figure 8). In early 1951, they wrote that they had been carefully studying the plans, "yet each time we look at it we discover something new—we feel the plans are satisfactory and well planned for our way of living."[57]

Wright designed a compact two-bedroom house with a two-car carport to the north, forming an L-shape. The office with lavatory is off the ample entry that steps down to the living space. The workspace and utility area are in the center, with the guest and master bedrooms aligned on the other side. Wright specified perforated concrete blocks facing the street, but on the other side the building soars (plate 18). The low pitched roof over the bedroom wing contrasts with the dramatic angle of the shed roof over the living space with abundant windows. Ample overhanging eaves provide shade to the large terrace on two sides.

After months of not hearing anything, Eugene Masselink, Wright's assistant, wondered

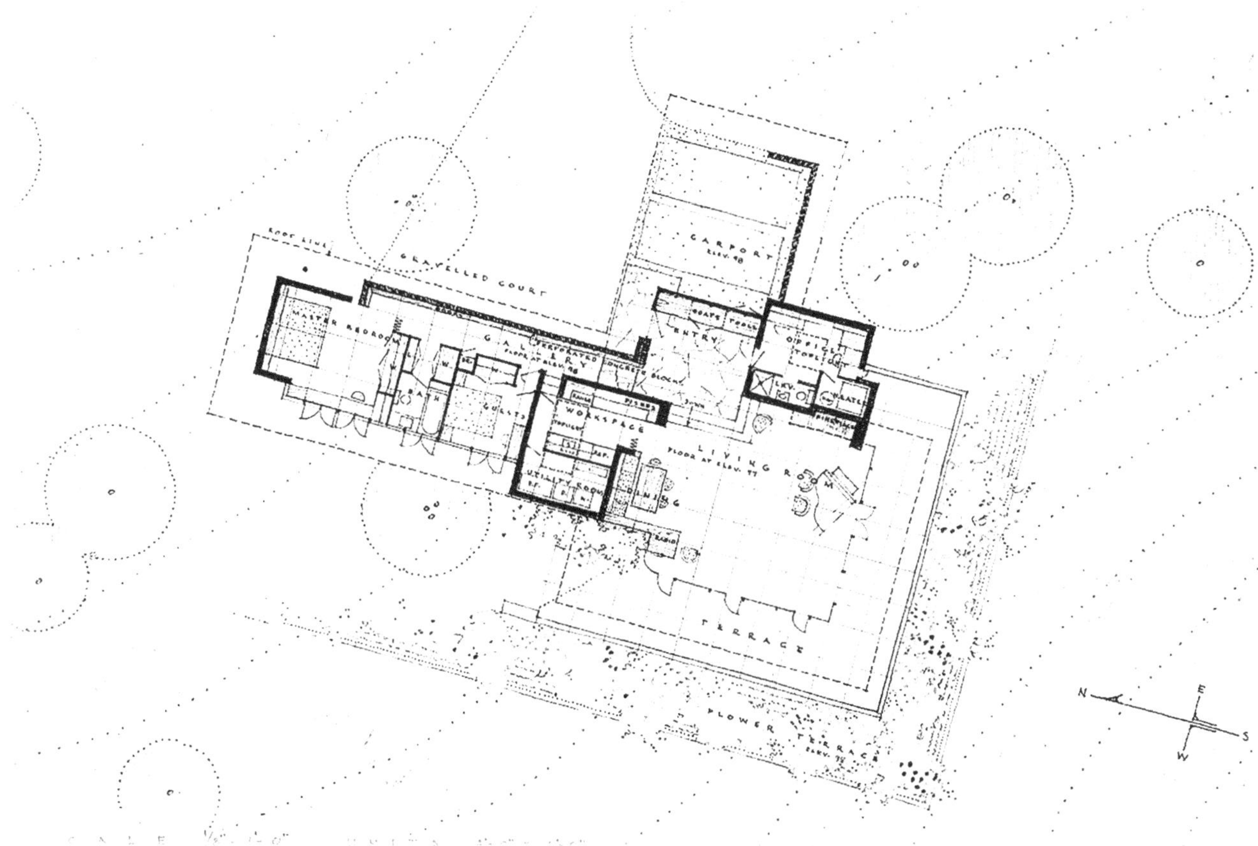

▲ **FIGURE 8.** O'Donnell House, Frank Lloyd Wright, plan, unbuilt. The Frank Lloyd Wright Foundation Archives (The Museum of Modern Art | Avery Architectural & Fine Arts Library, Columbia University, New York).

how construction was coming along.[58] The next correspondence, dated October 4, 1955, explained the long silence. With "deep regret," they were forced to postpone the house. Estimates by East Lansing and Lansing contractors between 1950 and 1954 were so out of line that "we became discouraged, decided to wait." They would carefully plan, do some of the work themselves, use some unskilled labor, and hoped to build a house for $17,000 to $20,000 as originally planned.[59] The response on October 15, 1955, was "Come again and better luck when you do."[60] So ends the story of the O'Donnells' Wright-designed home. Had it been built, it would have been one of the most striking and dynamic in the region.

The Clarence W. and Mary Muehlberger House

Another similarly fated project is the Muehlbergers' house (plate 12). Clarence W. and Mary Muehlberger initially contacted Wright in June 1946. He had been director of the Michigan Crime Detection Laboratory of the Michigan Department of Health since 1941.[61] "My husband and I are very good friends of Katherine [*sic*] Winckler and have been impressed with their house. We have bought 22 acres of land, south of here, and just as soon as we can get material, would like to build a house. . . . 11 acres of gently rolling field and 11 of woods, with about a mile of creek running through the woods. It is quite lovely."[62]

She added that "Mr. and Mrs. J. J. Garrison bought seven acres just adjoining us and plan also to build. At one time you designed a house for them which they were unable to build." This was a reminder to Wright that the Garrisons were original members of the Usonia 2 project.

In August 1947, the Muehlbergers received the preliminary studies for a $17,500 house. Their response was elation: "interesting and beautiful, in fact, as far as we are concerned the most beautiful house we have ever seen. . . . With one or two exceptions, your plans for our house are everything we have ever wanted."[63] By October 1948, the cost of the house had ballooned to $40,000, to the chagrin of the clients, who reiterated that as a salaried state employee, Mr. Muehlberger would find even a $17,500 house difficult to finance. He reviewed the costs: $10,000 to $12,000 in 1946; $17,500 by October 1947. "At that time we talked over the excessive cost of building and it was your suggestion that we delay construction until costs had receded somewhat. But we pointed out that in any event, we should have our working drawings. . . . But like Prof. Brauner, Alma Goetsch and Kathrine Winckler, we have looked forward to the pleasure of living in one of your houses even though it might throw our budget somewhat out of balance."[64]

Wright's response in November 1948 was that, indeed, the $40,000 was an error; the cost would be $25,000.

> To encourage you to believe your house would be less than that would not . . . be to my credit. . . . I have done all I could to bring the house within your means but no man should build less than 10 years ahead of himself unless he wants to live behind himself all the rest of his life. He has to stretch his limit. There is no prospect of prices coming down more than ten percent for years to come if that. We are all learning this the hard way.[65]

This seemed to satisfy the clients, who responded that $25,000 would be possible.[66] While enclosing a payment to Wright on January 3, 1949, Mr. Muehlberger wrote that he planned to spend the winter making a model from the working drawings. "In that way, we will be better acquainted with the architectural design of the house when we are ready to build."[67] The final letter from Masselink, dated June 30, 1951, is a bill for monies owed.[68]

Why the house was not built remains a mystery, but the cause likely revolves around the increasing costs. This was referenced by Mrs. Panshin in a letter to her architect, George Fred Keck, on September 30, 1947. She reported: "Another Wright plan for here for Dr. Muehlberger, who has 20 acres out on College Road. Turner intrigued with it and anxious to build it—he estimates it at $35,000, to Muehlberger's horror."[69]

Had it been built, the house would have been unique. In fact, one color drawing was reproduced in *Architectural Forum*, 1948.[70] The bedroom wing to one side of the entrance has a flat roof, and small windows beneath the eave (plate 12). On the other side, a deep overhang shelters the front of the house, the door, and three cars. But the most dramatic aspect was the steeply sloping roof towards the back of the house, where Wright canted most of the windows to slant downwards (plate 13). Although the land was fairly flat, Wright introduced movement and interest through the play of light and cast shadows, reflections on the slanted windows, and the deep recesses alongside.

Wright Associates and Wright-Influenced Houses

In addition to the four Wright houses that were built and the ones that were designed but not executed, there are a number of houses in mid-Michigan designed by architects associated with Wright, or inspired by him, as well as one outright copy. In addition, Wright's Prairie style influenced numerous one-story office buildings found across the region.

Taliesin Associated Architects fellow R. Joseph

Fabris (b. 1918) designed a distinctive home completed in 1971 for Harry and Betty Eckert at 124 East Sherwood Road, in what was then very rural Williamston. The house is set well back on the property and invisible from the road. While the design has two intersecting longitudinal shapes, rounded forms dominate. The living room ends in a curve; the indoor swimming pool at the other end is round (but inadequate ventilation led to it being floored over); and a two-story round tower houses a bedroom suite. The red roof is a series of pagoda tops with shallow slopes. Inside, the exposed curved wooden ribs of the living room ceiling have reminded people of the interior of a tent or the inside of a ship. The house has layers of Michigan sandstone on the exterior and Douglas fir plywood throughout the interior.[71]

Additionally, the house at 715 Red Cedar, Okemos, built in 1958, was designed by Theodore Van Fossen (1919–2010), who had worked as a builder and furniture maker on two of Wright's projects in 1939 and 1940. He later designed almost fifty homes in the Usonian community of Rush Creek Village in Worthington, Ohio, beginning in 1956.[72] The Okemos house is approximately 1,500 square feet, with a sloping roof and carport, on three-and-a half acres on the bluffs of the Red Cedar River.

Edwin Johnson (1903–1971), who designed the 1947 modernist house at 1913 Tecumseh River Drive in Lansing (plate 10), was described as studying with Frank Lloyd Wright. He practiced architecture in Cambridge, Massachusetts, and partnered with John Merrall Whitcomb in 1946. While Johnson is not listed either as an apprentice or a fellow at Taliesin, the influence of Wright's designs are evident in the project.[73] He was the brother of Rosamunde Hammond, who with her husband, Paul, commissioned this house. When the Hammonds first viewed the plans, they were thrilled.[74] Then they left for South America in their Airstream. Having lived for months in the compact space of this mobile home, they changed their minds about certain details of the house upon their return. Several revisions are recorded in the architect's drawings; the third set was dated July 31, 1947.

The L-shaped house is set on a rise of land high above the pond, which can be seen through the woods to the south. The southern elevation takes advantage of this view and is dominated by the large expanse of windows in horizontal bands, with fixed panes alternating with ones that open.[75] A large overhang keeps this side cool in summer. The short end of the house faces the street and is fronted by the detached garage, with a flat roof, that shields the entrance from view of passersby. Inside, the short set of stairs ascends to the main level or descends to the full basement. The living and dining area are on the south, as is a two-sided fireplace that opens to the living room and study; the kitchen and utility areas are on the north. Rather than

PLATE 1. Charles W. and Grace Bachman House. Alden B. Dow, 1937.

Photo courtesy of the Michigan State Historic Preservation Office.

PLATE 2. Mildred Hagberg Studio House, Barn, 1923.
Ralph Rapson design, 1940. Photograph © 2014 Kim Kauffman.

PLATE 3. Goetsch-Winckler House. Frank Lloyd Wright, 1940.

Photograph © 2014 Kim Kauffman.

PLATE 4. O. Lee and Genevieve Ricker House. Donald Hedges, 1940.

Photo by Natasha Crljenica.

PLATE 5. 164 Maplewood Drive, East Lansing. Architect unknown, 1941. Photo by Natasha Crljenica.

PLATE 6. John F. A. and Elizabeth Taylor. Architect unknown, 1946.

Photo by Natasha Crljenica.

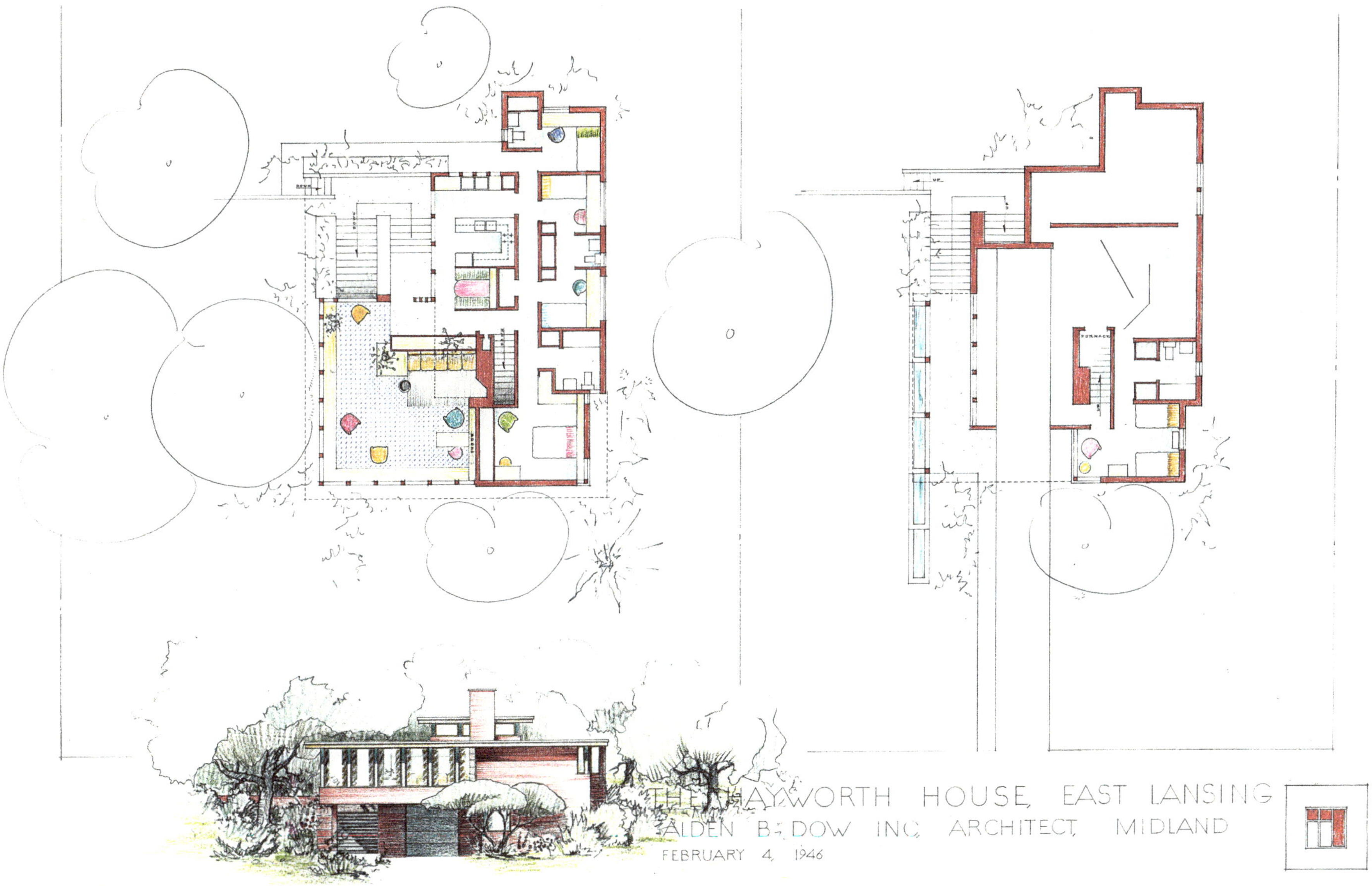

PLATE 7. Hayworth House, drawing. Alden B. Dow, 1946.

Courtesy of Alden B. Dow Archives.

PLATE 8. Donald and Betty Price House. Lee Black and Kenneth C. Black, Architects, 1946.

Photo courtesy of the Michigan State Historic Preservation Office.

PLATE 9. 901 Rosewood Avenue. Adrian Langius, 1947.

Photo by Natasha Crljenica.

PLATE 10. Paul and Rosamunde Hammond House. Edwin Johnson, 1947.

Photograph © 2014 Kim Kauffman.

PLATE 11. Alexis and Lucie Panshin House. Keck & Keck, 1947.

Photograph © 2014 Kim Kauffman.

PLATE 12 (*above*). Clarence W. and Mary Muehlberger House, drawing, front elevation. Frank Lloyd Wright, 1947. The Frank Lloyd Wright Foundation Archives (The Museum of Modern Art | Avery Architectural & Fine Arts Library, Columbia University, New York).

PLATE 13. Clarence W. and Mary Muehlberger House, drawing, rear elevation, detail. Frank Lloyd Wright, 1947. The Frank Lloyd Wright Foundation Archives (The Museum of Modern Art | Avery Architectural & Fine Arts Library, Columbia University, New York).

PLATE 14. Erling and Katherine Brauner House. Frank Lloyd Wright, 1949.

Photograph © 2014 Kim Kauffman.

PLATE 15. Harold H. and Gladys Anderson House. Alden B. Dow, 1949.

Photo by Natasha Crljenica.

PLATE 16. James and Dolores Edwards House. Frank Lloyd Wright, 1949–51; addition, Taliesin Associates, 1968. Photograph © 2014 Kim Kauffman.

PLATE 17 (*right*). Greyhound Bus Terminal. William Strudwick Arrasmith, 1950. Vintage postcard.

PLATE 18 (*below*). Dale and Beatrice O'Donnell House, drawing, rear elevation. Frank Lloyd Wright, 1950. The Frank Lloyd Wright Foundation Archives (The Museum of Modern Art | Avery Architectural & Fine Arts Library, Columbia University, New York).

being connected by a hallway, the rooms open into each other (figure 9). The bedroom wing is at right angles to the north and contains three small bedrooms and the larger master suite. There are built-in closets and storage in the bedroom-wing hallway. The focus of the house is the large living-room space, where the angle of the shed roof is the highest on the south end and makes the room light and airy. To enhance their enjoyment of this private lot, a large porch, lifted above ground level, was placed at the rear of the house. Influenced by Wright's organic approach, the architect placed the house at the highest point and away from the road. Surrounded on two sides by the extensive, hilly property, it is both open to nature and private.

The 1955 house at 416 Highland Avenue, East Lansing, was designed by Karl Frederick Krauss Jr. for Alice Griswold, a weaver, and Howard Griswold, who worked for the State of Michigan in food services and after retirement joined in her partnership. The Wrightian brick-and-wood ranch design with the short end of the garage facing the street does not fit with the rest of the earlier gabled homes in this area. At 1,900 square feet on one level with a full basement, the house has an open plan with varying ceiling heights and included a studio for Alice's power looms, where she created specialized fabrics for interior designers. Her curtains hung in the World Trade Center, and her work was included in a 1956 "Draperies for Art" Smithsonian

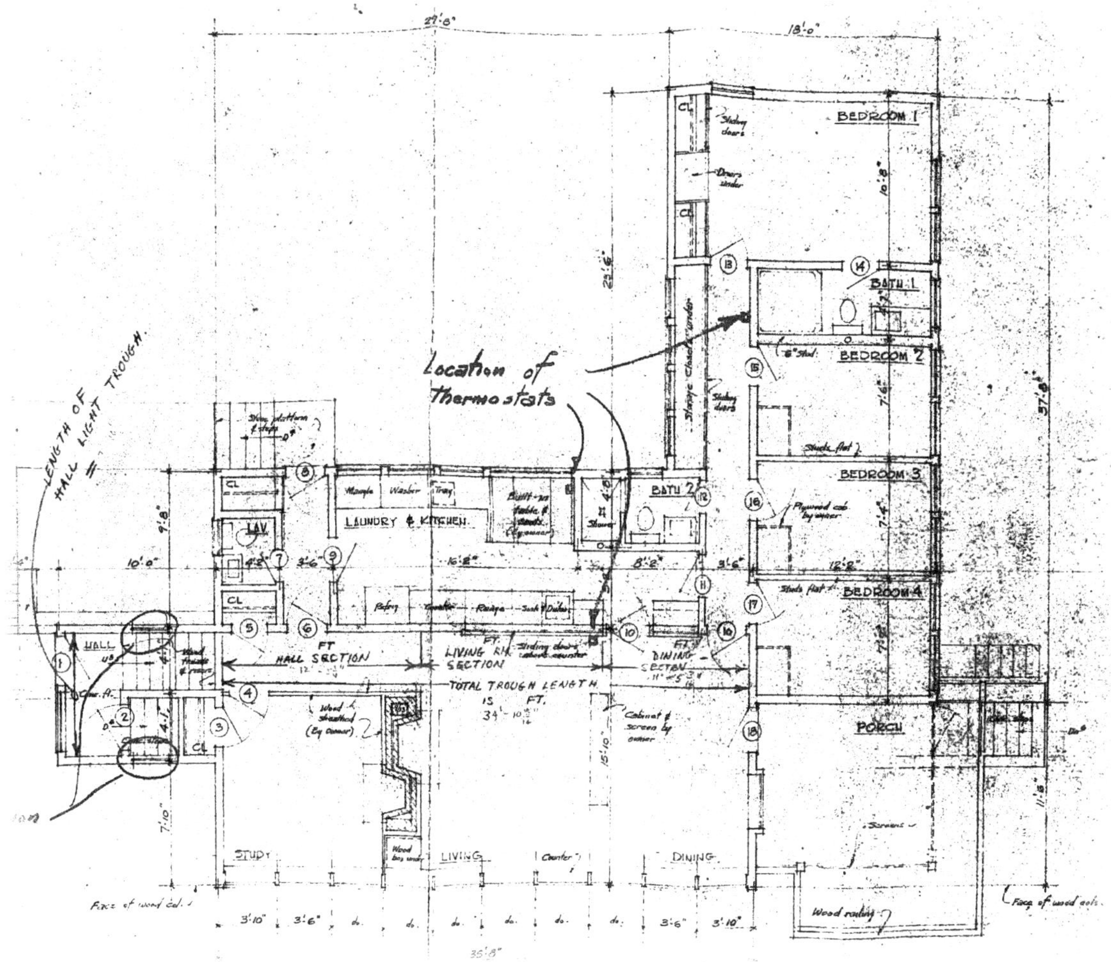

▲ **FIGURE 9.** Hammond House, Edwin Johnson, blueprint, detail, Lansing. Courtesy of Emily Tabuteau.

traveling exhibition.[76] For her home, she produced the fabric for the built-in seating as well as the drapes. Wood is used throughout for walls, ceilings, the angled display shelves near the entrance and hallway where clients could see her wares, and the many built-in shelves and storage units.

On the long south side, a walkway is sheltered by a generous overhang that leads to the entrance, placed away from the street and in the center of the house. Inside, stairs ascend to the main level, with bedrooms, separated by an accordion-pleated door, towards the front of the house. The house has extensive glazing at the back above the built-in benches that line the perimeter of the angled living room.

Architect Karl Frederick Krauss Jr. (1923–2008) supposedly studied under Frank Lloyd Wright. He obtained his architecture degree from the University of Michigan and started as a draftsman for Warren Holmes in 1940. He worked for a variety of firms until he founded his individual practice in 1953. The following year he opened Krauss and Farnsworth with an office in Lansing and then returned to a sole practice (Karl Krauss Jr., Architects) in 1957, the year he designed this house. He also practiced in Texas and by 1970 relocated to Arizona.[77]

Among early Wright-associated houses are two on Hamilton Road in Okemos. Hiram E. and Lena Wilson owned a large farmhouse at the corner of Hamilton and Charles Street (at 2236 Hamilton) that was built in 1926. As the neighbors recount, he divided part of his property and gave his two sons, Wallace and Roland, adjacent plots of equal size shortly after each married (Wallace in 1934 and Roland in 1935). The house at 2252 Hamilton, called "Longshadows" because of the deep overhangs, was built in 1936; the other, at 2254 Hamilton, was built in 1937. Though not identical, they both are one-story houses with large eaves, flat roofs, and horizontal lines, and are Usonian in concept. Longshadows has several half-levels in order to fit the family's requirements into the small house. The plots, which originally shared a common driveway, are narrow but deep, and the houses are set well into the property, making them invisible from the street. Both have had substantial additions and changes over the years, but their Wrightian aspects make them the earliest houses influenced by the architect, and predate the Goetsch-Winckler house of 1939–40.[78]

Roland and Wallace both studied at the University of Michigan in the early 1930s. Roland was listed as a clerk on his marriage certificate, and his wife, Jean Louise, was a stenographer. On his marriage certificate, Wallace was listed as a "designer."[79] As the story is told, Mr. Wilson sent his sons to Taliesin to study with Wright, and when they returned, they built their Wrightian homes. However, neither is listed among the apprentices or fellows at Taliesin, which opened to its first group of young students in 1932.[80] Although no direct connection with Wright can be verified yet, one can surmise that Wallace was the designer of the houses and must have carefully studied publications of Wright's Usonian homes and known about the Jacobs house in Wisconsin, built in 1936; he replicated the use of natural wood, overhanging eaves, clerestory windows, and other details. Further research may solve this mystery.

One further house should be mentioned. In 1952 Harry Lansing, the owner of a record shop in East Lansing and an amateur architectural designer, built a close copy of the Goetsch-Winckler house at 216 Oakland Drive in East Lansing for his family. The house repeats the horizontal lines, clerestory windows, and the orientation by placing the short end towards the street. The major differences are that the entire building has been flipped so that it is a mirror image of the original, and the carport was enlarged slightly and is held up by posts rather than the dramatic cantilever of Wright's building. The Lansings lived in the house until 1955.

Frank Lloyd Wright's connections to mid-Michigan are far deeper than the physical evidence of the four homes that were actually built. Had Usonia 2, the earliest project, been realized, it would have been the first manifestation of Broadacre City, his ideas for moderate-cost housing built on a communal rather than individual scale. From the small Goetsch-Winckler house to projects for their friends, colleagues, and neighbors, Wright's evolving approach to less modest structures can be seen, as well as his experiments with different materials, especially in the Brauner house. Each of the built and unbuilt houses evidenced his approach to organic architecture. The sites were large, often hilly, and the houses were carefully located to take full advantage of the connections between the land and building, the interior and exterior, nature and shelter. Extensive glazing, flat or low-pitched roofs, and low-to-the-ground structures make these continuing exemplars of the sensitivity of Wright's designed spaces.

CHAPTER 2

Alden B. Dow, Built and Unbuilt Houses

The Midland, Michigan, architect Alden B. Dow (1904–1983) designed five houses in mid-Michigan, of which four were built in East Lansing and Okemos. Additionally, he planned the first phase of Eastminster Church and was responsible for positioning the building on the site. Altogether, these structures range from early to very late in Dow's career, from modest to expansive structures, and from flat to steep roofs. By discussing them chronologically, one can gain an overview of Dow's aesthetic concerns.

Fortunate to be the son of the founder of the Dow Chemical Company, once he opened his architectural practice in 1934 in Midland, Alden created homes for many Dow executives, as well as numerous public buildings in the city. His home and studio, now a National Historic Landmark, not only retains his archives but is also itself the crowning achievement of the architect's career. The structure blends perfectly with nature in the most sublime example of his approach to relating a design to its site. It exemplifies his use of natural materials, unusual angles and shapes, bright colors, and the play of reflected light, all informed by a Japanese sensitivity that results in a harmonious and balanced whole.[1]

Because the majority of Dow's work is in Michigan, he is considered a Midwestern architect but deserves greater recognition. Like Frank Lloyd Wright, he embraced the ideas of using natural materials and of organic architecture. After graduating from Columbia University in 1931, Dow spent eight months as an apprentice to Wright in 1933. Comparisons with Wright are inevitable: their personalities, the way they

▶ **FIGURE 10.** Bachman House, Alden B. Dow, exterior, entrance, East Lansing. Early photograph, source unknown.

worked with clients, the influence on both of Japanese art and architecture, their use of color, and their mutual admiration.

Charles W. and Grace Bachman House

The first house Dow designed in mid-Michigan is the Charles W. and Grace Bachman House at 929 Roxburgh Avenue, East Lansing, designed in 1936 (plate 1). Charles Bachman was Michigan State College's football coach from 1933 until 1946. The two-story L-shaped structure is sited at the top of a rise in the land. The asymmetric design contrasts large solid-white walls with windows at the corners and patterned cement blocks. The flat roof emphasizes the horizontality of the house. The garage and porch (now enclosed) above jut out towards the street and shelter the entrance to the house (figure 10). On the back, the house is one story and very open, with larger expanses of glazing that connect the inside and outside. The living room, dining room, kitchen, and bedrooms are on the second story; the maid's room and garage are on the first.

This is the only one of Dow's mid-Michigan houses to use the "Unit Block" system that he developed in 1935, and for which he was granted a patent in 1938. Of the hundreds of houses he designed, there are only thirteen Unit Block structures, including his own. These precast molded masonry units are six-sided blocks that are laid in overlapping courses, one angled to the right, the next to the left so that a distinctive appearance is produced as well as a very strong bond.[2] The Unit Block's characteristic look can be seen on the exterior and interior of the Bachman house (figure 11). It was also used to make an interesting pattern on the edge of the two-story fireplace wall and to create cantilevered shelves and table bases. The strength of the Unit Block system was recognized; in a 1965 listing of the Bachman house by the Stebbins Realty Company, it was described as "solid as the Rock of Gibraltar."[3]

The two-story fireplace is the organizing feature at the center of the house. Stairs encircle the fireplace on three sides and provide interesting views of the interior as one ascends or descends. On the second level, the space moves fluidly around the open stair landing and the living and dining areas.[4] The use of white contrasted with cypress wood trim both inside and out reveals Dow's coloristic sense. He also specified bright-color carpets. There are many built-in shelves, closets, and even a bunk bed in one of the bedrooms.

When this house was built, there were only a few other flat-roofed homes in East Lansing, either in a Streamline or Art Moderne style, but this design was

929

nevertheless quite daring for the area. In using the Unit Block, Dow not only built a structurally sound and technologically innovative building but also gave the surfaces variety, texture, and visual interest.

Hayworth House

Dow's next East Lansing home, the two-story Hayworth house from 1946, is unpublished and unbuilt (plate 7). There is only one color drawing for the house in the Dow Archives, dated February 4, 1946, and no job file. Mr. Hayworth's first name is not given, but he likely is the same Donald Hayworth, a professor of speech, who contacted Keck & Keck of Chicago in September 1946, to design a house on Harrison Road in East Lansing. Why he did not build this Dow design therefore remains a mystery.

Dow's drawing shows the front elevation and plans for the ground and upper stories. The elevation emphasizes the horizontal with a flat roof, projecting entrance canopy, and clerestory windows in the upper pavilion. One bedroom and bathroom are indicated on the ground floor, but the main living space is above.

◀ **FIGURE 11.** Bachman House, Alden B. Dow, interior stairway, East Lansing. Early photograph, source unknown.

Here, four bedrooms, including the master bedroom, are aligned on one side of the house. On the other side of the hallway, there is a U-shaped kitchen and a small adjacent dining area. The majority of the space, however, is given over to the L-shaped living area with large windows on two sides of the room. On the side that is unseen in the elevation, there are exterior stairs that lead down to the patio below, which is protected by the overhang of the second floor. Many of the elements of this house, from the play of projecting and recessed parts, the placement of the main living spaces above, the large wall of windows, the second-story overhang, to the flat roof are recognizable from Dow's other houses from the late 1930s on. Unfortunately, the Hayworth house remained only a very preliminary idea.

Harold and Gladys Anderson House

Two years later, in 1948, Harold and Gladys Anderson began working with Dow to build a house at 340 Wildwood Drive in East Lansing (plate 15). Harold was head of the psychology department at Michigan State College. In contacting Dow about the project, the Andersons said they wanted "a home that a college professor could afford."[5] They asked for three bedrooms (for themselves, their son, Ted, and daughter, Janet), a study "in which two could work at the same time, a fireplace, plenty of space and light, and a window bench," but no dining room.

Dow sent sketches for the house on July 15, 1948, explaining:

> I believe it is about the best I can do in the light of present day prices, and it costs too much. It figures about 33,000 cubic feet which would probably run under $25,000. It is two stories, with a basement under the living room–kitchen area with part of the living room running two stories. The study is on the second floor looking down over the living room and could be arranged in any way to meet your particular needs for desk arrangement.

Dow explained that since each bedroom was to have a large wardrobe with drawers, they would save on the expense of furniture other than beds and a few chairs. By facing the garage and master bedroom to the street, the living and dining rooms would open on the backyard "as you desire. You will note that there is no service entrance to the kitchen. This could be provided but I feel that it is unnecessary."

> All of the heavy walls within the house would be built of standard cinder concrete blocks exposed inside and out. When these blocks are painted with the proper

> cement paint they make a really handsome wall that is durable, sound resistant and well insulated. In the last year we have built three houses using these blocks in this way and they have been very satisfactory. I think you will like this layout because it seems to suit your requirements, except, as I said before, the price and I don't know what to do about that.
>
> It just doesn't seem possible to get the cost down to the figure you are asking for, and make it really fit your lot. I suggest that you present these sketches to the builder you mentioned and see what he says about the price.[6]

Harold Anderson responded to Dow on July 24, 1949:

> Some of our friends have told us that building a house is just one series of headaches. If we are building a house I can only say that you are making it a thoroughly delightful experience. Of course building a house is not just dealing with cinder blocks and shingles. We found it very stimulating to discuss so many of these matters with you on Wednesday evening.[7]

Gladys Anderson, in a handwritten note to Dow dated August 7, 1949, wrote that

> Mr. Anderson says that in growth there are always new horizons. He is not sure whether it is more important to make a noise or to build a house, or whether they could be done at the same time. . . . We think your sketches have great possibility for a house we would enjoy living in. When we receive the list of specifications we shall begin at once with a new contractor.[8]

In "East Lansing Residence Lives up to Dow's Reputation," Warren Brintnall, the architecture writer for the *Lansing State Journal*, described the house on first glance as "ordinary" and "plain" because "the most striking feature is not visible from the street. At the rear, facing a spacious private yard dominated by three oak trees is a two-story wall made up almost entirely of double-panel insulating glass." These thirteen-foot-high windows admit light to the interior spaces. Brintnall described the colors as off-white on the walls; red in the rubber tiles on the floor; chartreuse linoleum on countertops, window benches, and bookshelves; and unpainted fir woodwork and trim. There is room for Anderson's extensive library and ample storage space. Brintnall pointed out that to make the 86-foot by 192-foot lot appear even deeper, Dow directed that the earth excavated for the basement was to be deposited near the rear property line. The resultant valley between the house and end of the lot is calculated to give the illusion of greater distance.

Brintnall also remarked upon the angle of the roof that provided space for another car (in addition to the attached garage) and sheltered the front door from the weather.[9] Indeed, this is the feature of the house that is most visible from the street and makes a statement about privacy and the house as refuge. When completed in 1949, the house cost $23,636, close to Dow's original estimate but nearly twice as much as the Bachman house twelve years before.[10]

Carleton W. and Heluiz Washburne House

In the 1950s, Dow designed the master plan for Eastminster Presbyterian Church on Abbot Road, of which the first unit was built. In 1960 he began working on the next house for Carleton and Heluiz Washburne (plate 52) at 2248 Kent Street in Okemos, built as a retirement home for the couple, who came from New York to be near their daughter who was married to an MSC professor. Dr. Washburne was a nationally known educational psychologist and theoretician and taught in New York. In retirement he became a Distinguished Professor of Education at MSC. His wife, Heluiz, was a children's writer.[11] He asked Dow to design a house that would be "an intellectually and emotionally satisfying environment" in which to continue his work throughout his retirement years.[12]

Washburne outlined a small home (five rooms, basement, attached garage, two bathrooms) that would meet their needs but allowed for the possibility of adding another bedroom at the east end.[13] The plot they chose has an unusual keyhole shape with only 15 feet on the street and required a variance from the township.[14] The narrow driveway leads up into the property where the house is sited on the highest part, oriented on an east-west axis.

On April 17, Washburne wrote to Dow: "In the nature of things, a letter such as this seems to be picking flaws and making criticisms. I think you know, however, that these are relatively minor functional details from the standpoint of our personal needs and way of life and that they don't in the least detract from our delight in the house as a whole—our enthusiasm, rather, grows as we see more fully what our new house will be like." He added a postscript: "How will we wash the clerestory windows, inside and out?"

The Washburnes had an urgency to build. They had moved out of their Manhattan apartment, were to spend several months in Africa, and hoped to return directly to their new home. However, this six-month time frame was too short for several contractors who declined to even bid on the project. On June 27, 1960, the Washburnes signed a contract with Modern Builders of Okemos.[15] The cost of the house itself would be $22,400, but with land, septic system, driveway, architect's fee (10 percent), and other items, the final cost was $33,500. Their accelerated time frame,

▶ **FIGURE 12.** Washburne House, Alden B. Dow, exterior, rear, Okemos. Photograph © 2014 Kim Kauffman.

however, turned out to be unrealistic and the house was not ready until spring 1961.

After they moved in, their enthusiasm continued. On March 20, 1961, Washburne wrote to Dow:

> We are eager to have you see the house now that it is finished and no longer a house but a home. It is beautiful beyond our fondest hopes and very functional. We keep finding new points of charm and care that delight us. As Phil Will [his friend who recommended Dow in the first place] said, when he visited us shortly after we got in, "It is a proud house!" But my wife says, "It's a serene house." Basically, we think it's a beautiful and wonderfully lovely home.[16]

With the emphasis on horizontal planes and placement on the site, the Washburne house has echoes of Frank Lloyd Wright's Goetsch-Winckler house, not too far away. However, Dow's house is white and bright, has a garage rather than a carport, an open kitchen area, larger rooms, and cement-block construction. The horizontal is further emphasized on the exterior by the deep overhangs and alternating horizontal bands of ten-inch blocks. The alternation was repeated on the interior, where cement blocks contrast with large sheets of Sitka spruce. The fireplace hearth is at the center of the structure, raised above the floor. There are many built-in shelves and storage units throughout the house.[17]

The front elevation has small windows in the bedroom wing, while on the garden side, the living room has floor-to-ceiling windows and miterless corners, and the ceiling is higher than the rest of the house (figure 12). A low cement-block wall demarcates a boundary for the outside patio and reinforces the planarity of the house. The subtle changes of the ceiling heights, the views outside, and the long vistas from one end of the house to another, as well as the harmonious placement of the house on the lot, are hallmarks of Dow's style.

In March 1960, the Washburnes asked Dow for a landscape plan. They had received as a gift from Chicago sculptor Alfonso Ianelli a small fountain with the figure of St. Francis that was to be the centerpiece of the landscape. Ianelli (1888–1965) had worked with Frank Lloyd Wright to produce the famous sprites that were part of the Midway Gardens in 1914. In an early drawing for the house, Dow had suggested placing a small pool outside the living room, but it was eliminated to save on costs. Now the Washburnes suggested a reflecting pool for the sculpture.[18] However, it was again eliminated based on questions of how to maintain it. One ornamental flourish that was provided is the elaborate outdoor wooden lamp. The Washburnes thought they were agreeing to a simple lamppost for the driveway, but were shocked when they received the bill. In the only disagreement they had with Dow, they

finally compromised on the cost and received a unique lamp that fits the geometry of the house.[19]

On April 29, 1961, after moving into the house, Carleton Washburne continued his earlier praise. "This house is certainly a joy—comfortable, functional, admirably constructed, and designed with attention to every detail as well as to its wholeness, wonderful balance and harmony of space proportions, materials, colors. We revel in its beauty."[20]

Michael and Rhea Dow House

Dow's two East Lansing houses were built on fairly small lots. The Washburne house in Okemos was built on an unusually shaped plot whose distance from the street afforded great privacy. The final house in the area, however, gave Dow his only opportunity to work with a large suburban lot of 3.8 acres (plate 81). Set on a cul-de-sac at 1172 Wrightwind Drive, it was designed for the eldest of Dow's three children, Michael, and daughter-in-law Rhea. The house would keep good company with the Schabergs' Frank Lloyd Wright design and others by prominent area architects already built or under construction.

The Dow house is one story with a partial basement, and as it steps down from street level towards the back of the property, there are several low-pitched roofs of differing heights. This 4,400-square-foot grand house has four bedrooms, three baths, and a two-car garage. The large "serendipity room" that Michael requested is adjacent to the kitchen and garage. Some other ideas he asked for were accommodated, including a workbench space, bookshelves, sewing area, reading corner, carpeting, high ceiling in part, good access to garage and kitchen, lots of storage space, game area, and a pool (which was enclosed in 1979).[21] One very modern feature was the central vacuum system. The original cost estimate in August 1968 was $99,045. By late November it had risen to $152,729, by May 1969 to $171,008, and then to $223,601. The family furnished the home with modern examples from Herman Miller, Knoll, and other design companies.[22]

Both the Michael and Rhea Dow house and the Corporate Hangar Facility for Michael Dow's company, General Aviation, at the Capital City Airport on the west side of Lansing, were designed very late in Alden B. Dow's career and were collaborations with designers in Dow's firm: William H. Gilmore (for the house) and James Howell (for the hangar). The hangar design was started in 1972; contracts were signed in July 1975, and the building was finished in 1976.[23] Howell succeeded Dow as chairman of the board of the company in 1974. Dow, Howell, Gilmore Associates, Inc. (DHGA), the successor firm, also designed Plymouth

Congregational Church in Lansing in 1975. Its design focus is the round sanctuary topped by a spire that rises 45 feet.

Throughout his career, Dow wrote, lectured, and spoke about his philosophy. Towards the end of his life, he codified it in a document called "A Way of Life Cycle" that can be summarized as being based on the encouragement of each person's innate creativity, which will lead to the development of finer standards.[24] Many of his ideas are manifested in his mid-Michigan architecture. These include that architecture should inspire its users; the outside is part of the inside; gardens never end and buildings never begin; a structure must have honesty, humility, and enthusiasm; space is not confined within four walls; and texture and color are uplifting.[25] In reading the various homeowners' glowing reports to Dow about how life-changing it was to live in their houses, it appears that he succeeded well. Through his architectural designs, he expressed his quest for composed order and for constructive solutions that would help the individual find their own creativity.

CHAPTER 3

Keck & Keck, Realized and Unrealized Houses

George Fred (1895–1980) and William (1908–1995) Keck began their architecture practice in the 1920s and became well known in the 1930s as a result of two houses they contributed to the Chicago Century of Progress Fair: the House of Tomorrow, 1933, and the Crystal House, which was added in 1934 for the second year of the fair.[1] These houses launched the Keck brothers' architectural careers and their reputation for innovative approaches to passive solar heating and the use of contemporary construction techniques. Of the hundreds of houses across the Midwest that they designed over the next decades, two were for mid-Michigan clients, but only one was built. Both, however, reflect the Kecks' novel ideas.

The House of Tomorrow was a pioneering twelve-sided, three-story structure commissioned by Century Homes, Inc., as part of a display of houses that utilized the very latest in building technology. Glass, steel, and concrete were used to create a wheel-like arrangement with spokes radiating from the central utility core. The main living space on the first floor had interior partitions that divided the space into a large living room, kitchen, children's room, bath, and bedroom. A deck and conservatory were on the floor above. However, the most unusual feature was on the lower level, where in addition to a recreation room, workspace, and porch, there was room to park a car and a plane. The latter was envisioned as the mode of transportation of the future.[2] The house was to rely on central air conditioning as a demonstration of a self-ventilating structure. To that end, the panes of glass on the upper two floors were stationary. However, during the blistering Chicago summer, the house became too hot, and for the second season of the fair, windows that could open replaced the originals. The house was visited by hundreds of thousands of fairgoers who saw not only innovative materials in use but also a completely furnished home with up-to-the minute time-saving devices such as a garbage disposal, an electric dishwasher, and electric eyes that controlled the doors of the garage.[3]

Keck & Keck's second house at the Century of Progress Fair was called the Crystal House because of the extensive use of glass. Large plates of glass were attached to a welded steel three-story construction. The first floor held the entry, hobby room, mechanical equipment, and garage. A stairway led to the second-floor living space with the dining room, study, living room, and kitchen, and then to the third-floor bedrooms and baths.[4] Photographs from the fair show that it was possible to see into the entire interior, which was furnished with reproductions of European modernists such as Mies van der Rohe and Marcel Breuer. Buckminster Fuller's Dymaxion car was parked on the first floor.[5] The Crystal House was built at the Kecks' expense for $15,000, but because its remote location was a deterrent to fairgoers, it was visited by fewer than those who experienced the House of Tomorrow.

The Century of Progress houses were inventive and radical, but following the war, the Kecks produced more modified structures in order to appeal to clients. They were consistent, however, in their experimentation with new technologies, seeking ways to improve modern living, and they developed the materials and techniques for which they became known. They pioneered the use of passive solar heating and were the first to consistently use Thermopane windows (a double-pane glass with insulating capabilities), wide sun-shading eaves, and exterior Venetian blinds. By 1940 the exterior blinds were replaced with ones on the interior.[6]

A majority of Keck & Keck's nine hundred modernist houses are in the Chicago area and in Wisconsin. In the late 1930s through 1969, they designed several summer homes along Lake Michigan in places such as St. Joseph, Benton Harbor, Muskegon, and Charlevoix.[7] The two residences for mid-Michigan clients are the Panshin house at 2515 Arrowhead Road, in Indian Hills, Okemos, 1947, and an unbuilt house for Donald Hayworth on Harrison Road, East Lansing, 1949.

The Alexis and Lucie Panshin House

The Keck & Keck house for Alexis and Lucie Panshin (plate 11) followed the couple's original foray into architectural design with Frank Lloyd Wright. The last to join the Usonia 2 project, they also were the first to withdraw. Alexis, who was a professor of forestry, was deeply concerned with Wright's use of untreated wood and the potential for exceeding their budget.

After the war, the Panshins renewed their interest in having an architect design their home. Already attuned to contemporary architecture, the Panshins would have learned about Keck & Keck in a wide variety of ways. In addition to seeing the Century of Progress publicity and perhaps visiting the fair, the Panshins undoubtedly read about the architects' solar heating experiments in popular journals such as *House Beautiful* (September 1943) or *Reader's Digest* (January 1944).[8] Beyond this, there was the Forest Products Laboratory connection. In 1942, Keck & Keck teamed up with the Green Company of Rockford, Illinois, a well-known leader in prefabricated buildings. The Forest Products Laboratory worked with the Green Company to improve the design and production of prefabricated wall panels.[9] Green's Ready-Built Homes, based on Keck and Keck's designs, were erected all over the Midwest from 1946 on. They featured high-quality products, flexible floor plans, folding partitions, flat roofs, south-facing Thermopane walls, deep overhangs, and gravity heat. The goal was to build a house for $6,122 in eight hours.[10] With twenty-one different models, variety was possible, but a shortage of materials, difficulty getting FHA loans, and union demands raised prices.[11]

Alexis Panshin had worked at Forest Products Laboratory in 1934–35 and likely kept up with Keck & Keck's news. Having expressed his concern about insulation in the Wright-designed house, Panshin probably found Keck's solar heating to his liking. In the 1940s, Keck & Keck became known as pioneers in solar homes, of which they designed over three hundred. Key to their success was to face the house to the south for maximum solar gain in winter. To the north, small rectangular clerestory windows below the roofline were used, as was an entryway protected by a berm.

The Panshins purchased a lot in the Indian Hills subdivision, adjacent to the Brauners, their good friends, and across the road from the Edwardses. Both of their houses were being designed by Frank Lloyd Wright and would be constructed at the same time. On January 12, 1947, Lucie Panshin wrote to George Fred (who was known as Fred) Keck thanking him for his interest in helping them and mentioning the two other families who had bought adjacent property in the Indian Hills subdivision: the Brauners, who were "still waiting for a reply to their second letter to Mr. Wright," and T. D. Stevens of the forestry department.[12] After meeting George Keck at his lecture at Michigan State College on January 16, the Panshins began exploring possible contractors.

Their detailed four-page letter of March 3, 1947, written by Lucie, who became the family's correspondent, put "on paper ideas as to how we live, and how we hope to live in our own home."

> Just living in general seems to come first, so to the living room. We think of the fireplace as the heart of the room, where we can have our usual sort of family evening, mostly reading or writing, or listening to a concert, and at the same time a place where we can entertain informally without a lack of comfortable place to sit. . . . My ideal of entertainment is for people to feel so much at home and a part of the family that they can do exactly as they please. I wish the fireplace could not be functional looking, but very much the center of the room, and not raised. . . .
>
> When I think about living, the outdoors comes into the picture. We like to sit outdoors . . . and in the living room, we wonder if it would be possible to be able to open some part to the outdoors, so we could hear the outdoor sounds. . . . [For the two boys] a space they'll never have to clean up their mess before dinner. . . .
>
> When it comes to provision for eating, I'd like our family meals in the kitchen, with space enough for one or two guests to join us, and with provision for storage of linen. . . .
>
> Whenever possible we'd like to eat outdoors. I've always longed for a porch directly accessible from the kitchen, where I could serve as easily as in the house. . . . the part of the kitchen that I am interested in is the work space. I really love to cook, and do more than the average family, for instance, we always have homemade bread and cookies, and we do not enjoy quick meals from a can.
>
> I am interested in the Purdue kitchen, scientifically planned to save steps. . . . It is arrangement of work space and cupboards that interests me especially, as well as all wood in a natural finish and no white woodwork to keep spotless. . . . Should I mention that I am tall, and would like work space higher than normal?[13]

Because Mrs. Panshin was undoubtedly thinking of some of the issues that others had working with Frank Lloyd Wright, she was very clear about her needs and desires. In mentioning her height, she may be recalling Sidney Newman, who was six feet tall and complained in vain to Wright on several occasions that the height of the ceilings in the rooms (6′6″ to 6′10″) and doors (6′5″) in his Usonia 2 design were totally inadequate.[14] For the canning of fruit and storage of fruits and vegetables, Lucie suggests a small underground room. Alma Goetsch and Kathrine Winckler had their builder put a small root cellar under the carport at their Usonian house just a few miles away. Wright almost divorced himself from the project as designer of the house as a result.[15]

The Panshins wanted a two-car garage with

storage. Rather than separate bedrooms for the two boys, Mrs. Panshin suggested dividing one room with a sliding partition, with a single bed, closet, drawers, a built-in desk, and bookshelves in each space. "Perhaps sentiment as well as dislike of tiny rooms influences me in hoping for no permanent separation." She also presented Keck with two problems to solve. One was how to ensure sufficient heat in the house. She recounted how she came to hate being cold because of horrible childhood memories of dressing in very cold unheated rooms in early winter mornings in New England. The second dilemma was to figure out how to provide enough sinks so that no one would have to wait to use one.

After detailing other wishes for storage, she added:

> I love to watch the morning and evening sky, and all my life I've had to work for an occasional glimpse of either. Out at Indian Hills, we'll have space and shouldn't have to do this. Will you keep my request in mind? I'm not sure that a western window would be pleasant with the setting sun striking people in the face, but would like to be able to watch the changing colors of the sky with the rising and setting sun.

By March the Panshins had secured the services of her brother, Tom Padget, an experienced builder then working in Florida.[16] George Keck sent a first sketch on March 29, 1947, explaining that

> We have followed first, your desires. We have paid no attention to budget. But, speaking of budget, the house will exceed the figure of $12,000 you gave me by a good deal I believe. But your brother will be of good help here. He is a man of good will, and can help get this house constructed along the lines of Wright construction in your vicinity. That method can bring costs down somewhat, but there always is a low limit.[17]

By "that method" he was perhaps referring to the use of prefabricated parts.

The Panshins were ecstatic about the plan. "I can't properly express our delight. It is our dream, and more," Lucie wrote on March 31. A follow-up letter on April 3 asked for clarification of the exterior treatment, which called for mainly wood with some brick. The Panshins were under the assumption that brick would be used.

> Incidentally, wood for siding is one of the scarcest items in local lumberyards. College construction is taking anything that can be had. . . . I'd like to say thank you again for the plan. We couldn't be happier, possibly. You seem to have thought of everything, and the plan shows such artistry and imagination. It is possible that cost will force us to postpone the bedroom wing for

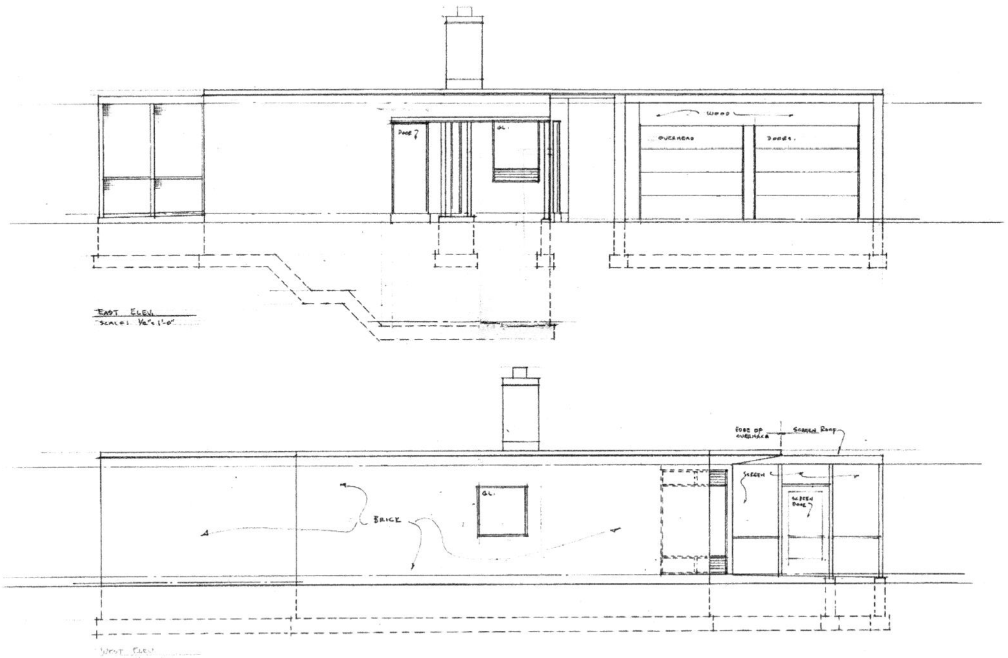

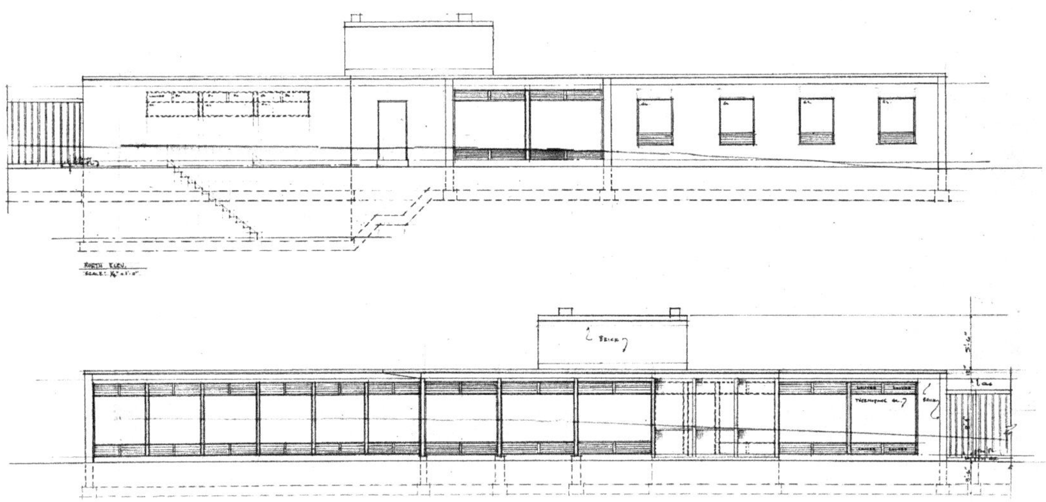

> the time being, but we are determined not to scale down the house. By the way, we had felt even before the plan came that we'd have to figure nearer $15,000 than our original figure. Beyond that the budget can't be stretched.[18]

Several quick sketches were enclosed with George Keck's March 29 letter. One indicates a long, rectangular building, but a more detailed drawing shows the obtuse angle of the bedroom wing as it was constructed (figures 13, 14, 15). Keck wrote on April 8 that he would start working on the perspective: "The south side of the house will be mostly glass and wood frames, and the north side mostly brick, with high horizontal windows except at the living room, where I would like one or two large panes. The view to the north is fine and should be seen from the living room."[19]

Throughout the spring and summer, letters went back and forth clarifying details. For example, Keck suggested leaving one bathroom unbuilt so that

▼ **FIGURE 13.** Panshin House, Keck & Keck, east and west elevations, Okemos. Wisconsin Historical Society, WHS-110759.

◀ **FIGURE 14.** Panshin House, Keck & Keck, south and north elevations. Wisconsin Historical Society, WHS-110758.

▶ **FIGURE 15.** Panshin House, Keck & Keck, floor plan. Wisconsin Historical Society, WHS-110760.

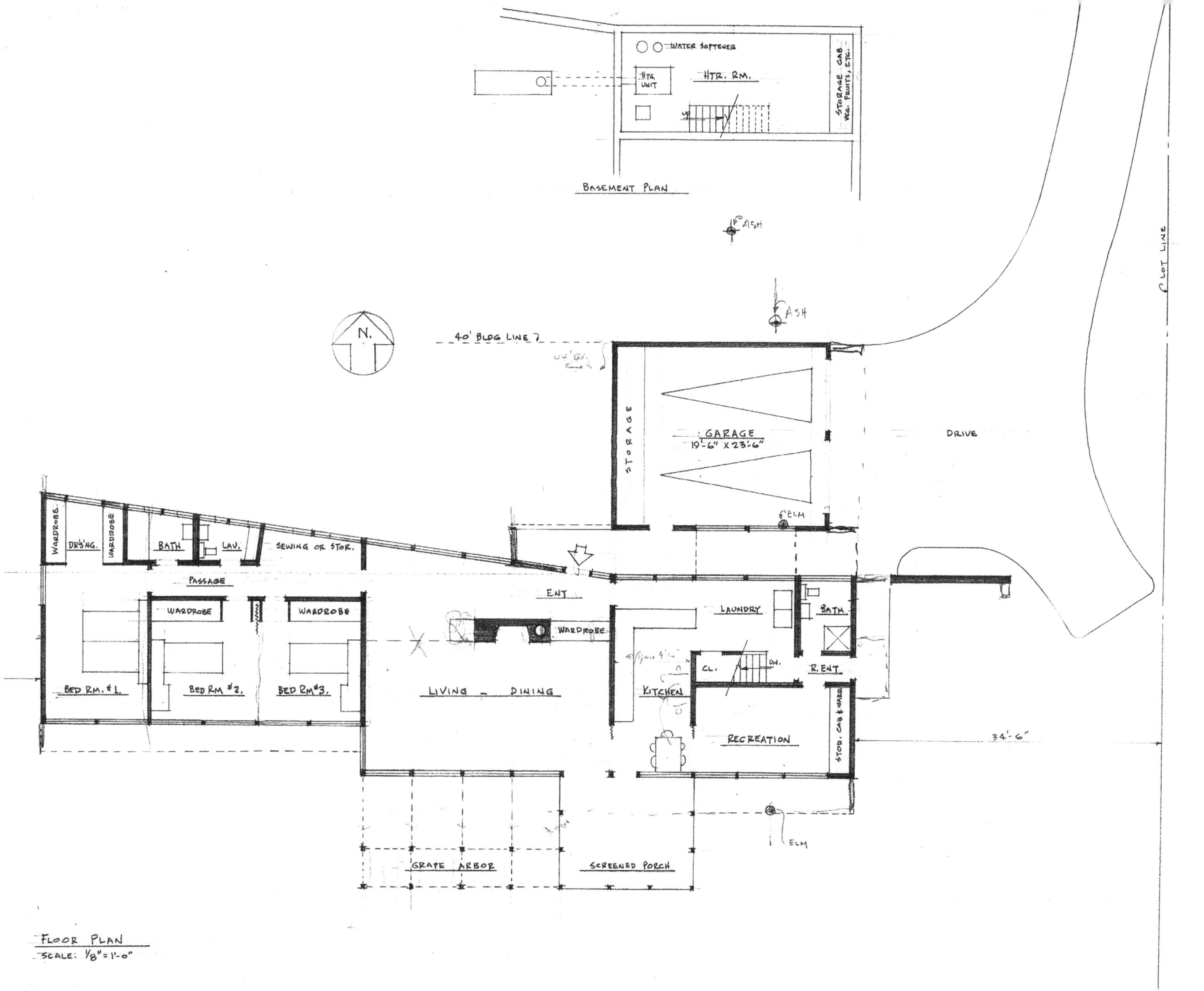
WATER SOFTENER
HTG. UNIT
HTR. RM.
STORAGE CAB. VEG. FRUITS, ETC.
BASEMENT PLAN
ASH
ASH
LOT LINE
N.
40' BLDG LINE
GARAGE
19'-6" X 23'-6"
STORAGE
DRIVE
ELM
WARDROBE
DRS'NG.
WARDROBE
BATH
LAV.
SEWING OR STOR.
PASSAGE
ENT
WARDROBE
WARDROBE
WARDROBE
LAUNDRY
BATH
CL.
DN.
R. ENT
BED RM. #1.
BED RM #2.
BED RM #3.
LIVING – DINING
KITCHEN
RECREATION
STOR. CAB & WARD.
34'-6"
ELM
GRAPE ARBOR
SCREENED PORCH
FLOOR PLAN
SCALE: 1/8" = 1'-0"

the house would not exceed the FHA rulings about maximum square footage (2,000) to qualify for a loan.[20] Other correspondence was about how to get the order for their Thermopane from Libby-Owens-Ford Co. back on schedule.[21] Contractor Tom Padget's letter on October 7, 1947, detailed all that was done and remained to be completed, with everything hinging on the arrival of the glass expected the following week.

The Panshins moved into their home in the late fall, and by Christmas 1947 Lucie wrote to Keck enthusiastically:

> I'll have to hold myself down but I break into rhapsodies. [It's a] new life for us all—we're still getting used to it and regretting every minute away from the space and light and freedom.
>
> To go to sleep looking out on a sky of stars, or as last night a fairyland of snow heavy in branches—our souls are still expanding to encompass it all. The boys are so happy that we feel like apologizing for having held them down and harmed them as we had to previously. It means everything to us to be able to have a more closely-knit family life up here, to be close to the outdoors together. . . . So grateful to you. . . . Not just a new house—it's a new way of living.[22]

The house they so enjoyed sits on a rise above street level; has three bedrooms, three baths, and 2,300 square feet; and is constructed of red brick. The solid brick wall of the detached garage facing north is the most visible part of the house from the street. It is approached up the driveway and shields the entry from view.[23] A segmented light roof between the walls of the garage and the house shelters the walkway and leads to the front door (figure 16). The north wall of the bedroom wing was angled outward to give visual interest to the long façade, as well as to vary the shapes of the interior spaces. As requested, a large fireplace is at the heart of the open space that flows from the dining area to the living room and out to the screened porch. The large areas of Thermopane glazing on the side facing the backyard brings the outside in. The glazed areas on the north are far smaller. Only one window in the entire house is operable. For ventilation, vents above and/or below the windows can be seen in the corridor outside the entrance and on the north façade. This novel system is evidence of the Kecks' approach to passive solar heating and self-ventilating systems.

Throughout the process of building their home, the Panshins frequently wrote to George Keck comparing their experience to that of the owners of the two Wright-designed houses that were under construction nearby, sometimes gloating over the difficulties of working with Wright compared to the Kecks. On January 12, 1947, Lucie reported that the

◄ **FIGURE 16.** Panshin House, exterior entryway, Okemos.

Photograph © 2014 Kim Kauffman.

▶ **FIGURE 17.** Hayworth House, Keck & Keck, elevation, unbuilt. Wisconsin Historical Society, WHS-110757.

Brauners were "still waiting for a reply to their second letter to Mr. Wright." On January 27, the Brauners "have still heard nothing from Mr. Wright even after asking him to acknowledge receipt of their contour map." On March 3, Lucie wrote a postscript to George Keck: "Believe it or not, Mr. Wright is at work on the house for the Brauners." On April 16, she mentioned that the Brauners' house would be brick too, and that "the two houses should blend well" (although when it was constructed, the Brauner house used cement block). "I'm glad yours is going up first." Writing on September 30, 1947, Lucie reported that Erling Brauner went to Taliesin with the house plan and "found His Majesty amenable and cooperative—result is a house vastly cut and very compact, though I still privately place it at $20,000." In the last letter in the Keck & Keck papers, dated March 21, 1951, Lucie wrote: "I think you'd be proud to compare your product with the two Wright houses that complete our trio. The second Wright house [the Edwardses' house], "scheduled for occupancy last November, still drags on, a long way from being finished. So much money has gone into it, with such a little bit of living space, and not even a large living room to compensate for cells as bedrooms. But perhaps you will come, and see for yourself."

Donald and Frances Margaret Hayworth House

Keck & Keck designed a second house that was to be built for Donald Hayworth and his family on Harrison Road in East Lansing, but its fate was less felicitous than the Panshins' (figure 17). In 1937 Donald Hayworth (1898–1982) was appointed professor and head of Michigan State College's Department of Speech. He left the university periodically to pursue other interests. He unsuccessfully sought the Democratic nomination for Congress in 1950. While he did receive it in 1952, he was defeated in the election. In 1954 he was elected and served in the U.S. Congress for one term. He returned to the faculty in 1957, but took leaves of absence to run again in 1958 and 1962. His politics were too liberal for the area, however, so he was not reelected. He resigned from the university in 1964.[24] In addition to his careers as an active Democrat and well-respected academic researcher on topics such as pubic speaking, he owned his own company, Michigan Plastics Manufacturing, from 1952 until 1963.[25]

In 1946 Donald and his wife, Frances Margaret Knight, began the process of building an architect-designed house. They first apparently worked with Alden B. Dow, and although a design was completed by February, nothing came of this project. By August, Hayworth was in touch with the Kecks to start anew. In a letter to George Keck dated August 9, Hayworth

explained that "On the advice of several architects in Detroit I am writing to ask if you are in a position to do a home for me and my family in the near future. I am cooperating with a number of manufacturers and will throw the home open to the public for two or three months. I propose to write a book and some magazine articles on it."[26] Indeed, his letterhead read, "The Hayworth House, a model home built to demonstrate postwar materials and furnishings."[27]

Hayworth proposed to purchase three lots in the Glencairn subdivision, which had been laid out in 1939. This would give him the corner lot on Harrison Road (running north) and Northlawn Street (running east). He enclosed an advertising brochure for Glencairn with the heading "See Glen Cairn Today—for Your Home of Tomorrow." Spacious lots, gracefully winding tree-lined streets with no through traffic, and picturesque plantings of trees were mentioned as enticements. Pictures in the brochure showed a range of architectural styles from Colonial to the modern Alden B. Dow–designed home for the Bachmans (see plate 1).[28]

Hayworth also enclosed a three-page statement of "certain ideas which have occurred to me." He realized that these would have to be pared down, given a budget of "something like $18,000 with which to work, and expect to borrow on the house as it is built. This amount includes what is available for site ($2,500), landscaping and furnishings." He went on to say they had no preference for the number of floors for their dwelling, and that the family consisted of himself and his wife and three daughters. He hoped to open the house in spring of 1947, or perhaps even a year later.[29] To accomplish his goal of cooperating with various companies, he asked for sketches so he could "take a trip east in December to make final arrangements with such manufacturers as Libby-Owens-Ford, Westinghouse, Johns-Manville, RCA-Victor and others."[30]

In September, Hayworth wrote of extending the option to purchase the lots and said that muck made choosing the building site somewhat tricky but there were no other lots available that were suitable for his purpose. Of concern to him was easy access from a main highway, "inasmuch as this is to be a model home."[31] Keck responded that although "it is difficult, in these days, to estimate the costs of a projected house . . . even in normal times the appetite outweighs the budget and in today's market the situation is worse."[32] He suggested some cost savings, such as eliminating the basement and building the radiant heating system into a masonry floor right on the ground. He also proposed to design the entire project, and if budget problems developed, only a part of the house would be built, with later additions.[33]

On January 11, 1947, Hayworth wrote with more

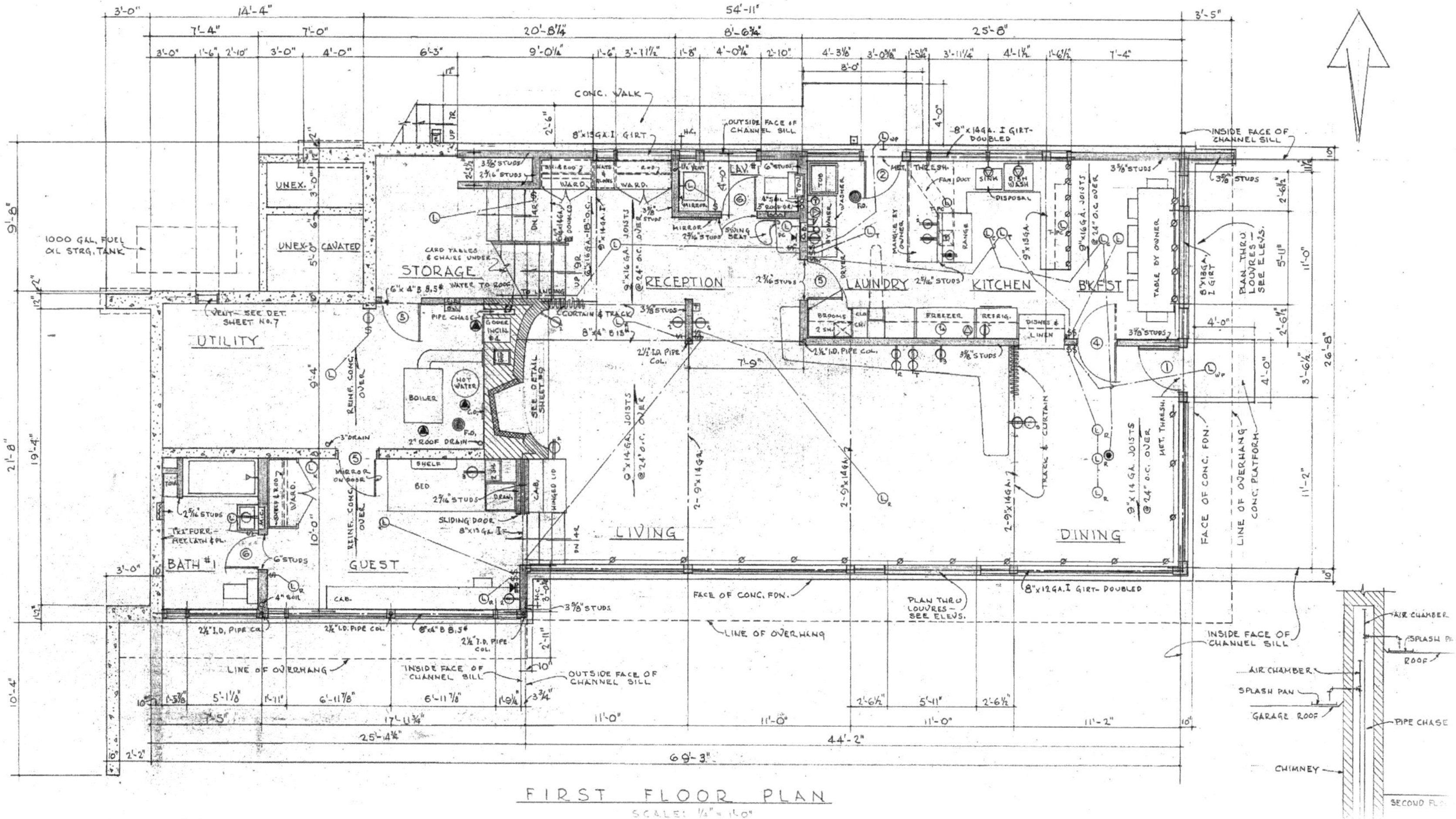

▲ **FIGURE 18.** Hayworth House, Keck & Keck, first-floor plan. Wisconsin Historical Society, WHS-110762.

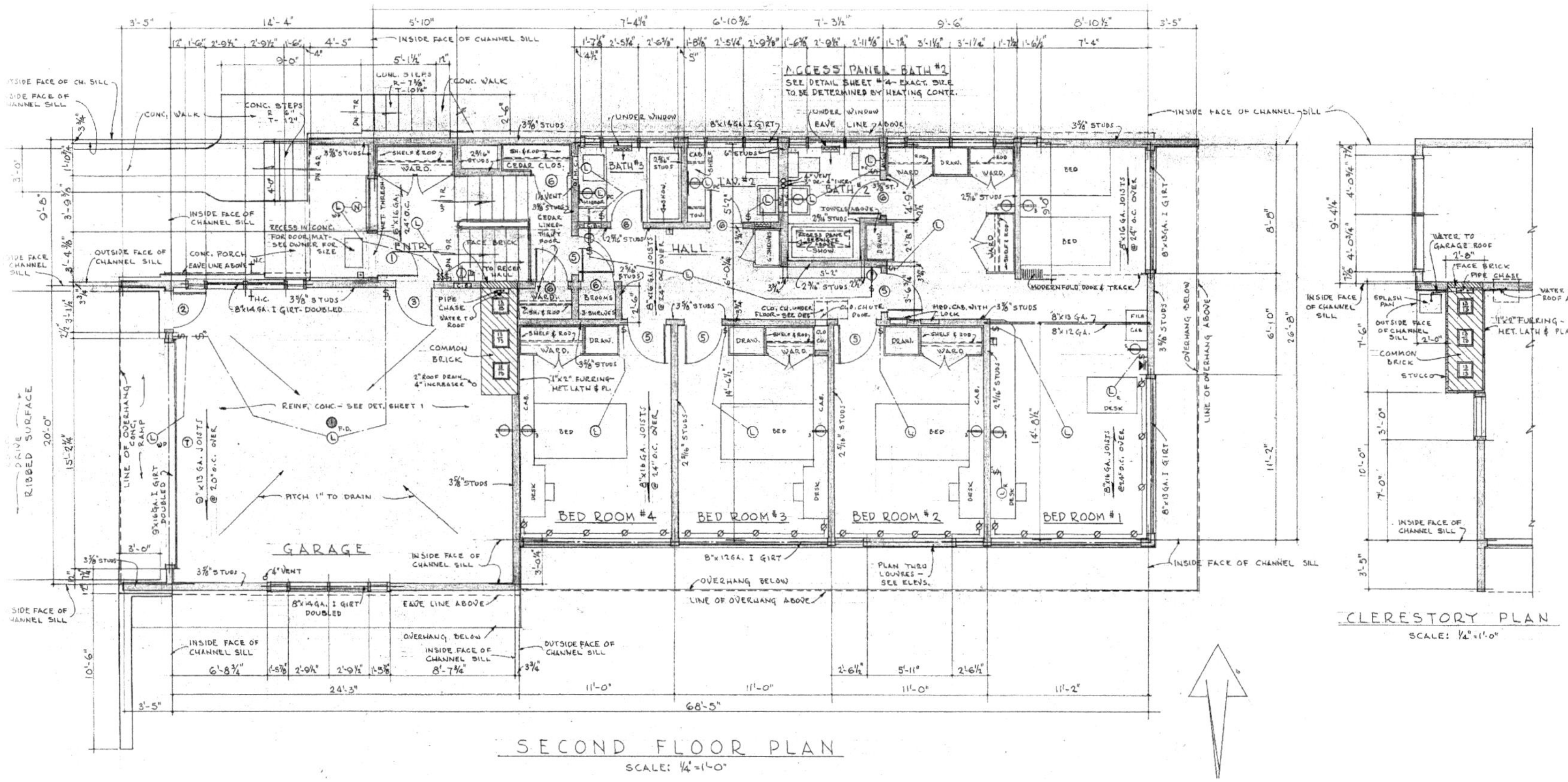

▲ **FIGURE 19.** Hayworth House, Keck & Keck, second-floor plan. Wisconsin Historical Society, WHS-110764.

information about the contours of the property, but added that he was in "no great rush for the drawings" as there "is a slight possibility we may move to another university." After a long hiatus, on September 14, Hayworth wrote again regarding the cost of the house per cubic foot (70 cents in Lansing), giving Keck permission to go ahead with the design, and specifying that he wanted a large shop and hopefully a two-car garage that could be combined with a children's theater with sliding doors.[34] In December, he explained that he would like to build in the spring, and that his wife's "children's dramatics" had "faded as a possibility" so the theater could be dropped. On the other hand, his plastic products were taking off, and while the company would be moving into a new building, he still wanted a good-sized workshop for "experimental purposes."[35]

Little happened in 1948. In August, Hayworth explained to George Keck, "We are in no greater hurry to build than when I last saw you."[36] Hayworth received blueprints by the end of the year and a watercolor drawing by February 1949.[37] In May, he sent a "potpourri of ideas for the house" covering minute details from where to put a light switch or built-in shelf, to the use of louver doors and a snow-melt system for the driveway. He also asked for a complete set of plans to send or take to Westinghouse in person to "see whether or not they want to make a project of it. . . . It would seem that the time is fast arriving when manufacturers will be glad for promotion which won't be expensive."[38]

Financing the project was a fraught issue. In an undated letter (probably early May 1949), Hayworth explained that he expected to finance the house with a $16,000 loan at 4½ percent from a life insurance company. He expected to have "not less than $15,000 including the lot at $2500." Things were moving along well towards the production of the final plans, including visits with Westinghouse and the local Stran Steele dealer, but on July 17, Hayworth hinted that financing was a problem. "One thing, which you cannot help me with, I assume, is the financing. There are complications which I did not anticipate."[39] Keck responded in October that "If you attempt to hold to your present budget, you will have to forego some of the refinements in the plan." He also compared the cubic feet (41,000) to the Panshins' (34,000), and while he never did know their final costs, he believed they were around $25,000. Hayworth's house would be more than that since the Panshins did not use steel.[40]

In one of his last (undated) letters, Hayworth wrote to Keck that "I thought I should let you know the situation at this end of the line, now that I have the plans. I thought I knew just how I was going to finance it, but I'm not sure now. I was getting the money from an insurance company, but it has a maximum of $16,000.

After investigating prices, I find that I may need quite a little more than that." He then compliments the plan by saying that inexpert friends are as enthusiastic about it as the experts he showed it to.[41] The contractor's estimate in early October was over $39,000. One can imagine how disappointed Hayworth was, but there are no further letters in the archives and the project seems to have come to a screeching halt due to the costs. The site itself was also probably an issue since no house was ever built on this corner lot, which now is the property of the house to the east.

As seen in the sketch of the south elevation in the Keck & Keck archive, this house would have had many of the features that can be considered the architects' trademarks (figure 17): a flat roof, south-facing façade for solar gain, and large fixed Thermopane windows with small horizontal louvers at the top and bottom edges for ventilation. The two levels are protected by flat overhangs to shade the windows below from sun. Drawings for each floor show the proposed layout (figures 18, 19). The two-car garage is on the west, accessed from Harrison Road, and a sidewalk on its north side leads to the unassuming entrance. Inside, stairs in the foyer ascend to the second level. The lavatory, utilities area, and small kitchen are aligned across the width of the house on the north, while the recreation, living, and dining spaces are contiguous on the south in an open plan. These rooms would have been well lighted by the floor-to-ceiling stationary windows. The private zone of the second floor consists of four bedrooms, three bathrooms, and a sitting room or "sleeping" quarters separated by a folding door. A deck to the east projects over the porch below.

While the Hayworth house was designed around the time that the Kecks' designs for Green's Ready-Built Homes were being constructed, this is a customized house with no mention of prefabricated components. Had it been built, it would indeed have been the "model" home that Hayworth proposed. The passive solar approach, flat roof, and other Keck characteristics can, instead, be studied and admired in the Panshin house. The Hayworths ended up living at 316 Kensington Street in East Lansing, in the oldest platted area of the city.[42] Like many in this area, this 1924 house has a steeply pitched roof, centrally placed doorway with a dormer window above, and small windows. It is a far cry from the house Keck & Keck designed for them.

There may have been another Keck & Keck house in the area. This possibility was mentioned by Tom Padget in a letter to [George] Fred Keck on October 7, 1947, regarding Ben Watson, a prominent local lawyer and his wife Helen, who owned forty acres next to the Muehlbergers, for whom Frank Lloyd Wright was drawing plans.[43] But instead, the Watsons hired the local architect Alfred C. Roth to design their house.[44]

PLATE 19. Auto-Owners Insurance Company. Lee Black and Kenneth C. Black, Architects, 1951. Photo courtesy of Michigan State Historic Preservation Office.

PLATE 20. Clarence H. and Marcella Rosa House. Clarence H. Rosa, 1951.

PLATE 21. Talbert and Leota Fry Abrams House (Wingspan). William H. Baugh with Grover M. Pratt, 1951. Photo courtesy of Jim Perkins.

PLATE 22. Malcolm and Harriet Williams House. Malcolm Williams, 1951.

Photo courtesy of the Michigan State Historic Preservation Office.

PLATE 23. John G. and Marjorie Goodell House. Architect unknown, 1951.

PLATE 24. Lantern Hill Model A2, drawing, exterior. Hugh Stubbins Jr., 1950.

Courtesy of the Frances Loeb Library, Harvard University Graduate School of Design.

PLATE 25. Lantern Hill Model A2, drawing, interior. Hugh Stubbins Jr., 1950.

Courtesy of the Frances Loeb Library, Harvard University Graduate School of Design.

PLATE 26. Walter and Pauline Adams House. Lantern Hill Subdivision. Hugh Stubbins Jr., 1950–52. Photograph © 2014 Kim Kauffman.

PLATE 27. Dr. Mahlon Samuel and Mary Sharp House. Laitala and Nuechterlein, 1952.

Photo courtesy of the Michigan State Historic Preservation Office.

PLATE 30. Jack and Evelyn Wolfram House. Lee Black and Kenneth C. Black, Architects, 1952. Photograph © 2014 Kim Kauffman.

PLATE 28 (*opposite, top*). Glencairn Elementary School. Laitala and Nuechterlein, 1952. Photo by Natasha Crljenica.

PLATE 29 (*opposite, bottom*). Clarke E. and Dora Harris House. Clarke E. Harris, 1952. Photo by Natasha Crljenica.

PLATE 31. Robin A. and Elizabeth Drews House. Trade Secrets House, 1954.

Photograph © 2014 Kim Kauffman.

PLATE 32. Merten Insurance Company Building. Lee Black and Kenneth C. Black, Architects, 1954. Photo by Natasha Crljenica.

PLATE 33. Zion Evangelical Lutheran Church. Laitala and Nuechterlein, 1954. 1954 image courtesy of Diane Sowash.

PLATE 34. Kenneth and Cornelia Hagberg House. Bernard J. Mayotte, 1955.

Photograph © 2014 Kim Kauffman.

PLATE 35 (*above*). Richard and Cheryl Maury House. Manson & Carver, 1955. Photo by Natasha Crljenica.

PLATE 36 (*left*). Stanley and Monna Lee Hartman House, drawing, front elevation. Frank Lloyd Wright, 1955. The Frank Lloyd Wright Foundation Archives (The Museum of Modern Art | Avery Architectural & Fine Arts Library, Columbia University, New York).

It was described as modern, low, with rambling lines, red brick and wood, broad sun-controlling eaves, and natural coloring of building materials that blend into the country landscape. Inside, every room was paneled in redwood, birch, or Philippine mahogany combined with brick walls. Even the two bathrooms were warm red, Mrs. Watson's "favorite color." The lessons of passive solar construction, so important to the Kecks, appear to have influenced this local architect and his clients.

The Keck brothers were known as experimenters with new technologies throughout their careers. After the Century of Progress, their aesthetics became less radical in the interest of satisfying clients. Nevertheless, the concern for passive solar heating that made its debut at the fair would continue as one of their major contributions. As soon as Thermopane windows appeared on the market in the 1930s, the Kecks embraced them for engineering as well as aesthetic reasons. The windows were good insulators because of the two layers of glass and trapped air space. As well, because they did not open, they provided large areas for views to the outside unimpeded by sashes or screens. The use of Thermopane glazing became a trademark of Keck & Keck houses, as seen in both the Panshin and the Hayworth examples.

CHAPTER 4

When Architects Design Their Own

Some of the most spectacular domestic buildings are the houses architects design for themselves. Yet when the title of this chapter was used for an article in the *New York Times* in 1931, the point was that many contemporary architects built in styles that were sentimental, eclectic, and traditional rather than the "new order" of flat roof and rejection of the past.[1] It would take a few more years for architects to embrace the new for themselves. The tide changed with Philip Johnson's 1949 Glass House in New Canaan, Connecticut, and Charles and Ray Eames's Case Study House of the same time in Pacific Palisades, California. In Michigan, eight architects designed modernist homes that are now in the National Register of Historic Places, including Alden B. Dow's Home and Studio in Midland, William Kessler's home in Grosse Pointe (replicated in Lansing), and Minoru Yamasaki's house in Oakland County.[2]

Mid-Michigan has quite a few homes designed by local architects for themselves and their families. As their own best clients, their houses are often more modernist and daring than those designed for others. This chapter will consider fourteen local architect–designed houses dating from 1948 through the 1960s. As will be evident, the 1950s examples tended to be moderately modern and understated, but as the years went on, the designs became more individual, idiosyncratic, and unusual.

The list of architect-designed houses actually begins prior to the modernist period with Darius Moon (1841–1939), Lansing's first native architect. His elaborate two-and-a-half-story Queen Anne–style house built in 1894 has an exuberance and abundance of decorative woodwork, numerous gables and

► **FIGURE 20.** Munson House, Orlie Munson, Lansing.
Photograph © 2014 Kim Kauffman.

dormers, a square tower, a variety of textured surfaces, as well as a deep porch that shelters the entrance. With embellishments such as turned woodwork, horizontal banding, polychromy, and decorative cornices and brackets, the Moon house, in effect, served as an advertisement for the architect's stylistic approach.[3]

Orlie J. and Jennie Munson's large home that Orlie designed at 1540 Lindberg Drive, Lansing, built in 1948, is an equally sumptuous example that sits across the road from the Red Cedar River (figure 20).[4] Munson (1892–1957) and Edwyn Bowd (1865–1940) joined forces in 1929 and became a prolific and well-respected Lansing-based firm. Bowd-Munson designed numerous churches and institutional, corporate, and municipal buildings. Their style encompassed Richardsonian Romanesque at the beginning of the century (when Bowd had his own firm), then Federal and Neoclassical, evolving into modern trends in the 1930s.[5] At 2,940 square feet, Munson's one-and-a-half story Colonial used redwood, cedar shakes, and large pieces of Indiana sandstone to form a busy pattern on the exterior. Several pitched roofs of differing heights and two dormers facing the street add to this effect. The sun porch at the rear was decorated with Flint Faience colored tiles and a sunken goldfish pool.[6] It is somewhat ironic that this house looks to the past, since Munson had already designed Lansing's most distinctive buildings of the late 1930s, including the very contemporary Streamline Moderne department store for the J. W. Knapp Company (1938), one of the finest examples of the style in Michigan, now owned by the Eyde Company, and the Art Deco Lansing Board of Water and Light Ottawa Street Power Station (1939), now the corporate headquarters of the Accident Fund Insurance Company of America.[7] Both have recently been sensitively restored and repurposed by their current owners.

Modernism made its appearance in houses built by architects for themselves by the early 1950s. Bruce M. Hartwick, who in 1953 became a principal in the firm of Simpson-Hartwick, designed his house at 2233 Cumberland Road in 1949 (figure 21).[8] It merited a lengthy article in the *Lansing State Journal* on July 15, 1951, titled "Architect Has Reasons for Design Features in His Home." "When an architect designs his own home, 'it's natural to expect there'll be a reason for features in it.'" Hartwick listed four key features:

1. To take advantage of the setting. This is accomplished by having the living room face toward and open to the rear yard, while more solid walls on the street side assure privacy from that quarter. . . .
2. To bring a portion of the out-of-doors into the house. A 32 foot stretch of windows in the living room faces the woods and river on the south while a wide roof

1540

overhang cuts off the summer sun while admitting direct sunlight in winter. A nine-foot planting box with its profusion of greenery separates the living room from the hallway.

3. Flexibility and ease of living. The plan gives access to any room without going through any other. Bedrooms for the Hartwicks' two children . . . are divided by a folding partition which can be drawn back to make a large play room by day. Also these rooms are large enough that both children can sleep in one, leaving the other as a guest room. The house has several storage walls. A counter in the kitchen doubles as a snack bar and housekeeping "office." There's a pass through in the wall between the kitchen and dining area. The fireplace, convenient to the eating space, can be used to broil steaks for the dinner table. Panel or radiant heating in the floor warms the house without drafts. The attached garage is heated and has been enlarged to accommodate the equipment and activities customarily found in the utility room. . . .
4. Warm and a pleasant feeling through the choice of materials, colors and textures. Floors . . . are of colorful flagstones . . . [or] of plastic tile in neutral colors. The tile brick surface of the exterior walls is brought into the living room and bedrooms. Other walls are plywood—mahogany veneered in the entrance and living-dining area; painted in the bedroom wing. The ceilings are cedar boards . . . [or] acoustic tile. . . . The glass areas

◄ **FIGURE 21.** Hartwick House, Bruce M. Hartwick, Lansing. Photograph © 2014 Kim Kauffman.

contribute by bringing in the texture and color of the scenery outside.[9]

Hartwick's home clearly spared no interior amenities despite its modest appearance from the street. The four key characteristics of modern design that it embodied were easy to embrace without being radical, and today are so commonplace as our legacy of modernism that they are taken for granted. Yet in 1951, they were so significantly different from the norm that they had to be pointed out.

Ralph B. Herrick (ca. 1895–1952), a partner in the firm of Herrick and Simpson from 1938 until 1952, built his house at 440 MacPherson Avenue, Lansing. Estimated at $18,200, it was one of the more expensive ones on a list published in the *Lansing State Journal* on August 13, 1950, under the title "Many New City Homes Costing in Five Figures." Most were under $14,000. Seven months later, the house was again in the news. On March 4, 1951, Warren Brintnall, *Lansing State Journal* architecture editor, wrote "Architect Plans Home for Leisurely Living, Third Stage of Family Development." Anticipating retirement as well as his and his wife Janet's later years, this one-story brick ranch (1,800 square feet) eliminated stairs and a basement. The unique part of the house, according to Brintnall, is the "family kitchen," an informal space opening off the dining ell and separated from the kitchen proper by a counter. A multifunctional space facing the rear yard, the family expected to use it for informal living, sometimes as a living room, dining room, den, or recreation space. In one corner, backing up to the main fireplace, is an indoor grill in a big hearth. Nevertheless, the house is understated, with a two-car attached garage, low-pitched roof, and overhanging eaves.[10] Unfortunately, Herrick was unable to enjoy his house for very long; he passed away on March 29, 1952.[11]

Elmer Manson (1913–1991), partner in one of the largest mid-Michigan architectural firms, designed his and his wife Marie's home at 2005 Cumberland Road in River Forest, a new Lansing subdivision in the early 1950s (figure 22). The house was set into the hillside with one story on the street but two stories in the rear. Warren Brintnall discussed the house in two *Lansing State Journal* articles: "Modern Design Shows Up Here" and "Modern Design Calls for New Appraisal Rules," Sunday, June 3, 1951. The latter describes an attempt to help local appraisers understand how to appraise modern homes. To that end, members of the Lansing Chapter Society of Residential Appraisers "made a thorough inspection last Tuesday night of the Elmer Manson home." Indeed, since the 929-square-foot house is quite modest and only one story above grade at the front, it was a good "case study" for the appraisers to see how some distinctly modern features

▶ **FIGURE 22.** Manson House, Elmer Manson, Lansing.
Photograph © 2014 Kim Kauffman.

could justify a higher appraisal. The caption for the illustration is:

> Modern in design both outside and in. . . . With its open carport and long breezeway, . . . the house gives the impression of a size much larger than its actual 22 × 35 feet. The same illusion is carried indoors . . . [living room] appears much larger than it really is because of the broad glass area extending around one corner, the distinctive light shelf along the length of the room, the higher than usual ceiling. . . . Terrace opens off the family room, . . . shows that the building fits into the knoll so that the basement is really at ground floor at the rear of the house. Naturally, the plans are by Mr. Manson, a local architect.

The article enumerated a number of these modern features, including the finished basement that turned into living space, which was not the case in a usual house.

> Perhaps the lower level should be called the ground floor rather than the basement. The house is set into a slope so that the "family room" at the rear opens out at grade level onto a terrace sheltered by a nine foot overhang of the living room on the floor above. . . . Built-in storage units make every cubic foot of space count to best possible advantage. Moreover, many of these units take the place of furniture, which the owner of a conventional house must buy in order to have his house livable.
>
> An open stairwell to the lower level in effect, adds space to the living room, increasing the value of several more cubic feet normally wasted in the stairway of the average house.
>
> A general feeling of roominess is achieved by raising the ceiling of the living room to a height of nine feet, and by a "light shed" which casts light down into the room through a translucent glass shelf, while giving indirect lighting by reflection from the ceiling.
>
> Electric kitchen equipment becomes part of the house, and an adjustment in valuation should be made not only for the cost of its installation but also for its usefulness.[12]

It is curious that such an unassuming, small house was chosen for the appraisers' lesson. Yet the architect used his considerable design skills to make it appear commodious. The self-effacing character of the house was apparently totally in keeping for this very accomplished yet reportedly modest architect. It is equally striking to realize how conservative the Lansing area was that it was necessary to do this exercise. The lesson was not only to inform the appraisers but also, by devoting a long newspaper column to outlining trends of modern design, to educate the readers and local buyers.

This article and the earlier one about Bruce Hartwick's key modern elements point to the important role that writer Warren Brintnall played in making modernist design acceptable in the Lansing area. While popular magazines such as *House and Home* and *Better Homes and Gardens* were significant in introducing modernism nationally, Brintnall did the same thing locally. In the 1950s, he often wrote about and illustrated new homes, although not all were modern. By mixing stories about traditional and newer approaches, Brintnall gently introduced those who read his columns to modernist trends.

The home designed by architect Malcolm (Mal) Williams (1912–1991) for his family on a large lot in the new Whitehills subdivision in East Lansing in 1951 is more obviously modern than Manson's house (plate 22). Williams recalled in 1975 that when he and his wife Harriet purchased the land, there were no surrounding buildings and the north-south street to the east did not exist. Neither were there any other houses in Whitehills with flat roofs or a contemporary design, and there was some question as to whether it would be financed.[13] His 2,600-square-foot brick house at 550 Whitehills Drive has a horizontal emphasis, with several flat and low-pitched roofs, numerous large windows, gravity heat, and a carport. Windows at the rear face the backdrop of the strip of woods about 26 feet wide across the property, one of the features Williams liked about the lot. The interior has an open plan, flat ceilings, and large wood beams. This home won Honorable Mention in the residential class in the annual competition by the Western Michigan Chapter of the AIA (American Institute of Architects), reported by the *Lansing State Journal* on Sunday, April 26, 1953.[14]

After receiving his architecture degree from Cornell University in 1935, Williams worked in New York until 1941. The next year he accepted a teaching position with the College of Engineering, Michigan State College. Two years later he joined the Warren Holmes Company, and in 1946 he was made a partner. Their business was booming after the war, and the firm became known as specialists in educational design.

Clarence H. Rosa's house, also built in 1951, was deemed noteworthy of a lengthy article in the *Lansing State Journal* as well. Rosa (1912–1990) was an architect for the state, and upon retirement, he went to work for Manson, Jackson & Kane.[15] His house at 1430 Lindbergh Drive in Lansing is 1,600 square feet, set into the slope of the property, making it two stories on the street and one at the back (plate 20). The house faces north on Lindbergh and has an unobstructed view of the Red Cedar River across the street.

The most distinctive feature of the house is the slanting glass wall of the living room, as noted in the *Lansing State Journal* on Sunday, April 8, 1951, in

"Here's New Slant on Picture Windows." The article compared three residences under construction that used slanted glass, which was more often found in storefronts, rather than the usual perpendicular large picture windows in houses.

> [Clarence Rosa is] thinking more about what happens to light on the inside surfaces of the glass at night.
>
> Angle of the window is to be such that a person sitting in the room and looking at a view outside will not be annoyed by reflections from within the room. This involves a good deal more than the position of the glass. Mr. Rosa says that the ceiling of the living room will have to be finished in a dark shade, and it will be necessary to avoid any kind of lighting that would highlight the ceiling.
>
> He says he got the idea from a friend in Grand Rapids, a lighting engineer, who has had outstanding success with such a window in his home. Mr. Rosa says it is possible to look out on the lighted garden with the view just as clear as though there were no glass at all in the frame.
>
> You don't see the glass, he points out. What you see is the reflection of light off it. Suppress the reflection and the problem is beaten.[16]

The owners of the two other houses with slanted glass windows (by unnamed architects) that were under construction at same time and discussed in the article gave different reasons for their approaches. The Charles Maxwell home, 1711 Tecumseh River Drive, Lansing, has a

> wide expanse of sloping glass across the front of the house, serving the living room and bedroom, and windows at the rear corner of the house also are at an angle. . . . Mr. Maxwell says the arrangement fills two main purposes. Tilting the upper edge outward gives an illusion of space to a narrow living room, in a manner similar to a bay window. Then there's the question of privacy. During the daylight hours, passersby see only the reflection of the lawn or driveway immediately in front of the house, instead of being able to look into the room. At night, of course, draperies must be drawn as with any window when the interior is lighted.[17]

The third, smaller, tilted window was in George MaDan's house at 1631 Roselawn Avenue, "east" of East Lansing. The owners purchased the house after construction was well underway, and they were indifferent to the window. Mrs. MaDan, in fact, was worried about how to hang the draperies and said that she did not see any advantage to the slanting window.[18]

At his house, Rosa divided the expanse of the tilted window into three rows of three panes each. He repeated the use of small glass panes alongside and above the entry door. Throughout the house, most of the windows have fixed glass panels. For ventilation, a narrower section to one side has louvers that can be opened.

The entrance is sheltered by a flat roof overhang creating a carport in front of the garage, supported by narrow metal posts. The main floor is elevated above ground level by four steps on the exterior and a flight of steps immediately upon entering the house (figure 23). This leads to the open plan of the dining and living areas. Even more spaciousness is possible by opening the folding screen doors of the bedrooms at the rear of the house.

The slanting window was the organizing principle for the interior, and it is echoed in a slanted horizontal mirror hung from the ceiling above the counter that separates the kitchen from the dining area. In it, one sees a reflection of the outside. Opposite the window, a long brick fireplace wall is angled at the end to give visual interest to the design. The rectangular plan of the house is extended into the back by bumping out the master bedroom wall. The house has cork floors, radiant heating, and an abundance of wood paneling.

Rosa also included a studio above the garage, with cabinets and horizontal shelving where he may have stored drawings and blueprints. Below the steps leading to the studio, he carved out a very small bedroom space for one of his sons. Because the shelving unit above overhangs the space below, the lowered ceiling in this part of the bedroom created a cozy nook for the built-in bed.

With the slight rise in the land, the main floor is at grade in the rear. In 1967, Rosa enlarged the kitchen with a small addition that he set at an angle to the rest of the house. The original porch area is now enclosed.

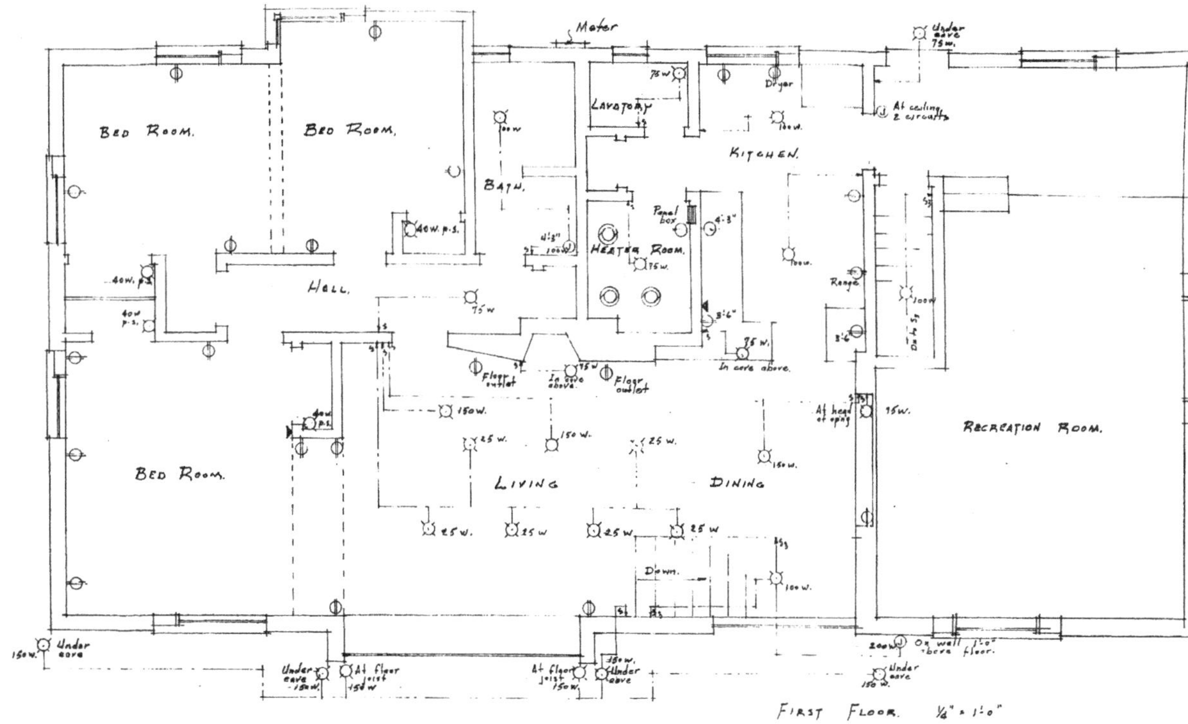

▲ **FIGURE 23.** Rosa House, Clarence H. Rosa, blueprint, detail, Lansing. Courtesy of Addiann Hines.

▶ **FIGURE 24.** DeWolf House, Howard DeWolf, East Lansing. Photograph by Natasha Crljenica.

The full basement has, among other spaces, a totally protected interior fallout shelter.

Rosa's individuality and personality is hinted at in some of the unique features of this house, such as the sleeping nook, the ventilation system, and the slanted window, as well as the scattered decorative tiles inserted into the brick wall at the entrance, the hand-crafted metal stair railing, and metal panels placed between the two vertical posts that support the carport.

Also in 1951, the architect Howard DeWolf (1922–2011) designed a Prairie-style house for himself, his wife Mary, and their family at 167 Maplewood Drive in East Lansing (figure 24). He was supervisor of Working Drawing Production and Architectural Design at the Warren Holmes Company.[19] The 2,200-square-foot, nearly rectangular brick ranch has a flat roof and a circular drive that leads to the carport on the north.

Finding the right site was important to the architect. By the time Clarke E. Harris (1906–1993) decided to build his house for himself and his wife Dora at 4681 Woodcraft Road, Okemos, in 1952, the Indian Hills subdivision already boasted homes designed by Frank Lloyd Wright and Keck & Keck.[20] Harris chose a large lot of almost an acre adjacent to the Wright-designed Edwards house in the back. His flat-roofed, one-story wood-and-brick building sits back from the road, with the garage at the south end and the bedroom wing to the north (plate 29). Sited on the highest spot of the plot, the house is low to the ground on this side, but sits high above it on the back as the land falls away quickly towards Herron Creek (figure 25). The basement level on this side of the house is at grade.

An open trellis projecting on the front façade provides shade, while a course of small windows admits light into the bedrooms and bathroom on this side. Larger floor-to-ceiling windows surround the back of the house (figure 25). The plan shows that the house is a series of rectangles that flow from one to the next (figure 26). The storage wall that divides the entry from the dining space and contains closet space on one side and a china cabinet on the other, stops just short of the ceiling, and the wood divider between the foyer and the living room is an open unit (figure 27). Other built-ins include chests and a drop-down desk in one of the bedrooms. The use of light oak veneer plywood paneling throughout, large windows, and an open plan in the living and dining area give this house a sense of openness, light, and informality. Perched high above the land at the back, surrounded by views of nature, Harris's house is a good example of contemporary ideas about organic architecture.

Connections to nature were also behind the decision of partners Walter Laitala (1917–1992) and Wilmer Nuechterlein (1920–2009) to purchase property

on Van Atta Road in rural Okemos to build their family homes. The plots were divided into irregular shapes because of the narrow frontage on Van Atta and the widening of the Red Cedar River to the south. The land was originally covered with trees, which the families cleared and milled, and the wood was used throughout the two houses. According to Laitala's daughter, building their house took a long five years, with family and friends working nights and weekends.[21] The Walter and Maxine Laitala house at 4051 Van Atta Road, constructed in 1959, is on 6.33 acres. The early photograph gives a sense of the original design and the placement of the house on the property (figure 28). The long, low-slung one-story wood ranch with a carport and flat roof has been substantially changed with several additions and remodeling, an added garage in 1994–95, and a change from the original flat to a pitched roof. Inside, the space was open, with large windows that allowed one to enjoy the changing seasons (figure 29).

The adjacent Wilmer and Lillian Nuechterlein house at 4045 Van Atta Road, also constructed in 1959, is on 2.34 acres. The house originally had a flat roof, with a carport between the house and a one-car garage. The west exterior wall was windowless and faced with brick, as was the wall perpendicular to the front entry.[22] Here, too, significant changes have been made. The carport was enclosed, a second story was

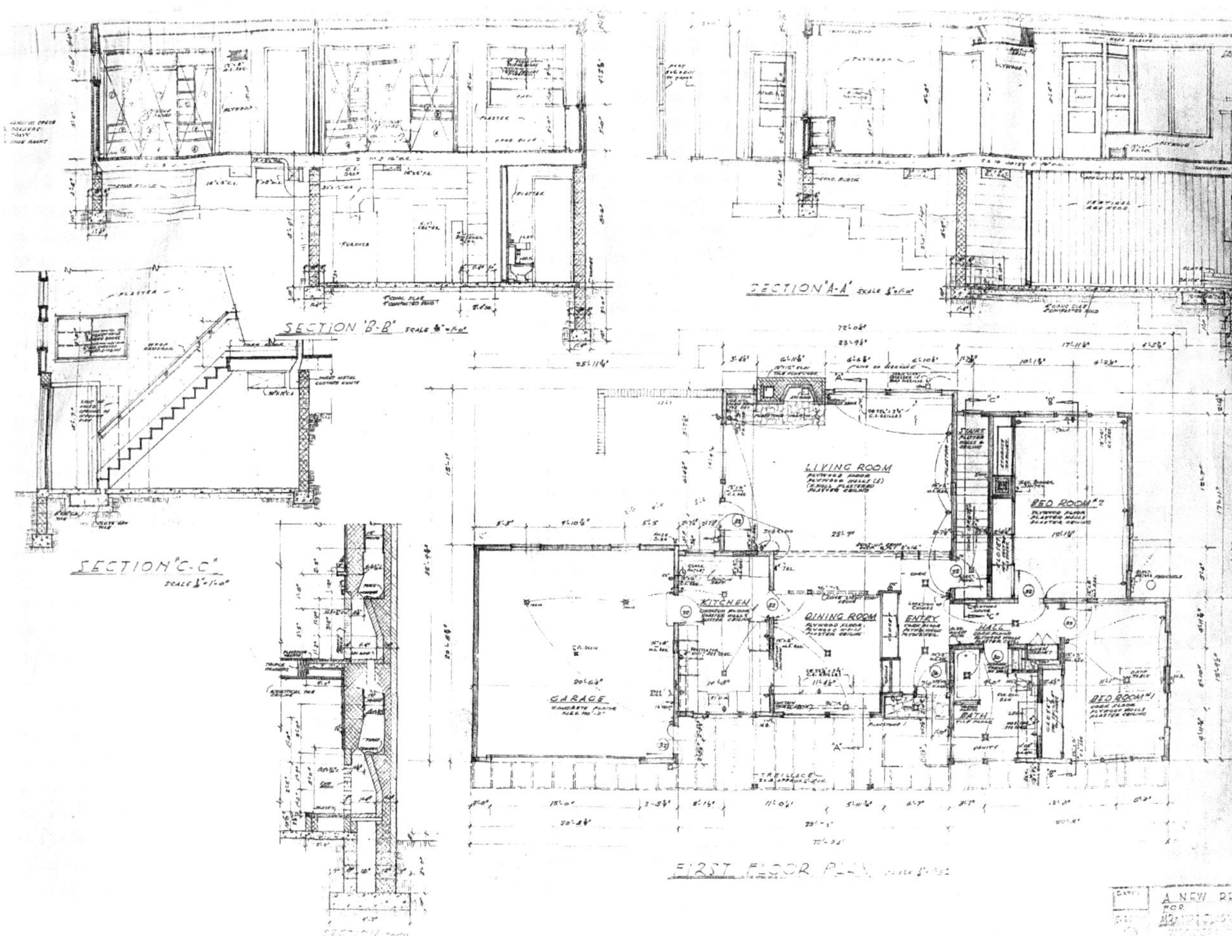

◄ **FIGURE 25.** Harris House, Clarke E. Harris, exterior, rear, Okemos. Photograph by Natasha Crljenica.

▲ **FIGURE 26.** Harris House, Clarke E. Harris, plan, Okemos. Courtesy of John and Mary Bresnahan.

ScanSnap

added, and the roof was given a pitch, substantially altering the structure and Nuechterlein's design.

This rural stretch along the river appealed to several other aesthetically inclined families who appreciated living in structures that blended in and were in harmony with the surroundings. Among them were several faculty members in the MSC Art Department. Ceramist Louis Benjamin Raynor (1917–1999) was hired in 1946 when the college was expanding rapidly. His fame in the art world quickly grew, and major institutions such as the Detroit Institute of Arts and the Metropolitan Museum of Art acquired his work. Despite his increasing popularity, Raynor kept his prices low to ensure that his ceramics would be readily available to people in Michigan. In 1962, he and his wife Sherry built a house just south of the river at 4086 Dobie Road. He designed and built much of the structure. The flat-roofed, single-story wood structure has four bedrooms and a separate garage on almost an acre of land. Nearby, MSU faculty member Jens Plum (1926–2002), a painter, and his wife Nancy, a potter, also built their house just north of the river at 4085 Van Atta Road (plate 82), designed by Birmingham, Michigan, architect Robert Hanamura in 1967. Jens had joined the MSU faculty in 1963. Clearly the wooded, steep land with river access in this relatively rural suburb appealed to a number of artists and architects desiring to build unique homes on large lots; but common to all of them was the way they worked with and in the landscape.

In the early 1960s, another wave of houses by and for architects was built in mid-Michigan.[23] These tended to be very individualized and more obviously modern than earlier ones when seen from the street. A good example is the house designed by John Crouse (1920–2009), a partner in Mayotte-Webb, at 1792 Walnut Heights Drive, East Lansing, in 1962 (plate 61). It started out as a rectangular plan with the carport at a right angle to the house. Two years later he added a 12-foot by 24-foot rectangular space to the rear of the house that extends it out into the yard.[24] This expanded the house to include a dining room and a sunken conversation pit with built-in seating on three sides and a large copper flue in the center. The house has approximately 1,800 square feet with three bedrooms on the main floor and a basement below grade (approximately 1,500 square feet) including a fallout shelter.

There are several other distinctive features about the house. First, at the entrance, the four steps that ascend to the large front door prepare the visitor for the elevation changes inside: up several steps to the living area, with a large fireplace and built-in seating, or down steps to the fire pit and the dining area. Another unusual feature is the treatment of the bedroom wing that faces the street. Small vertical slits of windows

◀ **FIGURE 27.** Harris House, living room interior, Okemos. Photograph by Natasha Crljenica.

divide the wall, providing light to the interior hallway. Between the windows are six built-in closets that cantilever out over the low brick retaining wall on the exterior. The wall creates a privacy shield for the bedrooms that are aligned on the other side of the hallway.

The architect Dixon Shaw Wilson (1923–2001) designed his family's 1963 brick house at 414 Ardson Road and Grand River Avenue, in East Lansing (plate 62). After graduating from Ohio State University in 1949 with a degree in architecture, he worked in Ohio and Michigan before joining Manson-Carver, Associates in 1954. He was made a partner in 1958 and then started his own firm in East Lansing in 1960.[25]

The brick-and-wood rectangular house faces west on Ardson Road, a residential street. The façade is distinguished by the cutback of the low overhang above the entrance area with its inconspicuous door. Car access into the property is from the busy Grand River Avenue to the south, from which the peak of the gable is visible (figure 30). At nearly 2,000 square feet, it has four bedrooms on one floor with a full basement and garage at grade. On this side, a narrow balcony runs the length of the dining room and is protected by the deep overhanging roof. A brick two-sided fireplace divides the dining and living spaces but allows views into each, while exposed wood beams and the wood ceiling provide interest.

▶ **FIGURE 28.** Laitala House, Walter Laitala, exterior, rear, Okemos, 1960s photograph. Courtesy of Diane Sowash.

The latest of the architect-designed modernist houses in the area is the most elegant, but Kenneth Black's 1964 residence at 1501 Cambridge Road, Lansing, was not the first of his homes. In the Society Notebook column in the *Lansing State Journal*, Sunday, March 19, 1950, the author noted that "It's interesting that while Mr. Black is an expert on modern design, indoor-outdoor floor plans and solar heat, the Blacks' own house is traditional in style. . . . It is built of white brick on charming Georgian colonial lines with a flowering crab tree by the front door. Within Canadian-born Mrs. Black had collected beautiful pieces of antique furniture."

Black's more modern new house on Cambridge Road, built in 1964, would have pleased the reporter (plate 69). It is an L-shaped, one-story house on a slab, with over 3,000 square feet, on an expansive lot that backs onto the Country Club of Lansing's fairway. It was built soon after Black's Lansing Public Library, dedicated in October 1964 (see plate 66). As in that building, he created texture by using decorative concrete blocks in repeating patterns. Both have solid sections that alternate with areas where the backgrounds were removed to allow light into the interior.

At his house, Black used two different repeating patterns of curves and counter-curves. The open pattern on the long façade also appears on the frieze

◄ **FIGURE 29.** Laitala House, Walter Laitala, interior, Okemos, 1960s photograph. Courtesy of Diane Sowash.

at the top of the brick wall on the other side of the entrance (figure 31). The second pattern wraps around the corner leading to the entry door, and shows up again on the separate privacy wall to the north of the house. The openwork section of the wall is balanced by a large glazed area. If one studies this asymmetric design, the subtleties of Black's decorative impulse become apparent. Another sensitive feature is the spur wall at the other end of the house, which shields the view of the garage from the street.

The interior entry hall leads to the spacious living room and adjacent library, beyond which (to the north) are the bedroom/dressing room, guest room, and two bathrooms. The dining area, pantry, and kitchen are on the other side of the living room.

In his firm's 1970 prospectus, Black illustrated his own house in the "Fine Arts Design" section as the exemplar of his philosophy. "Kenneth C. Black Associates encourages clients to enrich their building with appropriate landscape and with suitable sculpture, painting and ornamental metal work. These art elements contribute a distinction easily recognized by the public and at the same time enhance the pleasure of those who live and work in such surroundings." Views of the entrance hall, metalwork, and sculpture on the interior of the house were included, as was the 1965 landscape design by D. Newton Glick.[26] Additionally, a series of 1966 photographs of the house by Leavenworth

◀ **FIGURE 30.** Wilson House, Dixon Shaw Wilson, rear, East Lansing. Photograph © 2014 Kim Kauffman.

Photographics shows how the interior was decorated with contemporary and some traditional furnishings, including several Knoll tables, couches, floor-to-ceiling drapes, wood paneling, built-in bookcases, and recessed can lighting, plus a grand piano in the living room.[27] There also were oriental carpets on the floor of the hallway as well as one hanging on a wall, plus an elaborate bronze door salvaged from a Lansing building, an abstract mosaic, and fluted pilasters. As seen in his own home, Black's approach to architectural design was modern and holistic. It is also imbued with a sense of monumentality and presence. Black spent a year in Rome after graduating from the University of Michigan in architecture, and he seems to have absorbed something of the spirit of Rome's monumental marble structures that he translated into a modern sensibility. No one would label his architecture classical or even neoclassical, and deliberate historicism that would become the motivation of postmodernism is not at play here. Yet the solidity of his shapes and forms, the attention to ornament, the play of light and shade, and the light palette are part of his highly developed architectural affect.

While Black's house for Betty and Donald Price (plate 8) was influenced by Frank Lloyd Wright, and his City Hall design reflected the sleek International style of the 1950s (plate 39), by the 1960s, he had evolved a less stark and more decorative modern style, similar to Minoru Yamasaki's evolution seen in the Michigan State Medical Society building in East Lansing (plate 55) and his own Lansing Public Library building (plate 66). In the house he designed for himself and his wife Marie, Kenneth Black contributed significantly and differently to the many ways in which local architects embraced modernism.[28] For them, modernism was more than a passing fad, and many of the features they included in their own homes that were novel at the time made their way into mainstream design.

▶ **FIGURE 31.** Black House, Kenneth Black, Lansing.
Photograph © 2014 Kim Kauffman.

CHAPTER 5

When Architects Design for Clients

In addition to Frank Lloyd Wright, Keck & Keck, and Alden B. Dow, who designed houses in mid-Michigan, other nationally and regionally known architects made their mark with singular examples, such as Ralph Rapson and William Kessler. The majority of modernist residences, however, were the work of local architects. Indeed, most of the Lansing-based architectural firms active between 1940 and 1970 designed houses, including Laitala and Nuechterlein; Manson, Jackson & Kane (Manson & Carver); Mayotte-Webb; Kenneth C. Black Associates; and several others.

There are pockets of modernist design in the region: Lantern Hill, Walnut Heights, and more luxurious examples in Whitehills Estates in East Lansing; on Cambridge Drive and in River Forest in Lansing; and Indian Hills, Tacoma Hills and White Oaks Estates in Okemos. More frequently than not, however, the modernist house was sandwiched between Colonial two-story brick houses and bungalows. In this respect, the area is typical of many Midwestern cities. Even in new subdivisions, the mix of traditional and new continued in the 1950s and 1960s. Numerous pleasant but clientless ranch designs with open plans and large windows can be found in the area, but the houses considered here go beyond that norm to become architectural statements. If the architect was lucky, their clients had plots with interesting elevations and contours or perhaps a view of a river that could be used to advantage. It was also typical to design an understated street presence that belied the more expansive and open treatment in the privacy of the backyard.

Ralph Rapson

Ralph Rapson (1914–2008) espoused modernism throughout his long career. He studied architecture at the University of Michigan and did his graduate training at the Cranbrook Academy of Art from 1938 to 1940. Not only did he study architecture there with Eliel Saarinen, but also sculpture, ceramics, fiber arts, and painting with Harry Bertoia, Carl Milles, Maija Grotell, Marianne Strengell, and other illustrious faculty. His cohort included Charles and Ray Eames, Harry Weese, and Ben Baldwin. In this heady atmosphere, he experimented with a design for a fabric house (1939) and, with classmate David Runnells, a Cave House (1938) in which the building is half-sheltered in the earth. Rapson took a teaching position at the New Bauhaus in Chicago from 1942 until 1946, when he moved to the Massachusetts Institute of Technology. He returned to the Midwest to teach at the University of Minnesota from 1954 until 1984. Over his long career, he designed private residences, United States embassies, several small churches, performing arts centers (including the former Guthrie Theater), and furniture.[1]

Rapson's mid-Michigan connections are from his early professional years. He met Mildred Schoch Hagberg when both were students at Cranbrook. Her path to Cranbrook, however, was a circuitous one. She had been a widowed state employee living modestly in a white two-story house at 2239 Hamilton Road, Okemos, built prior to 1875 (demolished in the 1970s), which she had purchased in 1934. In 1937 when an automobile accident left her disabled, she became determined to regain the use of her injured arm. Using money she received from the insurance company's settlement, she enrolled at Cranbrook in late 1937. For four years she studied ceramics, metal crafting, weaving, and design. Around 1938 she had the opportunity to purchase a 1923 barn at 2231 Hamilton Road on the property adjacent to her house (plate 2). She was undaunted by the problem that while she gained ownership of the entire barn for $100, the lot on which it stood was not part of the deal. She apparently asked Rapson for a design to modernize the barn and turn it into a home and studio (figure 32). To do so, however, meant sawing the barn in half, then taking the half not on her property and repositioning it at the back of her building towards the Red Cedar River. In a dramatic retelling of the story, Mrs. Hagberg wielded the saw to cut the building in half when the carpenter she hired was too skeptical to do it.[2] The result was the "Studio House," completed in 1940.

Rapson included a color drawing of the studio house in a book of sketches he published in 2002.[3] Among the hundreds of drawings of his work, and those he did of buildings he admired around the world, he included only ten of his own house designs.

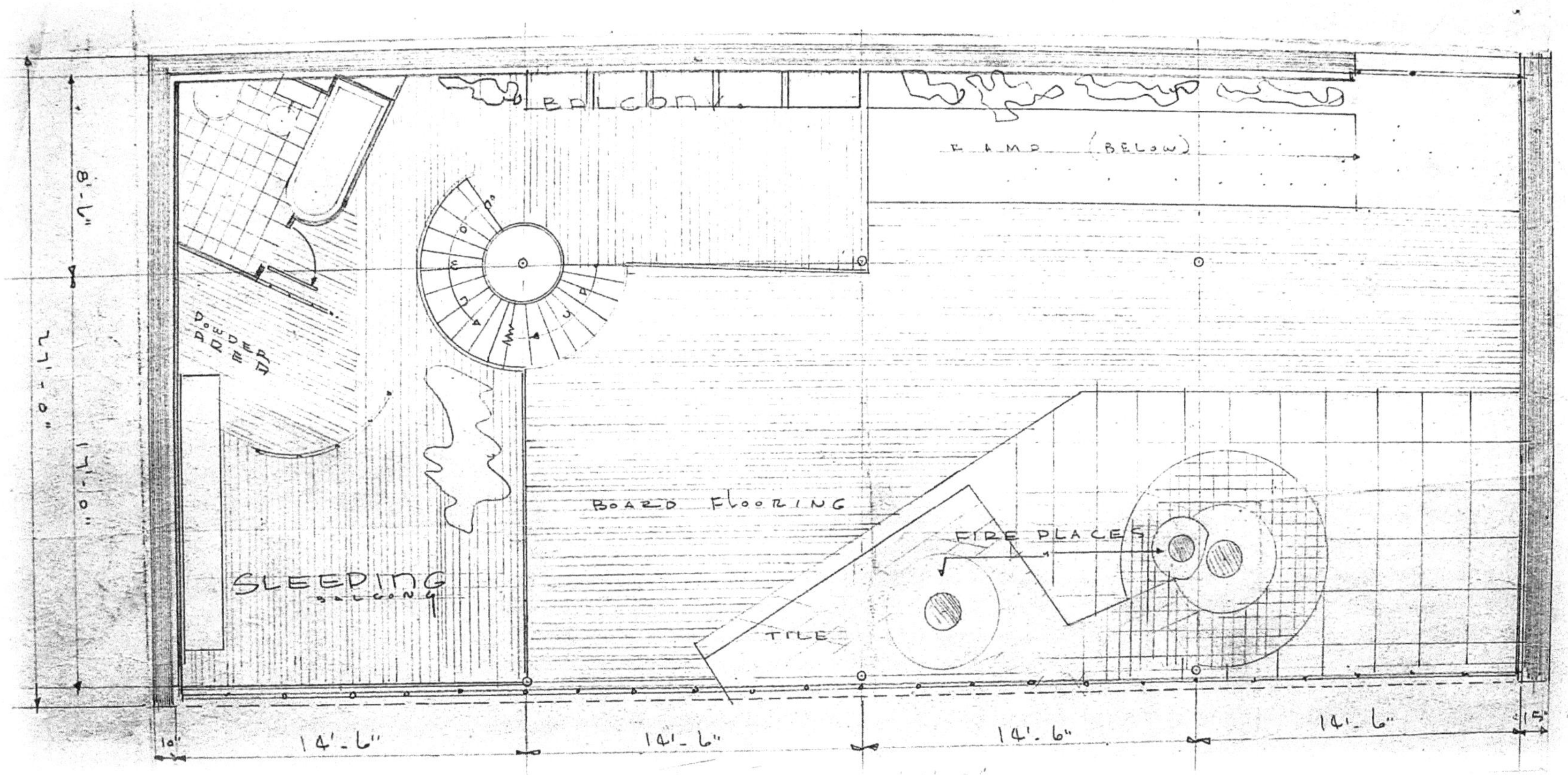

▲ **FIGURE 32.** Hagberg Home and Studio, Ralph Rapson, drawing, 1940, Okemos. Courtesy Cranbrook Archives, The Ralph Rapson Collection: 1935–1954.

Looking back on his long career, he must have had fond memories of Mildred Hagberg and the barn conversion project. However, his handwritten caption for the illustration erroneously located the studio in Mount Pleasant, Michigan. This sketch actually shows the entrance side of the building on the north (facing the street), and the west (side) elevation. On the north, there is a large glazed area on the lower left that included the door, sheltered by a horizontal canopy, and a second large glazed section in the upper right. In the street elevation with a "revised porch plan" in the Cranbrook Archives, Rapson added a second large window on the right at ground level that created an expanse of glazing from ground to just below the roofline and emphasized the asymmetry of the design.[4] It also shows that Rapson flattened the barn roof and added a

▲ **FIGURE 33.** Kenneth Hagberg House, Bernard Mayotte, elevations, Okemos. Courtesy of Betty Hagberg.

▶ **FIGURE 34.** Kenneth Hagberg House, Bernard Mayotte, rear, Okemos. Photograph © 2014 Kim Kauffman.

porch, seen in profile on the west. There are, however, numerous differences between the color sketch, the plans, and the building as it was constructed, especially in the placement, shapes, and number of windows. For example, in the color drawing in the book, one small window is placed above another on the west wall, plus there is a long awning that shades the ground floor, and on the terrace above the second level on the west, an open trellis sunscreen. As built, there are more but smaller windows, and no upper terrace.

For the interior, Rapson designed one large room with a fireplace and a sleeping loft, with a powder area and bath on the balcony above (figure 32). According to her daughter-in-law, however, Mrs. Hagberg slept on an old sofa in the living room or in her comfortable bungalow next door. The circular staircase he planned was replaced with a straight one off to one side, and there were floor-to-ceiling bookcases to the left of the entrance. Rather than a kitchen, there was a small sink with boards instead of cupboards. Likewise, the bathroom with a shower stall was very small. Hagberg kept her looms on the first floor and a lathe in the basement on which she made a variety of pewter and silver-plated objects that she sold. She approached the decoration and furnishing of the studio in a piecemeal fashion, using bamboo poles for the ceiling trim and window shades, and other cleverly recycled materials in addition to the mix of antique and contemporary

objects from her travels. Because the studio was not well insulated, she traveled extensively in the winter.[5]

Hagberg also owned the property on the other side of her bungalow. Rapson's drawing of a "Studio/ Residence for Dorothy Hageberg [*sic*], Okemos, Michigan," dated December 4, 1939, shows a "cave house," a concept that interested Rapson in the late 1930s.[6] This Hagberg design, however, was not executed here, no doubt because she could not afford new construction. The property stood vacant until her son, Kenneth, worked with a neighbor in 1955 to come up with ideas for a house. Once these were formulated, according to his widow, he hired the local architect Bernard J. Mayotte to produce the working drawings (figure 33). This 1,700-square-foot rectangular house at 2247 Hamilton is one story and low to the ground on the street side, with a flat roof and clerestory windows (plate 34). It does give the impression of being built into the ground, reflective of Rapson's ideas. However, towards the river it has two full stories above ground, constructed of wood above and cement block below, with large windows that provide views of the river. Exterior decks and stairs lead to the sloping ground below (figure 34). An abundance of wood is used on the interior, which was appropriate since Ken owned a landscape company: white oak on the walls, ash for the ceiling rafters, and pine for the floor. The living and dining rooms share a double-sided brick fireplace. By building a low-slung structure on the street side, the house has some affinities to Rapson's cave house design, but it uses a slightly different form of the modernist language of organic architecture to connect the building to its site.

William Kessler

Detroit-area architect William H. Kessler (1924–2002) is associated in mid-Michigan with the large Michigan Library and Historical Center that houses the state library, archives, and historical museum (1985–88).[7] In addition to many buildings in Detroit, such as the Detroit Receiving Hospital and the Detroit Science Center (now the Michigan Science Center), he designed a complex for Olivet College, Olivet, Michigan, although only the Lester K. Kirk Collegiate Center was erected in 1963.[8] A Harvard-trained architect, he studied with Walter Gropius and was imbued with the modernist aesthetic. Yamasaki recruited him to Michigan to join Leinweber, Yamasaki & Hellmuth. Eventually Kessler began his own firm: Meathe, Kessler and Associates in 1955; William Kessler and Associates in 1968; and Kessler Francis Cardoza Architects in 1999.[9]

The house he designed for himself, his wife Margot, and their family at 1013 Cadieux Road in

Grosse Point Park in 1959 is a strikingly modernist structure of light stainless steel with floor-to-ceiling glazing. Because of its location close to the street and a busy intersection across from Beaumont Hospital, Kessler placed a brick wall across the front of the house to create some privacy. Another distinguishing characteristic is the accordion roof that divides the one-story, almost-square building into three bays.[10] The public zone consists of the living room, parents' bedroom, and garden, while the private zone contains the children's bedrooms and play area.[11] Kessler used the same sawtooth roof construction in the 1959 Arthur Beckwith House in Farmington Hills.[12]

Kessler's house was published shortly after completion in the *Architectural Record*, March 1961 issue and became well known. He sold the plans to a number of people who requested them, as was likely the case with the replica that was erected in 1963 by Wallis M. and Norine Antuck on Lansing's west side at 3815 Waverly Hills (plate 65).[13] Although built well away from road traffic, the Lansing building is sheltered from view on the north by the brick privacy wall, with a repeated pattern of projecting bricks as in the Grosse Pointe house. A small enclosed garden is between the wall and house. The nearly square (40 by 43 foot) house is 1,730 square feet and oriented slightly off the cardinal points. The east and west brick elevations are opaque, while the north/northwest and south/southwest elevations, with floor-to-ceiling glazing, are fully transparent. The carport on the west ends in a small shed and connects by a breezeway to the inconspicuous entrance into the house.[14] The plot slopes gently south, and from the living and dining room areas, there is a view of the Grand River in the distance. There are few minimalist glass-and-steel residences in the area, making this a most unusual example for mid-Michigan.

Lee Black and Kenneth C. Black, Architects

Houses by Lee Black and Kenneth C. Black, Architects (and after Lee's retirement in 1958, Kenneth C. Black Associates) are recorded from the 1930s through the 1960s. While early examples were traditional two-story homes,[15] beginning in 1945, they designed modernist split-levels or one-story houses in Lansing and East Lansing for a distinguished clientele. In East Lansing, two of these designs merit discussion: the Henry E. and Mary Crouse house, 1045 Rosewood Avenue, 1945, and the Donald and Betty Price house at 417 Clarendon Road, 1946.

The Society page of the *Lansing State Journal* on Sunday, March 19, 1950, mentioned that one of the prime examples of Mr. Black's modern design is the "handsome functional house of their friends, the Henry

Crouses." This split-level on two-and-a-half lots has a wide façade facing east with an off-center entrance. The living quarters above the garage have small windows under large eaves. The rest of the house is stepped back and one story. Two lower bedrooms and a bathroom suite, and an upper bedroom suite and a screened terrace are on the back. Photographs of the exterior from the 1960s show brick on the lower half of the façade, and vertical and horizontal wood siding above. The siding has been substantially changed since then. One of the selling points when the residence was on the market in 1969 was that it was the home of Michigan's forty-third governor, George W. Romney, and his wife Lenore, and had an up-to-date kitchen with two stoves.[16]

The Donald and Betty Price house at 417 Clarendon Road (plate 8) was built nearby in 1946 for the owners of Liebermann's, the downtown Lansing store that specialized in modern design housewares and gift items. (The store was designed by George Nelson; see plate 77.) When told by Frank Lloyd Wright that she would have to wait several years for a design by him, Mrs. Price decided to work with Kenneth C. Black instead. The 2,600-square-foot home, brick with red trim, is one story with four bedrooms and was the only house on this block when it was built. The garage is at street level while the living space is several steps up from the street. Because of the rise of the land, the back of the house is level with the ground, and this variation enabled Black to alter the height of the rooms and the ceilings. On the back, the large living room has a 40-foot-long wall of glazing facing the small enclosed yard. The large fixed panes of glass are bracketed by smaller rectangular windows at the floor that open, and by fixed panes above that form a large triangle that follows the rising slant of the ceiling. Because the bedroom wing angles out from the rest of the house, the short wall at the far end of the living room reflects that angle, in effect making the room into a pentagon. Built-in bookcases along two walls with indirect lighting above and the red brick fireplace make this an inviting, warm, and informal space. The dining area on the other side, separated from the kitchen and large pantry, also has recessed lighting. Polished and stained cement floors that contain the radiant heat system continued the modernist approach, as did the original furnishings that included iconic Eames and Hans Wegner chairs and table, Nelson's Atomic clock, and other Herman Miller pieces.[17]

To spread the word about modernism, Kenneth Black penned an article in the *Lansing State Journal* on January 1, 1951, in which he gave a brief history of architectural design and encouraged readers to embrace the potential of the new. As an illustration, he recounted the recent remarks of an unidentified client who might easily have been Mrs. Price.

> I am only going to live once and I don't want to live my one life in an imitation of a Colonial house, surrounded by imitations of antique furniture and other gadgets reminiscent of days that are long dead and gone. I want to live today's life today. I want my house and my office and my furniture to be as different from my grandfather's as my car is different from his horse and buggy. Then I will feel that I am really living a contemporary life instead of simply existing in an atmosphere of phony antiquity.[18]

As a result of the Price house, Kenneth and Lee Black must have earned a reputation as the architects to go to in mid-Michigan for a Wrightian design. The following year, they designed another for Mr. and Mrs. R. B. Harvey, who called their raised ranch "High Hollow." Perched high on the land, well back from the road at 4355 Hulett Road, in Okemos, surrounded by wetlands and woods, it is just south of Wright's Goetsch-Winckler house. At approximately 2,000 square feet, it has two bedrooms, a large siting room with a wall of windows facing south, and a carport (now enclosed). Some of the Wrightian details are the red cedar shiplap wood on the walls, built-in furniture and storage, gravity heat in the concrete floors, a massive brick fireplace that anchors the siting room, a flat roof, and horizontal emphasis. The adaptation of many of these details apparently caused a rift between the Harveys and their neighbors Alma Goetsch and Kathrine Winckler.[19] Nevertheless, the Blacks put their own stamp on the building. Unlike at the Goetsch-Winckler house, the clerestory windows open, and while wood is used extensively on the walls and ceilings, in the living room and two bedrooms, patterns of concentric diminishing squares create intriguing designs.

For Jack F. (1899–1971) and Evelyn Wolfram, the Blacks designed a large, sprawling ranch at 1341 Cambridge Road, Lansing, in 1952 (plate 30). The Riverside Homes Association had developed this exclusive subdivision in the 1920s and the architecture is a mix of traditional, revival, and contemporary styles. The winding streets are bounded by the Grand River, Francis Park, and the Country Club of Lansing's fairways. Lots are large, wooded, and fairly flat, as well as expensive, and they appealed to automobile executives and successful Lansing business owners.[20] Wolfram was chief engineer at Oldsmobile and then general manager from 1950 through 1964. His elegant, large tan-brick residence has floor-to-ceiling windows in many of the rooms facing the golf course. The living, dining, and sun rooms are at the heart of the house, and the open flow between them can be closed off with a sliding curtain. The shared brick wall has a smooth surface and fireplace in the living room, but is textured in the dining area, where bricks of different widths and heights were used. The more intimate and darker television room at the front of the house is lined with built-in bookcases that rise to the clerestory windows. From this space, the stairway that leads to the bedrooms above or the basement level below is visible.[21] Recent additions at either end have greatly expanded the original building to 5,574 square feet. Twelve years after this house, Kenneth Black designed his own residence nearby at 1501 Cambridge (see plate 69).

The Abrams House known as Wingspan

Wingspan, the home of Talbert and Leota Fry Abrams at 1310 Cambridge, Lansing, is also known as the airplane house (plate 21). Abrams was the founder of the Abrams Instrument Corporation and Abrams Aerial Survey Corporation. The one-story ranch has two intersecting rectangles, one longer than the other, and each of the ends of the arms is rounded. The design, according to Mr. Abrams and recounted in several articles as well as oral histories, was inspired by the shadow of an airplane on the upper surface of a cloud bank that he and his wife saw as they were flying at 15,000 feet.[22]

To execute the idea for the house, the Abrams first engaged the local firm of Herrick and Simpson, who rendered the idea on paper.[23] After this stage, working drawings were executed by Grover M. Pratt, "designer," an assistant professor of engineering drawing at Michigan State College, and Willard H. Baugh, "architect." Final revisions were dated August 15 and September 1, 1950 (figure 35).[24] The house was completed in 1951.

Although the design was unusual, as pointed out in the *Lansing State Journal*, Sunday, July 16, 1950, "Seen from Above, Abrams Home Has Airplane Shape,"

> The passersby will not recognize this airplane-like shape. They will see an attractive modern house, which Mr. Abrams says is neither radical in design nor extreme in size. "A lot of plans have a wing off the main body of the house [he says;] simply put another wing on the opposite side, lined up with it, then round off the corners and you have something like an airplane."

From the entrance, one moves into the "reception room" with a large two-sided stone fireplace wall shared with the dining area behind. The fireplaces on either side are actually separate, and the wall is deep enough to contain a telephone booth on one side (since dismantled) and shelving on the other. The reception room window looks like the nose of a plane and is in three sections that form the 22-foot-long arc rising six feet high. In the dining area, the corresponding arc was a semicircular slate terrace for outdoor dining (which has since been enclosed) with seven fluted limestone pillars.

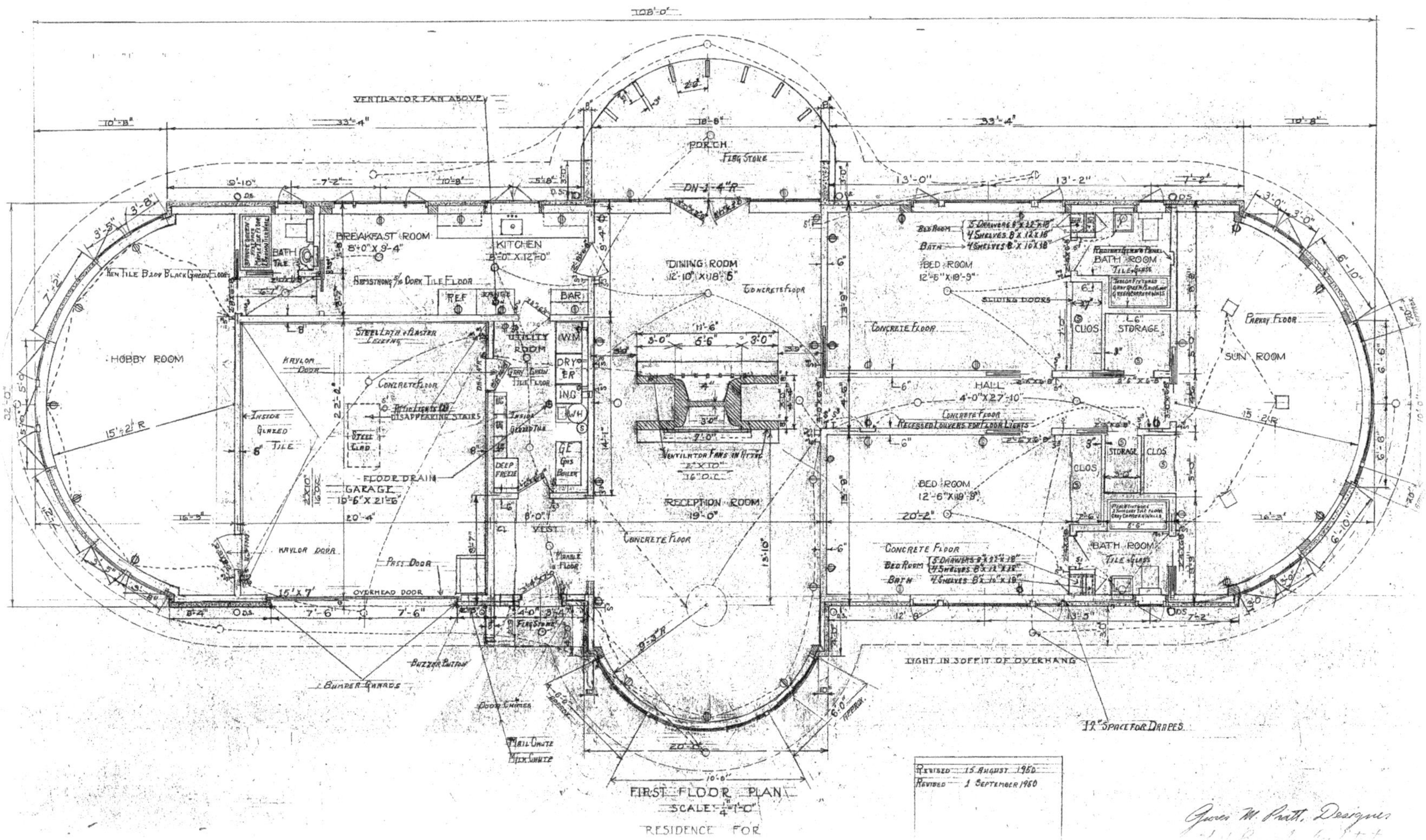

▲ **FIGURE 35.** Abrams House, William H. Baugh and Grover Pratt, floor plan, Lansing. Courtesy of Jim Perkins.

The north wing has the master bedroom and guest room suites, each with its own bathroom. At this end, another living room called the sunroom has a large curved window looking towards the Grand River (figure 36). At the opposite end of the house, the hobby room has a large wall of built-in storage, bookshelves, a drafting table, and other cabinets, and a semicircular enclosed porch. It connects to the two-car garage. The windows in the curved areas of the sunroom and living room were of plexiglass manufactured in New York by a company that made transparent plastic for aircraft for cockpit covers and airplane runners. Nevertheless, the house has more conventional features, such as the use of stone for the exterior walls and plaster on the interior. There is no basement, and the radiant heat is in the ceiling rather than the poured concrete floors.[25] When it was built, the costs were estimated at $30,000, making it one of the more expensive houses under construction in 1950.[26]

▶ **FIGURE 36.** Abrams House, William H. Baugh and Grover Pratt, interior, Lansing. Photograph © 2014 Kim Kauffman.

Manson & Carver/Manson, Jackson & Kane

Mid-Michigan architects Manson & Carver, and the successor firm from 1960, Manson, Jackson & Kane, had a large, thriving office.[27] They designed schools, offices, the East Lansing Public Library (see plate 63), and many residences in East Lansing. The range was

quite extraordinary depending upon the desires of the client. Some were brick Colonials; others were sprawling ranches. Their firm's approach was confident and resourceful without entirely reinventing each new project.

Manson & Carver designed a 2,045-square-foot, five-bedroom, three-bath house for Richard and Cheryl Maury and their family on a corner lot at 809 Harrison Road in 1955 (plate 35). Guests approach the house along the circular driveway where it appears as a small one-story building. Rising above the flat roof is a clerestory with small windows that is key to the unique ventilation system of the house. The rear of the house is two stories with a two-car basement garage accessed from Southlawn Avenue (figure 37). On this elevation, the center of the building is accentuated vertically by a two-story glazed section that angles out. The design takes full advantage of the corner lot and the sloping ground.

To the west of the Maury house, Manson & Carver designed a large 3,644-square-foot brick structure at 820 Southlawn Avenue for Albert and Ethel Redmond, completed in 1956 (plate 40). The firm successfully provided the clients with what they requested, in this case a combination of modern and traditional features. For example, an antique fireplace in Albert's bedroom and the traditional molding in Ethel's bedroom contrast with the more modern open plan of the public spaces of the dining and living room. Mr. Redmond had made his fortune in the

◄ **FIGURE 37.** Maury House, Manson & Carver, exterior, rear, East Lansing. Photograph by Natasha Crljenica.

automobile industry. When they commissioned this house, the Redmonds had already raised two sons and this was their future retirement home.

The U-shaped house sits majestically back from the road on a lot-and-a-half and is approached by a long circular driveway, past the sunken garden area. A long covered walkway leads to the front and protects the door, which is up several steps. To the east are the service area (kitchen and maid's quarters) and carport, and to the west are the couple's bedroom suites, each comprised of a bedroom, study, and bathroom. In between is the 11-foot-high-ceilinged public space, with a wall of glazing facing the back patio and yard, and narrow vertical windows at the front of the house.[28] Hand-blown glass blocks, grass-cloth-covered walls, and leather flooring in the dining room are some of the distinguishing modern features that are mixed with traditional details.

Manson & Carver were the designers of choice for many families in the late 1950s that bought land in the new subdivisions of Walnut Heights, east of Hagadorn Road, and Whitehills Estates, north of Saginaw Street. Both areas were annexed by the city in 1958. With larger lot sizes than in the older parts of the city, they appealed to increasingly affluent families who desired expansive residences. At the same time, financing of "modern" homes became easier than in the previous decade.

From the late 1950s to 1960s, the firm often used butterfly or shed roofs and an open living/dining plan. One example, at 1631 Walnut Heights Drive, was designed for Edward and Dorothy Hertel, who owned Builder's Hardware in East Lansing. Built in 1958, their house is a quad-level L-shaped house of 2,700 square feet with four bedrooms and three baths (plate 46). The two-story wing on the west extends forward towards the street. The sloping roof over the entrance links to the flat roof of the garage and carport. In "New Home with More Rooms Fitted into Old Neighborhood" in the *Lansing State Journal* on September 21, 1962, Kenneth Harkness wrote that the Edward Hertels

> describe their house as a compromise between contemporary and traditional. Mr. Hertel favored traditional styles and Mrs. Hertel says she likes modern. They turned their ideas over to an architect, who reconciled the differences into one set of plans. The house has a two-car carport in front of the two-car garage . . . where guests could park and stay dry even if it was raining. . . . Another feature of the home is a five-zone hot water heating system, which allows separate control of temperature in five areas of the house, even the garage is heated in the winter.

The article was illustrated with several pictures: of the brick fireplace that takes up one wall in the living room, a sunken patio off the second level, and the open stairs leading between two of the four levels.

Several other Manson & Carver designs were built nearby in the Whitehills Estates development. For example, there are two on Curtis Road across the street from each other.[29] The three-bedroom, 2,150-square-foot brick ranch at 508 Curtis was designed for Theodore and Florence Levy (of Shinberg Insurance) and their family in 1956. Across the street at 527 Curtis, Leland N. and Nora Jones's 1957 house originally was a two-bedroom, two-and-a-half-bath ranch; a recent addition added a second floor above part of the house. Leland Jones was in administrative services in the State Department of Conservation. Their house has a characteristic butterfly roof and open plan. At the rear, large windows overlook a wooded area that slopes quickly downwards and creates privacy for the house. In general, Manson & Carver designs are stately yet understated, with a refined sense of proportion, marrying some modernistic tendencies to more traditional aspects.

John Crouse, Mayotte-Webb Architects

In addition to his own home on Walnut Heights Drive in East Lansing, built in 1962 (plate 61), John Crouse designed three large residences on White Oaks Drive and Wrightwind Drive in Okemos. Donald Schaberg and Stanley Hartman had purchased twenty-five acres and divided them into large lots varying from one to seven-and-a-half acres. In 1955 Stanley and Monna Lee Hartman engaged Frank Lloyd Wright to design their home at 1185 Wrightwind Drive on the plot adjacent to the Schabergs, who were also working with Wright on their design. The Hartmans continued working with Wright through 1958, when the correspondence abruptly stops.

Several years later, the Hartmans asked John Crouse to redesign their Wrightian home, which was completed in 1965 (plate 74). Crouse's design is very much in the spirit of Wright's. It is a low-slung T-shape, with a carport at right angles bisecting the house proper into two almost equal parts. Wright had oriented the house on the property from the southwest to the northeast; Crouse modified this a little while still turning it off the cardinal points. By moving the bedroom wing to be in line with the kitchen and away from the driveway, he made room for another bedroom. The living room, dining area, and workspace are to the west; the bedroom wing is to the east. Crouse gave Hartman the large storage/tool shed at the end of the carport that he had asked Wright for several times. He removed the large oak tree that was at the center of Wright's house. He retained the low roofline, but the roof was made of crushed marble with copper flashing as a way of retaining heat. Over time, rain and snow washed the small chips into the yard and eventually the material was replaced.[30] As built, the house has a very Wrightian feel, with low-pitched roofs, a central brick fireplace stack, and large overhanging eaves. Crouse echoed Wright's ideas of organic architecture by giving this house a low sense of gravity that makes it feel at one with the landscape.

The Richard and Sharon Taber house at 1190 Wrightwind Drive (plate 80), completed in 1967, is a long rectangle approximately 3,000 square feet, set on three-and-a-half acres of woods across from the Hartmans' house and adjacent to Michael and Rhea Dow's house designed by his father, Alden B. Dow (plate 81). Unlike those, however, where the horizontality relates the structure to the land, here Crouse used a prominent mansard roof that emphasizes weightiness. Mansard roofs are unusual in the area, but were used to good effect here. A smaller one is over the lower wing of the house containing the master bedroom and garage. On the larger central block, the roof is more pronounced and the lower portion has a steep, almost vertical pitch. Rather than soaring upwards, it anchors the house.

The treatment of the exterior is echoed on the interior in the large living space that rises almost two stories. In the center, a double-sided, massive brick fireplace divides the living area from the family room

▶ **FIGURE 38.** Hay House, John Crouse, exterior, rear, Okemos. Photograph © 2014 Kim Kauffman.

behind. Large brick piers emphasize the ends of the hallway and kitchen walls at the point where they enter the space of the living room. To add to the sense of mass, a wide horizontal band of redwood trim was placed on the upper portion of the walls and lit from below. Wood trim was also used around the large windows facing the back.

If Frank Lloyd Wright's organic and planar approach inspired the Dow and Hartman houses, his cement-and-concrete "Mayan" phase, seen at the Alice Barnsdall residence in Hollywood, 1920, may have influenced Crouse's ideas here. That building's massive forms create a fortress-like impression. Here, too, the building looks inward, enclosing and protecting the spaces within.

Crouse used a different approach for Dr. Kent and Donna Hay's tan-brick and wood house nearby at 1234 White Oaks Drive; built in 1967, it has 2,950 square feet with five bedrooms and three baths on 1.58 acres (plate 73). It is a cross between a T and L shape, with projecting bedroom wings to the north and east. There are several informal living spaces. On the main floor, a rectangular area, with a fireplace on the exterior wall, has a half-wall with built-in seating that opens the space up. This openness continues in the nearby stair landing. The most unusual aspect of the house, however, is seen from the backyard (figure 38). Here it becomes clear that most of the main floor is dramatically elevated on piers, and the open spaces underneath create a large protected patio.[31]

Each of these designs by Crouse is quite different. The house he designed for himself (plate 61) can be added to this list of intellectually interesting and dramatically varied ways of using materials, volumes, and shapes that show a sensitivity to site and client.

Laitala and Nuechterlein

Laitala and Nuechterlein, and the successor firm Laitala, Freeman, Smith and Fowler, were responsible for a number of spectacular homes in mid-Michigan in addition to many churches and schools. According to his daughter, Walter Laitala considered his own home at 4051 Van Atta Road, built in 1959, to be his masterpiece.[32] It was adjacent to the home built by his partner, Wilmar (Nick) Nuechterlein, for his family at 4045 Van Atta, also in 1959.

Their house designs for clients from the late 1940s and early 1950s tended to be brick-veneer structures of varying sizes depending upon the lots. By the mid-1950s, they preferred wood, flat or shed roofs, and open designs, and they created some of the area's more interesting modernist homes, among them the 1952 Sharp house, the 1961 Hayes house, and the 1964 Crites house.

One of their early designs, on view when the River Forest subdivision in Lansing was being developed, was seen by several thousand people when it was opened as a display house by the developer, the Walter Neller Company. This house at 2636 Cumberland Road was designed for "Luxury Living in the Upper Price Brackets." As described in the *Lansing State Journal* on April 24, 1949, it reflected typical expectations at this time: "A single story brick veneered residence with full basement and attached two-car garage . . . living room and dining room have large picture windows and a third bedroom or den can be partitioned off by drawing an accordion partition across the living room."

The architects' design for George Foster III at 900 Southlawn Avenue has features similar to the display house in River Forest, albeit on a much larger scale: a 4,432-square-foot brick ranch on two lots and placed deep into the property. Built in 1951, it was the first house in this area of Southlawn and set the design aesthetic for the homes that followed (including the two adjacent Redmond and Maury houses by Manson & Carver discussed earlier).

Laitala and Nuechterlein used some of these features for the Harold J. and Hazel Garrison house at 1135 Abbot Road, built in 1951, where the challenge was the small third-of-an-acre lot and the location on the busy road. For Garrison, who was division chief in the State Department of Aeronautics, and his wife and their family, the architects turned the house at an angle to take advantage of views of the adjacent lot's gardens. At 1,194 square feet, it is a modest wood-sided house of one story, with a basement and garage below. Nevertheless, it caught the interest of the *Lansing State Journal* the following year. In an extensive article subtitled "Upstairs on the Ground Floor," the writer pointed out the flexible layout of the house—in particular, that other than doors to the basement and bedrooms, there were none. Accordion-fold partitions were used to open the den to the living room. A dining ell, the living room, and the kitchen were "grouped around a center wall dominated by a colorful stonework fireplace." Other adaptable features, such as kitchen cabinets that open from both the kitchen and dining area, a linen closet that opens from the bathroom and bedroom wing, and large windows in the dining and living areas, make the house seem larger than it is.

The article is also interesting in that it offers a definition of "Michigan modern" in the early 1950s.

> Mr. and Mrs. Harold J. Garrison use the term "Michigan modern." . . . The modern label is appropriate because of the open planning and flexibility of the living areas, the way the house fits into contours of its site, and the large window areas that make the most of the view. The

▲ **FIGURE 39.** Sharp House, Laitala and Nuechterlein, east side and rear, East Lansing, 1960s photograph.

▶ **FIGURE 40.** Sharp House, Laitala and Nuechterlein, interior, East Lansing. Photograph © 2014 Kim Kauffman.

> Michigan touch is in the use of materials and type of construction well suited to Michigan's climate.[33]

After these "Michigan modern" homes, Laitala and Nuechterlein were given the chance to design several truly modernist homes with shed roofs, very open spaces, and other interesting design features. In 1952, they designed a home for Dr. Mahlon Sharp and his wife Mary, who trained as a lawyer. Mrs. Sharp is remembered today as a forward thinker, a courageous leader, and an aggressive advocate for civil rights in the Greater Lansing community. She was a member of the East Lansing City Council and was instrumental in the passage in 1968 of the Open Housing Ordinance, following shortly the federal Fair Housing Act that banned discrimination in home purchases.[34] Until then, much of the established older parts of East Lansing were closed to Jews and minorities.[35]

"Modern is the word for the M.S. Sharp residence, 950 Audubon Road, East Lansing" (plate 27). This is the beginning of Warren Brintnall's description in the *Lansing State Journal*. "The house nestles into the contours of its sloping lot, becoming a part of the site." Indeed, from the street side, the house appears to be one story, fairly modest and shy, with a roofline that extends past the building and keeps the front door out of view. Because of the slope of the land, there is a full story below in the rear (figure 39). This southern

exposure has a large wall of glass and a porch (now enclosed) that cantilevers out from the upper level. The children's rooms are off the lower level. There is a swimming pool in the steeply sloped, landscaped backyard.

Brintnall continues, "There's a good example of open planning in the uninterrupted flow of space from the entrance hall, through the living room and into the dining room and study. The only interior wall in this entire area is a large storage unit separating the dining area and hall. Even this storage wall does not extend the full height of the ceiling" (figure 40). Early photographs of the exterior clearly show the butterfly roofline that dips towards the center of the structure and peaks at the edges. On the interior, large beams emphasize the slant as the height increases towards the back. In the center of the house, facing the living room, is a large open brick fireplace with a massive copper awning. Instead of air conditioning, a series of louvers or vents were placed high and low on the walls and can be opened to ventilate the house. The large eave on the southern side shields the floor-to-ceiling glazing from the sun's rays in the summer. In winter, the radiant floor heating is supplemented by the passive solar gain through the windows.[36]

At 6292 Skyline Drive in Meridian Township, Laitala and Nuechterlein designed a luxurious home in 1961 for the H. N. Hayes family, whose company made

◄ **FIGURE 41.** Hayes House, Laitala, Freeman, Smith and Fowler, interior patio, East Lansing. Photograph © 2014 Kim Kauffman.

▶ **FIGURE 42.** Hayes House, Laitala, Freeman, Smith and Fowle, interior, living room, East Lansing. Photograph © 2014 Kim Kauffman.

parts for the auto industry (plate 59). With a home on Marcos Island and his own plane, Hayes provided the architects with a generous budget for the new house facing the Walnut Hills Country Club fairway. In addition to the main house, there is a detached "mother-in-law" guest unit and garage. The approach to the house is under a covered, flat loggia that leads to the large front door. This type of loggia was also used by the architect at Edgewood United Church in 1957 and later at the Crites house. From the entry, one sees across the span of the house to the golf course beyond (figure 41).[37] Originally the porch area at the center, which divides the public and private spaces of the house, was open, but it has since been enclosed.

The house is divided into three parts, each with a separate gable roof (figure 43). Most of the interior walls are nonstructural and stop short of the ceiling, adding to the sense of openness (figure 42). The large, open living room with a wall of glazing facing the back has a wood ceiling with dark wood beams and varying heights. The room still has the original plastic hanging light fixtures in aqua and white. In the bedroom wing, several narrow rooms for the family's children had spring-loaded beds that dropped down from the walls. The master bedroom is on the other side of the hall and faces the fairway. In 1966, Hayes asked Lewis L. Fowler, of Eagle, Michigan (who had been a partner with Laitala) to design another bedroom wing that would have been

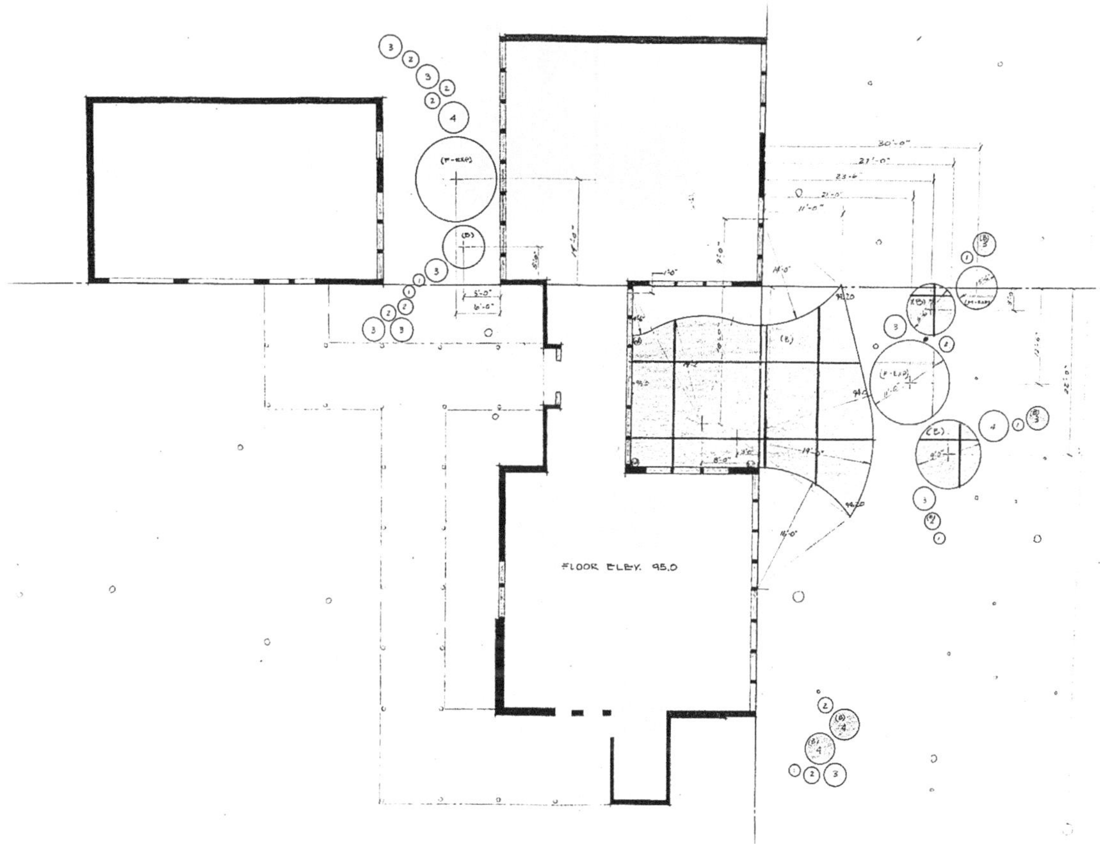

added to the south, towards the garage. This would have necessitated removing the signature fireplace in the living room, and in the end it was not built.

Drew and Skidmore, a prominent local landscape-architecture firm, drew up the plan that used circular concrete discs of differing sizes and colors that dot the area behind the house and the space between the main house and the separate smaller guest/mother-in-law

◄ **FIGURE 43.** Hayes House, Laitala, Freeman, Smith and Fowle, exterior, rear, East Lansing. Photograph © 2014 Kim Kauffman.

▲ **FIGURE 44.** Hayes House, Drew and Skidmore, landscape plan, East Lansing. Courtesy of Bill and Chris Triola.

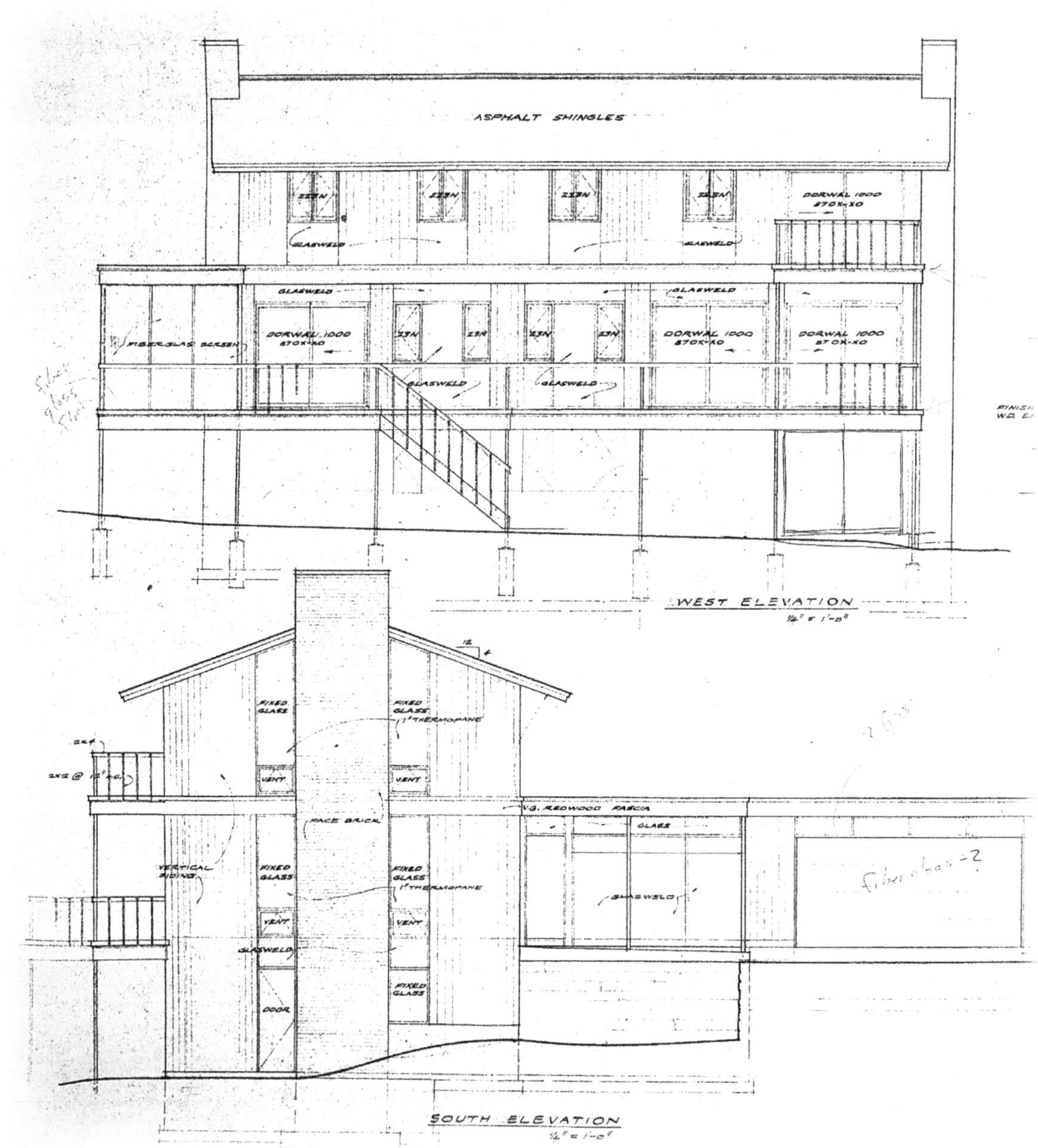

► **FIGURE 45.** Crites House, Laitala and Nuechterlein, west and east elevation, Okemos. Courtesy of Marcia Aldrich and Richard Isomaki.

cottage (figure 44). They tie the buildings together in a unique and humorous way. The firm had also done the landscape design for the Michigan Education Association building for the Warren Holmes Company and most likely designed the landscape for the Sharp house.[38]

Laitala and Nuechterlein also designed a large two-story house for the Dale and Hope Crites family of seven in the Tacoma Hills subdivision in Okemos in 1964, and worked again with landscape designers Drew and Skidmore (plate 72). The house at 4317 Tacoma Boulevard is located at a bend in the road and on the highest part of the property, which slopes down to the Red Cedar River in the back. The house has a play of vertical and horizontal elements on the exterior. The flat-roofed garage on the right and the covered walkway leading to the front door emphasize the horizontal. In effect, the loggia masks the more conventional-looking two-story rectangular house with a gable roof behind (figure 45).

On the inside, however, it is decidedly modern with an open floor plan, asymmetrical and free-flowing with few internal dividing walls (figure 46). The entrance area is double height, with an open stairway rising to the upper-level bedrooms (a master bedroom suite and four additional bedrooms of varying sizes), and descending to the full basement with a game room, laundry, and sewing room that is below ground on the

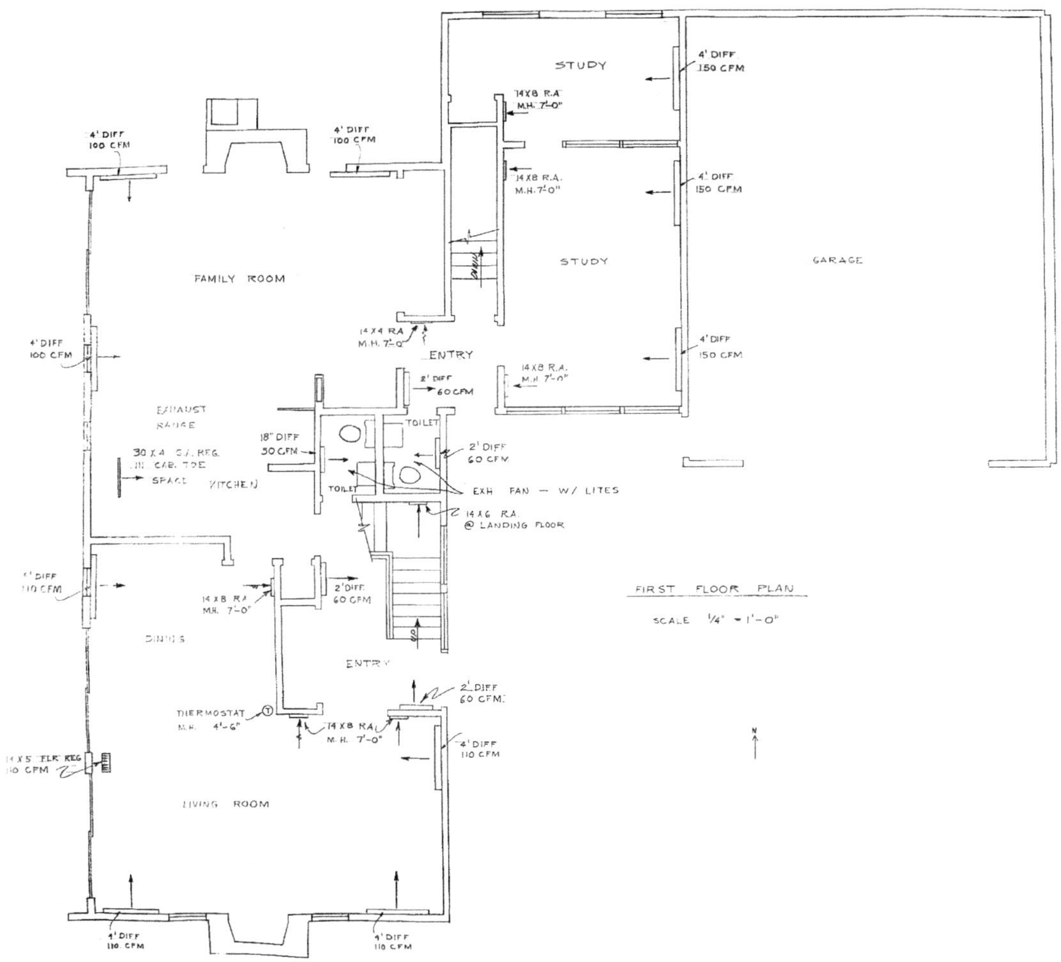

▲ **FIGURE 46.** Crites House, Laitala and Nuechterlein, plan, first floor, Okemos. Courtesy of Marcia Aldrich and Richard Isomaki.

north but at ground level on the rear. There are several balconies on the back and sides.

The living and dining areas are on the south near the U-shaped kitchen that opens to the family room. The plan, the Japanese-influenced front, and the transparency of the first-floor rooms are decidedly modern. This house, like the two discussed above, provides an excellent example of the ways Laitala and Nuechterlein employed volume, open and closed spaces, a sense of proportions, and the importance of sightlines and vistas, as well as the use of natural materials.

Earl Vaive

While Earl Vaive (1924–1999) worked as an architect for the State of Michigan for forty-one years before retiring in 1988, he designed a number of houses in East Lansing and Okemos.[39] Among the most interesting and well sited is the 1957 one for Herbert Weisinger and his wife at 4351 Wausau Road in Tacoma Hills, Okemos (plate 41). It is on slightly more than an acre of land at the end of a cul-de-sac and on the banks of the Red Cedar River in the back. Weisinger was chair and professor of English at MSC, and his wife owned a wholesale electric company. The original brick-and-redwood design, with Plyoform concrete, had an indoor pool for his wife, a recreation room, fireplace, kitchen, one bedroom and one bath on the first floor, and another bedroom and bath on the second floor. The carport has a flat roof, while the house's shed roof rises to the highest point at the back and enabled Vaive to put in a three-story wall of glazing that affords views of the river. Vaive was inspired by Frank Lloyd Wright in many small touches, including 5′7″ doors with hinges that allowed the doors to swing freely, radiant heating in the floor, and other passive solar heating ideas.[40]

When Mr. Weisinger left MSU in 1966, he sold the house to the Stranahans. He was a physics professor who taught at MSU, and she founded the Montessori schools in the area. With four children, they needed a larger home, and they hired a local builder in 1967 to add the tower wing, a significant feature of the house now. This turned the smaller house into 2,900 square feet with six bedrooms and four baths.[41] The tower, with its flat roof and large windows, is unique. Inside, each bedroom reflects the fanlike opening of the circular shape.

Vaive designed several homes in the East Lansing Walnut Heights subdivision, which was developed during the 1960s, including 1684 Walnut Heights Drive, completed in 1961 for Erle Verdun Leichty (1905–1983) and his wife Mary (Woollcott) (d. 1977), MSU professors of English and psychiatry (plate 58). This modified

◀ **FIGURE 47.** Leichty House, Earl Vaive, interior, East Lansing. Photograph © 2014 Kim Kauffman.

A-frame has the short ends turned away from the street, and instead of the sloping walls that end directly at ground level, the design has partial vertical brick walls as the base.[42] Glazing fills the short end on the east. The interior reflects an expansive A-frame treatment. On the first floor, the entrance opens to a hallway with an open stairway leading to the half-floor above and the full basement below. To the right is the kitchen, adjacent to the large living/dining area with a wall of glazing facing the backyard. On the other side of the hallway is a bedroom and bathroom. On the half-floor above, the balcony overlooks the double-height living room (figure 47), with a small study area to the south and bedrooms to the north. Because of the open spaces and the one-and-three-quarters height, the house feels larger than 1,685 square feet.

A-frames were most often used for church construction as well as rural cabins and getaways, because they were easy to construct and economical, and their designs were very flexible.[43] The small 960-square-foot A-frame at 6268 Ridge Street in Haslett, built in 1965, is located a short block-and-a-half from Lake Lansing. As a weekend cabin, the A-frame construction makes sense, as does the rural setting at 2510 Haslett Road, Haslett, described in the *Lansing State Journal* in "Downs Home has Individuality," on April 11, 1965. The owners prized the open feeling, 30-foot high ceiling, and the fact that very little finished carpentry work and skilled labor was required to build it. A more unusual setting for an A-frame is the house at 2052 Tomahawk, Tacoma Hills, Okemos, in the middle of a suburban subdivision. The longtime owners were Anthony and Ellen Battaglia. He was a graduate of MSU and was president of Capital Advertising Company. Similar in size to the Walnut Heights house and built a year later, in 1962, the slanted exterior walls are on the north and south sides, and the shorter sides have glazing. Because of the corner lot, a brick privacy wall shields the glazed wall on the west. The house has a rectangular plan consisting of two bedrooms and two baths, a metal spiral staircase providing access to the upper level, and a breezeway linking the house to the carport. It represents typical A-frame construction, while the Leichty home is a far more subtle adaptation of this plan.

Close to the Leichty house, Vaive designed a split-level home at 1844 Walnut Heights for Paul and Betty Strassmann, professors at MSU. Paul Strassmann, an economist, wrote his master's thesis at Columbia University on the building industry and was always interested in buildings and homes. When he came to East Lansing in 1956, he and his growing family of three rented a small nondescript house before deciding to build in the Walnut Heights development. Given Paul's academic interests, there was no question that they would build a modern home. They signed a contract with Earl Vaive in 1962 and built in the following year. Strassmann had definite ideas about what he wanted in his house and made several drawings to show the relationships and placements of the rooms that then guided the architect. On the main floor, there is a large living room with a high ceiling. Behind it is a two-story rectangle with bedrooms on the floor above and the kitchen and bedrooms below, with access to the sloping backyard and stand of aspens.[44]

These three examples show Vaive's versatility as an architect and his attention to the site. There are undoubtedly additional examples that he designed that remain to be identified.

Adrian N. Langius

The situation is similar with Adrian (Gus) Langius (1903–1991). Trained at the University of Michigan, he was employed by the State of Michigan from 1939 until he retired in 1971, including as director of the Building Division, Bureau of the Budget. In this capacity, he was in charge of existing state buildings and new construction.[45] As the state architect, he made an impact in preservation, planning, and construction codes rather than in physical structures.[46] He did, however, design at least two modernist houses in East Lansing in addition to his own from 1936.

Known as the "bookends," these two small spec houses are mirror images and stand side by side where two streets come together on a curve; one is at 901 Rosewood Avenue (1952) (plate 9) and the other at 910 Roxburgh Avenue (1947). Over the years, each house has had several additions, but enough remains of 901 to provide a sense of the original structure. The plan is rectangular, tri-level with a shed roof and carport. The living room was on the ground level with floor-to-ceiling windows. The main floor was half a level up and connected by an open staircase from below to the upper level. There were three bedrooms and one bath, with an extra toilet in the furnace room, although there was no real basement.[47] These houses are near Alden Dow's Bachman House (plate 1) but are otherwise surrounded by typical two-story bungalows, so it was unusual that the architect would build these very contemporary structures on speculation.

Sanford Farness House

Sanford S. Farness (1917–2006), professor of urban and regional planning at MSU, made his home at 730 Grove Street in East Lansing (plate 70). Built in 1964, the sprawling house of over 3,800 square feet sits on a narrow but deep lot and rises from one story towards the street to two stories into the property.

Originally the carport was open, and elaborately patterned wood slats were visible. The extensive use of wood throughout; the broad, sweeping eaves; the different roof levels; balconies on the second floor; and the horizontal planes are reminiscent of California bungalows. This makes sense, since Farness came to East Lansing from California. He may have worked with the architect Robert Pond, who was an apprentice at Taliesin in 1949, in designing this house.[48]

Davidson House, also called the House of the Future

The Lansing area has its share of folklore, which includes many stories about the "House of the Future." Constructed in the mid-1960s at 4918 Delta River Drive, on a secluded lot of over forty-five acres that had a pond and barn, this sprawling house had five bedrooms and seven baths. The original owners were Richard (Dick) and Sally Davidson.[49] Richard worked with his father L. A. Davidson, who had a bridge-building and construction company in Lansing. Davidson specifically wanted the house to look like a bridge with high concrete arches (figure 48). To that end, the bridge-building technique of cast-in-place reinforced concrete was used rather than typical home construction (figure 49). Davidson hired Charles Harper, a Milwaukee architect who was recommended by a fraternity brother, Robert Greaves, who was a landscape architect in Milwaukee. Harper translated Davidson's ideas into a building plan. The result was a large, roughly U-shaped asymmetrical structure with convex and concave walls and a fluctuating roofline. A series of interlocking domes and buttresses created large areas below that were filled with huge sheets of dark tempered glass held in place by aluminum frames. The large panes of glass had to be lowered into place by derricks.

The front of the house had a large patio and faced a man-made pond. To the left was the game room and four-stall garage. In the center was a large living and dining room, and on the right, a guest suite. The kitchen was on the back. Wide stairs near the entry led to the second floor, which had four bedrooms to the left, and a balcony that looked down to the kitchen/dining areas and connected to the master bedroom suite with two baths on the right. In the basement, described as tunnel-like, there were large wine cellars. No expense was spared, including finding purple granite in Virginia that was used to face the large fireplace.

Plans for the building dated August 2, 1963, show the elaborate wood-frame forms that were used for the poured concrete, as well as the extensive amount of rebar required to reinforce the oval and round shapes of the individual roof domes (figure 49). As seen in the model (figure 48), the roof floated and swooped

PLATE 37. Gordon H. and Catherine Stow House. Gordon Stow, 1955.

PLATE 38. George H. and Elizabeth Arbaugh House. R. B. Sloan Jr., 1956.

Photograph © 2020 Kim Kauffman.

PLATE 39. Lansing City Hall, 1956–58; Lansing Police Headquarters, 1958–59.
Lee Black and Kenneth C. Black, Architects. Photo courtesy of Michigan State Historic Preservation Office.

PLATE 40. The Albert G. and Ethel Redmond House. Manson & Carver, 1956.

Photo by Natasha Crljenica.

PLATE 41. Herbert Weisinger House. Earl Vaive, 1957; tower addition, 1967.

Photo by Natasha Crljenica.

PLATE 42. Durward and Paula P. Varner House. R. B. Sloan Jr., 1957.

PLATE 43. Lawrence L. and Frances J. Boger House. R. B. Sloan Jr., 1957.

Photograph © 2020 Kim Kauffman.

PLATE 44. Edgewood United Church. Laitala and Nuechterlein, 1957; sanctuary wing, Gordon Cornwell, 1966.

Photo courtesy of the Michigan State Historic Preservation Office.

PLATE 45. Donald and Mary Lou Schaberg House. Frank Lloyd Wright, 1958; addition, Taliesin Associates, 1966.

PLATE 46. Edward and Lisa Hertel House. Manson & Carver, 1958.

Photograph © 2014 Kim Kauffman.

PLATE 47. Gordon and Angela Fineout House. Gordon Fineout, 1958.

PLATE 48. William Sylvester and Margaret Jeannette Gamble House. "ACH," 1958; garage addition, 1970.

PLATE 49. Lloyd and Fern Marie Miller House. Donald Scholz, 1958.

PLATE 50. Kresge Art Center, rear. Ralph Calder Associates, 1958; additions 1966, 1973.

Photo courtesy of the Michigan State Historic Preservation Office.

PLATE 51. Maynard and Betty Simmons House. Gordon Fineout, 1959.

PLATE 52. Carleton W. and Heluiz Washburne House. Alden B. Dow, 1960.

over the space, held aloft by the vertical and slanted buttresses. The organic flow reminds one of commercial rather than domestic architecture, and Davidson used his bridge-building crew and equipment to erect the house. He may have had in mind the Eastman Kodak pavilion at the 1964 New York World's Fair, which was under construction.[50] There was great fanfare when its design was unveiled to the public at the time of the groundbreaking in August 1962. Press releases called attention to the poured concrete, freeform, undulating roof referred to as a "floating carpet," a "moon deck," or lunar landscape, using space-age terminology that was in vogue. At 363 feet in length, the building was one of the largest at the fair and was meant to signal Kodak's cutting-edge technology. It neared completion in the winter of 1963–64, around the time that Davidson was working on the ideas for his house.

There are sketches and numerous plans for the house from 1963, as well as many construction snapshots taken by the family. It was under construction for roughly a year, and just before the scheduled move-in day after Labor Day, 1965, one of the daughters, who was riding her horse on the property, was involved in a serious accident. With the focus on her recovery, which took many months, the family did not move into the house, and neither was it completely finished. A divorce followed and the house was basically abandoned.[51]

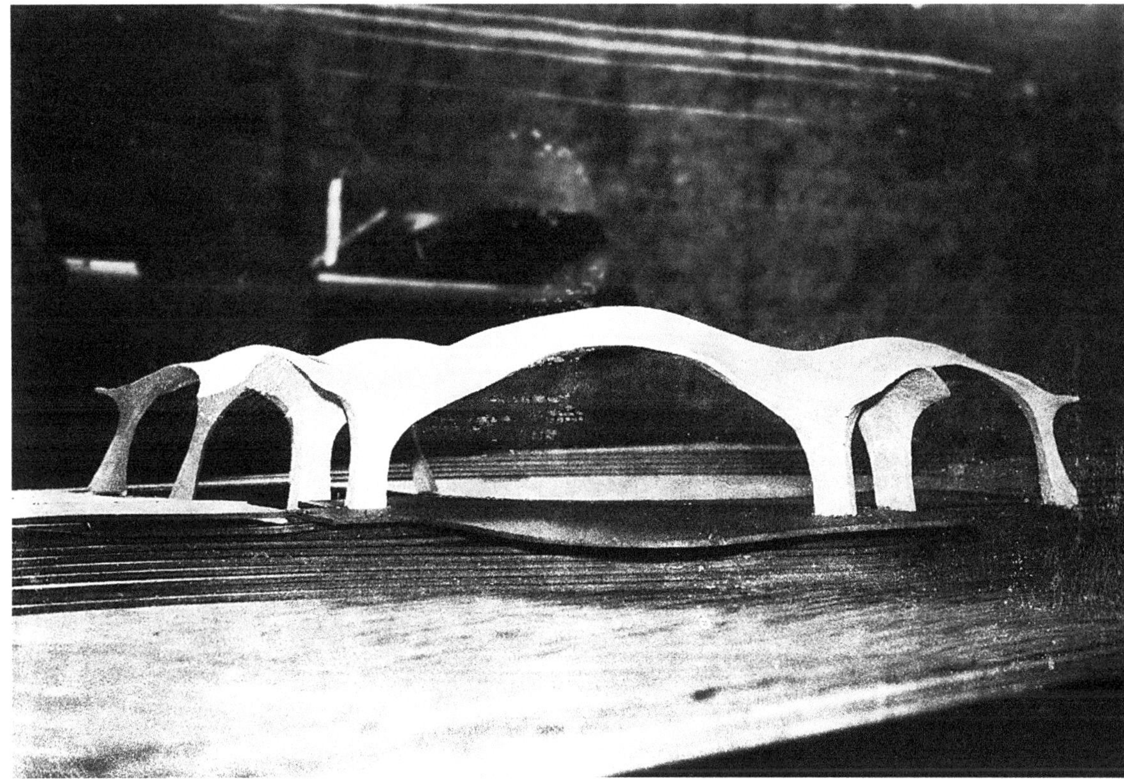

▲ **FIGURE 48.** Davidson House, Charles Harper, model, Lansing. Courtesy of Sally Davidson.

Subsequently, vandals broke most of the glass, and the structure became a favorite getaway for many local high school students.[52] Eventually it was purchased and finally completed in 1984, but with more wood and less glass than originally intended.[53] Even in its present altered state, it remains one of the most unusual houses in mid-Michigan.

Several additional architect-designed and unusual houses in mid-Michigan deserve mention. These include

▲ **FIGURE 49.** Davidson House, construction photograph, 1964. Courtesy of Sally Davidson.

the compact streamlined house at 164 Maplewood Drive from 1941, at the tail end of the popularity of the Art Moderne style (plate 5); the 1940 O. Lee and Genevieve Ricker house designed by Donald Hedges, a Pennsylvania architect (plate 4); the John G. and Marjorie Goodell house from 1951 that has features in common with houses designed by Manson, Jackson & Kane (plate 23); and the later, very elegant Harold and Wilma Good house designed by Florida architect Alfred Browning Parker in 1967 (plate 83). The John and Margaret Henderson House (plate 76), known in the neighborhood as the "fishbowl" house because of the extensive use of glass, was designed by Mrs. Henderson. Unbeknownst to her, her husband had her ideas executed while they were in Europe on a Fulbright grant.[54]

This survey of architect-designed houses in mid-Michigan has unearthed a lot of information about singular homes; their owners, who for a myriad of reasons chose modernist designs; and their architects. The range is equally impressive. No doubt, however, there are many more stories and houses to be discovered.[55]

CHAPTER 6

Hugh Stubbins Jr. and Lantern Hill, an East Lansing Community

The history of Lantern Hill in East Lansing was recounted in 1999 by Alan Grimes, one of the original corporation members, on the occasion of the fiftieth anniversary of the first appearance of the project (plate 26).[1] The fourteen-page description, "Remembering Lantern Hill, 1950–52," has drama, despair, and hope as the story of this cooperative building project became a reality. It began with the critical housing shortage brought about by the G.I. Bill of Rights (1944), which dramatically increased student enrollment not just at Michigan State College but across the country. When Myles Boylan, professor of landscape architecture and urban planning, spoke to the Newcomer's Club about "Helpful Housing Hints" in February 1950, his mention of cooperative housing projects elsewhere led to an ad hoc group that explored a similar venture in East Lansing. Subgroups studied possibilities of financing, legal aspects of setting up a corporation, cooperative construction programs, and possible sites.

By May, "Home-Sites, Inc." was incorporated and the hunt for land started in earnest. After looking at property to the south of the campus,[2] they eventually chose twenty-three acres of farmland north of Burcham Drive (beyond the city limits at that time, but within walking distance from the campus) that were purchased for $850 an acre. As word of the project spread, more people wanted to participate, and an additional seven acres were bought. Boylan drew a plan that divided the land into forty-one half-acre lots on gently curving roads (figure 50). Of the new roads, Lantern Hill Drive is the longest, starting at Burcham Road and winding

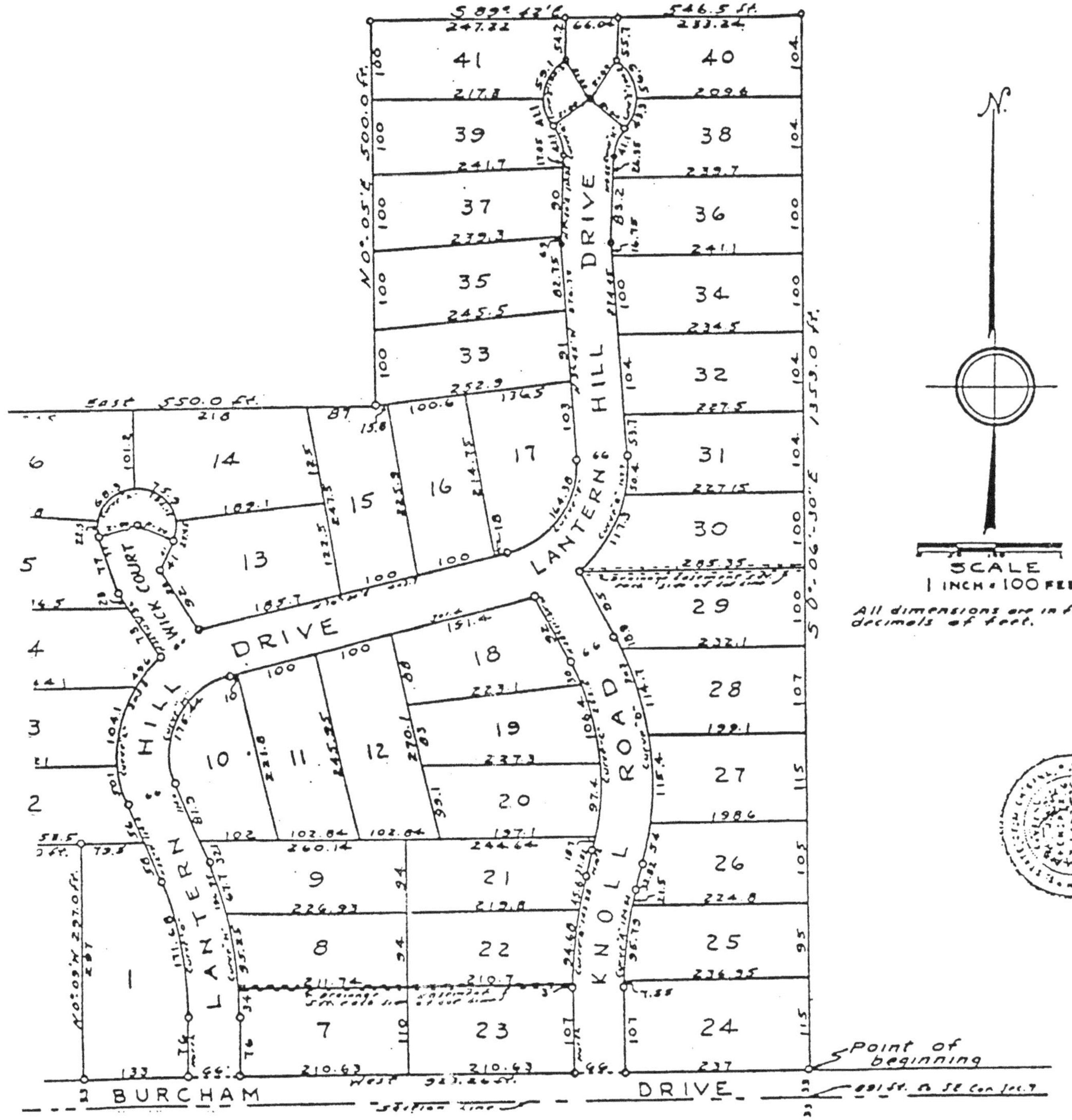

▶ **FIGURE 50.** Lantern Hill plot plan, Myles Boylan, East Lansing.

north. Wick Court is a cul-de-sac off Lantern Hill, and the short Knoll Road starts at Burcham Road and intersects with Lantern Hill.

According to Warren Brintnall in the *Lansing State Journal*, participants saved about 50 to 60 percent of the probable market value of the homes, in part because there were no promotion costs for the project or costly sales programs, and no business overhead.[3] To take advantage of the economy of scale, Home-Sites members agreed to build at the same time and to use the same architect. Boylan's recommendation of Hugh Stubbins Jr., with whom he had studied at Harvard University, was accepted. Of the forty-one families, twenty-four decided to work with Stubbins. Their lots would be on the western side of the plat; the remaining seventeen would make their own arrangements and build on the east side.

Hugh Stubbins Jr. (1912–2006) was born in Birmingham, Alabama, and educated in architecture at the Georgia Institute of Technology (1932) and the Harvard Graduate School of Design (1935), where he studied with Walter Gropius and then worked for him. In 1949, he formed Hugh Stubbins, Architect, practicing in Cambridge, Massachusetts.[4] Lantern Hill was one of his earlier projects, and he went on to gain international acclaim, constructing buildings across the globe. Among his best-known designs are those for the Berlin Congress Hall in West Germany (1957), Citicorp Center in Manhattan (1978), Reagan Presidential Library in California (1991), and the Landmark Tower in Yokohama, Japan (1993).[5]

In hindsight, Stubbins proved to be the appropriate architect to become engaged with Home-Sites. He was well aware of cooperative housing developments recently completed or underway in Massachusetts by the TAC (The Architects Collaborative), the partnership founded in 1945 by Walter Gropius with seven other architects. Their Six Moon Hill development (1947–1951) and Five Fields (1951–59) in Lexington were based on the idea of building low-cost ($15,000) affordable houses with small bedrooms on lots of equal sizes, utilizing utilitarian modern construction.[6] These were probably among the cooperative projects that Boylan lectured about in 1950. Additionally, numerous other mid-century modern communities were being constructed and discussed in the early 1950s.[7]

Stubbins also had designed low-cost military housing during the war, and participated in the design of two houses for the Ingersoll Village project in Kalamazoo in 1947.[8] The latter was a project of architect J. Fletcher Lankton and the Ingersoll Steel and Disc Division of the Borg-Warner Corporation. The idea was to develop a unit measuring two-and-a-half-feet wide, seven-and-a-half-feet long, and six-and-a-half-feet high that contained all of the utilities, plumbing, electrical, and ventilation connections needed in a house. It could be inserted into the structure as it was being built and thereby speed construction and save money. Stubbins, Alden B. Dow, Keck & Keck, and Edward Durell Stone were among the eight nationally known architects who were asked in 1945 to design a house using the unit. Their designs varied; some were Cape Cods, others two-story Colonials, and some were stripped-down modernism. Stubbins's one bedroom, single-story house at 1111 Crown Street was built around 1946. His second house at 1115 Crown Street was a compact, three-bedroom structure with a low sloping gable roof.

Stubbins's pragmatic approach emphasized function, logic, and relationship to the surroundings. Years later, he was quoted as saying that architecture is not just individual buildings, but "the whole fabric of our physical environment. Architecture is the man-made world in its totality." As such, he viewed architecture as an "approach towards life . . . a social art."[9]

For Home-Sites, Stubbins was asked to provide three different plans from which the participants would choose (figure 51).[10] All but three selected Plan A. Although the basic features were set, as Grimes wrote, individualization of the design was possible. Plan A had a slab foundation, a rectangular plan with the entry placed just off-center, and a small study off the entrance. Two or three bedrooms were at one end, with a small bump out from the straight line of the rectangle to enlarge the space of one bedroom and the bathroom. A free-standing fireplace was placed in the large living room, which had 18 feet of glazing (windows and doors) on the backyard side. The U-shaped kitchen had a counter rather than a wall to open it up to the dining and living areas. A utility room was provided near the kitchen for the oil furnace and other utilities. Options included an activity room and an open or enclosed carport. Plan B had a small basement and was suited to sites on a hill; two of these were erected. Plan C differed slightly in the placement of the dining area and kitchen near the entrance; one was constructed.

Stubbins made three pairs of colorful presentation drawings so that the Home Sites participants could envision life in these houses.[11] Model A2's exterior is a bird's-eye view showing the rectangular shape, a sheltered walkway to the carport, and privacy fences in the yard (plate 24). The interior is a wide-angle view from the back, emphasizing the open plan and flow between inside and outside (plate 25). The space is divided visually rather than physically, and the furniture is clearly contemporary. A slick curved red fireplace is especially noteworthy although in the model B3 drawing, there is a traditional brick fireplace, and in the blueprint, a freestanding fireplace (figure 51). These drawings visualize the minimalist, functional décor that clearly suggests a modern way of living.[12]

▶ **FIGURE 51.** Lantern Hill, Hugh Stubbins, blueprint, detail. Courtesy of the Frances Loeb Library, Harvard University Graduate School of Design.

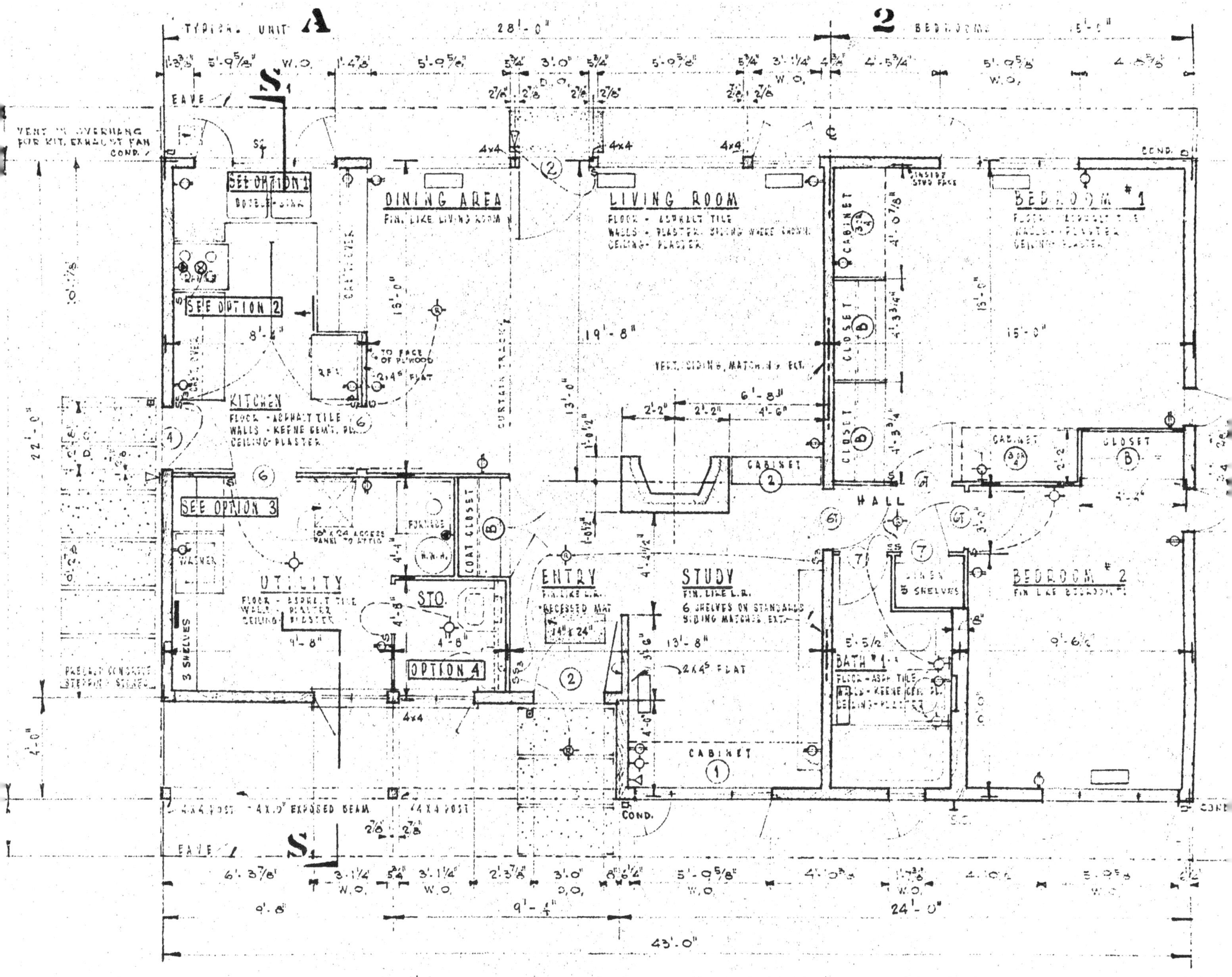

TYPICAL UNIT A
2 BEDROOMS
28'-0"
EAVE
VENT IN OVERHANG FOR KIT. EXHAUST FAN
SEE OPTION 1
SEE OPTION 2
SEE OPTION 3
OPTION 4
DINING AREA
FIN. LIKE LIVING ROOM
LIVING ROOM
FLOOR - ASPHALT TILE
WALLS - PLASTER, SIDING WHERE SHOWN
CEILING - PLASTER
BEDROOM #1
KITCHEN
FLOOR - ASPHALT TILE
WALLS - KEENE CEM'T. PL.
CEILING - PLASTER
CURTAIN TRACK
VERT. SIDING, MATCHING EXT.
CABINET
CLOSET
HALL
UTILITY
FLOOR - ASPHALT TILE
WALLS - PLASTER
CEILING - PLASTER
WASHER
3 SHELVES
FURNACE
W.H.
COAT CLOSET
STO.
ENTRY
FIN. LIKE L.R.
RECESSED MAT
24" x 24"
STUDY
FIN. LIKE L.R.
6 SHELVES ON STANDARDS
SIDING MATCHES EXT.
LINEN
5 SHELVES
BATH #1
FLOOR - ASPH. TILE
WALLS - KEENE CEM. PL.
CEILING - PLASTER
BEDROOM #2
FIN. LIKE BEDROOM #1
PRECAST CONCRETE STEPPING STONES
4x4 POST
4x4 POST
COND.
2x4S FLAT
43'-0"
24'-0"

Many features and construction methods were modern, including the slab foundation, interior partitions rather than load-bearing walls, forced air system with clay supply tubes under the floor, flat roofs on the separate garage, and low gables on the house itself, as well as large areas of glazing.[13] In addition, the way each of these low-profile houses was placed on the lot followed ideas of organic architecture. The Walter and Pauline Adams House shows the original characteristics of Plan A, with the exception of the later addition on the left (plate 26).

When the FHA office in Grand Rapids refused to approve Stubbins's plans because they were nontraditional, the entire project was almost derailed. Stubbins appealed to the Washington office, which overturned the Michigan decision.[14] This was especially fortunate. At this same stage in the Usonia 2 project fifteen years earlier, the FHA, as the lender of last resort, had refused to fund Frank Lloyd Wright's designs and that project came to an abrupt end.

To cut costs, Home-Sites members did a lot of the labor themselves and acted as subcontractors. They bought appliances in bulk. Large parts of the houses, including trusses and sides of the houses, were fabricated in Grand Rapids and trucked to the site. This method sped the construction process, and many of the houses that were started in spring 1951 were ready for occupancy by the fall.

A *Lansing State Journal* article on Sunday, July 15, 1951, "Homes Built for Faculty, Co-operative Development Near East Lansing Shows Progress," opined that

> It is doubtful if the Lansing area has had any other subdivision that has shown such a rapid spontaneous growth as has Lantern Hills . . . [the] common choice of the same model by most of the families, . . . along with the fact that all of the Stubbins-designed houses there have natural finished wood siding, account for a notable similarity of the houses at the present stage of construction. However, residents expect to achieve individuality in the finished homes through variations in the landscaping in plans and placement of screen fencing.

The Home-Sites Articles of Incorporation were specific about where future additional structures could be placed on the lot, the maximum number of stories that could be built, and other details that succeeded in keeping the original aesthetics of the project.[15] As starter homes for young faculty, Stubbins's designs were modest, but over the decades, most of the houses have been enlarged and the interiors rearranged. Original redwood siding has been painted, cork or linoleum flooring has been replaced, rooms have been combined, and the landscape has matured. Indeed, each has been individualized, as was expected, so that now it is fairly hard to find traces of those modest beginnings. What remains unchanged, however, is the sense of community that developed early on as a result of the necessity of working together physically and financially. Most of the original group were the same age and raised their children together. They had already worked together to develop several cooperative enterprises—a grocery store, nursery school, and cashless baby-sitting service—through which members of the group became friends, tackling these smaller projects before the larger one. They were of like minds politically as well. Current residents recall that at times Lantern Hill owners were referred to as "commies," confirming the left leanings of the close-knit community. In fact, cooperative projects at this time tended to attract people who were liberal politically and socially conscious.[16]

The keys to the success of this project, as opposed to Frank Lloyd Wright's failed Usonia 2 in nearby Okemos, were in both limiting the design choices and the creation of a corporation. For Usonia 2, each person contracted separately with Wright and received a unique design that typically stretched their limited budgets and time frames. Lantern Hill's covenants, bylaws, and formal incorporation gave its members a structure that enabled them to move ahead swiftly and work together. In addition, the personalities of the architects came into play. Wright's infamous ego got in the way of providing his clients with some of their requirements within their financial constraints, whereas Stubbins, as a young architect, seemed more willing to address the clients' needs.[17] As of this writing, two original Home-Sites members still live in their houses, as do several children and two grandchildren.[18] Lantern Hill remains prized for the large lots within the city, the park-like atmosphere (with no sidewalks), walkable distance from the MSU campus, and the pride the homeowners have in the neighborhood and its history.

CHAPTER 7

Trade Secrets Revealed

The choices people had in the postwar period were to buy an older house, purchase a newly erected one, or pick a design or designer to build a custom house. The majority of new homes in the Lansing area, as elsewhere in the country, were modest and traditional, built on speculation by developers. Each January 1st issue of the *Lansing State Journal* often summarized the previous year's building trends and made projections for the new year. On January 1, 1950, "1949 Proves Busy Building Year," the most significant trend was the shift to low-cost houses—that is, those priced between $5,000 and $7,000 and sold with small down payments—while those costing more than $10,000 represented a relatively small proportion of the total number.

"Factory-built Houses Unknown Back in 1900," in the same issue, discussed the fading stigma against prefabs as a result of the housing shortage following World War II, which made production of assembly-line housing not only possible but necessary.[1] Indeed, the Lansing City Council had amended the building code on May 27, 1946, to permit the erection of factory-produced houses, provided they could pass tests proving their strength and durability. Additionally, federal support to makers of prefabricated houses led to plants springing up across the country. This, however, did not guarantee success, as in the case of the ill-fated Lustron house.[2]

The enormous building activity in the Lansing area provided opportunities for local developers of new subdivisions to work with national or regional prefabrication firms. One of these was the National Home Corporation of Lafayette, Indiana, described as the largest producer of prefabricated houses in the United States. They opened a model in Lansing in 1950 of a "thrift home" that could be erected in a few hours by a crew of eight to ten men and was ready for occupancy within ten days, for an average price of $6,300.[3]

Pollman Homes from Toledo, Ohio, a rival national company, made their first appearance in the area in 1951 in the Homestead Terrace subdivision in East Lansing, east of Hagadorn Road, where twenty-seven of these were planned and quickly built. The prices for these "homes in a hurry" (the caption for the pictures in the *Lansing State Journal*, September 30, 1951) ranged from $11,500 to $12,500, including the land. A Pollman home came directly from the Thyer Manufacturing Corporation in Toledo, with walls in ten sections and items such as columns for the porch ends, parquet oak squares for the flooring, and a double closet that formed the wall between two of the bedrooms.[4]

Of the many examples of models available that used prefabricated components, perhaps the most intriguing is the Trade Secrets house. According to *Changing Times Magazine*, "The most talked about house of 1953" was a *Life Magazine* project intended to cost around $20,000 and specifically targeted at young couples.[5] It caught the attention of one such couple in East Lansing. Robin A. and Elizabeth Monroe Drews decided to build a Trade Secrets house at 1410 Sherwood Road in 1954 (plate 31).[6] Some of the "secrets" included the use of preassembled trusses, prefabricated closets that rise the full height of the

► **FIGURE 52.** Drews House, Trade Secrets, interior, East Lansing. Photograph © 2014 Kim Kauffman.

interior space, and thin partitions separating the spaces rather than internal supporting walls. All of these made the house feel decidedly modern and much larger than the 1,340 square feet it contained.

In 1952 *Life Magazine* sponsored a conference of leaders of the building industry, coordinated by the National Association of Home Builders. The results were presented to the public in the January 5, 1953 issue. The goal was to design a "good looking, skillfully engineered, $15,000 house." Putting together features people preferred with quality materials, and using the latest tested engineering techniques, the "Trade Secrets" houses were neither cheap nor very expensive.[7] Each would use assembly-line techniques to keep costs down. One of the characteristic features was the triangular framed trusses that spanned from one outside wall to the other, freeing up the interior space and eliminating the need for interior supports.[8]

Changing Times published a five-part series on the Trade Secrets houses between May and September 1953. The May issue listed 139 builders and building organizations in thirty-three states that were constructing them. Of these, the largest numbers were in Texas (nineteen), Ohio (thirteen), and California (thirteen). Nine were listed in Michigan: four in the Detroit area, two in Grand Rapids, and one each in Flint and East Lansing.[9] At $20,000, *Changing Times* made it clear that this type of house was

> not planned for austerity living or "just scraping along." It's meant for comfortable living in the modern manner. It is spacious . . . and has many of the conveniences that most moderately well-off Americans want in their houses today but don't always get. Such living doesn't come at cut rate.[10]

The National Association of Home Builders collected data on the selling prices of the first of these homes. The highest was $26,900, the lowest was $15,000, and the average was $21,900. Some of the variables cited were the cost of land in different parts of the country (15 percent of the total cost) and the wide choice of equipment that came with the house (garbage disposal, kitchen fan, clothes dryer, refrigerator, washer, dishwasher, etc.).[11]

The *Changing Times* article elaborates on what is intriguing about the house in terms of contemporary cost-cutting construction techniques, such as dry walls of painted wallboard instead of plaster, which is costlier and takes longer to apply; commodious prefabricated storage walls "not only save on the cost of the closets, but nearly do away with interior partitions entirely." Additionally,

> Exterior framing is assembled on the floor slab, then tilted up into position, a simpler, faster way than building framing vertically. The preassembled triangular

> roof trusses save carpenter time and are quick to instal [*sic*]. The crew simply lifts them to the top of the framing, allowing them to hang point down. Then they are flipped over to point up. It takes little more than a twist of the wrist.[12]

Over the course of six months, *Changing Times* reported on the case-study house built by Carl M. Freeman in Bethesda, Maryland, a seasoned builder in that area. Interest was so high that when the house was ready for public inspection, nine thousand people toured it in a single day. The August article reported people's reactions.[13] About the outside appearance, a frequently heard comment was "Pretty, isn't it?" This was "freely interpreted" to mean that the house was a successful "design compromise." It had a familiar warmth, even with an open plan, to satisfy

> those who usually favor more traditional architecture and looks trim and structural enough to appease the partisans of all-out modernity. . . . absence of a dividing wall between the living room and the dining kitchen area . . . prompted some mothers to approve, seeing how easily they could attend to kitchen chores and still keep an eye on the youngsters' deviltry in the living room or out on the terrace.[14]

Visitors admired the "indoors-outdoors" connection between the living room and the outdoor patio area, the storage in the carport, and the massive storage walls that were "deftly designed and neatly engineered to make every inch count."

Objections were raised to the openness of the kitchen, although this was intentional on the part of the designers to "meld various functions of the modern family." Bedrooms were deemed to be too small. The builder's retort was that the function of a bedroom is to "provide a private place to sleep and dress in," and that since the built-in storage walls eliminated any need for "such half-forgotten objects as bureaus and chiffoniers, a bedroom must only be large enough to accommodate a bed, a chair or two, and perhaps a chest of drawers. These bedrooms serve their purpose without squandering an inch or a dollar." Larger families wanted a permanent divider rather than an accordion door between the "den-library" and the adjacent living room. And finally, the 28 feet of floor-to-ceiling glass was "too much to take" for some (figure 53).[15]

In the final article in the series, "How the Buyers Fit It into Their Budget," the author profiles a typical potential purchaser of a Trade Secrets house: a young married couple in their mid-thirties, one annual income of $9,600 but anticipating future increases, one three-year-old with more expected in the future,

currently renting and putting aside savings each month. Financing could be obtained through the builder at 5 percent for twenty years for $13,500 and a down payment of $6,450.[16] The Drews of East Lansing fit this profile. He was born in 1914, had served in the military during the war, and began teaching social science at Michigan State College in 1948. He was promoted to assistant professor in July 1953, around the time his house was taking shape. He remained at the university until he resigned in 1965.[17]

The Drews' L-shaped house faces west on a corner lot; the attached carport with storage is to the north, and the bedroom wing, with two bedrooms and two baths, is on the west. The path to the front door is sheltered by the roof overhanging the entry courtyard between the carport and the house (plate 31). The roof rises to form a gable, and the outer edges facing the back are supported by wood posts, providing a shaded area below and protecting the living room from the high summer sun (figure 53). In addition to gardens on two sides of the house, there is another small "secret" enclosed outdoor space at the end of the bedroom wing that is accessed from both bedrooms. To create a sunshade, the trusses on the end were left exposed. On the interior, one end of the living room has a large raised brick fireplace, but the dominant feature is the long wall of windows on the east that truly does meld indoors and outdoors (figure 52).

◀ **FIGURE 53.** Drews House, Trade Secrets, exterior, rear, East Lansing. Photograph © 2014 Kim Kauffman.

The house followed the Trade Secrets model with only a few exceptions. A wall was used to separate the kitchen from the dining area, but a spacious, open flow was created by omitting the accordion door that could close the den/guest room from the living/dining area. Countering the idiom that too many cooks spoil the broth, in this case the sharing of the latest ideas by many home builders led to the very successful experiment of the Trade Secrets house.

Over the years, *Lansing State Journal* writers found the ways in which homeowners sought ideas for their houses of sufficient interest to warrant discussion and illustration. For example, in 1950, it was reported that Mr. and Mrs. Alten Hager admired a plan in Atlanta, Georgia, illustrated in a national magazine, that they replicated at 846 Wildwood Avenue at the corner of Harrison Road in East Lansing.[18] Likewise, J. F. Rupperts used blueprints from the *Better Homes and Gardens* "5-Star" home for January 1950 at 175 Maplewood Drive.[19] There were many other examples that were reported and others that were not, such as John and Martha Seaman, who admired a split-level house in another widely circulated magazine; contacted the New York designers, the husband-and-wife team of Louis E. De Respinis and Lucia E. Neumann; and built it at 529 Southlawn Avenue in 1958.[20] Popular magazines like *Better Homes and Gardens* and *Popular Mechanics*, "how-to" books by *Sunset*, builders models and expositions, and model homes at World's Fairs responded to the widespread interest in home design. Even the *Lansing State Journal* published a "model home" plan in each Sunday section of the newspaper in the 1950s. Information about construction, materials, room and closet sizes was available free by contacting the Home Building editor. But these ideas were not always modern. The Drews were not alone in choosing their house plan based on magazine coverage they read, but they were the only ones in the area to choose the latest trade secrets.

CHAPTER 8

City Hall, Associations, and Commercial Buildings

Local governments, trade associations, and businesses explored modernism to broadcast that they were up-to-date and future-oriented. Yet, in mid-Michigan there are less than a handful of International-style buildings that made visible the modern technologies that reinforced this message. The purest of these are Lansing City Hall and the Police Headquarters in downtown Lansing, from the mid-1950s. Many of Lansing's office buildings are from earlier in the century when the automobile industry, in particular Oldsmobile, was the economic driver. The Knapp's department store building, an iconic example of Streamline Moderne from the 1930s, reflects the period when people shopped and worked downtown. While this remained true at mid-century, especially with the seat of state government at its center, businesses and government-related concerns routinely moved away to spread out rather than up. This was the case with two professional associations that built East Lansing's two most important modernist buildings: the Michigan State Medical Society and the Michigan Education Association. Minoru Yamasaki's elegant white building with slender arched columns for MSMS, and Warren Holmes's noteworthy subtle detailing for the MEA both successfully used a modernist vocabulary to convey their organization's goals and values. Each of these and City Hall fit the dialogue that was occurring nationally and internationally about the advantages of modern design.

At the opposite end of the architectural spectrum are examples of vernacular "Googie" commercial roadside structures, such as Dawn Donuts and Arby's, that were meant to call attention to themselves as motorists whizzed by. Their universal corporate designs were instantly recognizable to customers. The rapidly

▶ **FIGURE 54.** Dorothy Barden, Lansing City Hall, painting, ca. 1960s. Photograph courtesy of Jim Perkins and the Greater Lansing Historical Society.

expanding automobile culture and move to the suburbs were responsible for spawning these businesses, as well as drive-in banks, takeout restaurants, and large supermarkets that brought services to where their clients lived. Beyond these individual structures, shopping malls developed at the eastern and western edges of Lansing and in Okemos, as they did in many American suburbs at mid-century.

As the population moved to suburban communities in mid-Michigan, new business corridors started to develop. Abbot Road in East Lansing, for example, marched northward while Grand River Avenue went east. Along both there are numerous, very competent one- to three-story buildings of glass, steel, and brick built for local businesses. Individualized design can also be seen in a number of small, understated one-story Prairie-style structures built for insurance companies, dentists, and banks that were described by some as "homey" and meant to express welcome and familiarity.

This chapter will explore the plurality of modernist styles of commercial and government structures in the 1950s and 1960s. These include internationally known architects such as Yamasaki and George Nelson who produced significant designs for their mid-Michigan clients. More frequently, the local large architectural firms such as Lee and Kenneth Black, Warren Holmes, or Manson, Jackson & Kane received the commissions and applied their formidable talents in the production of buildings that married the clients' requirements with a modernist approach.

Lansing City Hall and Police Headquarters

Lansing City Hall at 124 West Michigan Avenue, designed by Lee Black and Kenneth C. Black, Architects, 1956–58, is one of the few office buildings in Lansing in the International style characterized by an abundance of glazing, curtain wall construction, steel framing, and sleek design (plate 39). It replaced a massive, elaborately ornamented 1890s Richardsonian Romanesque building a block to the north. As early as the late 1930s, the idea for a new city hall was under discussion. In the mid-1940s, Lee and Kenneth Black submitted a model for a brick building that was not modernist at all.[1]

The idea was revived several years later by the ambitious Mayor Ralph W. Crego as a focus of his modernization program, which included a civic center, fire stations, an airport terminal, a new central library, and police headquarters. The choice of the site—across the street from the State Capitol—was deliberate and critical to the mayor's message. This time the Blacks designed a nine-story rectangular

barden durst

block built of glass and steel. Set back from the street, it fronts onto a plaza that opens on two sides. The east side is bordered by the new six-story Lansing Police Headquarters (1958–59) at 120 West Michigan Avenue, designed by the Blacks at the same time. The two buildings form an L-shape.[2] The smaller rectangular building has solid walls faced with limestone, and small, square plate-glass windows that create a foil to the City Hall's transparency. The ground level is faced with pinkish mauve granite and slightly recessed, with a ramp to the right leading into the building.

City Hall's first-floor lobby uses the same pinkish granite on the columns that support the cantilevered upper building. On the narrower west end and on the north, the building is faced with Indiana limestone. The portion of the building facing south has courses of clear and bluish-green glass.[3] To advertise the building, Dorothy Durst Barden, a local artist, made a painting that captured the dynamism and excitement of the complex (figure 54). She painted the sky bright yellow and orange, and light streaks down the glass façade, turning it into shades of yellow, green, purple, and blue. By exaggerating the angle of the larger building as it recedes into the painting, she dramatically increased its height.[4] The spirit rather than the veracity of the image speaks to the optimism of the age in which City Hall was built.

An early sketch for the proposed steel, concrete, and glass building was published in the *Lansing State Journal* on October 2, 1953, with a caption that compared it to the United Nations building in New York, begun in 1947 and completed in 1952. Designed by Wallace Harrison and Max Abramovitz, this complex consists of the tall, thirty-nine-story Secretariat building, a semitransparent slab of green glass with end walls clad in stone, and the smaller horizontal General Assembly structure. It became immediately well known for its striking International style and the sculptural effect of the connections between the buildings.

Justly proud Lansingites also compared City Hall to Lever House in New York, the iconic office building completed in 1952, designed by Skidmore, Owings & Merrill. In "Two New City Buildings to Solve Growing Pains," *Lansing State Journal*, 1955, officials were quoted saying that City Hall was "another step toward the maturity and development of a metropolitan community." Touted as "the first of its type in the Midwest . . . the construction will be similar to the Lever building."[5] This reference is especially revealing in the way Lansing city officials sought to position themselves. Lever House was the first curtain wall office building in Manhattan, and at twenty-four stories, it stood out from the surrounding limestone and brick structures. It was noteworthy not only for the use of stainless steel in the curtain wall and a blue-green glass façade but also for the innovative plaza design with gardens and walkways. In actuality, it was two buildings: one vertical and one horizontal, both of which were elevated on pylons above street level. Lever House was immediately copied across the country in countless glass boxes with varying degrees of success. Its influence was felt elsewhere in Michigan as well, where government complexes were being erected in a similar International style. Detroit's downtown City-County Building, designed by Harley, Ellington & Day, 1955, combined a nineteen-story tower with a contrasting fourteen-story office section using black and white marble.[6] Grand Rapids's Vandenberg Center, 1966–68, designed by Skidmore, Owings & Merrill, and O'Bryon and Nachtegall, consists of a ten-story City Administration building and the low, three-story Kent County Administration structure. In the plaza between, Alexander Calder's large stabile titled *La Grande Vitesse* (1969) adds color and vibrancy seen against the rectangular masses of the buildings.[7] As part of this larger national trend, the Blacks' Lansing design of two buildings of differing heights, colors, and textures that complement each other, plus the pedestrian plaza that humanizes them, fits the modern approach embraced by many cities, although not all of them succeeded as well as this complex.

Liebermann's

Another significant, albeit much smaller, International-style building is a few blocks away at 113 South Washington Square (plate 77). Liebermann's was designed for Betty Price by George Nelson and reflects his modernist aesthetic. Nelson (1908–1986) trained at the Yale School of Fine Arts and rose through the ranks at *Architectural Forum* to become managing editor in 1943. He opened his design firm in 1947 while serving as design director at Herman Miller, Inc. from 1946 until 1972. In addition to his well-known furniture pieces and graphic design, he designed buildings and interiors, but Liebermann's was his only extant retail store.

Nelson worked with Betty Price three times in downtown Lansing.[8] The first project, in 1947, was the design of the lower level of her father's leather-goods store at 107 South Washington Square. In 1952 he designed a remodel of that store, but it was not carried out. In 1964 he was invited to design a new store by totally remodeling an older 1862 building. This revamping of 113 South Washington Square was completed in 1966.[9] Using modern materials, he created an International-style building with four huge 22-foot-high windows hung on the steel frame, with the frameless glass entry door placed off-center. The upper projecting cornice faced with concrete panels is the same height as the building to the south, but slightly shorter than the one to the north. The sidewalls are actually party walls with the adjacent buildings, but the Liebermann's structure is set back about four feet from the street. These sidewalls are covered with jade green and multicolored slate pieces that continue inside, obliterating the division between them.

This exterior treatment and the view into the store announced to the shopper the modernist aesthetic to be found inside. Looking through the store windows, items for sale could be seen on the floating glass shelves that were held in place by tension rods. This was the first use of Nelson's new CSS (Comprehensive Storage System) shelving units in a retail setting. Some shelves were open, some were closed with glass fronts, and others used under-shelf illumination. Further into the space is an open, suspended staircase with a small Japanese garden beneath the lowest treads. Upstairs the balcony is set back about eight feet from the front of the building, creating a two-story open space at the front of the store.[10]

Betty Price took seriously her role of introducing modernist design to mid-Michigan. Sandra Seaton's "Betty Price and George Nelson, Spreading the Word about Modern Design," an interview with the nonagenarian about her fifty years in retail, records how she got started in her uncle's dry-goods store in Saginaw, then worked in her father's store in downtown Lansing in the 1930s.[11] During this time she saw the landmark exhibition of *Organic Design in Home Furnishings* at the Museum of Modern Art, New York, in 1940, visited Frank Lloyd Wright's Goetsch-Winckler House in Okemos, and read George Nelson and Henry Wright's book, *Tomorrow's House*, 1945.[12] Influenced by her ongoing interest in modernist architecture, Mrs. Price commissioned a final Nelson-designed project in 1972 for her store at 107 South Washington Square, which modernized the façade and renovated the interior. This building has been greatly modified since then.[13] Although Liebermann's closed in 1991, the building at 113 South Washington Square remains unchanged. Betty and Donald Price had earlier shown their consistent modernist interests by commissioning Kenneth Black to design their East Lansing home (plate 8), which was filled with contemporary furnishings.

Michigan State Medical Society Building

The Michigan State Medical Society (MSMS) headquarters built in 1961 at 129 West Saginaw Street in East Lansing is another significant building by a well-known architect (plate 55). It was designed by the firm of Minoru Yamasaki & Associates, started by architect Minoru Yamasaki (1912–1985) in Birmingham, Michigan, in 1949. The MSMS building, which is in the National Register of Historic Places, is an elegant white structure with lofty, slim columns across the front and back elevations.[14]

The commercial corridor of Saginaw Street and Abbot Road, where the building is located, was being developed rapidly in the early 1960s. Further south on Abbot, there are several one- to three-story modernist office buildings, including the one-story glass-and-steel structure that was designed by, and served as the home of, the Mayotte architectural firm. To the north, Eastminster Presbyterian Church was under construction (see plate 56), and across Abbot Road to the east, the Michigan Education Association headquarters was rising. Land was plentiful in this northern reach, which was then just beyond the city borders in Lansing Township, and the large plots had many acres to spread out on.

The MSMS was founded in 1866 in Detroit. Its mission is to "promote a health care environment that supports physicians in caring for and enhancing the health of Michigan citizens through science, quality, and ethics in the practice of medicine."[15] After moving to temporary quarters in Lansing, it was evident by 1951 that MSMS needed a larger, permanent home. The goal was to build a structure that would be symbolic, "a serene and inviting building to express the idealism and humanity of the medical profession."[16]

Yamasaki's building is two stories, measuring 155 feet long by 55 feet wide, set back from the busy road on a small rise of the land. The circular drive off Saginaw Street leads to the prominent southern entrance placed slightly off the center of the building. The corresponding secondary entrance from the parking lot on the north side, however, is most often used. Because of the slope of the property, the north side of the building rises higher above grade than the south, where terraces with several landings and steps lead to the door.

Each of the north and south façades has thirty-two slender columns, made of quartz-aggregate cast concrete, that rise to small arches at the top. Between the columns are large glass windows. The entrance lobby, which has walls of the same surface as the exterior columns, rises the full height of the two stories and has a bridge connecting the two parts of the building on the second floor. Offices on this upper floor are set back from the window wall and connect along the windows as well as along the interior hallway. The large wood-paneled conference room uses, as elsewhere on this floor, a decorative treatment of the repeating arches of the vaulted ceiling. Throughout, the building is furnished with the original Knoll and Herman Miller furniture.

The building is well documented in the National Register of Historic Places Registration Form filed in 2011, which explains its significance in terms of Yamasaki's developing exploration of the New

Formalism, characterized as a return to past styles to inform modernist design. The use of columns and arches, an interest in pattern and symmetry, as well as smooth and glossy wall surfaces are hallmarks of this style.

Yamasaki, who was educated at the University of Washington and New York University, arrived in Detroit to work for Smith, Hinchman & Grylls in 1945. In 1949 he started his own firm with George Hellmuth and Joseph Leinweber.[17] Most of their work in the 1950s was in the Detroit area, where the New Formalist style developed. Yamasaki designed a master plan for Wayne State University (1956–64), and several of his buildings, including the award-winning McGregor Memorial Community Conference Center, completed in 1958, provided ideas for the MSMS building. McGregor is a two-story white structure divided by a glass two-story atrium; it has thin columns with triangular capitals, and a reflecting pool on the exterior.[18]

Although his buildings are found throughout the world, Yamasaki is best known for the World Trade Center (1971) in New York City, whose towers rose 110 stories high. There the reference to pointed Gothic arches was evidence of his embrace of historic styles, but updated through the use of new technologies of steel and concrete. At the MSMS building, this sensitivity is seen on a much smaller scale, as is his careful attention paid to landscaping and locating the building on the site. The MSMS building has a commanding presence on the northwest corner of the heavily trafficked thoroughfare, standing sentinel and quiet.

▶ **FIGURE 55.** Michigan Education Association, Warren Holmes, aerial photograph, 1964, East Lansing. Courtesy of the MEA.

Michigan Education Association Building

Yamasaki's gentle form of modernism was one of the modifications of the International style in the 1950s. A similarly moderated approach can be found in the nearby Michigan Education Association (MEA) building at 1216 Kendale Boulevard, East Lansing, opened in 1964 (plate 67). This is the home of the professional association for teachers and education support staff. It was fittingly designed by the Warren Holmes Company, a Lansing firm that specialized in educational buildings in Michigan, Indiana, Ohio, and Illinois.

The MEA was started in 1852, and it expanded rapidly in the postwar years, when the staff was housed in Lansing in cramped quarters in several buildings on North Washington Street. In the mid-1950s, the membership agreed to assess itself special fees to pay for a new building that would bring the entire staff under one roof. Originally it was to be built on the south side of Saginaw Street in East Lansing, but the property was exchanged for the location to the north. The Warren Holmes Company was named architect of

► **FIGURE 56.** Michigan Education Association, Warren Holmes, reflecting pool, 1964, East Lansing. Courtesy of the MEA.

the building in 1959; construction began in 1963, and the building was dedicated in 1964.

The MEA headquarters is actually a complex of two buildings; the main one is clearly visible from Saginaw Street across a wide expanse of lawn, and it makes a strong visual statement (plate 67). This rectangular two-story building has three similar façades. It connects to a smaller one-story brick building to the north that houses assembly rooms and storage. The latter was treated more simply and is not visible until one turns onto Kendale Boulevard on the west (a new street laid out for this project) (figure 55). The main entrance to the primary building is on this side, with a subsidiary entrance on the north. By moving access into the building to the west, the architects were able to concentrate on pure design on the highly visible southern elevation.

In "More Than an Office Building," the booklet produced by the MEA for the opening of the building, the Warren Holmes staff provided six pages of detailed descriptions to their architectural approach. The building was to "visually represent a proud profession in the public eye as well as functionally and inspirationally provide both indoor and outdoor space in which to perform the Association's varied tasks and functions."[19] The accompanying black-and-white photographs show some of the handsome features described by the architect.

> The exterior of the building was created to establish a feeling of welcome and sophistication and still maintain the necessary functional aspects of good design. Materials used are simple: brick, glass and precast concrete with exposed aggregate, which is used as sculptured concave panels on the upper level of the building. These panels set a definite design theme with their contrast and rhythm established with the alternating vertical windows. They also serve to cut down on heat gain and loss as well as to diminish interior glare at the upper periphery of the building.[20]

The second-floor south façade facing Saginaw Street is divided into three equal parts; the panel-and-glass patterned sections towards the corners are stepped back at the center and hidden by a solar screen in front of the recessed Board of Directors room.

The main building is surrounded by a depressed plaza, halfway between the ground and first floors (figures 55, 56). The first floor projects forward approximately eight feet to shelter the plaza from the weather and the road. The steel channels, with glazing in between, support the cantilevered second floor above and end in the reflecting pools below that flanked the main entry. The pools could be enjoyed from the bridge leading from the parking area to the west entrance, but unfortunately they have been

removed. Nevertheless the effectiveness of this design element, as well as the attention to and crispness of the details, can be judged in 1960s photographs. Without the pools and with the aging of the structure, some of the finesse of the architect's ideas has been diminished.

This commission gave Holmes an opportunity to include some extraordinary and sensitive aspects that were out of place in the design of typical functional schools, the firm's bread-and-butter projects. Holmes undoubtedly had Yamasaki's recently completed MSMS building in mind. Perhaps he also thought about Yamasaki's McGregor Center. Holmes would have been interested in McGregor's reflecting pools, the steel-frame and concrete construction, placement of sunscreens on portions of the façade, and the use of a two-story atrium as the organizing feature, as well as Yamasaki's careful employment of textures and patterns. Yamasaki's Helen L. DeRoy Auditorium, also at Wayne State University, begun in 1962 and completed in 1964, could have served as a model for Holmes as well. Here, the square building, surrounded by a sunken plaza with a reflecting pool on all four sides, was approached by several small bridges.[21]

The interior of the MEA building revolves around a central two-story courtyard with a Japanese-influenced garden that has a semicircular bench, fieldstones of differing sizes and colors, and

◄ **FIGURE 57.** Michigan Education Association, Warren Holmes, interior courtyard, 1964, East Lansing. Courtesy of the MEA.

various plantings (figure 57). The hallways on both floors afford unimpeded views of the garden through the tinted glass windows. This openness aids in a sense of spaciousness and quietude. The garden area was designed by local landscape architects Drew and Skidmore and has been well maintained as it was designed, while the rest of the interior has been renovated several times. Some of the original materials, "carefully selected to give a warm, interesting, subtle effect as a background for the finish [*sic*] interior décor," remain. Warm gray brick is featured in the main lobby and in many rooms, with teak paneling in the board room, while off-white and a muted color palette were specified for the Steelcase furnishings, the walls, and carpets. Moveable floor-to-ceiling partitions were used for flexibility. Although the total cost of the building was $1.7 million, the budget was nevertheless an issue for the architects, so they approached the challenge of a design that provided flexibility for the future, functionality, and a feeling of openness and welcome for staff and visitors.

Business Headquarters and Commercial Structures

The Auto-Owners' office building (now the Ingham County Courthouse, called the Grady J. Parker Building) at the intersection of Kalamazoo Street and Townsend Street (303 West Kalamazoo Street) was the first of four buildings by Lee and Kenneth Black Associates in downtown Lansing (plate 19). When it opened, the *Lansing State Journal* dedicated several pages of the June 5, 1954, issue to the building's fine points: "Fixtures Win Praise," "New Home of Auto-Owners Is Dedicated as Example of Faith in Future of City," "Mayor Praises Achievement," "Offices Are Ultra New," and "New Headquarters of Auto-Owners Called City's Finest Building." Great hopes were placed on the message of the new building, which opened on the thirty-fifth anniversary of the company, founded in 1916. Speaking on behalf of Governor G. Mennon Williams, state comptroller Dr. Robert Steadman declared that the building was an inspiring example of modern office construction and that the company was "symbolic of the vigor and enterprise of Michigan's financial institutions."

The four-story reinforced concrete building was hailed as "not only one of the city's most attractive on the exterior, but it is the last word for efficiency, convenience, comfort and good working conditions."[22] The exterior is faced with squares of Indiana limestone, and glass blocks and strips of clear glass were used throughout. An elevated garden area (40 feet wide by 140 feet long) outside the lobby continued to the east and west, while a sunken garden outside the basement

PLATE 53. Henry E. and Mary Crouse House. John E. Crouse, Mayotte-Webb, 1961.

Photograph © 2020 Kim Kauffman.

PLATE 54. University United Methodist. Earl Confer, Wesley Foundation, 1961; sanctuary, 1963. Photograph © 2014 Kim Kauffman.

PLATE 55. Michigan State Medical Society. Minoru Yamasaki and Associates, 1961; addition 1979. Photograph © 2014 Kim Kauffman.

PLATE 56. Eastminster Presbyterian Church. Alden B. Dow, 1961 (west side); addition, Manson, Jackson & Kane, 1969. Photo by Natasha Crljenica.

PLATE 57. Capitol Savings and Loan Association, Okemos Branch. J. Wesley Olds, 1961.

Photo by Natasha Crljenica.

PLATE 58. Verdun Erle and Mary Leichty House, rear. Earl Vaive, 1961.

PLATE 59. H. N. Hayes House. Laitala and Nuechterlein, 1962; landscape: Drew and Skidmore.

PLATE 60. Lansing Teachers Credit Union (now Michigan Press Association). Charles V. Opdyke, 1962.

Photograph © 2014 Kim Kauffman.

PLATE 61. John and Marguerite Crouse House. John Crouse, 1962; addition 1964. Photo courtesy of the Michigan State Historic Preservation Office.

PLATE 62. Dixon Shaw and Madeline Wilson House. Dixon Shaw Wilson, 1963. Photograph © 2014 Kim Kauffman.

PLATE 63. East Lansing Public Library. Manson, Jackson & Kane, Inc., 1963; addition 1975.

Photo by Natasha Crljenica.

PLATE 64. Dawn Donuts (now Bell's Pizza). Architect unknown, 1963.

Photo courtesy of Amanda Seeger.

PLATE 65. Wallis M. and Norine Antuck House. William Kessler, 1963.

PLATE 66. Lansing Public Library (Clarence H. Rosa Public Library). Kenneth C. Black Associates, 1964.

Photo courtesy of Michigan State Historic Preservation Office.

PLATE 67. Michigan Education Association. The Warren Holmes Company, 1964.

Photograph © 2014 Kim Kauffman.

PLATE 68. Martin Luther Chapel. Charles Stade, 1964.
Photo by Natasha Crljenica.

PLATE 69. Kenneth C. and Marie Black House. Kenneth C. Black Associates, 1964; landscape: D. Newton Glick.

PLATE 70. Sanford Farness House. Sanford Farness, 1964.

Photo by Natasha Crljenica.

recreation room admitted light into that space. In "Lobby Receives Special Design," the author noted the walls of paneled white oak, the green terrazzo floor divided into squares with aluminum stripes, large floor-to-ceiling Thermopane glass windows, and red granite pylons at the entrance. "The whole effect . . . is to give the lobby an openness in which both exterior and interior materials are blended so as to make a gradual transition from outside to in." The other public spaces were on the fourth floor in the executive suite, where no expense was spared to make them "ultra-modern," including built-in bookshelves, large visible lighting fixtures, and also some recessed lights. Publicity photographs of this floor from the opening of the building show Herman Miller and Knoll furniture as well as Mies van der Rohe's iconic Barcelona chair.

Another article, "New Headquarters of Auto-Owners Called City's Finest Building," commends the building's appearance of

> dignity and stability which reflects the sound financial position of the company. . . . It is an excellent example of the results which can be achieved when the planning of the building, its surroundings and its interior decoration and furnishing are all carried out under the guidance and supervision of the architect. The landscape architects and the decorators were told to "provide the company with the most efficient and, in appearance, most modern home office building of any insurance company in the United States."

The result is "the creation of a unity of design between the building, landscaping, furniture, furnishings and color which is seldom achieved." The Auto-Owners building was far more than a statement about the company. It showed off the architects' holistic approach to design—even the neon sign at the top of the building was designed by them—as well as encompassing the hopes and dreams of many in the city of Lansing for the continued and increased prosperity of the region.[23]

New construction techniques of visible steel framing and large areas of glazing were used by local architect Charles V. Opdyke (1918–1990) for the Lansing Teachers Credit Union (now Michigan Press Association) in 1962 at 827 North Washington Avenue (plate 60). This small one-story building is elegantly proportioned and used floor-to-ceiling glazing extensively. The all-glass southern entrance façade is sheltered by a covered loggia supported by steel posts, while on the east side, the glass is continued for two-thirds of the wall and then is replaced by a solid wall of limestone. The emphasis on horizontality, lack of ornament, and sophisticated balance of parts took as its inspiration examples of Mies van der Rohe's International style.[24]

▲ FIGURE 58. Michigan Avenue Dental Office, East Lansing. Photograph courtesy of Michigan State Historic Preservation Office.

Prairie Style Office Buildings and Drive-in Banks

Glass-and-steel structures of several stories were typically not what was required by the many smaller Lansing-area businesses that sought new buildings in the 1950s and 1960s. Instead, the majority reflect the scale of domestic architecture and the influence of Frank Lloyd Wright's Prairie style. The Merten Insurance building on a corner lot at 935 East Grand River Avenue, East Lansing, designed by Lee and Kenneth Black in 1954, is one such example (plate 32).[25] The horizontal emphasis, flat roof, wide overhangs, and brick facing, as well as the stone planter in the front, are Wrightian design elements. The dental office at 604 East Michigan Avenue, East Lansing, 1957, is another (figure 58). In these, the similarity to residential architecture helped the businesses convey messages of comfort, familiarity, and "home." Many similar Prairie-style one- or two-story buildings can still be found across the area, and through them, Wright's ideas about modernism were introduced to the mid-Michigan population.

The Warren Holmes Company's new headquarters at 820 North Washington Avenue in Lansing, built in 1959 (now the Central Free Methodist Church Training Institute of East Michigan), was characterized in the *Lansing State Journal* as "more like a home than an office," and the inviting scale and design were compared favorably to larger office buildings closer to the Capitol (figure 59). The building was praised as an example of the latest contemporary thinking in the use of materials, heating, and electrical systems.[26] The one-story section facing west onto Washington Street used fieldstone close to the ground, brick, and curtain wall construction with large panes of glass above. The entrance on the south side of the building

▲ **FIGURE 59.** The Warren Holmes Company, Warren Holmes, entry façade, Lansing. Photograph © 2014 Kim Kauffman.

is hidden from the street and opens off a small patio with a pool. Yet, this impression of a small, homey office is deceptive; the building actually stretches east to the next street, where there is a two-story metal and glass annex that faces Grand Avenue (figure 60). This larger functional structure is nearly invisible from Washington Street. Its open plan, movable partitions, and minimalist aesthetic allowed the firm to consolidate offices and to house the seventy employees in one place. The differences between the two parts was intentional. The smaller residential-scaled building addressed the firm's public identity, while the private no-frills work area responded to the firm's contemporary work atmosphere. Here two aspects of modernism showed the different styles the architectural firm was capable of producing. Within a few years, steel-and-glass

construction came to the foreground on North Washington Avenue when the Lansing Teachers Credit Union built their one-story building across the street (plate 60).

Frequently a Prairie style was chosen for small branch banks. The Capitol Savings and Loan Association (now Independent Bank), Okemos Branch, built in 1961 at 2119 Hamilton Road, near the busy intersection of the "four corners" in Okemos, is a nicely proportioned example (plate 57). It features the requisite characteristics of large windows, flat roof, a clerestory with tinted plate glass, brick, and horizontal planes. By including the covered drive-up window and a community room in the basement, the goal was to entice people not only to bank locally but also to think of the bank as a community center. The architect, J. Wesley Olds (1917–2010), had his offices just down the block. He trained in architecture at the University of Michigan, started practicing in Detroit, and then worked for the Warren Holmes Company before opening his own practice in Okemos with Morris Stein, an engineer.[27]

◄ **FIGURE 60.** The Warren Holmes Company, Warren Holmes, annex, Lansing. Photograph © 2014 Kim Kauffman.

This was one of many branch banks to open in the 1950s as the bank wars were heating up. Location and ease of access were paramount as people moved further away from the city centers and became more dependent on the automobile. In response, small branch banks with drive-up windows started to dot the

▶ **FIGURE 61.** Michigan National Bank, architect unknown, Lansing. Photograph © 2014 Kim Kauffman.

edges of town and the suburbs to be closer to their clients, who wanted and expected convenient, nearby banks with parking and drive-up services. These were the same people who frequented the increasingly ubiquitous drive-in movie theaters and fast-food restaurants.

Kenneth Black designed numerous small drive-in banks as early as 1950,[28] and others for American Bank and Trust in the 1960s.[29] He became Michigan National Bank's favored designer as it aggressively expanded into the suburbs. He and his father had earlier designed one of Lansing's most iconic bank/office towers in downtown Lansing. The Bank of Lansing, 1931–32 (Manufacturer's Bank of Lansing/Comerica Bank) at 101 North Washington Square and the corner of Michigan Avenue rises fifteen stories and was richly ornamented with Romanesque motifs, limestone, carved marble sculptures, and bronze, as well as cast-iron grillwork by Samuel Yellin. The interior banking hall was equally embellished with details characteristic of the contemporary Art Deco style.[30] The slightly earlier twenty-two-story Capitol National Bank and Loan building (Michigan National Bank and now the Boji Tower) at 124–126 West Allegan Street, built between 1929 and 1931, was designed by the New York firm of Hopkins and Dentz. As the tallest building in the downtown, it was built for Ransom E. Olds to house his company's offices above, in addition to the bank and rental spaces below and at street level. The exterior is fairly austere and blocky with a combination of Italian Romanesque and Art Deco details. The arched main entry has terracotta reliefs and columns and prepares the visitor for the lofty two-story banking space inside, with painted ornaments and a coffered ceiling.

These two examples were typical of bank buildings erected before the Great Depression but after the era when banks looked like classical temples or Italian Renaissance palaces. With the high cost of real estate in prominent downtown locations, the office-tower/bank structure became popular. After the stock market crash of 1929, the failure of many banks, and the resultant banking reforms, national banks were granted branching privileges that started the proliferation of smaller banks located away from the downtown. Since the classical fortress or palace-like architecture did not guarantee the safety of a person's money, a stylistic break with the past was required. Banks now had to project modernity and less extravagance than in the past. Skidmore, Owings & Merrill's Manufacturer's Trust in New York, 1953–54, designed by Gordon Bunshaft, set the bar for opening up the building to the passerby with the use of extensive glazing and steel framing as well as a view of the impressive vault.[31] Rectangular glass-box banks became commonplace thereafter, as did poured concrete forms that allowed for curving walls and pleated roofs; by the 1960s these trends merged.[32]

In mid-Michigan, Kenneth Black extended the vocabulary for banks beyond the usual Prairie style seen in Olds's Capitol Savings and Loan Association (plate 57). For example, he used accordion-pleat roofs for several of his designs for Michigan National Bank,[33] and he may have been the architect of that bank's round branch buildings from the 1950s. At least four are still in existence in Battle Creek, Port Huron, and Lansing, but they have all been repurposed.[34] One of these at 2017 West Saginaw Street (address changed in 1968 to 2001 West Saginaw), Lansing, opened in 1954 (figure 61), followed by a second on North Larch Street in 1955. The choice of these sites was strategic; in both instances the location is at the intersection of major Lansing thoroughfares (Saginaw Street and Oakland Avenue, and Cedar Street and Larch Street). Each small building was round on three sides with a square entrance. Three drive-in windows protruded from the curves. On the interior, a skylight dome, surrounded at its base with small windows, let abundant light in. The shape also is seen as reflecting the dawning of the space age and the interest in satellites and flying saucers.[35] The Saginaw branch retains the original cast-stone exterior with polished red granite around the foundation, dome, and skylight. The Larch Street branch was likely the same, but today is covered with blue-and-white striped wood and houses a Chinese restaurant.

Michigan National Bank's ad in the *Lansing State Journal* on January 28, 1955, invited people to a preview of the Larch Street bank and touted the merits of the design. The three drive-in windows offered better, faster service from the "comfort of your car. No walking in bad weather. No standing in line. And no risk of walking with large sums of cash." Accompanying illustrations show a woman in the driver's seat with a young child, reaching for cash at the drive-in window. A sketch of the interior of the bank also made it clear that all of the usual facilities for complete banking services were offered. In addition, the two fashionable women in suits and heels, and the suited man transacting business implied the upscale, affluent suburban clients the bank hoped to attract.

Schmidt's Food Market

Just as banks moved to the suburbs, so did supermarkets. A prime example is Schmidt's Food Market (now Playmakers) at 2299 West Grand River Avenue, Okemos, designed by Manson, Jackson & Kane, Inc. (figures 62, 63).[36] It was the fourth Schmidt's supermarket in the Lansing area, but unlike the others, this was the "Store of Tomorrow . . . Today," according to their advertisements. When it opened in 1958, it was to serve people who had moved east to the burgeoning suburb of Okemos.

▲ **FIGURE 62.** Schmidt's Market, Manson, Jackson & Kane, exterior, Okemos, 1958 photograph. Source unknown.

"New Schmidt Store Ready for Opening," a *Lansing State Journal* article on January 26, 1958, explained why this was "one of the area's most modern supermarkets." With more than 16,500 square feet, the unique architectural design has "dramatic character, which is achieved by laminated wood arches rising to an interior height of 16 feet above the floor, making possible a clear span of 110 feet." In addition, the store had automatic doors (with "magic door carpets"), air conditioning, and modern shelving using the latest display techniques for the merchandise. A plastic sky dome on the roof admitted light into the interior (figure 63).

The building is set back from the heavy traffic of Grand River Avenue and has ample parking. To attract customers, a tall flashing neon sign at the road featured a striding woman with a shopping cart and the

▲ **FIGURE 63.** Schmidt's Market, Manson, Jackson & Kane, interior, Okemos, 1958 photograph. Source unknown.

supermarket's name in big letters beneath.[37] This sign still exists, but instead of groceries in the cart, books were added in 1991 when the building briefly housed a Barnes & Noble store.[38] Another feature that was intended to catch the eye was the large expanse of glass on the front façade divided by steel frames. On top of this, five-by-six-foot light blue plastic-coated panels served as background for the name "Schmidts."

The advertisement in the *Lansing State Journal* announcing the open house on January 26 read:

> Dad will want to study the new structural design of the building with its huge laminated wood arches. . . . Mother will thrill at the spacious interior with its dramatic décor and myriad displays including more than 350 feet of refrigerated cases for fresh meat, dairy products, frozen foods, ice cream and produce.

The advertisement then tells the story of the Schmidts as the fulfillment of the American Dream. From the humble beginnings when Paul Schmidt returned from World War I, "the expansion of the Schmidt Brothers Super Markets has paralleled the growth of Lansing itself." It notes that the small stores from 1926 and 1930 were replaced with larger ones starting in 1948; "and now, the newest and largest . . . The Store of Tomorrow—TODAY."

In comparison to Schmidt's three extant conventional rectangular box stores, the new one was indeed unusual for supermarket design. The closest parallels to the large, vaulted space devoid of internal support can be found in railroad terminal construction and contemporary bowling alleys.[39] Like those marvels of technology, this new store used modern construction techniques, scale, and daring contemporary architectural design to entice customers to stop, and then to lure them in to explore the merchandise.

Googie Architecture meets Mid-Michigan

This type of flashy architecture that calls attention to itself has been referred to as Googie architecture. This trend was started by Michigan native John Lautner in Southern California and became popular in the 1950s, when the car culture spurred architecture that was unpretentious yet highly visible. Exuberant, unrestrained, and optimistic, these examples of vernacular architecture did not take themselves very seriously. Neither, unfortunately, do those interested in "high" architecture. Unloved as time has passed, many examples have been demolished. In mid-Michigan only a handful of Googie buildings remain, but in the 1950s and 1960s, many car washes, car dealerships, diners, and bowling alleys were built in this flamboyant style.[40]

The best Googie example in the Lansing area is Dawn Donuts (now Bell's Pizza) at 1135 East Grand River Avenue in East Lansing, built in 1963 (plate 64). Dawn Donuts was headquartered in Jackson, Michigan, and made its name as the nation's first industrial bakery-mix company. As the company continued to grow in the 1950s, it opened local stores to serve individual customers.[41] All of the Dawn Donuts shops, which were ubiquitous in Michigan in the 1960s, had the same steeply pitched, sharp-angled roof.[42] Repetition bred familiarity and comfort, and when people saw them on the road, they knew exactly what they could expect in terms of convenience and quality of the product.

This was the same for the national fast-food chains as well. The former Arby's (now Biggby Coffee since 1995) at 270 West Grand River Avenue in East Lansing, 1966, was one of the earliest of this chain's restaurants (plate 78). Founded in 1964 in Boardman, Ohio, the company was named by the brothers Forrest and Leroy Raffel using initials from "Raffel brothers." The first franchise was granted in 1965; the East Lansing Arby's was the eleventh and opened the following year.[43] All of the restaurants used the same Googie design, that is, a curved roofline designed to resemble a Conestoga wagon from the old West. Inside, the ceiling was also curved. The original neon ten-gallon-hat sign, similar to the logo still in use, announced the restaurant to those driving by. The sign is long gone, and the building, too, is slated for demolition to make way for a mixed-use development.

Along the same lines of uniform corporate architecture, the 1950 Greyhound Bus Terminal (now the Centennial Group) at 511 South Washington Street, at the edge of downtown Lansing, was designed by William Strudwick Arrasmith (1898–1965) in a Streamline Moderne style (plate 17). Arrasmith was the architect of choice for the company and was commissioned to design over fifty terminals between 1937 and 1958.[44] The Streamline style deliberately evoked the sleek aerodynamics of the buses themselves. The Lansing building was planned before the war but not realized for another decade, by which time this Streamline style was outmoded. Nevertheless it continued to be used by the Greyhound Corporation because the building was immediately recognizable to travelers. While the "sign pylon" of the Lansing building retained the signature curve of this style, as did the assymetrical design, the building became a bit boxier than earlier examples. The entrance canopy, signature round window, and irregular spacing of the windows across the long façade were characteristics of the Greyhound design. Inside were the spacious waiting room with seats for eighty-four passengers, four ticket windows, baggage storage, and the 125th Greyhound Post House restaurant. Eight bus docks were at the back of the L-shaped building for the convenient embarking and disembarking of passengers, and a cab stand was adjacent to the terminal. All of these amenities made visible Greyhound's projected image of efficiency, comfort, and modernity.[45] When constructed at a cost of $300,000, there was a building abutting the terminal to the north that has since been demolished.

Had the terminal been built earlier, it might have had an exterior of blue porcelain-enamel steel panels that was typical of the prewar designs, rather than the tan bricks that were used. It would have looked more like Lansing's Streamline masterpiece, the J.W. Knapp Company Building, just a few blocks to the north at 300 South Washington Square. Here architects Bowd-Munson produced their masterpiece in 1937–39, at the height of the style. With its horizontal emphasis and cladding in blue and yellow Makota tiles, the round edges make it appear like a sleek cruise ship. This large department store anchored the downtown and would have had a distant cousin a few blocks away rather than looking decidedly different than any other building in the area. But by 1950, the Streamline style evoked the past, and Greyhound sought to project the future with its revised design.

Geodesic Domes

As fast-food chains became ubiquitous across America in the 1960s, geodesic domes did as well and the Lansing area had several. During the 1950s, Buckminster Fuller (1895–1983), the visionary inventor, thinker, and architect, developed the geodesic dome as a self-supporting structure that could be erected quickly and inexpensively. It became his most popular and successful structure, using geometric principles to solve issues of lightweight and economical housing. The

first dome was constructed with help from students and colleagues at Black Mountain College in North Carolina, where Fuller began teaching in 1947. In the 1950s, full-size geodesic domes were built by the Ford Motor Company in Dearborn, Michigan (1953), and at the Museum of Modern Art in New York (1959). The large domes at the New York World's Fair in 1964 and Expo '67 in Montreal brought widespread attention to Fuller's ideas. At first the domes were manufactured by only two companies, but by the 1960s, over two hundred companies were licensed to manufacture and build them using Fuller's patent.[46] According to his estate, over 300,000 geodesic domes exist today.[47]

Two geodesic domes were erected in Haslett, Michigan, in 1971–72 (figure 64). The idea of owners/partners Tom Young, Louise McCagg, and Russell

▲ **FIGURE 64.** Geodesic domes, Buckminster Fuller, aerial view, Haslett, 1971–72. Photograph courtesy of Tom Young.

McGee was to develop an Art Park on twenty-three acres of land. They purchased a kit from Geodesic Domes, Inc., in Davison, Michigan.[48] As the original dome was going up, the owner of a second dome in north Lansing offered his to the group. The two domes existed side by side into the 1990s, along with a studio building with a shed roof, and another structure that housed the Lansing Potters Guild.[49]

Pictures taken as one of the domes was erected show the wood frame to which plywood tetrahedron sections were attached (figure 65). No exterior scaffold was needed and, true to the advertising, no special building skills were required. One dome was covered with blown foam for insulation. Since they did not need internal support, they were spacious inside, albeit drafty in winter. The domes sat back in the woods and for several decades served as studios for local artists. The dream of the Art Park, however, never materialized.[50]

In summary, businesses, governmental units, and professional associations in the mid-Michigan area approached the question of modernist architectural design in a myriad of ways, each of which provided clues to the potential visitor or client about the purpose and personality of the concern. Government was forward-looking and optimistic. Professional associations were sophisticated and attentive to the new. Insurance companies and doctors were familiar and welcoming. Banks were up-to-date and convenient. And fast-food restaurants and grocery stores were inviting, loud, and often humorous. None of these approaches were unique to the area, but each was appropriate within its context.

◀ **FIGURE 65.** Geodesic domes, construction photograph, Haslett, 1971–72. Photograph courtesy of Tom Young.

Academic Buildings, Schools, and Libraries

After the war, the expanding population in mid-Michigan, as elsewhere, required new schools at all levels. The housing market was booming, young families were growing, and cities were moving beyond their boundaries. Michigan State College (MSC) experienced unprecedented growth as returning veterans took advantage of the G.I. Bill of Rights and enrolled in the university in astonishing numbers. This led to hiring more faculty, who required offices, laboratories, and classrooms in new buildings on the campus as well as housing nearby, plus schools for their burgeoning families. In this chapter the modernist architectural style of academic buildings erected on the MSC campus and in schools in the community will be considered by studying a sampling of 1950s and 1960s academic structures as well as three major libraries in mid-Michigan built within a ten-year period that exhibit a range of modernist styles.

Michigan State College Becomes a University

Enrollment at MSC skyrocketed between 1945 and 1970, from 9,197 to nearly 35,000 students.[1] In recognition of its expansion from a college focused on agriculture and the sciences to a multidisciplinary, multi-college, and research-based institution, several name changes occurred during this period. In 1955, the Michigan State College of Agriculture and Applied Sciences (MSC) became the Michigan State University of Agriculture and Applied Sciences, and Michigan State University (MSU) in 1964.

▶ **FIGURE 66.** Kresge Art Center, Ralph Calder, exterior, southwest stairwell, MSU, East Lansing. Photograph © 2014 Kim Kauffman.

Prior to World War II, most buildings were north of the Red Cedar River, and their placement related to a campus plan originally developed by the prominent Boston-based landscape architects Frederick Law Olmsted Jr. (1870–1957) and John Charles Olmsted (1852–1920) in 1915 and modified later.[2] Buildings were designed in a Collegiate Gothic style using brick and limestone, and were sited on winding roads in a deliberately park-like setting. Lansing-based Edwyn Bowd designed many of these as the university's architect at the beginning of the century. His favored relationship with the university continued after he formed a partnership with Orlie Munson; Bowd-Munson was responsible for numerous structures through the 1940s.

In the postwar period, Quonset huts were erected on the campus as a temporary fix for the need for more classrooms. For a permanent solution, a moderate International style began to be used in the 1950s as the campus expanded to the east, west, and south. By 1967, the number of buildings erected doubled what had been on campus previously.[3] Ralph Calder Associates was engaged by John A. Hannah, president from 1941 to 1969, to design many dormitories and administration and classroom buildings that have International-style elements. A graduate of the University of Michigan, Calder founded his Detroit-based firm in 1945. In addition to his extensive work at MSC, his buildings can be found on the campuses of Western Michigan University, Michigan Technological University, and Wayne State University.[4]

Rather than individualizing buildings, Calder's approach was for visual consistency across the campus. The results were variations on a theme that typically included curtain wall construction, floating stairs, horizontal banding, green-tinted glazing, rectilinear patterning, and flat surfaces. Asymmetrical organization, cantilevered canopies, and broad plazas were also hallmarks. A few examples suffice to provide evidence of his aesthetic, which clearly was in tune with the administration's.

Kresge Art Center

The Kresge Art Center, sited just north of the Red Cedar River, will serve to exemplify Calder's design approach to multi-story buildings (plate 50). It is between the WPA-funded Auditorium building to the west and the 1952 Collegiate Gothic Alumni Chapel by Calder on the east. For the Kresge, which was built to house the studio art and art history department with classrooms, studios, offices, and a small gallery, the modern style was fitting. Illustrative of Calder's typical design features, it has a flat roof, smooth walls of glass on the north and south organized in patterns of green spandrels and clear sections with aluminum trim. A light orange-red brick was also used. This building, as well as other International-style ones on the campus, sits on a large plaza with broad stairs (now a ramp) that lead to the canopied entrance. Most notable at Kresge are the two four-story curtain-wall stairwells on the east and west sides of the building (figure 66). Inside, the stairs seem to float with minimal visible structural support.

The south side of the building takes advantage of views of the Red Cedar River. Here there are three levels of cantilevered balconies; those on the third level are ornamented with large enameled panels of solid bright colors (orange-yellow, off-white, bluish green, purplish brown, yellow-orange, and green) that serve as sunscreens and dividers between the studio/offices for the art faculty. These secondary colors relieve the otherwise monotone and usual palette of Calder's buildings and create visual interest.[5] Calder used similar but smaller color panels on the vertical row of balconies at Owen Graduate Hall (1961), where they function as barriers rather than screens.[6] Kresge's green glass pattern and cantilevered entrance canopy were repeated at Bessey Hall (1961).[7] Calder's slightly earlier Student Services Building (1957) has many similar features,[8] as does the MSU Library discussed here.

Buildings that did not quite fit the mold are two single-story domed structures on the campus: the

circular kiva at Erickson Hall (1957, 1964, 1974), a large conference and lecture space; and Abrams Planetarium (1963). They are placed diagonally across from each other on Farm Lane, although they are not visible from each other.[9] Nevertheless, they are related in scale as well as stylistically in the use of a patterned green copper dome. They also fit well with, and reflect, the International style of the adjacent buildings. While none of Calder's structures makes an individual statement (that would come much later with Zaha Hadid's Eli and Edythe Broad Art Museum of 2012), together they project a unified approach to modernist sensibilities.

All of the larger Lansing architectural firms in existence in the mid-twentieth century contributed one or more buildings to the campus, including the Warren Holmes Company, Mayotte-Webb, and Manson, Jackson & Kane, Inc.[10] Nevertheless, it was Ralph Calder who was best able to translate into reality President Hannah's vision and expectations for the campus expansion.

Glencairn Elementary School

Almost all of the local architectural firms also benefited in the 1950s and 1960s from the need for new kindergarten through twelfth-grade schools, additions, or renovations of existing buildings. Most of these were modest, no-frills rectangular buildings with straightforward plans for classrooms and had few amenities.[11] The small budgets—the average cost for a new elementary school was $150,000—did not allow the architect to stray from typical designs. In "Grade School Projects Launched," the *Lansing State Journal* in 1951 reported that nearly a half-million dollars in new grade-school construction was anticipated for Lansing. It listed three schools, each of which would have four classrooms for kindergarten through third grades. They were Lyons (architect Warren Holmes), Willow (architect Manson & Carver), and Maple Hill (architect Laitala and Nuechterlein).

All the buildings listed above were in Lansing. In the first half of the 1950s, five building projects in East Lansing were completed: the new Red Cedar School, 1948, addition, 1951 (Warren Holmes); Bailey School additions (Laitala and Nuechterlein); Central School alterations (Laitala and Nuechterlein); and Glencairn (Laitala and Nuechterlein).[12] This reflects the great increases in elementary school enrollments post–World War II. In East Lansing the numbers represent nearly a 13.8 percent jump from 1,139 in 1950 to 1,295 in 1952.[13]

Only one public school, Glencairn Elementary at 939 Harrison Road, is noteworthy architecturally, and it was recognized as such when completed in 1952 (plate

28). Architects Laitala and Nuechterlein were lucky to be given a generous budget of $301,770, almost twice the usual amount, albeit for a larger building. They were charged with creating a friendly and inviting place of learning for children in kindergarten through sixth grade. The architects designed a single-story brick building, measuring 215 feet long by 161 feet wide, with eight rooms, set on a five-acre site adjoining a city park on Harrison Road and Saginaw Street, then at the northern edge of the city. The expected enrollment when it opened in September 1952 was two hundred children. In 1954 two more classrooms were required and added to the north.

Retired school teachers Jeanette Sloan and Carolyn Lee recounted in interviews years later what made the school special.[14] Mrs. Sloan recalled the numerous teachers and school board members from elsewhere who visited to see the "modern" building. Specifically she mentioned the varied color schemes that were quite different from the battleship gray that so often appeared in schools, as well as the inviting lobby and unique fireplace.[15] Miss Lee spoke about sitting around the fireplace, especially at Christmastime, when they would read Christmas stories. Eventually electric logs replaced the wood after a law was passed that banned open fires in schools. With a large round rag rug in front of the fireplace, children were encouraged to come in and play games as they waited for their classes to begin. "We tried to have a very warm and pleasant atmosphere. One time a little four-year girl came in and looked around and she said, 'Why, this is nice, it looks just like home.'"[16]

An advertisement for school furniture in the *School Board Journal*, April 1954, adds further to the understanding of what made this school "progressive." It was

> as attractive as it is functional, making it ideal for teaching and learning. The classrooms are spacious and filled with light to reduce eyestrain and encourage concentration. The entire school is done in soft, relaxing colors, complemented by the trim, modern design and light finishes of Heywood-Wakefield Tubular Steel Furniture.[17]

Just how different this was from the usual design can be gauged by comparing the inviting atmosphere of Glencairn to the more spartan Maple Hill School in Lansing, also designed by Laitala and Nuechterlein. The June 3, 1952, dedication brochure for Maple Hill made note of such features as asphalt tile floors, the foot-scraper grating at the main entrance, green chalkboards and tack boards, a folding partition between two kindergarten rooms, the steel deck, finished acoustic ceiling, and individual heating and ventilating units.[18]

Okemos High School

Laitala and Nuechterlein were also responsible for the design of the new Okemos High School (now Chippewa Middle School) at 4000 Okemos Road and Kinawa Drive, which opened to classes in 1961. It was significant for the conceptual approach to teaching that was reflected in the design rather than the architectural style. A special section of the *Meridian* newspaper on January 18, 1961, was dedicated to the new school. The caption for one photograph read:

> The new is represented by the ultramodern high school, built at a cost of roughly $1,250,000. Utilizing new and modern architectural design, the school is built as a structure-cluster, often called a campus plan building, which provides maximum square footage and versatility while offering close, personalized surroundings for students and teachers.[19]

Classrooms for related subjects were grouped together in units with a central media space. This approach, also referred to as a "house plan," eliminated the need for space-wasting corridors, as explained in a comparison of floor plans printed in the paper.[20] Modern materials were used, such as cement blocks and the metal, barrel-vaulted walkways between units (now enclosed) and bus shelters. The atypical metal-framed windows set flush with the walls made the overall design appear somewhat different from other schools built at the time.

The design approach for elementary through high school buildings in the Lansing region was similar to that taken in countless Midwestern cities where function and cost to the taxpayer were paramount concerns. The result was a unified but modified International-style variation of flat-roofed, rectangular-shaped, brick and often metal one-story structures. On the MSU campus, the aesthetic was decidedly more sleek and modern yet equally efficient and expedient, and produced a uniform modernist, future-oriented look that contrasted with the prewar campus.

Lansing Area Libraries

Along with academic buildings, three large public libraries were built within a ten-year period in the area: the Michigan State University Library, 1955, by Ralph Calder Associates; the East Lansing Public Library, 1963, by Manson, Jackson & Kane, Inc.; and the Lansing Public Library, 1964, by Kenneth C. Black Associates. While all three were modernist in design, they range from the strict geometry of the International style to a more decorative approach. All are also quite different from earlier libraries in the area. In fact, the new Lansing library replaced the 1905 Neoclassical Carnegie

Library on Shiawassee Street, which typically had a flight of stairs leading to the imposing columned portico entrance.

Michigan State University Library

The 1955 International-style university library at 366 West Circle Drive is the earliest of this group. Located in the heart of the campus, just north of the Red Cedar River, it made a bold statement in comparison to the surrounding Collegiate Gothic limestone and brick buildings (figure 67). The library was funded in 1953 by an appropriation approved by the Michigan Legislature in response to President Hannah's request. He saw the lack of a central library on the campus as the "single greatest barrier to the combined educational advancement of this institution."[21] When it opened in 1956, it was the nation's fifth-largest university library in terms of floor space under a single roof, and was concrete evidence of Hannah's quest to increase the university's academic stature.[22]

Unlike the pointed arches, ornamental details, horizontal stone courses, and projecting piers of the neighboring buildings, the new library had flat wall surfaces, an abundance of glass, and steel framing. The use of horizontal bands of green-tinted glass, the geometric linear pattern of the exterior, the curtain wall construction visible in the north stairwell, and the open plan can be found in other buildings by Ralph Calder Associates on the campus. The library is especially dramatic at night, when the stairs of the projecting pavilion appear to float above the open space of the stairwell. The library was built on a modular basis to allow for future additions, of which there have been several designed by Calder in 1967 and 1995.[23]

East Lansing Public Library

The need for a new East Lansing Public Library was very evident by mid-century. The library was established in 1923 and housed in the original Peoples Church building. In 1931 it moved into two rooms in the expanded East Lansing City Hall. By 1951, responding to the rapid growth of the city and increasing use of the library, East Lansing voters were asked to pass a millage rate that would fund a new library and an enlarged city hall.[24] The design by Lee and Kenneth C. Black was published in the *Lansing State Journal* several times to generate interest.[25] This two-story brick structure with numerous windows, plenty of stacks for books, and a music room was to be built just north of city hall. It was to be "bright with color, a cheerful place to read, to browse."[26] Librarians anticipated that the new building would allow them to

double the number of people served. The East Lansing proposal to borrow $500,000 for the two projects developed into a controversial topic. Some objected to spending money on these before a new high school or sewer system; some balked at considering the library as a unit of city hall; still others did not want increased taxes.[27]

Voters eventually did approve a bond issue, and a new building was constructed in 1961 on property that is further north at 950 Abbot Road, which rapidly had become the main north-south commercial thoroughfare in East Lansing (plate 63). A typed manuscript history of the library noted that "Resisting the temptation to make the library into a colossus of stone and brick, the city selected a quiet, wooded site on Abbot Road. The building design was adapted to that sylvan mood—from just about anywhere in the library, a person could look out on trees."[28]

The sentiment expressed about the library in the Manson, Jackson & Kane Inc. prospectus was widespread:

> The opening of this building marks a new era for East Lansing and its public library, an era of opportunity for the city's residents of all ages.
>
> Here is an open door to the wisdom and experience of the past and the expanding discoveries of the present. The hospitable reading space beckons the

◀ **FIGURE 67.** MSU Library, Ralph Calder, exterior, East Lansing. Photograph © 2014 Kim Kauffman.

> reader to come and enjoy the great ideas in books and the cultural values it places on literature, pictures and music.[29]

To make sure that the library was not a "colossus of stone and brick," the architects included several modernist features and materials, the most obvious being the pleated roof (figure 68). Its lively zigzag line and the bluish-green panel that runs along the cornice just below the roof convey movement, energy, and dynamism not usually associated with staid, quiet libraries. Similar roofs could be found on 1960s commercial structures such as hotels, drive-in diners, and residences, although there were not many in the Lansing area. A 9,000-square-foot library addition in 1975, plus another small expansion and complete overhaul of the interior completed in 1998 have obscured some of the original aesthetic. However, parts of the original 12,000-square-foot building can be glimpsed in the design of the façade and the zigzag roofline and can be seen in period photographs.

The library sits on a large podium with broad stairs, several low brick walls, and landscaped areas with benches (plate 63). The principal façade of brick, concrete, steel, and glazing conveys modernity. The asymmetrical treatment placed the glass entry doors off-center, sheltered by the deep recess below the screen, a large mesh grille on the upper portion hung from the roof to provide a permanent sunscreen for the floor-to-ceiling windows behind. Inside, in the high-ceilinged open space, reading areas at the front and back are light-filled and have views of the surrounding landscape. The building does indeed succeed in conveying calm and contemplation, modernity and vitality.

Lansing Public Library

The Lansing Public Library (Clarence H. Rosa Public Library)[30] at 401 South Capitol Avenue, Lansing, is considered one of the area's finest modernist structures (plate 66).[31] It was designed by Kenneth C. Black Associates and landscape architect D. Newton Glick in 1964.[32]

Like the East Lansing Public Library, it took a long time to realize. Proposals were generated in 1951 but not approved for another decade. The *Lansing State Journal* article on January 1, 1951, "City Library Building Bursting at Seams," explained that the library was making the case for an expansion to their 1905 building as well as several branch libraries. Planning started again in 1954 for a new structure and was reactivated in 1959. A vote was taken in 1961 to allow the school district to bond itself, and ground was broken in October 1962. Finally the building opened in

◀ **FIGURE 68.** East Lansing Public Library, Manson, Jackson & Kane, exterior. Photograph by Natasha Crljenica.

▶ **FIGURE 69.** Lansing Public Library, Kenneth C. Black Associates, exterior. Photo courtesy of Michigan State Historic Preservation Office.

June 1964. The new building became the processing and distribution point and central storage for the library system, then consisting of fifty elementary and secondary schools as well as five public branches and the main library itself.

The location in downtown Lansing was significant, as explained in the brochure produced for the dedication. The entrances "are no more than three-fourths of a block from entrances to all three main downtown department stores and within a radius of one or two blocks from the highest concentration of parking space in the downtown area." Unfortunately, downtown Lansing has changed substantially since then. The department stores are long gone and the library now stands at the southwestern edge of the downtown activity.

The library building has three floors, with a mezzanine and basement level, and occupies approximately 75,000 square feet. The dedication brochure described it as "contemporary but with a traditional warmth and dignity so often lacking in modern buildings. . . . Planned to be servant, not master of the flow of people and materials, the building can deliver more service with the same staff than was possible in the old building."

The façade and the two gardens distinguish the building. The upper façade has precast square panels with designs of the colophons of eight well-known contemporary book publishers in the United States (figure 69). These printer's marks vary from figurative and symbolic to the use of a firm's initials. They create an interesting pattern across the façade. On this entrance side, the overall pattern is divided into three sections. On the building's longer west side on Capitol Avenue, the rhythm changes to three wide, solid sections alternating with narrower ones that emphasize the vertical. This overall treatment masks the number of floors of the building.

The building sits six steps above street level. The entrance is sheltered by a cantilevered canopy that juts out towards the street.[33] Above the entrance, the solid backgrounds of the concrete panels were cut out to allow light to enter into the building. At night, the building glows from the interior lighting visible through the gray plastic panes of these windows. During the day the small pieces of marble embedded in the cast cement catch the sunlight and make the building sparkle. Around and under the canopy, small pieces of quartz aggregate were put into the wet concrete to create Fulget tiles. Here, too, the effect is to lend visual interest and texture to the material. The canopy shelters the semicircular, floor-to-ceiling-glazed foyer area and affords a view into the interior, where terrazzo, wood, and different colors of stonework were used in abundance.[34]

Although designed at the same time as the

building, the two gardens as well as the auditorium and local history room in the basement were left unfinished. The building itself was paid for by taxes, but these other areas were not considered functional, and controversy ensued over how to fund them. Eventually private donations were solicited, but it took several years after the building opened to complete them.

The sunken plaza on the west side of the building was completed first. A rectangular space, 32 feet wide by 162 feet long, it extends the length of the building on Capitol Avenue. Placed a step below street level, the space is visually and physically separate to provide "a dramatic and colorful visual barrier between the reading room and the heavy street traffic."[35] With cement benches and rectangular planters, the space fits the rectilinear character of the building.

The east garden has a totally different feel. It is hidden from the street by a high wall and accessed only from the library's interior. Described as "jewel-like" and Japanese in character, it "provides a profusion of greenery, blossoms, and a bit of rippling water in the heart of downtown."[36] With its path that meanders past trees, rocks, and benches, the space is serene, creating an oasis to look at from the interior of the main reading room, or to enjoy in warm weather.

Kenneth Black's ornamented approach to the façade, the play of textures, and the different characters of the outdoor spaces make this a highly successful and unique architectural statement. By the 1960s, Black had moved away from the starker, sleek International style of his Lansing City Hall (plate 39) and aligned himself more closely with Minoru Yamasaki's decorative modernism, seen in the recently completed Michigan State Medical Society building in East Lansing (plate 55). Like Frank Lloyd Wright and Alden B. Dow, Black was cognizant of the widespread interest in Japanese architecture and garden design. Black's Michigan colleagues (as seen in the MSU Library and the East Lansing Public Library) were in tune with other contemporary modernist approaches, and in these three buildings, a snapshot of those differing concerns is evident.

CHAPTER 10

Sacred Spaces

As population expanded, prosperity increased, and people moved away from the downtowns, new postwar congregations were formed to be closer to potential constituents. Permanent buildings were the next step. In mid-Michigan, numerous new congregations erected churches between the late 1940s and the mid-1960s, and by the end of this time, the area's first synagogue was built, followed in the next decade by the Islamic Center. The overwhelming majority of these sacred buildings were churches of various denominations that are the focus of this chapter. By 1969, however, the church building boom tapered off.[1] Most often the churches were built in phases. An affordable "first unit" functioned as the temporary sanctuary until the congregation became more established, grew, and had additional funding. Then they erected a permanent sanctuary and repurposed the first unit for education and administrative needs.[2] This was a national, and specifically American, pattern that happened locally, for example, at Eastminster Presbyterian Church, Edgewood United Church, and St. Thomas Aquinas, all in East Lansing.

The style of church architecture at mid-century was varied and confusing. Many local examples were discussed as being modern and traditional at the same time. Budgetary constraints often drove design decisions with the result that construction methods were conservative, ornament was minimal, buildings were fairly modest in size, and plans were simple. This chapter will consider four examples in depth, plus several others, in order to characterize both the typical and the unusual in church architecture in mid-Michigan. Many of the 1950s and 1960s buildings have been expanded and renovated. For example, at the Martin

Luther Chapel, the original structure is easy to discern, while at Eastminster Presbyterian Church, Alden B. Dow's design is more difficult to pick out. To reconstruct these mid-century buildings, to understand the liturgical requirements and the congregations' needs as well as the relationships with their architects, documents and plans in the church archives were consulted and proved most helpful.

Zion Evangelical Lutheran Church and the Ubiquitous A-Frame

Mid-Michigan churches tended to be designed by local or Michigan architects, among whom Laitala and Nuechterlein earned their reputation as ecclesiastical designers. Several of their numerous local examples took the form of an A-frame, which was ubiquitous across the country in the 1950s (plate 33). Among the reasons for its popularity are economics, ease of construction, and flexibility of plan (figure 70). Additionally, with its steeply rising sides, there was no need to add a separate tower structure. Less recognized now are connections to tent structures and tent revival meetings.[3] According to the 1954 *Architectural Digest* article "The Tent Form—A Village Gothic for Today," the simplicity of the form had widespread appeal, and while modern, had deep roots in churches in northern Europe where steep wooden roofs were used to shed heavy snows. The symbolism of the form was also significant. The triangular shape is a symbol of stability, shelter, and prayer.[4] Others note the structural comparisons with hands raised in prayer, an inverted ship, or even a fish.[5]

In the 1950s both Frank Lloyd Wright and Eero Saarinen designed A-frame chapels, thereby sanctioning the use of the form for religious structures. Wright's First Unitarian Society Church in Madison, Wisconsin (1951) and Saarinen's Kramer Chapel at Concordia Senior College in Fort Wayne, Indiana (1953–58) were noted immediately and featured in many journals and books, such as Albert Christ-Janer and Mary Mix Foley's *Modern Church Architecture* of 1962, one of the early attempts to provide an overview of contemporary ecclesiastical architecture. The A-frame was already popular for commercial and resort structures, but with Wright and Saarinen as exemplars, A-frame churches began to dot the landscape.[6]

A-frames are characterized by a steep-pitched roof with slanting walls. Glazing is often restricted to the shorter gable ends and sometimes added at the low edges of the slanted walls. How successfully the architect brings light into the interior often distinguishes one building from another. In this regard, Laitala and Nuechterlein's Zion Evangelical Lutheran

▶ **FIGURE 70.** Zion Evangelical Lutheran Church, Laitala and Nuechterlein, construction photograph, 1954, Lansing. Courtesy of Diane Sowash.

EXIT

Church at 4001 South Pennsylvania Avenue in Lansing, dedicated on November 7, 1954, the congregation's thirty-fifth anniversary, stands out (plate 33). The congregation's rapid growth had led to the appointment of a building committee in January 1951, the purchase of six lots, and, at the end of 1953, the selection of the architects.[7]

The long western side of the building is visible on Pennsylvania Avenue, one of the major north-south thoroughfares in the city. The short ends face north and south. When the church was built, the entrance was in the northwest corner and the door, which was placed off-center, was emphasized by a horizontal canopy. The effect was as if the architects had lifted up the slanting wall to form this welcoming entrance. They left the ends of the diagonal steel framing beams in place and inserted a vertical brick wall behind to create a triangular entry space. Triangles also are formed by three smaller diagonal supports that hold up the canopy.

The rest of the sharply pitched west wall, like the east wall, has windows inserted at the lower end. Additionally, light enters the sanctuary through the window placed at the gable peak and the skylights towards the altar. Shadows are cast on the interior as light filters through the patterning of the windows onto the wood paneling, creating warmth and mystery (figure 71). Attention to details such as these won the

◄ **FIGURE 71.** Zion Evangelical Lutheran Church, Laitala and Nuechterlein, interior, Lansing. Courtesy of Diane Sowash.

architects a state award for excellence in public and religious building design.

In the *Lansing State Journal* article "Churches Lean toward Modernism," on May 17, 1964, Thelma Harnett described Zion as simple structurally but instantly recognizable as "in the modern trend." An early photograph shows the architects' original intent (plate 33). This was altered, however, in a renovation and expansion campaign in 2000 when an addition reoriented the entrance from the north to the south, that is, from the street to the parking lot. As the population across the country was becoming increasingly mobile, arriving by automobile rather than on foot, most churches built in the 1960s placed the primary entrance near the parking area.[8] At Zion, the northern canopy, which was no longer needed, was removed, and the original church evolved from a stand-alone structure into a complex of buildings.

There are numerous A-frame churches in the Lansing area from the 1950s and 1960s.[9] Plans were readily available and prefabricated materials could be used, so they could be built very quickly and cheaply. They fit the vernacular trend seen across the country where functionality and frugality were the topmost concerns. But their popularity bred numerous undistinguished buildings. Moreover, while originally considered modern, as other more modernist approaches became popular, the A-frame came to be regarded as traditional, as modern "Gothic," inflexible and not cost-effective.[10] Therefore, by the mid-1960s, when new liturgical approaches took hold, the long, narrow orientation of the A-frame began to be replaced by more centrally planned structures.

Edgewood United Church

Edgewood United Church at 469 North Hagadorn Road in East Lansing is a prime example of a central-plan sanctuary, as is the decision-making process that led to its selection. Because of its proximity to the Michigan State College campus, Edgewood drew its membership from the faculty, and it was known as a liberal congregation from its beginnings in 1954.[11] For the first construction phase, the Building Study Committee, appointed in 1953, interviewed seven architects and selected Laitala and Nuechterlein in November 1954. Their church-school unit facing north on Beech Street opened in March 1957 (figure 72). It comprised an auditorium seating three hundred that served as the temporary sanctuary, offices, classrooms, kitchen, choir room, and meeting rooms, and cost $237,270. The configuration and construction were straightforward and functional. The rectangular brick building has a flat-roofed portico leading to the entrance. Flat roofs are also over the two wings, while a low sloping roof

▲ **FIGURE 72.** Edgewood United Church, Laitala and Nuechterlein, entrance, East Lansing. Photograph by Natasha Crljenica.

with clerestory windows and a small steeple covers the auditorium.[12] Although the interior of the sanctuary is a spartan rectangular space, the laminated wood arches provide visual interest (figure 73). Laminated products had been developed before the war but became widespread following it because of their cost effectiveness, strength, and ability to be bent into new shapes, as seen here. Edgewood's first unit is similar to many erected at mid-century when church architecture paralleled the widespread, inexpensive, and quick construction techniques also seen in school buildings. In fact, it was common for many urban local architects like Laitala and Nuechterlein to design both schools and religious facilities.[13]

Edgewood's second phase, completed two years later, added the educational wing at a cost of

EXIT

$21,000, but by the mid-1960s, the need to expand and build a large, permanent sanctuary became clear. Planning for this third phase (the sanctuary, atrium, chapel, and fireplace room) to the south of the existing structure was especially deliberate (plate 44). The very thoughtful and inclusive process is recorded in typed histories, numerous handouts, and other church publications in the Edgewood archive.[14] It began in 1960 with study groups formed to understand church architecture historically and decide upon the most appropriate shape and form for Protestant worship. Members researched, wrote papers, and gave lectures through 1962.[15] They read Rudolf Schwarz's seminal book *The Church Incarnate*, which had been translated from German into English in 1958 and gained widespread influence in Europe and America. Schwarz advocated architecture based on the liturgy rather than construction materials, the use of modern materials in a modern idiom, and sanctuary shapes that bring the congregants close to the center of the celebration.[16]

To address the enormous need for church structures at mid-century across the country, various denominations developed national architecture committees and published numerous books and directives on appropriate church design. Beginning in the 1940s, American Protestant groups renewed their interest in participatory worship that emphasized active rather than passive congregants, and communal rather than individual concerns. The typical church plan with a long nave ending in a raised altar, where the priest had his back to the congregation and the congregants observed rather than participated, was no longer acceptable. Instead, the desire was for each person to be as close to the altar as possible. This necessitated reorienting the plan to place the altar in the center of the room, with the pews (or often moveable seats) arrayed around it.[17]

This was the national context that explains the discussions and decision made by the Edgewood congregation to build a round sanctuary (figure 74). Their instructions to the architects were that the building should express their faith in the "continuity of the Judeo-Christian heritage and the utilization of new materials and new forms . . . their Protestant beliefs and the mutual ministry of its people."[18] The memorable, stirring, and erudite address given by MSC philosophy professor and congregation member John F. A. Taylor on Sunday, May 15, 1966, "on the occasion of the dedication of its new sanctuary" explains this further: "It is fitting that on at least this inaugural occasion we should pause over it and meditate, in an essay of self-knowledge, what it is we have attempted in this building, to do."[19] He described the miraculous transformation of the raw materials of wood, steel, and stone into a soaring, weightless presence. "This

◀ **FIGURE 73.** Edgewood United Church, Laitala and Nuechterlein, Fellowship Hall, East Lansing. Photograph © 2013 Kim Kauffman.

building, our luminous bright miracle, is but the outward form by which we seclude our community of promise, by which we set it apart, in reverence and tenderness, for its free and unhindered development." He referenced Le Corbusier's definition of a building as "a machine for living," which Taylor defined as "a large-scale tool," and how good the tool is depends upon how efficiently or inefficiently it functions.

Edgewood's distinctive atrium space was explained by Taylor by referring to Early Christian churches where the atrium serves as an important transition between secular and sacred spaces. At Edgewood,

> the hexagonal of the atrium is already an anticipation of the shape of the sanctuary you are about to enter; its lights are a jeweled transformation of the white physical light of the parlor you have left behind. It is, musically, the statement of a theme, a base premonitory intimation of the grand orchestral variation which is about to be run upon it in the sanctuary.

The sanctuary then enlarges this hexagonal theme, but "erupting and enlarging into a luminous space, filled with color . . . pierced by a vertical shaft of light no longer physical at all, sweeps in solemnity aloft in one majestic rise in which heaven and earth are joined climactically."

► **FIGURE 74.** Edgewood United Church, Gordon Cornwell, sanctuary, East Lansing. Photograph © 2013 Kim Kauffman.

At the center of the circle is the communion table.

> It is the positive central focus of this space, as the communion is the positive central motive of our assembly. The form and the function are congruent. They visibly coincide, the one following the other. Vertically, the table occurs beneath the oculus, the eye, which opens to the sky. Horizontally, it radiates outwards upon ourselves. And we are gathered in each other's presence, related to each other through our common relation to it.

In a round sanctuary, Taylor wrote,

> it matters not where you sit; we are all alike related to one center. And from that center which we share, the radii, themselves infinite in number, spread infinitely outward—through us, through those walls that screen the privacy of our communion, through all space beyond the walls; so that at last, if you will but reflect upon it, there is nothing in all the illimitable ocean of space which is not related, or at least relatable to this center about which we are gathered in quiet reverence.

He explained further that this is "the purest expression of all Protestant principle[s]," referencing Luther's phrase "the universal priesthood of all believers." "No priest, no organization, no rite is intruded between you and that center." Taylor concluded by reminding the congregation that the building is just that, a way to house the church, but that the church extends far beyond the physical structure—that the interior light in the church is the exterior light filtered, but the church's work extends into the world.

To choose the architect to carry out these carefully delineated ideas, the Sanctuary Building Committee, appointed on January 23, 1963, wrote letters to sixteen architects. Of the twelve who expressed interest, six were interviewed: Nuechterlein, Dixon Shaw Wilson, Webb, Mayotte, Gordon Cornwell, and Harold Fisher. Several committee members drove to Ann Arbor to hear a lecture by Marcel Breuer, but his fees were too high to be considered. Breuer had already begun to work with the St. Francis de Sales parish in Muskegon on their spectacular concrete Brutalist building that would cost $1 million when completed in 1966. After the Edgewood committee visited one of Gordon Cornwell's churches in Traverse City, his home base, he was recommended as architect.[20] His preliminary plans were approved in May, detailed plans and specifications were sent to bid in December 1964, and groundbreaking occurred on February 21, 1965.[21]

To transition from the old to the new building, Cornwell placed the atrium at the center of a Y-shape, connecting the first unit to the north, the small hexagonal chapel to the west, and the large sanctuary to the southeast. While the interior of the sanctuary is circular and built of concrete block, the brick-faced exterior was made hexagonal to save costs (plate 38). The sanctuary roof is supported by large, curved Douglas fir rafters from Oregon. These laminated wood trusses visible on the interior are characteristic of modern construction techniques and relate to their use in the first unit (figure 74). Wood paneling between the rafters, the wood pews arranged in circles on the inclined floor, as well as stained-glass windows in geometric patterns of different colors create a warm, inviting atmosphere.[22] The symbolism of all of the adornments of the church, even the colors chosen for the carpet and bench pillows, was explained in church publications and handouts.

Edgewood's inclusive and very articulate approach to the design process, and the extensive research that was conducted to deeply understand trends in contemporary church architecture were unusual for a congregation. Cornwell matched its desires through his sensitive church design.

Martin Luther Chapel

Other congregations in mid-Michigan were less involved in the design process than Edgewood was and instead followed directives from their mother church or synod. This was the case at Martin Luther Chapel on 444 Abbot Road, built in 1963 (plate 68). It took the congregation (of the English District of the Missouri Synod) three years to find a suitable location in East Lansing that was close enough to the campus to fulfill their mission of ministering to students. All Saints Episcopal Church had purchased a site on Abbot Road, but when they decided to erect their church further north on Abbot, their original site became available. This property contained a fraternity house that was used temporarily for services. Eventually six lots were put together to expand the site, the fraternity house was razed (1960), and the new Martin Luther Chapel was constructed and opened in 1964.

Planning began formally in March 1962 for a building to serve 350, which was based on the projection of MSC's increasing student enrollment. The Mission Board of Detroit, rather than a local group, served as the building committee "responsible for planning and ultimate construction and furnishing of the plant."[23]

Although architect Charles Edward Stade (1923–1993) was young, he had already made a name for himself as a designer of Lutheran churches. He had attended a Lutheran seminary, received his architectural degrees from the University of Illinois and Princeton University, and opened his practice

REJOICE

in the Chicago area in 1951. His background as well as the fact that his brother was a Lutheran pastor in Des Plaines, Illinois, probably made him appealing to the Lutherans. He was a member of the Church Architecture Guild, an affiliate of the American Institute of Architects started in 1958, and became president of the American Society of Church Architecture, which had begun in 1959.[24] Four of his designs between 1961 and 1963 (three of them for Lutheran churches) received awards from the Chicago chapter of the American Institute of Architects.[25]

The Martin Luther Chapel sanctuary is square and aligned with the streets to the north and east in the northeast portion of the lot. The offices, library, and other rooms extend diagonally to the southwest. "The structure [of the sanctuary] is 'tied' to the earth with its low masonry planters and truss anchors and soars into space with its steeply pitched roof and tower."[26] It was also described as "strong with monumental forms and heavy texture," and with furnishings in the sanctuary and throughout the building that continue the massive outdoor characteristics.[27]

While square on the exterior, the sanctuary is pentagonal on the interior (figure 75). This was achieved by cutting off the south and west walls and joining them on the diagonal. This also created space for the narthex from which one sees the baptismal font, altar, and pulpit on an axial alignment in the sanctuary. The altar is the focus, placed in the center, below the oculus of the spire. Six large wood trusses, anchored in steel (visible on the exterior), rise to form the skeleton of the tall 107-foot spire.

Numerous printed sources in the church archive describe the architectural influence as Norwegian or Scandinavian.[28] For example, a *State News* article on the opening of the building in September 1964, "Chapel, Center Are Unique," stated that it is a "replica of a high roofed Scandinavian stave church." The reference is to wood churches found in Scandinavia in the early eleventh century when Christianity was first introduced there. Stave architecture is characterized by steeply pitched roofs, roof shingles, timber construction, and the use of poles (or staves) in the post and beam construction. The tower or spire rises above the central mast rather than being a separate structure. The steep pitch of the roof is designed to help shed the heavy snows.

The idea of attributing architectural influence to a venerable Old World tradition also figured in discussions about A-frame construction in general, as we have seen. Stade himself used it to justify his basilical design for the Valparaiso University Chapel of the Resurrection, 1958. As architectural historian Gretchen Buggeln points out, referencing historical styles often made the building more acceptable to the client. Nevertheless, the use of new materials such as

◀ **FIGURE 75.** Martin Luther Chapel, Charles Stade, sanctuary, East Lansing. Photograph by Natasha Crljenica.

steel, concrete, and laminated woods paradoxically made the building decidedly contemporary.[29]

While it may be true that committee members thought about early Scandinavian churches, there were more contemporary examples with which Stade would have been familiar, in particular Eero Saarinen's North Christian Church in Columbus, Indiana, designed in 1955 and completed in 1964. Saarinen's church sits low to the ground in a greensward and is hexagonally shaped with a centrally rising needle-like spire. The oculus below admits light into the sanctuary, and rows of pews surround the altar in the center. The sanctuary itself is elevated several steps, as Saarinen wrote, to reflect that the experience in reaching the spiritual is difficult.[30]

Stade was well aware of contemporary architecture and had traveled to Germany and across the United States after receiving the Valparaiso Chapel commission in the late 1950s.[31] For that chapel he used a traditional rectangular basilical plan with a separate baptistery and raised chancel. Its large scale was necessary to accommodate all the university students who attended services. Stade's Martin Luther Chapel is far smaller and feels more intimate inside, despite the description of the exterior as strong, monumental, and "masculine."[32]

At Martin Luther Chapel, the sanctuary is lit from the oculus as well as spotlights cut out in the ceiling that create random, interesting patterns. Abstract patterns of small, irregularly placed rectangular pieces of different-colored glass are used very effectively in the oculus, the windows in the library, and several of the offices. The horizontal course of glass along the upper edge of the brick walls of the sanctuary seems mysteriously lit from below. In fact, the warm glow is the result of lights on the outside below the wall that reflect up on these windows.

Reverend Theodor K. Bundenthal, the pastor, stated that he had suggested using the random checkerboard of colored glass squares after seeing something similar in a Finnish church.[33] Stade, however, had already used them in his A-frame church designs.[34] These in turn were based on designs by Frank Lloyd Wright, an architect Stade greatly admired.[35] Additionally, the large planters that Stade used at the Martin Luther Chapel have precedents in Wright's early Prairie style in Chicago.

In "Churches Lean toward Modernism," the headline in the *Lansing State Journal* on Sunday, May 7, 1964, Thelma Harnett wrote that architects were describing the Martin Luther Chapel as the only ultramodern church edifice in the area. They were likely referring to construction materials, the stylistic and design influences of Wright and Saarinen, and the fact that the building looked totally different from any other structure in the area. But the idea of tradition that was so important to the church hierarchy is manifest in numerous ways, including the handmade bricks and cedar shakes that show an attention to craftsmanship often missing in minimalist International-style examples. Martin Luther Chapel successfully illustrates ideas of the liturgical reform movement in its proportions, structure, and plan. There is no ambiguity about the building's function. In a dignified and eloquent way, the large trusses of the exterior tie the building to the earth. Yet the contradictory sweep of the steeply rising roof dramatically points to the heavens.[36]

Eastminster Presbyterian Church

Eastminster Presbyterian Church at 1315 Abbot Road, East Lansing, at the northern boundary of the city when it was built in the 1960s, is another example of a phased structure (plate 56). Because the congregation was new, they could not possibly have raised all of the money needed for the larger building. The congregation had only recently been formed by the Lansing Presbytery in April 1957 and held its first services in borrowed space at All Saints Church on Abbot Road. Originally the congregation had purchased three-and-a-quarter acres on the north side of Saginaw Street near Abbot, but in 1959 exchanged the property with developer Albert White for nine-and-a-half acres on the west side of the road. The new site was preferred because it offered unlimited possibilities for expansion; wonderful natural features, including many trees, that minimized the need to landscape; and the variations in contours and elevation that would greatly aid the architectural design.[37] Indeed, the church is located well into the property at the top of the rise and is not visible from Abbot Road, but comes into view from the long uphill driveway.

Brainstorming for the new building proceeded in 1958. The new congregation received guidance from the Department of Church Building, New York. The Eastminster Archives contain a "Suggested List of Architects who have shown an interest and competence in church work," with names in Pennsylvania and Ohio; "Literature on Church Building: Getting Ready for the Building Program"; and "A Report on the Architectural Setting of Presbyterian Worship," presented to the Presbytery of Chicago, January 13, 1953.[38] Building-committee members charged themselves with "describ[ing] the feelings we want the church to exhibit towards others; old, young, children, newcomers . . . also the purposes and functions of a church. Start with people in a meadow, then visualize their functions, purposes, activities, feelings . . . and let the design evolve from them. . . . Come up with a series of adjectives."[39]

In late April 1958, a request for proposals was sent to over ten architectural firms, mainly in

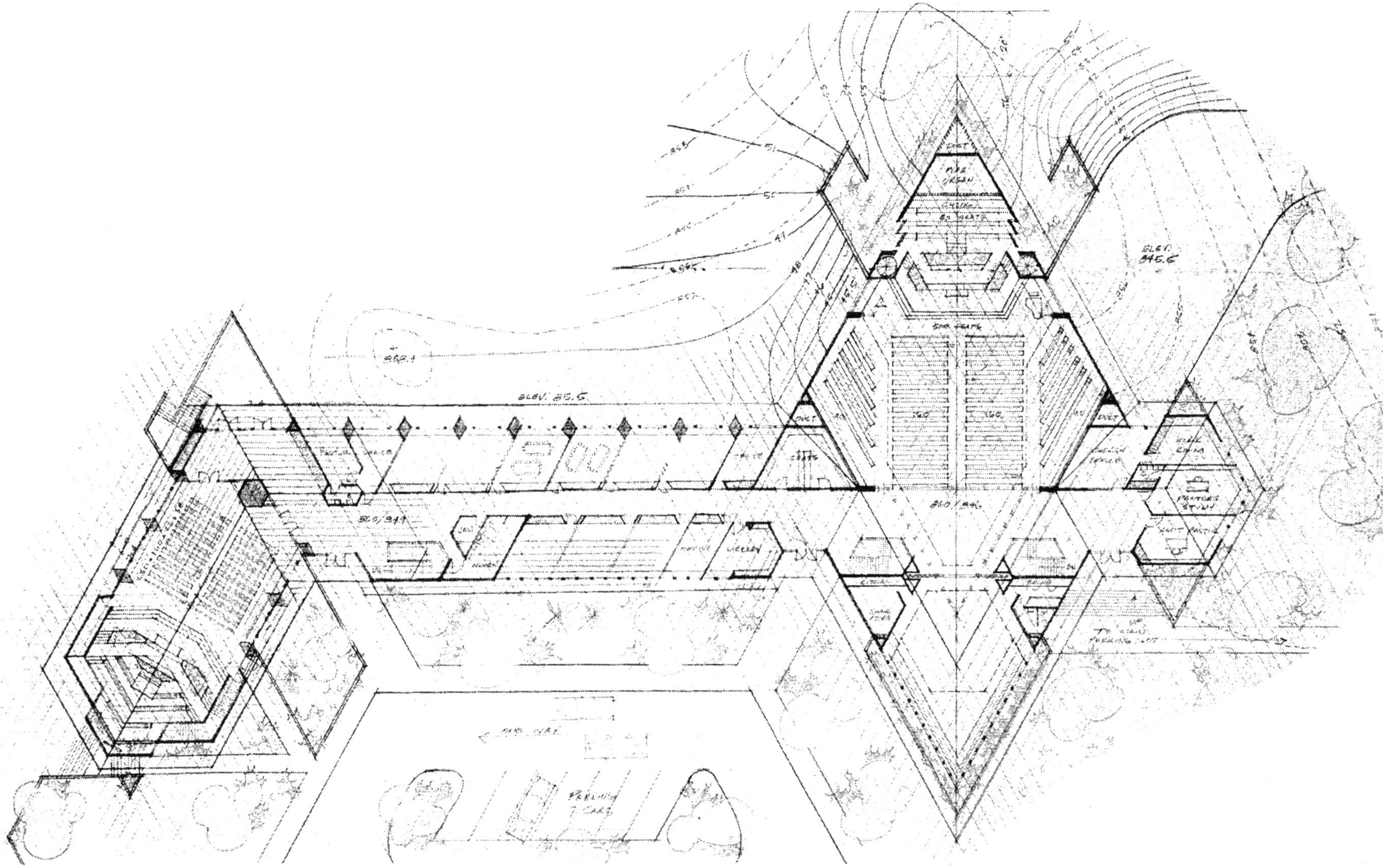

Michigan, including Laitala and Nuechterlein; Alden B. Dow; Manson, Jackson & Kane (who would later be responsible for the 1967 building); and Eero Saarinen, who replied that the office was too busy to meet the proposed deadline. Of the architects who submitted their credentials, the majority had designed A-frame churches in the late 1950s, including Gordon Cornwell (who would later design Edgewood), Harford Field and Associates, Mano and Associates from Detroit, and Charles V. Opdyke, Lansing.[40]

By way of introducing his firm's work, Alden B. Dow wrote:

> We have found that a good building requires a client just as creative in values as the architect is creative in his representation of these values. Consequently, we're very aware that this creative union between client and architect is fundamental in the development of a really significant building.[41]

After visiting many churches and a "lengthy period of study and evaluation," the building committee chose Dow. He was asked to design the entire project, but was charged with building only the first unit.

At this time, the northern reach of the city at the intersection of Abbot Road and Saginaw Street was buzzing with activity. To the south of the future church, the Michigan State Medical Society (MSMS) building designed by Minoru Yamasaki was nearing completion (see plate 55). In the building committee minutes for January 27, 1960, T. C. Cobb of the church committee recounted his meeting with Dr. Kenneth Johnson, president-elect and member of the MSMS building committee, for the purposes of getting acquainted with their neighbor, to share plans and open communication. The real purpose, however, speaks volumes about the significance MSMS gave to architecture's ability to make an impression on its members and the community. Cobb noted that the society was very concerned that the neighborhood be made and kept as attractive as possible, and "he thought we felt the same way." MSMS desired

> to protect the aesthetic nature of the approaches to their building and to keep other interests out of that site . . . Mr. Yama has been quite concerned about all the trees and had each tree tagged and its location carefully plotted and not a tree was touched without his specific permission. The present grove of evergreens is being carefully preserved, although future plans provide for expansion to the west and to the north . . . the Medical Society is vitally concerned with their public relations and in the dedication of their new building they plan to emphasize their role as a good citizen in the community. I feel that we will find them to be good neighbors.

◄ **FIGURE 76.** Eastminster, Alden B. Dow, complex plan, 1959, East Lansing, Eastminster Archive.

In contrast to Yamasaki, Dow did not have the luxury of an unlimited or even an adequate budget, and from the start, financial constraints were made obvious to him. Minutes of the building committee recorded that "The Building Committee and architects want to emphasize that in no respect should there be any expectation of a 'plus' building or of luxurious appointments. Simplicity and tasteful design geared only to the most immediate and vital needs of our church programs are our objectives."[42] On the other hand, the desire for an aesthetically pleasing building was also apparent. In a letter to Dow on April 2, Cobb wrote, "Come prepared for a hot discussion of windows. Committee is now divided between aesthetics and aluminum. Cost is held not to be the deciding factor."[43] Focusing on how to site the building on the property, Cobb wrote on April 13 to Dow, "We are not looking for the cheapest way out. This roadway will be the approach to a million dollar structure in a few years and we feel that it should be built now so as to last indefinitely."[44]

The "million dollar structure" refers to Dow's estimate for the master plan that he sketched in August 1959 (figure 76). It was divided into three phases: the first included the upper temporary sanctuary and lower education spaces; the second, the upper-floor classrooms and lower nursery, and offices; and the third, the upper sanctuary for five hundred and lower fellowship hall. The total project costs were $1,225,000.[45] Dow's drawing of all three components was used for publicity and fundraising purposes, and the building depicted would have been spectacular. His proposed diamond-shaped sanctuary would have soared above the land on the north, suggesting the prow of a ship. This large sanctuary was placed to the east, the office and education wing in the center, leading to the chapel on the west. Dow's complicated geometries in the sanctuary and chapel were the result of his use of a very carefully orchestrated and consistent module. This can be seen in the placement of the outer walls of the chapel, which parallel those of the sanctuary. Even the walls in the offices were angled to fit this grid. Dow had already used diamond shapes, as had Frank Lloyd Wright for the Annie Pfeiffer Memorial Chapel, Florida Southern College, Lakeland, 1941, and the large complex of the Unitarian Meeting House in Madison, Wisconsin, designed in 1946 and constructed in 1949. Each of these used an underlying design based on geometric units to give unity to the parts.[46]

Unfortunately, the Eastminster congregation had to start small. They tasked Dow with the first phase, a 10,670-square-foot building, with a working budget of $130,000 plus site development and the architect's 8 percent fee ($11,200). In his preliminary ideas for the temporary chapel and for the lower-level fellowship hall illustrated in the fundraising brochure, he drew a rectangle, with two rows of diagonally placed pews and a center aisle. He then angled all of the corners. On the shorter sides he placed the narthex and stairs opposite the chancel and altar.

This idea was scaled back further to a wider but shorter space oriented east and west.[47] Angles and triangles still predominated. Dow angled the corner walls of the sanctuary outwards and continued the diagonals in the offices and used a triangle in the stairwell. This was ultimately what was built. The exterior elevation, seen in an undated drawing in the Dow Archive, shows his proposed treatment (figure 77). The three large windows with dividing brick piers on the front were duplicated at the rear on both levels. On the exterior he used pink brick with spandrels in white stucco, and on the interior he used cement blocks. These set the proportional model that dictated the scale as well as the materials used for the subsequent building phase. In addition, Dow designed the chancel table and the chancel choir furnishings, and he even chose the color of the choir robes. To save on costs, the chancel window was pared down from three to two shades of blue plastic. Construction finally began on June 17, 1960, and the building was dedicated on January 22, 1961.

Dow's building served the congregation for five years until 1967, when they were ready for phase two. According to minutes of the (new) building committee's first meeting on June 5, 1967, the members wished to preserve the aesthetic quality of the existing building and were concerned about how various parts of the building, added a piece at a time, would fit together. "We need some aesthetic control."[48]

By July, with a programming document ready, the committee scheduled meetings with several local firms: Manson, Mayotte-Webb, Howard DeWolf, and Freeman and Smith. Warren Holmes declined. All had worked on churches in the area, most of which were additions to older structures. Alden B. Dow was interviewed on July 19, and expressed that he "would feel badly if [he] could not finish the building." He proposed a diamond shape for the sanctuary, as he had in his original plan, because of its flexibility.

> It goes into a hexagon . . . the present building has a lot of directions it is itching to go . . . the master plan is open ended for change and growth. . . . We want the church to work in a composed order, rather than an organized order. We must keep compositing (as in a flower arrangement). It is dynamic, grows on its own, but needs leadership as to where it goes. . . . The new building should pleasantly relate, in as many ways as possible, to its surroundings—to [the] original building, surrounding land, people that use it, neighbors.[49]

▶ **FIGURE 77.** Eastminster, Alden B. Dow, elevation drawing, East Lansing, ca. 1959. Courtesy of Alden B. Dow Archives.

Those familiar with Dow's design philosophy would have recognized his use of the term "composed order" and the frequent analogies he made to a bouquet of flowers "where each flower is so placed that it contributes the most to the total form," and that each commission's specifics of site, climate, and budget needed to have a creative response from the architect.[50]

By July 24, the committee narrowed their choice to two: Manson, Jackson & Kane, and Dow. But with Dow's fee at 9.4 percent, compared to the 8 percent they paid him for his first phase, and Manson's at 6 percent, the decision was ultimately based on economic concerns. Nevertheless, it took two votes and a second interview with Manson for the committee to decide in his favor. In the minutes of the October 15, 1967, session, the process was disclosed:

> In brief, it may be said that the Council was to ultimately choose between the "competent technician" and the "artist"; and in so doing displayed an obvious sensitivity to the difference in fee schedule.
>
> There was little or no dispute over the expressed belief that Alden B. Dow would in all probability better explore the alternate methods for our church to fulfill its building needs and could guarantee continuity of design. However, it was the majority opinion that the Eastminster Presbyterian Church did not need to buy that kind of insurance; and that another competent architect experienced in church design could quite adequately fulfill the aesthetics and the structural needs of our church. In this decision making process we constantly kept before us three basic principles, namely 1) gross cost, 2) repayment capability of the congregations, and 3) quality. We responded, we trust, to a deep sense of responsibility to the entire congregation.

Of the two designs that Manson presented, the one that was chosen provided a hexagonal-shaped sanctuary facing north. The alternative design was an elongated diamond shape that expanded the building longitudinally to the east. Both sensitively enveloped the original building so that the two are indistinguishable, and it is hard to discern where Dow's original was. Proportions, angles, materials, and colors defer to Dow's ideas (plate 56, figure 77). Despite its larger size, Manson's sanctuary is a warm, intimate space with a relatively low ceiling, brick walls, dark wood rafters, wood pews, and groupings of windows on both sides that allow the congregants to see out. Instead of Dow's prow-like design, the building appears to be anchored to the ground, especially on the entrance side. On the north side, the two full stories of the structure are obvious. As seen here, Manson was adept at responding to the client's

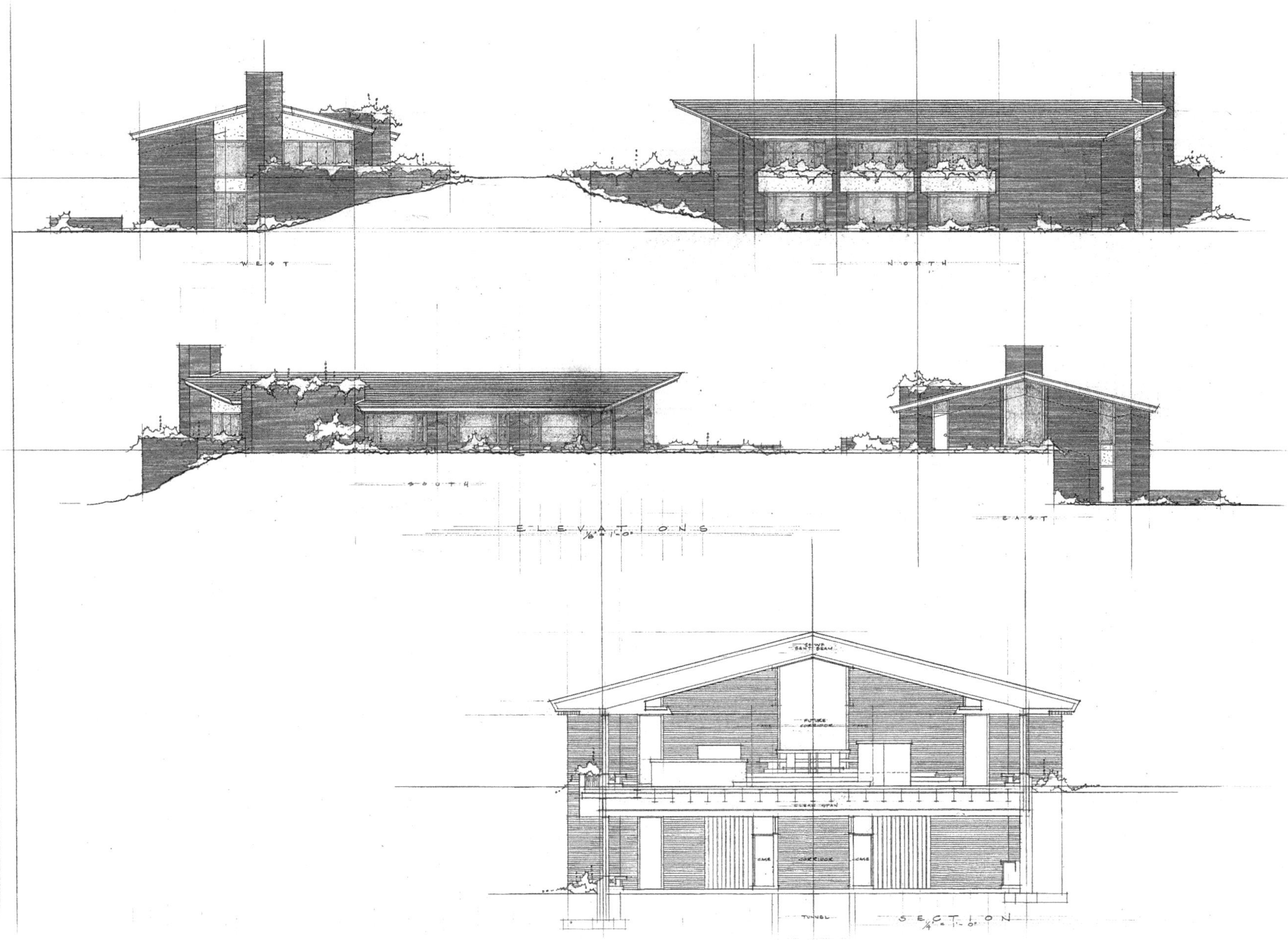
WEST
NORTH
SOUTH
EAST
ELEVATIONS
SECTION
TUNNEL

needs. Whether designing a Colonial or a ranch, the Manson firm was as successful as it was because of its flexibility and ability to listen to the client. Here Manson was asked for a design that would relate seamlessly to Dow's original, and the result succeeded well in paying homage to it.

The building's real achievement, however, is the way it sits on the plot. Early on, there had been a lot of discussion about how to place Dow's building on the site. Dealing with the extensive amount of muck became an issue of logistics and cost. At one point the building was turned on the site so that the center line of the chapel was in the north-south direction with the main entrance exposed to Abbot Road and the service portions hidden.[51] However, as built, the entrance is on the south and the building was almost invisible from the road. Recent landscaping and a large sign and cross at the roadside have addressed the desire for better visibility. Although not articulated in any of the documents, the long approach is important symbolically. Turning off the busy road into the church property, one is forced to slow down and make the transition from the secular world to the sacred one. As the land rises to the level of the parking lot and the church comes into view, this ritualized procession has prepared the congregant to enter the worship space.[52] This ritual of arriving, which is impossible for churches that are more centrally located in the city such as the Martin Luther Chapel or Edgewood Church, is especially effective at Eastminster.

Alden B. Dow's firm was responsible for another church in mid-Michigan. Plymouth Congregational Church at 2001 East Grand River in Lansing was built in 1975 for a congregation that had a long history dating to 1864, as well as several different structures in the downtown area. Although plans to expand its downtown location were contemplated in the 1960s and ground was broken in 1971 for an addition, a devastating fire on February 25 destroyed the building. A new site with plenty of space for parking was selected north of downtown. After considering six architectural firms, Alden B. Dow Associates was hired.[53] In the history of the church prepared for its 125th anniversary in 1989, the congregation's consideration of different architectural styles was discussed. Neo-Gothic was too expensive, as was Colonial, and the choice of modern reflected the desire to be representative of the time and project into the future. There was a heated debate about a centrally planned versus a cruciform shape, and the former won out. The result is similar to the Martin Luther Chapel in appearance, with the tall spire rising from the center of the building. Above the altar is an enlarged chandelier based on the design of the old church building. These are aligned below the oculus, which is filled with faceted glass pieces of red, blue, green, and yellow, creating a warm glow that is augmented by the dark wood on the interior, an intentional feeling of "insideness" focused on prayer. The centrum is enclosed within the building, surrounded by a wide corridor. Airy, light-filled offices, meeting rooms, and other spaces encircle the corridor and have windows that relate the church's mission to the outside.[54]

Okemos Community Church

At the earlier Okemos Community Church at 4734 Okemos Road, Manson & Carver (the predecessor firm to Manson, Jackson & Kane) showed what they were capable of when not saddled by the constraints they had at Eastminster (figure 78). The congregation dates to 1840, when Methodist services were first held in people's homes. Their first building was erected in 1870. In 1957 a large two-story light-tan brick and stone building was erected to accommodate 475 members, and in 1967 the original structure on the site was razed to make room for an education unit.[55]

The sanctuary designed by Manson & Carver is a longitudinal space with a raised altar at the west end and a balcony on the east. On both the exterior and interior, there is a play of contrasting textures. The most distinguishing feature is the west exterior wall that faces Okemos Road. Here rough-hewn stones are at the base, smooth bricks above, and projecting bricks higher up, with small openings that were filled with red glass that filters the light on the inside. Narrow windows in the chancel area also create patterns of light and shade on the interior where the chancel is separated from the nave by a wood altar rail and a tall, open wood screen on one side. Modernist materials and ideas include the large rounded wood rafters that rise to meet the ceiling, and the division of the wall behind the altar into three uneven vertical sections. This asymmetry was caused by the placement on the exterior of the entry and covered walkway on the south side of the building. An angled canopy (no longer extant) projected horizontally and was a visual counterpoint to the vertical gable of the chancel wall.

The location of the church near Okemos's original downtown was important when the church was built. However, as strip malls and the large Meridian Mall to the north took shoppers away from downtown, and new subdivisions were opened in different directions, access to the church from the main street, Okemos Road, was no longer useful or needed. A recent addition and remodeling moved the main entrance from the street to the parking area on the east. When the cantilevered entry canopy which no longer served a function was removed, one of the characteristic traces of modernist detailing disappeared.

4734
OKEMOS
Community
Church

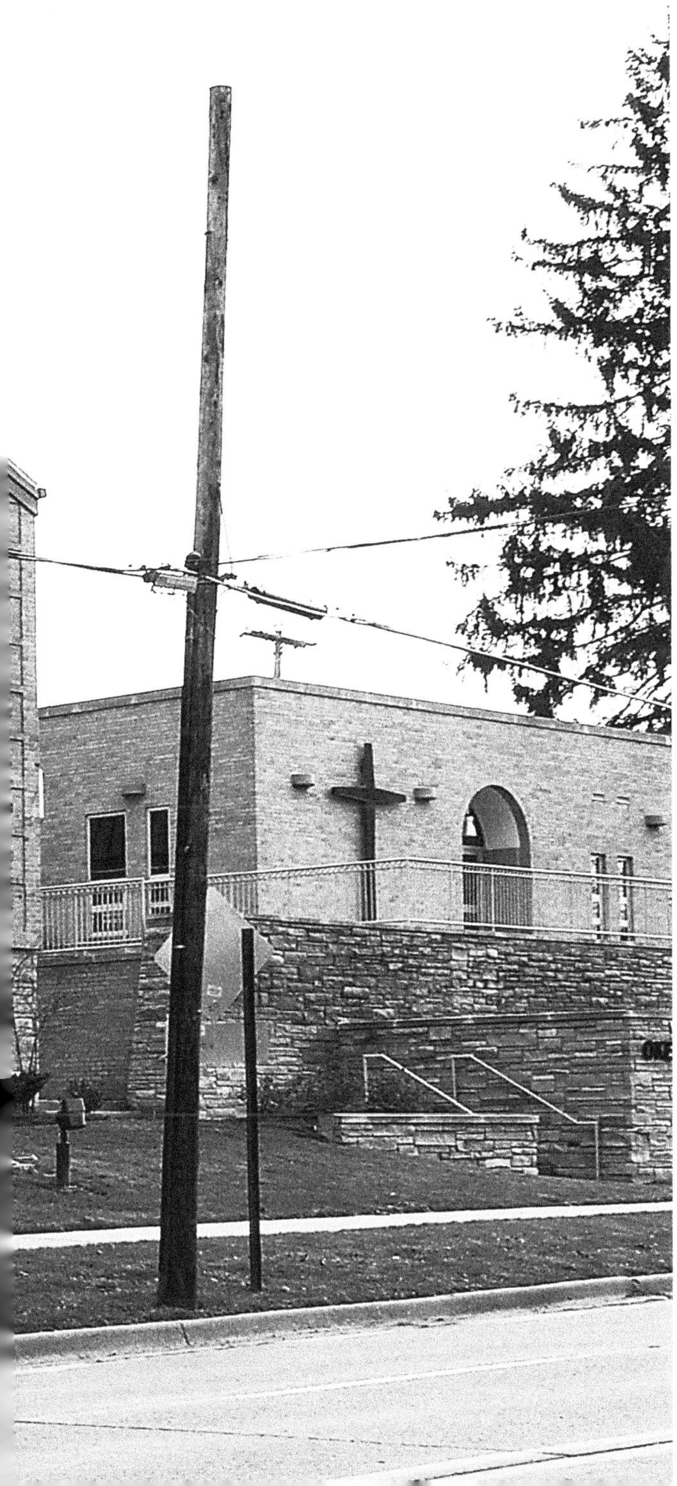

◀ **FIGURE 78.** Okemos Community Church, Manson & Carver, Okemos. Photograph © 2014 Kim Kauffman.

St. Thomas Aquinas

St. Thomas Aquinas is a further example of building in phases (plate 86). The church was formed in 1940 to serve Catholic students and families in East Lansing, and it held services in temporary locations for several years. By 1948 Father Mac (Jerome MacEachin) had purchased twenty-five acres on Alton Road. The first building constructed was the parish school (1949) designed by Laitala and Nuechterlein and expanded in 1956.[56]

When it came time to build the church, Bernard Joseph Mayotte (1923–2006), of Mayotte-Webb, was the obvious choice. Not only was he a member of the congregation, but he was also well-versed in post–Second Vatican Council (1963) discussions about religious architecture, and had already built a number of churches for the Diocese of Lansing. As a result of his earlier involvement with the St. Gerard project on the west side of Lansing, he became good friends with Bishop Albers.[57] Mayotte-Webb also designed Catholic churches in mid- and central Michigan, in Grand Ledge, Flint, Brighton, Howell, and Pinckney.

Looking back on his career in 2006, Mayotte stated that St. Thomas Aquinas, completed in 1968, was the finest church that he designed personally.[58] He worked closely with Father Mac, whom he persuaded not to place the church close to the road with parking behind, but to reverse the order so that the public would see the building rather than just drive by. Indeed, the large parking area in front of the building serves as its forecourt, building anticipation of entering the interior. From this vantage point, one sees the imposing east façade with its large stained-glass window measuring 60 by 50 feet.

Mayotte also recalled that the "Grande Window" that dominates both the exterior and interior was the Father's idea and became the pivotal design element for the building. The decision to place it on the east wall rather than behind the altar was deliberate; Father Mac did not want it to distract the worshiper from the priest and the service at the altar. But this, in effect, meant that the entrance, which would usually be in the center of this wall, had to be moved to the side. People enter on the left or right or follow an indirect route through a hallway/foyer past the small Chapel of Our Lady of the Blessed Sacrament, then enter the church proper. Here the baptismal area in front of the window is to the right (or east); the longitudinal, rectangular space of the nave is to the left, ending in the elevated chancel area.

Mayotte undoubtedly knew of architect Pietro Belluschi and Skidmore, Owings & Merrill's design for Trinity Lutheran in Walnut Creek, California, from 1956, where a similarly placed large stained-glass window fills the entire entry wall, and the roof is also gambrel-shaped.[59] However, Belluschi lifted the structure up on a base in order to insert the entrance below the window. The slightly rounded shape of both roofs is distinctive and almost barnlike. The closest parallels are airport terminals, schools, and bowling alleys where large expanses of space are spanned without internal columns for support.

Although the interior of St. Thomas Aquinas is capacious, the scale is not overwhelming. To achieve this, the space above is constricted by angling the poured concrete walls inward as they rise and adding visual interest with rows of rectangular reliefs. Decoration in the nave is otherwise limited to several relief sculptures, vertical faceted glass windows on the lower portion of the walls, and larger ones placed near the altar.

Compared to the off-white and light wood palette in the nave, the large window made of faceted pieces of slab glass embedded in epoxy is a burst of deep reds and blues. The overall theme of this window is the Paschal mystery based on St. Thomas Aquinas's writing about five steps to the existence and knowledge of God.[60] The figure of Christ is a large, powerful presence in the center. In addition to Adam and Eve, the hands of Moses receiving the tablets, and the crib of the Nativity, more contemporary symbols emphasize Christ's presence in the world. These include a scientist, factory worker, parents and children, faces of people of all races, electronic orbits, a rocket, and Sputnik.[61]

At mid-century, in addition to the Protestants,

the Catholic Church also was discussing how to design sacred spaces for the contemporary age. For Catholics, the papal encyclical *Mediator Dei*, issued in 1947, was seminal in that it acknowledged the earlier Protestant reforms that sought to transform onlookers into active participants. In terms of architecture, as we have seen at Edgewood Church, this resulted in designs that brought the priest closer to the congregants and promoted a sense of community.[62] The Second Vatican Council continued these discussions and issued a "Constitution on Sacred Liturgy" in 1964 that gave explicit ways to bring the clergy closer to the laity both through the use of the vernacular rather than Latin in services, and by the physical structure of the church itself. The priest was to face the people to officiate, rather than the altar, and the altar was to be in close proximity to the worshippers rather than closed off from them.

Father MacEachin wrote about the guiding principles behind the design of St. Thomas Aquinas in the dedication brochure referencing Cardinal James Lercaro's "Documents for Sacred Architecture."[63] These include distinct areas for Eucharistic adoration, the administration of the sacraments, and penance—each requiring its own architectural treatment.

> The external design of the building should express the supernatural divine character of the worship that transpires within and at the same time to adapt the edifice in harmony with its surroundings. They tell us that the main portals should be of impressive design to suggest to the faithful the symbolism . . . as representing the gates of heaven. The architecture and the decoration of the Sanctuary should be so designed that the eye will not be distracted but rather drawn to the Altar and to the action of the Eucharistic Sacrifice. . . .
>
> It would be a mistake to arrange and decorate the interior of the church in such way as to create the atmosphere of a comfortable and cozy bourgeois residence; and a mistake to wish to imitate the poverty of a proletarian dwelling.
>
> The church interior should be neither bourgeois nor proletarian. It should bespeak forcibly the grandeur of God which surpasses all earthly measure, so that it may exalt the worshiper above the sphere and atmosphere of his daily private life; and yet, it must still leave one with the friendly feeling of "the goodness and kindness of our Savior." . . . The decorative scheme of the finished house of God should present to the view of the congregation an ensemble of the theme of our holy faith, not in a fragmentary way, but with a certain completeness and in significant proportions and with right placing of accent.

This, in effect, is a summary of the contemporary thinking about what makes a space sacred. When it opened, St. Thomas Aquinas was described as

> Contemporary American—mingling the rich traditions of the past with the *aggiornamento* of today and tomorrow . . . a bold architectural statement of glass, precut stone and masonry. Its contemporary style and sloping roof areas were carefully detailed and executed to blend harmoniously with the other campus buildings and the surrounding neighborhood. . . . To meet the demands of the new liturgy, the seating is arranged in a fan shape surrounding the altar in a column free nave.[64]

The church project cost $1.2 million and included new administration offices and priests' residence, as well as the 65-foot-tall separate bell tower.[65] A member of the congregation wrote to Bishop Zaleski to object to the lavishness and scale of the building, expressing concern that if the nearby communities of Okemos and Haslett were to separate and build their own churches, or if a recession were to hit, the church would be saddled with a large debt. He declared that he would rather see "a more modest building . . . rather than erect a monument, in 1966, to a view of parish life that is anachronistic."[66] The bishop responded diplomatically that there was general approval of the design and "many people eagerly awaiting the plan to be fulfilled."[67] Indeed, the lavishness of the structure is in its scale and the large window rather than in the materials used, which included brick (to a height of ten feet), plaster on lath, and terrazzo for the floors.

▶ **FIGURE 79.** University United Methodist, Earl Confer, East Lansing. Photograph © 2014 Kim Kauffman.

The foregoing case studies of the processes used by several mid-Michigan congregations to explicate their needs reveal their awareness of the current liturgical debates about church design. Mid-Michigan architects did not contribute any new solutions; rather they sought guidance in existing successful design ideas that they could incorporate. The extent to which the architect's design for a religious building makes a gradual transition from the everyday to the spiritual, the way it builds expectation through architectural components that speak to and reinforce ritual and create a sacred atmosphere, determines how successful the structure is.[68] Although the circumstances of each differed, St. Thomas Aquinas, Martin Luther Chapel, Eastminster, and Edgewood United are only a few of the Lansing-area churches that met these expectations.

Many other Lansing-area churches were built at mid-century, and many had modernist features. Among those worth mentioning is the University United Methodist complex at 1120 South Harrison, which Detroit architect Earl Confer (1901–1968) designed.[69] The first unit was the Wesley Center, dedicated in 1961 (figure 79). This one-story, flat-roofed structure with large windows was the education wing and resembles one-story International-style steel-and-glass structures as well as school construction. It culminates in the round Chapel of the Apostles to the north. In 1963, the adjacent sanctuary and bell tower were built (plate 54). A *Lansing State Journal* article on May 7, 1964, enthusiastically opined that "Also contributing majestic beauty to the East Lansing community is the $500,000 of combined modern and Gothic architecture." Confer carefully placed the bells and the cross of the slender, diamond-shaped tower so that the light was most intense on the bells, "but as one lifts his eyes heavenward, the top of the cross fades into the mystery of the night."[70]

Church construction in this area in 1957 totaled nearly $3 million on seventeen projects.[71] In 1958, another seventeen projects were completed. As reported in "Religious Construction Exceeds Million Dollars" in the *Lansing State Journal* on January 1, 1959, new congregations built modest churches, education units, a convent, and schools. Several were described as "contemporary" or "modern" in design, others as "modified contemporary," one as Gothic-type, and another as a "modified Gothic" stone structure. Local firms Manson & Carver, Laitala and Nuechterlein, Mayotte-Webb, Simpson and Hartwick, and Charles Opdyke were each involved in a building. Although twenty-four churches had building projects in 1960, including a Byzantine style (Eastern Orthodox church) and a Colonial style (Second Church of Christ Scientist), Thelma Harnett reported in "Greater Lansing Churches Expanding Again" that the story in 1960 was not about modern design since the largest percentage of these churches were in traditional styles.[72]

A few years later, however, she was finally able to talk about modernism. Her headline in the *Lansing State Journal* on Sunday, May 7, 1964, was "Churches Lean toward Modernism." "Leaning toward" is an apt phrase to describe the area churches' somewhat shy embrace of modernist aesthetics, even though they did frequently utilize modern construction techniques including steel, laminated wood, and cement block. Nevertheless, some of these churches erected between the postwar years and 1970 discussed in this chapter are distinguished, sensitive buildings that used general modernist features, relate well to their surroundings, and responded to the congregation's budgetary and spiritual needs.[73]

While the vast majority of religious buildings in mid-Michigan are Christian, and of those most are for various Protestant denominations, other religious groups began to have a physical presence by the mid-1960s. Of particular note is the Shaarey Zedek synagogue in East Lansing (plate 87). The congregation dates back to 1918 in Lansing and merged in the 1930s with the new Reform Temple Beth El congregation, resulting in a mix of Conservative and Reform traditions. However, it was not until the 1960s that the Jewish population had sufficiently grown to contemplate a permanent structure for their services. The congregation received a donation of ten acres on north Coolidge Road in East Lansing from builder Francis Fine, who was a member and also would be the builder of the synagogue. Fine was erecting residences in the new Pinecrest subdivision, where there were no covenants that prevented Jews from purchasing houses as there were in older areas of East Lansing. It was not until 1968 that the Equal Opportunity Housing Act in East Lansing opened the way for African Americans and Jews to purchase houses in older areas that were previously off-limits to them. Here, in the far northwestern edge of the city, Jews could not only live but also worship in their nearby synagogue.

Smith, Hinchman & Grylls, the august Detroit firm, designed the sprawling 32,000-square-foot brick building at 1924 Coolidge Road. While not known as synagogue designers, it is Michigan's largest and oldest firm. Shaarey Zedek's building consists of the sanctuary and fellowship hall to the north, connected by a glass atrium to the classroom and office wing to the south. The original intent was to put parking in the back and for people to enter the building through the atrium. Instead, however, since parking is on the north, most enter through an inconspicuous side door.

The long, one-story brick façade facing the road is severe and unornamented, except for periodic projecting brick pilasters that break up the flatness of the wall, and the vertical tower of the sanctuary that sweeps upward in a large curve (plate 87). Between the two curved supports is a slanted wall of glass panels that allows light to penetrate to the bimah or rostrum area below where the service is conducted. In addition, clerestory windows admit light into the flat-roofed sanctuary. The untitled bronze sculpture on the outside near the tower, by Israeli artist Aharon Bezalel (1925–2012), was commissioned specifically for the building and is integral to the design. The group of elongated, abstract figures form an arch through which one can walk. They stretch their arms up to support a platform on which is placed a menorah, while Moses's tablets of the law are on the building behind it.[74] These two symbols identify this as a Jewish building.

It is customary for congregants to face east during prayer, towards Jerusalem and the site of the ancient temple, and as a result, most synagogues in the Western Hemisphere have the bimah and ark for the Torah in the east. At Shaarey Zedek, however, they are placed in the west. This reversion of the typical orientation was likely a design decision necessitated by the desire to have a visual focus for the building that could be seen from the road.

Inside, wood is used throughout, including the long benches facing the altar in the wide sanctuary. For High Holy Days, when there is a need to accommodate more people, the temporary wall partition separating the main sanctuary from the fellowship hall is opened, doubling the space for worship. At Shaarey Zedek, Smith, Hinchman & Grylls designed a simple, subdued building that conveys solidity, assertiveness, and integrity.

Among other religious groups to build permanent structures, the Islamic Center, at 920 Harrison Road, East Lansing, designed in the late 1970s by Robert W. Smith of Freeman, Smith & Associates, deserves mention.[75] By that decade, there was a proliferation of religious groups that had not previously been present in the area. Some repurposed older buildings, including commercial spaces, while others erected purpose-built structures. A more extended look at sacred spaces in mid-Michigan would add to this brief review of select mid-century modern buildings and the relation between structure and worship.

PLATE 71. Robert E. and B. Katherine Brown House. Earl Vaive, 1964.

Photograph © 2020 Kim Kauffman.

PLATE 72. Dale and Hope Crites House. Laitala and Nuechterlein, 1964; landscape: Drew and Skidmore.

Photo by Natasha Crljenica.

PLATE 73. Dr. Kent and Donna Hay House. John Crouse, Mayotte-Webb, 1964.
Photograph © 2014 Kim Kauffman.

PLATE 74. Stanley and Monna Lee Hartman House. John Crouse, Mayotte-Webb, 1965.
Photograph © 2014 Kim Kauffman.

PLATE 75. Frank and Martha Couchois House. Gordon Fineout, 1965.

Photograph © 2020 Kim Kauffman.

PLATE 76. John P. and Margaret A. Henderson House. Margaret A. Henderson, designer, 1965. Photograph © 2014 Kim Kauffman.

PLATE 77. Liebermann's. George Nelson, 1966.

Photo courtesy of Michigan State Historic Preservation Office.

PLATE 78. Arby's (Biggby Coffee). Lester H. Weinberg, engineer, 1966; addition 1975.

Photo courtesy of Amanda Seeger.

PLATE 79. Myles and Virginia Delano House. Alexander William Dempsey, 1966; addition above garage, 2007.

PLATE 80. Richard and Sharon Taber House. John Crouse, Mayotte-Webb, 1967.

PLATE 81. Michael and Rhea Dow House. Alden B. Dow, 1967.

PLATE 82. Jens and Nancy Plum House, rear. Robert Hanamura, 1967.

Photograph courtesy of Nancy Plum.

PLATE 83. Harold and Wilma Good House. Alfred Browning Parker, 1967.

Photo courtesy of the Michigan State Historic Preservation Office.

PLATE 84. Edward and Mrs. Pratt House. Couchois and Miller builders, 1967; addition behind garage, 2006.

Photograph © 2020 Kim Kauffman.

PLATE 85. Dr. Carl W. and Mrs. West House. Arai and Hummel Architects, 1967.

PLATE 86. Saint Thomas Aquinas. Mayotte-Webb, 1968; education wing, Laitala and Nuechterlein, 1956. Photo by Natasha Crljenica.

PLATE 87. Shaarey Zedek Synagogue. Smith, Hinchman & Grylls, 1969.

Photo courtesy of the Michigan State Historic Preservation Office.

CHAPTER 11

Life Along the Water

In the Sunday, September 20, 1964, issue of the *Lansing State Journal*, "Picturesque Homes Line Winding River," the women's editor, Virginia Redfern, tells us to "pack up a picnic lunch, find a friend with a pontoon boat and go cruising on Grand River. . . . One might take a book of verse also, for the scenes of beauty along its shores, especially in the stretch between Waverly Hills and Dimondale, inspire poetic moods." Following her suggestion, houses along the water provide the organizing theme for this chapter that explores modernist architecture not only on the Grand River, Michigan's longest river, but also the Red Cedar River, and other bodies of water (man-made or natural) in mid-Michigan. Water front properties were highly desirable, tended to be large and consequently more expensive than other sites, and owners sought unique designs. Several designed by architects for clients have already been noted: for the Hagbergs (plate 34), Abrams (plate 21), Plums (plate 82), Raynors, and Weisingers (plate 41). Local architects found these sites especially appealing for their own residences as well, including the Munson (figure 20) and Rosa (plate 20) houses in Lansing, Clarke Harris's on Herron Creek (plate 29), and the Laitala (figure 28) and Neuchterlein houses on the Red Cedar. But there are more to discover. This chapter also introduces additional mid-Michigan architects and several architectural designers not discussed previously. We will at times venture inland to discover other examples by these architects and related and notable houses.

▶ **FIGURE 80.** Arbaugh House, R. B. Sloan Jr., interior, date unknown, Lansing. Courtesy of Bruce Bower and Christine Altese.

Locust Lane

Redfern's river tour begins along Moores River Drive and passes the Antuck House (plate 65). "Ducking down in the boat" below the Waverly Bridge, we emerge on the south side of the river to see "a beautiful point of land with large houses built on large lots sloping down to the river. This is the Locust Lane section, all built by families who have been friends for many years; the W. S. Nugents, the Horace A. Sarvises, the Richard B. Fosters, the Guy Shumways, and the Richard Stones."[1] She signals out the newest house built by the George H. Arbaughs at the head of the little road.

Locust Lane is a private street with the Grand River on the north and west sides. Originally a rural road, it was an enclave for the Arbaughs, one of Lansing's most distinguished families. The name was associated with the oldest as well as one of the largest department stores in downtown Lansing. The F. N. Arbaugh Company, which went through several name changes, was begun in 1905 by Frank Arbaugh (1872–1955) and his partner Basil Cameron. By 1909, Arbaugh bought out Cameron, and expanded and modernized the store. Arbaugh brought his son George H. (1900–1989) into the business. In 1953, they sold it to Sperry and Hutchinson of New York. They remained in charge for several months until they both resigned that August.[2] George then became president of the VanDerwoort Hardware Company and secretary of Stratton's Sports Car Corporation.[3]

The Locust Lane acreage was purchased by the families of George and his sisters, Frances (Foster) and Ruth (Shumway). The Shumways and the Arbaughs built the two earliest houses (4 Locust Lane in 1929 and 5 Locust Lane in 1930). Two more were built in the 1940s (2 in 1945 and 3 in 1949). The Fosters built 1 Locust Lane in 1957, and in 1956, George built a second house at 6, the subject of this discussion. The most recent house dates to 1988 (4.5). These range from very large houses with multiple stories to smaller single story ranches.

George and Elizabeth Arbaugh's first house originally was 2,900 square feet, but in recent years, additions on either end have doubled its size.[4] The Arbaughs lived here until 1956 when they moved into the ranch right next door designed by R. B. (Bob) Sloan Jr. (ca.1903–1995). [5] He worked as a draftsman for the State Highway Department in 1934 and went on his own by 1948 as an architectural designer. He designed the Arbaugh's 2,600 square feet house with a slightly irregular shape on 1.2 acres (plate 38). On the east side, two unequal projecting wings form a U shape with the entrance at the center. The attached garage on the south end is at an angle to the shorter arm. Facing the river on the back, the southern end is carved back to create a terraced area off the dining room. At the opposite end, the house takes a slight jog to the north.

The land-facing side is treated texturally with a solid massive Tennessee stone wall adjacent to the garage, and small windows on the brick walls. It is closed and private, yet the vertical pane of glass next to the entry door allows a glimpse through the house to the river bank. The horizontality of the lower roof line, echoed by the clerestory windows above that stretch the length on this side, gives way to different angles of the shed roofs on the sides and the back. The back is mainly a mix of large fixed glazing, and windows and doors. One can best appreciate the careful siting of the house from this side, at the point where the land extends out into the river, which flows into a lagoon on the south.[6] The narrower north side has large windows that also face the water.

On the interior, the ceiling of the living and family rooms slope down towards the exterior walls. The formal room was wood paneled, and the fireplace is faced with marble (figure 80). In the adjacent family room, two brick walls meet at an angle, and next to the brick fireplace is a built-in, floor-to-ceiling, wood storage cabinet. While this is a sprawling basement-less ranch, the multiple roof heights and numerous angles, varied wall textures and projections, and extensive glazing provide great visual interest. Moreover, the setting of the house takes full advantage of the natural surroundings and the privacy of being on the water.

Leaving Locust Lane, Redfern points out "two more lovely ranch-style houses overlooking the Grand River on the south side built high on a hill and spaced well apart." These were the houses of close friends in the medical profession. Dr. Jesse F. Harrold, the chief of staff at St. Lawrence Hospital, was a specialist in urology, and his wife was a former dietician. Dr. Frederick W. Tamblyn was an obstetrician and gynecologist and chief of staff of Edward W. Sparrow Hospital, while his wife was a former nurse. In 1958, Redfern wrote that the two families had become "next-door neighbors" on Grand River, just off South Waverly, where they share beautiful views and rolling land abounding with pheasants.[7] She described the Harrolds' house as the "striking modern home they spent all last year building. . . . The house is contemporary in style, reflecting the influence of Frank Lloyd Wright with oriental overtones."[8] While no address is given in the frequent society page mentions of events at the house, it can be identified as 4228 Pinetree Lane, built in 1958, on over two acres of land with the river to the north.[9] It shares many characteristics of houses designed by Manson, Jackson, and Kane, and, indeed, Dr. and Mrs. J. F. Harrold are listed among their clients, although neither a date nor address is provided in Manson's list.[10]

The large one-story broad house has a complex shape resembling a splayed V with a gable roof at the center that intersects the longer cove roofs. The focus on both front and back is the center where the walls project forward. They meet in a wide angle on the back. On the front tall narrow windows are inserted between six vertical masonry jambs that support the peaked gable. The entry is inconspicuous to the right, near the kitchen, which is adjacent to the garage. Windows on this side of the house are small and high up on the walls, sheltered by the eaves. The circular driveway as well as the angled projecting walls with windows were used by Manson in a two-story version at the 1955 Maury House (plate 35 and figure 37).

The Tamblyns' "spacious . . . modern brick home with many picture windows making the most of the ever-changing panorama of nature outside," is likely 4300 Pinetree Lane, the only other older house in this area that is on the river and near the Harrolds'. At over 3,000 square feet on almost two acres, it is a rambling one-story brick house with a large basement.[11]

The Henry E. and Mary Crouse House

On the north side of Grand River, Redfern points out the delightful hidden cove formed by a lagoon west of Waverly Road off Lansing Road. It comes up suddenly, "a mirror-smooth little harbor with many pleasure boats" including one owned by Mr. and Mrs. Henry E. Crouse whose property on Bittersweet Lane borders this part of the river (plate 53).[12] Henry (Heinie) Crouse (1907–2001) was president of the Heatherwood Farms Company and an active volunteer in Lansing civic life, serving as a Jaycee, president of the United Community Chest, on the boards of the Lansing Symphony, Lansing branch of Michigan National Bank, Plymouth Congregational Church, and the YMCA.[13] Mary Crouse was also very engaged with local groups including the Edward W. Sparrow Hospital Guild, Visiting Nurses board, and Junior League. The teas and get-togethers she hosted in her home for various groups were often reported in the society pages of the newspaper.

The Crouses had a deep interest in modern architecture. In 1945, they had commissioned Kenneth Black to design a modern, split-level house at 1045 Rosewood Avenue in East Lansing (discussed in chapter 5). Mary, in particular, was described in the *Lansing State Journal* as sharing her son John's interest in modern architecture.[14] Indeed, he was serving his apprenticeship with Mayotte-Webb in East Lansing when his parents asked him to design the new house at 4400 Bittersweet Lane. In an article in the *Lansing State Journal* on April 2, 1961, when they had just moved in, Mary Crouse tells her friends, "It's a happy house," which she explained refers to the harmonious working relationship between the designer; builder, William J. Clark; and decorator, William Denler of Grosse Pointe.[15]

Unlike Redfern's water view, the typical approach is by land but the only thing apparent from the street is the private drive and a glimpse of the hip roof of the detached garage that seems to hover over the ground. Slowly the house on the other side of the ample drive comes into view; first the two-car garage and then the sheltered entrance and the large overhanging eaves of the hip roof. To the west is the upper-story bedroom wing with alternating panels and windows, the same treatment as on the back of the house.

The gracious, large wood entry doors open into a foyer area with high brick walls (figure 82). The kitchen is to the left; straight ahead are the large dining and family rooms as well as stairs down to the lower level. Stairs to the right lead up to the bedroom wing. There is an abundance of warm, brown-toned woodwork throughout the house, including many built-in storage units with rows of louvered doors and drawers and a very large mahogany buffet that spans one wall of the dining area and wraps around into the hallway. From here, several steps lead down to the living room with a brick fireplace on the narrow wall. Large windows on the opposite side and the windows and glass doors on the longer walls look out towards the patio and the river. Outside, numerous levels and terraces create several seating areas and balconies, and sliding doors provide further access to the yard and the panoramic view (figure 81). Some of the custom features mentioned

► **FIGURE 81.** Crouse House, John E. Crouse, river side, Lansing. Photograph © 2020 Kim Kauffman.

in the article include the mitered corners wherever either glass or wood is used, the beamed cathedral ceilings in the living and dining rooms, indirect lighting just below the ceiling's lower edges, and clerestory windows above the shelves in the living room. An enclosed porch on the east side of the house is down several steps and faces a little channel "where the Crouses will build a dock for their boat."[16]

The bedroom wing upstairs is "complete with two bedrooms, dressing rooms and baths as well as balconies overlooking the river." The level below "includes a spacious and practical 'second' living room with picture windows . . . overlooking the river." Son Barney's quarters (living room, dressing room, and bath) open off this level and are used only when he is on vacation from Cranbrook. It is clear that, in this expansive house, design, aesthetics, and attention to details were the foremost considerations over budget.

This is undoubtedly John E. Crouse's earliest house design from the very beginning of his illustrious career. After graduating from University of Michigan in 1959, he joined Mayotte-Webb in 1960. In 1962, he designed his own house in East Lansing also using level changes to vary the floorplan (plate 61). Throughout the 1960s, he designed large houses in Okemos on White Oaks Drive and Wrightwind Drive (plates 73, 74, 80). Additionally, he is very likely the designer of his brother Edward and his sister-in-law Patricia's large country

◄ **FIGURE 82.** Crouse House, John E. Crouse, interior, Lansing. Photograph © 2020 Kim Kauffman.

house at 4920 Country Drive, in a rural part of Okemos, built in 1967.[17] In 1970, he again designed a house for his parents, this time in Sotogrande, Spain, on the Costa del Sol.[18]

Mr. and Mrs. Robert J. Schultz, owners of the Bittersweet Lane house in the 1970s, commissioned local architect Malcolm M. Williams to design a bedroom addition in November 1977. Had it been executed, it would have added one bedroom on the first level and a second above it on the front of the house.[19]

After the Crouses' house, Redfern mentions "one of the newest and most elegant" houses on nearby Thornapple Lane, a short northeast–southwest street parallel to the river. Mr. and Mrs. Earle R. Wilson's red brick and white frame rectangular house at 4733, built in 1963, is "on contemporary lines" with views of the river from the living and family rooms and the sun deck. Mrs. Wilson designed the house herself rather than working with an architect and claimed that of the three houses she designed, it is her masterpiece."[20]

The adjacent house at 4741 Thornapple Lane is decidedly more modern and was under construction at the time of the boat ride. It was likely built for Dr. P. J. Oschner and his family.[21] The designer has not yet been identified but his/her interest in Frank Lloyd Wright's architecture is apparent. The flat roof and angled storage at the end of the carport and the clerestory windows on the front side are evidence. At 2,000 square feet, the house is one story and low to the ground on the front with decks on the back to enjoy the river.

River Forest and West

If Redfern's pontoon boat could have traversed obstacles and roads, her journey would have continued north and west to the River Forest area where several architect-designed houses had been built, although not on the river, for example, Bruce M. Hartwick's house, 2233 Cumberland Road, 1949 (figure 21), and Elmer Manson's at 2005 Cumberland, 1951 (figure 22). Tecumseh River Drive is to the south of Cumberland and winds through the neighborhood, paralleling the Grand River to its south. It dips down from the high point at Paul and Rosamunde Hammond's 1947 house (plate 10) to the low point opposite the park. As the drive continues west, the terrain levels out. In the first half of the 1950s, large lots were purchased in this section and custom-designed houses were going up. At 3517, architect Richard (Dick) G. Snyder (1913–2012) built his family's two-bedroom, two-bath ranch in 1953 on 0.6 acres of land that slopes down to the river at the back of the property.[22] Snyder started out at Warren Holmes Company as a draftsman and field supervisor from 1935–1941, received his undergraduate degree in architecture at the University of Michigan in 1943 and became a registered architect the following year. He served in the U.S. Army's antiaircraft artillery battery in 1941–1946 and returned to Warren Holmes as an architect in 1950.[23]

On the adjacent lot at 3505, Snyder's coworker Gordon H. Stow (1913–2007), designed his own house (plate 37). Stow was also educated at the University of Michigan. Except for four years in the U.S. Army (1942–1947), his professional career was spent at Warren Holmes starting in 1937, eventually becoming president of the company by 1970.[24] He was very active in the Lansing community and held numerous elected positions in the YMCA as well as president of the international YMCA. Mrs. Stow was equally busy in the local chapter of the American Association of University Women, and she assisted libraries and church groups. Many of her parties at their new house were mentioned in the newspaper.[25]

The Stows moved into their 2,400-square-foot brick ranch in January 1955. It is basically a rectangle with a main level and a walk-out basement. One distinguishing feature is the series of pierced roof openings to admit light into the kitchen. To the left of the entry is an office area that thrusts forward about twelve feet from the rest of the house. The bedroom wing extends past the office, with the master bedroom facing the river. From the brick wall of the entrance hallway, there are two steps down to the living room with a wall of windows facing the back. The windows continue in the dining area, which is up two steps and separated from the living room by a low unit of shelves and drawers. The abundance of brick continues in the stairway to the basement, which also has brick walls and large windows. In style, it is close to the slightly earlier Hartwick ranch. These ranches, as well as the Arbaughs', fit the Midwest style that derives, in part, from Wright's Prairie houses. The use of brick, hipped roofs, wide eaves, clustered windows, and broad rectangular shapes are typical but offer a vocabulary with infinite possible variations depending upon the client's needs and the site.[26]

Eastern Suburbs

Backtracking along Grand River, one can follow the river trail by foot, bike, canoe, or kayak through the heart of Lansing. Just south of the downtown, it meets the Red Cedar River, a tributary that originates about fifty miles to the east. Here architects Orlie Munson (figure 20) and Clarence Rosa (plate 20) built their own residences facing the river. The Red Cedar continues through the middle of the Michigan State University campus and on to the nearby eastern suburbs. Okemos, in particular, was developing quickly in the 1950s and

1960s, and lots on the water attracted many affluent owners who worked with local architects or designers in Herron Acres, Indian Hills, Indian Lakes Estates, and Tacoma Hills, among other new developments.

Herron Creek and Frank Lloyd Wright

Herron Creek is a tributary of the Red Cedar River that runs primarily north and south near the eastern edge of East Lansing. Seventeen of forty acres southeast of the creek and north of Mount Hope Road were to be the site of Wright's Usonian community (see chapter 1). In 1939, Wright advised on organizing the triangular land in the center enclosed by the U-shaped Hawthorne Lane (also spelled Hawthorn). By the early 1950s, a second road, Herron Road, paralleled the creek on the west, heading north from Mount Hope and then northeast. As a result, the creek formed the far boundary for houses on the east side of Herron Road and the west and north sides of Hawthorne.

After Wright's project failed by 1939, it took about ten years before the area fully developed. In the first half of the 1950s, residences were erected in a variety of styles and sizes from smaller 1,440-square-foot houses to double that. Lot sizes also ranged from less than half an acre to almost two, depending upon the topography. One of the worries that led Alma Goetsch and Kathrine Winckler to build their Wright house elsewhere fully emerged at this time. The landowners complained about refuse dumped on A. M. Johnson's adjacent farm to the east. "'Piggery' Thumped by Landowners," from the *Lansing State Journal*, March 10, 1951, is the caption of a picture showing an East Lansing Public Works truck dumping garbage near Robert Snyder's house on Hawthorne Lane. A second picture is of a group of pigs devouring the refuse on Johnson's farm, which had operated the piggery since 1935. In the accompanying article by Carlisle Carver, "Landowners Declare War on Meridian Pig Farm," the property owners complained about the rats, flies, and stench from the dumped garbage. The Dennys had just moved into their new house that past September, apparently unaware of the piggery. The Snyders were aware of it, but the hogs typically had been fed at the back of the property and the refuse was plowed under. A change in management was the issue as was the condition of the unpaved roads in the spring, which made it necessary to dump the refuse close to the Hawthorne houses.[27]

Among the earliest and most modern styled houses on Hawthorne are 2472 and 4565. The former was built in 1950 for MSU psychology professor Al Rabin and his wife Beatrice. Their two-acre lot (that was originally part of Goetsch and Winckler's land) is narrow and extends deep towards the north. Their small one-story house has since been expanded, and the carport has been enclosed.

The property at 4565 Hawthorne is now on an unusually shaped 1.9 acre lot with only forty feet on the road, but it widens to about two hundred feet into the property. The one-story, wood-sided, flat-roofed house is set far back from the road and closer to the creek at the north. The year 1939 is given for this house in the Meridien Township assessing records, signaling the year a building permit was filed, although the house appears to have been built later. Piecing together the story provides one explanation for the discrepancy.

The first owners of this lot were Sidney H. and Althea Newman, members of the original Usonian group for which he was the spokesperson. His correspondence preserved in the Wright Archives relates to the project in general as well as his own house. Polite, but frustrated, Newman asked several times for ceilings higher than six feet, six inches since he was six feet tall himself, and for more insulation, among other items. Harold Turner, Wright's master builder in Michigan between 1938 and 1943, became involved with the group in summer 1939.[28] The unanticipated problems in obtaining financing and the escalating costs of each house that led to the project's demise by spring 1940 are recounted elsewhere.[29] With Turner's help, however, Newman continued to tweak his Wright design in order to keep to his allotted budget, but when Wright heard about this, he became furious. In a letter to Newman, he demanded, "Return my plans. . . . Then ask Turner to make you a plan he will personally guarantee to build for you under contract without extras for $6,000. If he is such a good builder, he might not be a bad architect?"[30] Following up with a terse telegram dated April 18, 1940, Wright wrote that Turner had wired him "informing me whether I like it or not he is going ahead to build your house. I must warn you that you cannot use my plans that way. If necessary an injunction will stop such piracy."[31] Newman responded with a long conciliatory letter on May 24 explaining that on his salary and without financing, he could not spend more than $3,000 on his house but neither could he afford to pay rent and he had to build, even if only a one bedroom. "I realize I can't expect much, but then, I can't afford much."[32] Although in June Turner began work on the Goetsch-Winckler House, he may have helped Newman build a small house on his property. Newman spent the war years in government service in Washington, DC, and Connecticut, and left the university for good in 1946.[33]

Maurice (Ray) Denny (1918–2001) and his wife became the owners of the house from at least 1950 until 2001.[34] He taught psychology at MSU from 1945 until his retirement and was a colleague of Newman as well as Rabin. The question remains how to interpret Carver's statement in 1951 that the Dennys had moved into "their new house" the previous September. Was it new to them, or were they the ones who significantly changed the 1939 design? According to architectural historian Anatole Senkevitch Jr., the house was "remodeled several times, thus making it difficult to assess either the character of Turner's work or its indebtedness to Wright's original design."[35]

In the early 1950s, several of the original Herron Acres lots were subdivided, creating new sites for additional homes, and this was probably when the odd shape of Denny's lot took form. Local contractors Claude Hinman and his son Robert designed several houses on Hawthorne. Robert's own 1951 house is at 4527, a 2,099-square-foot modern house. He also designed 4512 (1955) and 2782 (1956) although neither is modernist in style.[36]

Indian Hills

About a mile to the east, the Indian Hills subdivision is bordered on the west by Herron Creek, and on the north and east, by the Red Cedar River. Wright's Brauner (plate 14) and Edwards (plate 16) houses and architect Clarke Harris's house (plate 29) are on the creek. The two Hagberg houses (plates 2 and 34), while not in the subdivision, are on the north side of the Red Cedar. With long curving roads paralleling the water, there was ample opportunity in this area for lots with frontage on water.

Indian Hills is one of the older developments in Okemos. It was started by the Ehinger Realty Company in the late 1920s on the old Evert family farm, but it bloomed after World War II.[37] By 1950, there were thirty-six new housing starts with another twenty-one in 1951.[38] Parts of Huron Hill Drive and Nakoma Drive intersect twice, and curve as they follow the river, which makes a large looping run north and south. Houses on the east side of both roads are on large lots with the river at the back. Several of these were built on speculation, such as the 1955 split-level at 4720. However, others were custom designed for clients.

One example is 4702 Huron Hill, built for dentist Dr. Richard E. and Joyce Bailey in 1960 on two and a half acres and barely visible from the street.[39] It was designed by George Williams of Haughey, Black, and Williams, a Battle Creek firm, with landscaping by Jack Drew.[40] The most striking feature is the large square living room at the center of the house. The peaks of four hip roofs intersect in the middle to create a dynamic star-like pattern with ridges and valleys that rise and fall around the room. Each gable end is glazed. A huge stone fireplace is on one wall; another is wood paneled but stops below the gable. At the back of the house, large sliding glass doors lead to a balcony above the expansive yard. The light, openness, and large scale of this room contrasts with lower ceilings, smaller windows, and wood-planked walls and ceilings in the rest of the house that create more intimate and warm spaces, clearly delineating the public and private portions of the house.

Indian Lakes Estates, Comanche Drive

Lakes, man-made or made by damming rivers and streams, also provided many possibilities for proximity to water. Indian Lakes Estates, to the west of Indian Hills and east of Herron Acres, began in the 1960s. In the first phase in 1964, houses were built around the lake in the center formed by damming the Herron Creek.[41] In this upscale area, there are large brick ranches amid more traditional Colonial designs.[42] In 1966 and 1967, most of the houses on Comanche Drive were under construction; four designed by architects at the north end demonstrate the variety in contemporary plans.

Houses bordering the lake typically appear to be one story on the street side but rise a full story above it on the other where long decks take advantage of the water views. The house at 4595 Comanche is a sprawling Wrightian U-shaped brick and redwood house on two lots totaling over 0.8 acres. It was built in 1965 for James S. and Frances Schultz, of Schultz, Snyder, and Steele Lumber, a wholesale lumber company with locations in mid and northern Michigan.[43] The architect was Harold Jack Begrow (1930–2019), a University of Michigan–trained architect who started his career at various Detroit-area firms including working for Minoru Yamasaki. In 1957, he joined with Jack W. Brown to form Begrow+Brown. He designed the Comanche house after moving north in 1962 to Charlevoix where his own firm designed the Shanty Creek Lodge in Bellaire as well as houses and condos.[44]

The 1966 brick ranch at 4569, three houses to the south, was designed by local architect Howard DeWolf. This 2,770-square-foot U-shaped house has five bedrooms, a full basement with a recreation room and bomb shelter, and access to the sandy beach. The landscape was by Jane L. Smith, a well-known and respected local landscape architect.[45] She and her husband Edwin E. formed Smith Tree Service in Lansing in 1948 and had clients throughout the area. She returned to school and earned her landscape degree at Michigan State University in 1957 and became one of very few landscape architects in mid-Michigan. She was active in the profession, serving as president of the Michigan Association of Landscape Architects in 1959, among other roles.[46]

These two are among many one-story ranches along this body of water. The gable roof, asymmetric façades, open plans, and multifunctional rooms could be combined in endless ways. Sturdy and low to the ground, at least on the front side, these houses are modern in their use of new construction techniques, but traditional in the use of brick and wood. They project family stability, comfort, and the good life attained in mid-twentieth-century America. Recognizable and familiar, it is clear why this style was widely accepted. By contrast, two nearby houses on Comanche show very different approaches.

On the other side of the street, on a little less than a half-acre V-shaped lot with the point in the south, 4600 Comanche Drive was designed for Myles (1921–2011) and Virginia (Jinnie) Delano in 1966 (plate 79). He was a professor of accounting and financial administration at MSU; she is an artist. The multilevel house appears to have two stories facing the road and sits high above a dramatic drop at the back to a swale and the flood plain of the Red Cedar River. The lowest level, accessed from the front of the house down a flight of stairs with an awning above the door, has a studio, kitchen, family and double-height dining rooms. On the next level, even with the street on the front, one enters into the foyer and a large living room on the south. Stairs beyond the entry lead to the four bedrooms above. The first of these, labeled "study/bedroom" on the plan, is open to the living room below and the dining area on the lowest level (figure 83). Originally, there was a carport for two cars

▶ **FIGURE 83.** Delano House, Alexander William Dempsey, interior, Okemos. Photograph © 2020 Kim Kauffman.

but a 2006–2007 addition enclosed the garage and added another bedroom, small kitchen, and bathroom above. On the back of the house, there were patios (now decks) overlooking the steep slope down to the swale. The house has extensive redwood outside (now stained) and inside, on the high walls and ceilings, plus the many built-ins.

Many details and desires were specified by Virginia in lists she made for the designer Alexander William Dempsey (1929–1989). In a seven-page, typed document, she explained that the orientation of the house was of major importance.

> We definitely do want the house to have one major wall area facing South to allow maximum sunlight into the house in winter, while keeping it out in summer. This means that there must be sufficient overhang on first and second story roofs to protect from summer sun. . . . The view windows need to face North East to look directly back into our own lot and North into the swamp. The North East would seem most desirable for large window area, in that winter storms seem to come from the North West. . . . Myles does not care for my idea of the major area for outdoor living being on the South side of the house. I will still use this for sitting in the sun, shielded behind a fence or plantings. Some kind of screened porch or patio in another area would be used a great deal, especially for eating.[47]

◄ **FIGURE 84.** Delano House, Alexander William Dempsey, exterior, south and southwest sides, Okemos. Photograph © 2020 Kim Kauffman.

An early pencil sketch shows the original east–west orientation of the house with a detached carport in the north.[48] When built, the house was oriented northwest to southeast to parallel the road. As requested, there is a large wall of windows facing northeast with the patios on this side rather than on the south (figure 84). "When it comes to landscaping I love big rocks. Are they expensive in this area?"[49] Large rocks were eventually added to create a privacy mound in front of the living room floor-to-ceiling windows.

Virginia's list is evidence of concern for aesthetics, costs, and logical details. "I do want doors—to the living room, dining room, kitchen, etc. Most desirable to slide back into the wall, perhaps to fold back unobtrusively to the wall. Not full width doors that intrude when they are gone. . . . Recognizing the difference in cost—if it can be worked into our budget, I would prefer a garage to a car port." To that end she wrote that their "cars are never new, fancy or washed, so I would like them out of sight." For bedrooms, "We like the slant roof bedroom, closet and storage arrangement of this house." An artist, she specified that "the studio needs cupboard and closet. . . . The dining room will probably be the most refined room in the house." After further tweaks to the plan, Dempsey drew up the bidders instructions, on April 1, 1966.[50]

Dempsey worked in Lansing as a designer, which is how he signed the blueprints for this house. In 1973, he became a member of the American Institute of Architects.[51] In 1965, he provided the design of a U-shape ranch called "The Horizon" for Tom Plumhoff Builders in west Lansing.[52] This and the Delano House are the earliest of his designs to be identified so far. Others date from the 1970s including the Myron Beal House at 4650 Sequoia Trail, 1975, in the same subdivision.

Arai and Hummel Architects

The house for Sparrow Hospital radiologist Dr. Carl W. and Mrs. West at 4609, between the Delanos' and Schultzes', completes the northern terminus of Comanche (plate 85). Like the Schultzes', the Wests picked an "up north" architect known for designing houses on the water. This large four-bedroom house was designed in 1967 by Arai and Hummel Architects, based in Suttons Bay.[53]

The house sits on 1.19 acres of land that extend north to woods and end near the dam that forms the lake. The Herron Creek channel runs north to south on the east. The house itself is angled to the west off the north axis. The entrance on the south side is inconspicuous from the road (figure 85). It is past the garage and connecting utility room on the west and a planter on the other side, then down several steps

▶ **FIGURE 85.** West House, Arai and Hummel Architects, entrance; Jack A. Drew Associates, landscape, Okemos.
Photograph © 2020 Kim Kauffman.

to the entrance court and front door. The detailed landscape plan from the road to the entry was by Jack A. Drew Associates.[54] The house is L shaped with bedroom wings of the main and upper floors to the west and the living, dining, and kitchen spaces angled to the east.

Once inside, the space is dramatic, rising two stories in height to the gabled ceiling. From the southeast corner of the living room, the view encompasses the upper bedroom and study balcony, the kitchen and formal dining area on the same level, and the water beyond (figure 86). High ceilings and multiple views from one space into the next activate the interior. This is a complex arrangement based on careful geometry and the use of a module, which the architects often employed. The large volume of the living room space is made more intimate by an open wood grid above. Hefty square posts with visible joints and hardware support crossbeams that extend from the kitchen across the living room, continuing the height of the kitchen ceiling and functioning to lower the perceived height of the living room.[55] A balcony ledge that rests on the beams is counterbalanced on the opposite wall by the ledge above the fireplace. Verticals and horizontals entice views beyond but also interrupt and fracture the vistas complicating the visual movement through, around, and above the room. Many of the wood walls stop below the ceiling, and walls

◀ **FIGURE 86.** West House, Arai and Hummel Architects, interior, Okemos. Photograph © 2020 Kim Kauffman.

move in and out of adjacent spaces. By these means, the space is energized, creating endlessly interesting vistas and angles. Likewise, on the exterior, the numerous and different sized gables and multitude of staggered walls reflect this activation and compound the visual interest.

The bedroom wing is to the left of the entry up a flight of stairs that lacks a banister. This master bedroom suite is half the length of the lower bedroom wing and has a very large dressing area at a right angle. From there, the low walls of the long balcony study open it to the space below as does the large cutout in the bedroom's interior wall. Numerous windows of varying size throughout the house provide glimpses or full views of the lake.

The lowest level of the house is unexcavated below the living and dining room due to the sloping site, but it is full height below the bedroom and family room. The plans called for separate storage, game, and recreation rooms, two bathrooms and a space designated as "shelter," although by the late 1960s fallout shelters per se had disappeared.[56]

Asian American architect Glenn Tsutomi Arai (1925–1998) received a BA in architecture from University of Illinois in 1947 and practiced in Chicago from 1950–1955, before settling in northern Michigan.[57] With Roger A. Hummel, a University of Michigan graduate, he opened Arai and Hummel Architects in

▶ **FIGURE 87.** Sheathelm House, Arai and Hummel Architects, Okemos. Photograph © 2020 Kim Kauffman.

1965, based in Suttons Bay, Michigan.[58] The majority of their work was in the Leelanau Peninsula and Traverse City areas in northern Michigan. The Wests' house with its sculptural treatment of space has many characteristics for which the firm was known, including a preference for natural materials such as stone and wood, lots of angles, multiple levels, complex spatial arrangements, and "teasing views" from one space into another.[59] In 1976, they received a patent for their "modular building construction" that used preformed box units to create a building. Although it was not used here, one can detect the way the architects thought modularly in putting together the different parts to form the whole.[60] The use of large timber pieces with visible bracing and the fragmented vistas may also reflect the influence of Japanese art and architecture on Arai's style.

Wind-N-Wood

Arai and Hummel Architects provided only one other mid-Michigan design. This was in 1975 for Mr. and Mrs. Robert Sheathelm at 125 Wind-N-Wood Drive in the Wind-N-Wood Estates in Okemos (figure 87).[61] Mr. Sheathelm worked for the Schultz, Snyder, and Steele Lumber Company, a mid and northern Michigan wholesaler.[62] Although smaller than the house on Comanche, it is still a substantial, sprawling structure of over 2,000 square feet. Its site is two acres, bordering the man-made lake in the center of the development. When it was featured in the Kresge Art Gallery annual Home Tour in October 1977, Mrs. Sheathelm said that the rooms in the house "'cannot be counted . . . as I did not want to be stuck in the kitchen while the family watched a football game.' So the architects did away with the conventional living room, combining a family room, dining room, kitchen, and solarium into one big open area."[63] For Mrs. Sheathelm, a ceramist, the solarium was outfitted with a sink as well as enough electrical plugs to power her kiln. The plans also designate a "sewing" area in front of the windows on the south, which are at ground level. The house has several levels: there are a few steps down from the kitchen to the solarium, and, at a right angle, several steps up from the solarium to the intersecting bedroom wing. The half-wall of the master bedroom opens it to the solarium below and views of the water beyond. Additionally, there is a large guest or sitting area in the loft above the family room, reached by a spiral staircase. As in the house on Comanche, interior walls are lined with cedar with occasional accents of rough, white plaster. Similarly on the exterior, the complex plan is evident in the numerous roof heights as well as many projecting and recessed walls. Two thick white plaster walls jut out to create a forecourt at the entry and to add privacy. This type of wall was also used at the Wests' house and in other Arai and Hummel Architects designs.[64]

Tacoma Hills

The Red Cedar River continues southeast from Indian Hills to become the western and southern boundaries of the Tacoma Hills subdivision that was started in 1956. Eighty lots were sold quickly by Ehinger Realty developers, and thirty-one houses were built, mainly on speculation. In the next phase, many lots were sold to individuals who chose their own designs. The most desirable locations were along the spring-fed lagoon in the west that the developers had created as well as on the banks of the river.[65]

In 1959, Maynard Simmons, the plant manager at Standard Block and Supply Company, worked with designer Gordon Fineout to build his own house at 4359 Wausau Road using various cement products made by the company (plate 51).[66] Standard Block frequently partnered with local builders to erect model homes that were opened during the annual Parade of Homes in order to get the word out about new approaches to construction. The *Lansing State Journal* would be full of stories about and ads placed by a variety of home building businesses. For example, the 1957 home show featured Standard Block's "House of 101 Ideas," built at Hagadorn Road just north of Grand River Avenue, east of East Lansing. After Design HW-60 appeared in the newspaper on December 9, 1956, Standard Block obtained the blueprints and built the Hagadorn version "with maximum use of materials made or sold by Standard. For example, exterior walls are finished with Manor Haven masonry units . . . manufactured at the Aurelius Road plant," and the glazed blocks, patio tiles, the fireplace surround, and kitchen and two exterior walls of exposed concrete block were in a "new eight inches square."[67]

Upon completion, Simmons's cement house in Tacoma Hills was open for one day. The quarter-page advertisement in the *Lansing State Journal* on October 4, 1959, invited people to "See Today's concrete materials used in this contemporary home." The goal was to have people "learn more about the advantages and versatility of concrete materials. . . . See how the combination of beautiful concrete masonry and rich, natural wood blends a flair for the traditional with the practicality of modern."

Perhaps Simmons was also motivated by the example of the American Concrete Institute that had commissioned Yamasaki to design their international headquarters building in Detroit, showcasing the capabilities of concrete and meant to be a "demonstration model and teaching tool."[68]

Begun in 1955, it was completed in 1958 and garnered international publicity. The elaborate building has a folded plate roof, screens of concrete pipe sections, precast concrete panels, and poured in place concrete walls.[69]

Simmons engaged designer Fineout (1922–2010) who was gaining a reputation in Lansing for his "California"-style houses. After studying industrial design at the Chouinard Art Institute in Los Angeles on the GI Bill following World War II, he returned to Lansing and established Gordon D. Fineout Associates in 1953. He became known for his "L for Living" residential design developed in the 1950s that included a full basement, carport covered by extending the main roof line, and large windows.[70] His and his wife Angela's own house at 2512 Delta River Drive, built in 1958, is almost 2,000 square feet on a long narrow lot slightly less than a half acre (plate 47). The one-story, almost square, design is built on a slab; the L shape of the residence wraps around the carport (now enclosed) on the side and back. With a flat roof and entrance portico held up by thin supports, the emphasis is on horizontality. Additionally, the wall of windows on the front reflects his interest in the California case-study houses as well as Wright's architecture.

▶ **FIGURE 88.** Simmons House, Gordon Fineout, interior, Okemos. Photograph © 2020 Kim Kauffman.

Fineout's admiration for Wright is also evident in Simmons's house on Wausau, especially in the way it fits naturally into the setting and melds together inside and outside space (plate 51). Several rooms have clerestory windows, and the deep orange-red color used for the wood trim is reminiscent of Wright's Cherokee red. This low-slung house is on a wooded lot, oriented northwest to southeast to parallel the Red Cedar River. It sits low on the ground on the front, and above the riverbank at the back. From the separate carport for two cars, an open walkway connects to the entrance and continues past it. The walkway's flat cover is held up by narrow wood posts. The house is screened from the road by a wall of perforated architectural concrete blocks that stops near the door and then resumes on the other side past the house itself. This allows only a glimpse of the low peak of the house as it nestles on the site. The lacy screen wall as well as the carport wall partially enclose the concrete patio (poured using ready-mix concrete from Standard) that opens off the living and dining area.[71]

Inside, the rectangular plan is divided by a cement wall placed lengthwise with communal living spaces on one side and the slightly longer bedroom wing on the other. The living room is separated from the kitchen by a wall that stops short of the ceiling (figure 88). The horizontal shelf at its top contains indirect lighting on both sides that make it appear to float above the space. Original cabinets line both sides of the kitchen. Their sliding glass doors were specifically requested by Betty Simmons to "avoid bumping heads, a hazard

▶ **FIGURE 89.** Brown House, Earl Vaive, first-floor plan, Okemos. Courtesy of Sarah and Andrew Finley.

with conventional cupboard doors."[72] They hang on patterned cement "shadow" blocks, showcasing another of Standard Block's new and varied products. In this case, a repeated hourglass pattern projects slightly from the block. Opposite it, the angled brick wall continues into the dining/family area facing the river, where the two-way fireplace also opens in the living room. On the other side of the kitchen is the bedroom hallway lined with closets. Between two of the bedrooms is a storage room about half the size of a small bedroom that Betty Simmons found particularly convenient given the lack of a basement.

Outer walls have an equal amount of cement block and floor-to-ceiling windows.[73] The latter are in the living and dining areas and the master bedroom at the back of the house. These provide views of the riverbank beyond. The roof is flat over the bedroom wing but peaked over the living and kitchen areas. Large muscular redwood beams encase steel beams that support the steel decking of the roof. These beams slide beyond the glass to the outside of the house to hold up the deep eaves on the back, and create a dynamic play of interior and exterior.[74] The Simmons liked the architectural patterns and shadow effects created by the cement blocks. Indeed, the combination of wood, large windows, strong beams, warm bricks, and the angles of the ceiling create an intimate, cozy, and human-scaled residence at one with the natural surroundings notwithstanding the modern construction materials.[75]

Up the hill and just beyond the Tacoma Hills lagoon, MSU history professor Robert E. Brown and his wife B. (Bessie) Katherine Brown, also a historian, built a house designed in 1964 by local architect Earl Vaive, who had earlier designed 4351 Wausau Road, next to the Simmonses' house (plate 41). Approaching the Browns' house from the northwest, it appears to be one story, nestled into the top of the hill with the lagoon in the distance. As the land descends, the house reveals itself as two stories, the upper one rising above a full-story basement level. Farther into the property, terraces make use of the slope of the lot leading down to the riverbank (plate 71).

Brown (1907–2001), a well-known scholar of colonial history, began his teaching career as an assistant professor at Michigan State in the history department in 1947. In 1951, he was promoted to associate professor and in 1956 to professor.[76] In anticipation of his retirement in 1977, the house was put on the market. Real estate ads pointed to "the panoramic view from the hillside wooded lot" and "an original expression of contemporary design and landscaping to capture fantastic views of the Lagoon and Red Cedar."[77]

The house has a complicated shape of two abutting rectangles with projecting walls, placed off

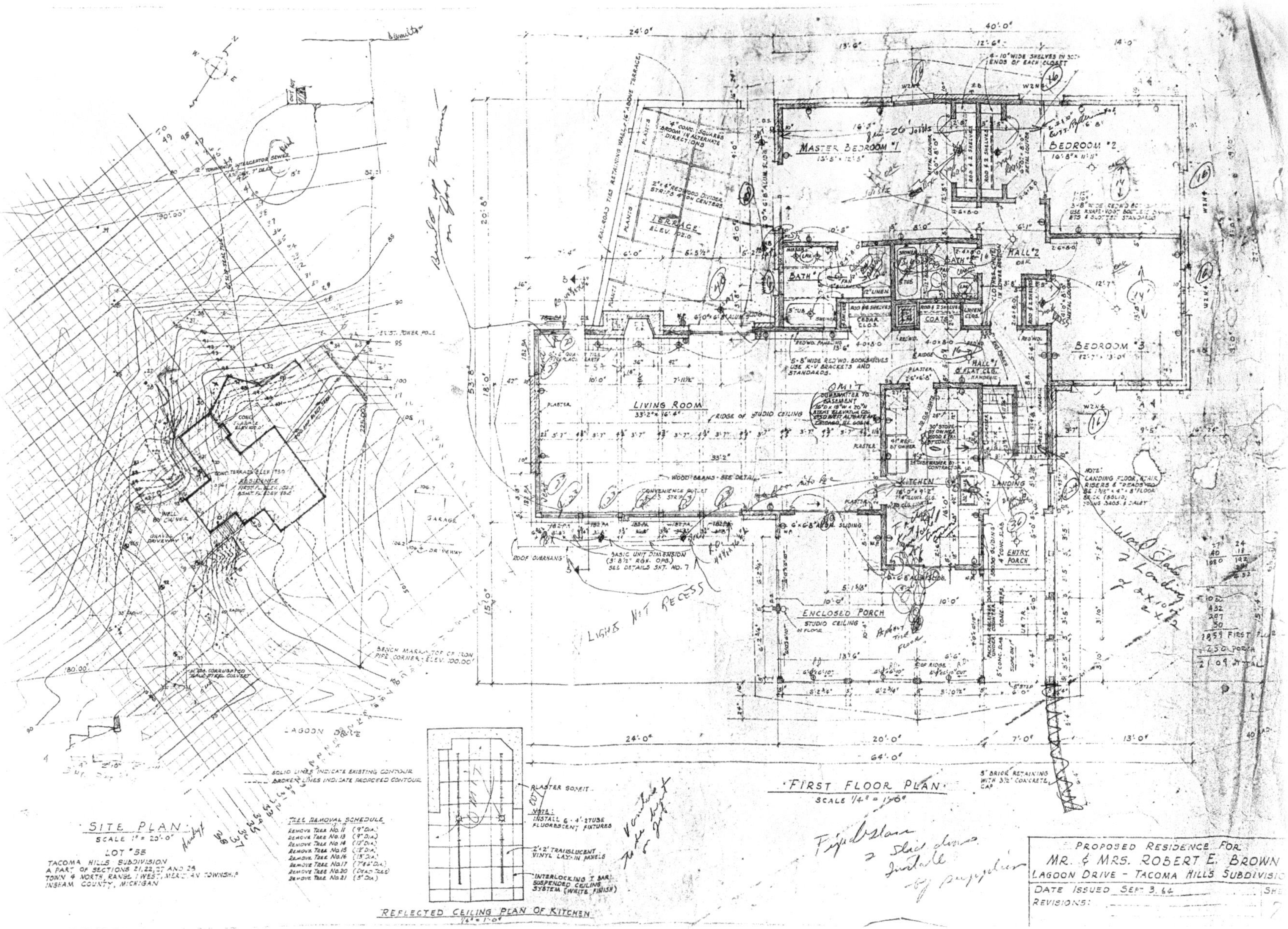

SITE PLAN
SCALE 1" = 20'-0"
LOT "58"
TACOMA HILLS SUBDIVISION
A PART OF SECTIONS 21, 22, 27 AND 28
INGHAM COUNTY, MICHIGAN
TREE REMOVAL SCHEDULE
LAGOON DRIVE
SOLID LINES INDICATE EXISTING CONTOUR
BROKEN LINES INDICATE PROPOSED CONTOUR
MASTER BEDROOM #1
BEDROOM #2
BEDROOM #3
TERRACE
BATH #1
BATH #2
HALL #1
HALL #2
LIVING ROOM
KITCHEN
LANDING
ENTRY PORCH
ENCLOSED PORCH
OMIT
FIRST FLOOR PLAN
SCALE 1/4" = 1'-0"
REFLECTED CEILING PLAN OF KITCHEN
PLASTER SOFFIT
INSTALL 6 - 4' - 2 TUBE FLUORESCENT FIXTURES
2'x2' TRANSLUCENT VINYL LAY-IN PANELS
INTERLOCKING T BAR SUSPENDED CEILING SYSTEM (WHITE FINISH)
24'-0"
40'-0"
20'-0"
7'-0"
13'-0"
64'-0"
PROPOSED RESIDENCE FOR
MR. & MRS. ROBERT E. BROWN
LAGOON DRIVE - TACOMA HILLS SUBDIVISI
DATE ISSUED SEPT 3, 64
REVISIONS:

the north–south axis at the highest point of the lot. Brick and redwood were used extensively on the exterior and interior (figure 89). The front door is up a flight of stairs the landing of the covered entry porch (figure 90).[78] Once inside, the bedroom wing is along a hallway on the northeast side of the house, at ground level. The kitchen and large living room are to the west, above the above-grade basement. The spacious living room has a cathedral ceiling with redwood beams and a wall of floor-to-ceiling windows on the southwest. The opposite wall has a large brick fireplace and doors that open onto the upper terrace, which is also accessed from the master bedroom. The porch on the southwest side of the house (above the garage) had a mix of fixed screens and glass units and was accessible through sliding doors from the living room and kitchen. It is now fully enclosed and more integrated into the rest of the house. The basement level on this side of the house has the same window and wall treatment as the living room area above. In addition to utility rooms, the basement design indicated a guest room or recreation room with a hearth and a fruit room.

In April 1975, floods engulfed many areas of mid-Michigan and the Browns' neighbors, who lived close to the lagoon but at lower ground, were driven from their homes as the road became "a four-acre lake . . . replete with canoes and ducks."[79] On higher ground, the

Browns' house was safe from the waters and became a haven for stranded neighbors. Indeed, approaching it from the south, it seems to be a beacon, rising up from the land on this side and sheltering on it from the other.

Couchois and Miller and Donald Scholz

Business partners Francis Alfred (Frank) Couchois and Lloyd Miller were well-known builders in the area who were very active opening up new suburban developments in the 1950s and 1960s. Each built their family's home in Tacoma Hills; one on water and the other inland. Both chose "California-contemporary," and both are connected directly or indirectly to Donald Scholz (1920–2000), a popular national designer of prefabricated houses, who founded Scholz Homes in Toledo, Ohio, in 1946.[80] Their 1966 catalogue of prefabricated "upscale" houses ranged from colonial to very modern offered in different sizes and with many options. As the demand for these designs grew, seven factories were opened across the country in Long Beach, California; Long Island; St. Petersburg; Durham; Kansas City; Houston; and Toledo.

A Scholz Mark '58 design was erected in 1958 in Forest Hills in Okemos. Prefabricated materials such as the wood panels, wood tresses, interior partitions, and other component parts were manufactured at the Toledo plant, trucked to Michigan, and assembled at the site. The house at 4391 Greenwood Drive, built by John W. Mercer Jr., was the smallest version. It was the subject of several articles in the *Lansing State Journal* on May 25, 1958, when it was opened to the public. This was coordinated with showings of the model in seventy-five communities throughout the country and a national TV and radio campaign including an extensive fourteen-page article in *House Beautiful* magazine that June.[81]

Lloyd (1904–1980) and Fern Marie Miller obtained the plans in 1958 for the largest version (plan C) to build in 1959 at 2019 Osage Drive (plate 49). The 2,500-square-foot, three bedroom, two-and-a-half bath house is on a third of an acre of land and faces north. The garage is closest to the street but turned away to open onto the circular driveway. Characteristics of the Mark '58 are an asymmetric gable with inserted glass in the peak to bring light into the garage; brick screen wall extensions on either side of the house that mask it from view and allow teasing glimpses of the upper glazing of the kitchen and family room gable wall; and open beams and a studio-type ceiling. The designer considered the glass gables in the kitchen and family room as the "crowning glory" of the house.[82]

Although Warren Brintnall was writing about the Forest Hills example, his description fits the Millers' house in pointing out other celebrated features, such as

◄ **FIGURE 90.** Brown House, Earl Vaive, entry, Okemos.

Photograph © 2020 Kim Kauffman.

the "dramatic entrance foyer with wide double doors." Indeed, these doors that are flush with the wall and in the center of an expanse of glass were unique at this time to Scholz's design and used in almost every Mark model thereafter. Its theatricality has been connected to the influence of Hollywood on Scholz's California style.[83]

The gabled entry and sheltered patio lead into a roomy foyer, "brightened by big windows and decorated by the foliage from planters recessed in the floor. . . . The sweeping design flourish that marks Scholz homes is apparent in the living and dining areas. Massive wood beams, cathedral ceilings, full floor-to ceiling sliding glass doors, create a feeling of space, open the house interior to the outdoors. . . . Eliminating wall partitions between the living and dining room, and the use of large areas of glass, created the sense that the space was larger than it was, visually extending beyond boundaries."

At Osage, the living room is ahead, the family room and kitchen is on the west, and the bedroom wing is to the east. The sunken living room has floor-to-ceiling windows and its own gable that extends into the backyard and creates a covered porch (figure 91). Plans also called for a "quiet patio" outside the master bedroom to ensure privacy, and another patio on the other side of the living room to continue connections between indoors and outside. The formal dining room

▶ **FIGURE 91.** Miller House, Donald Scholz, interior, Okemos. Photograph © 2020 Kim Kauffman.

is several steps up from the living room and opens into the kitchen and family space. There is ample storage throughout the house including an unusual arrangement of a closet/dressing room off the master bedroom, which is a feature of plan C, and a large built-in cabinet in the basement. This lower level has another family room with a fireplace that were not in Scholz's design.

The level changes, varied ceiling heights—from low to soaring—views from one space into another, and extensive glazing characterize the modern residence. Whereas other houses discussed in this chapter reveled in the extensive use of wood on walls and ceilings that created intimacy and warmth, the light, open, and airy approach here is connected to the "California contemporary" style. The success of Scholz's designs was due to the livability of his plans, their curb appeal, and the fact that models of the houses were often furnished with traditional furniture, enabling even those who did not fully embrace modernism to envision living in them.[84]

Couchois (1920–2000) and his wife, Martha, built their Tacoma Hills house a few years later to fit their family of nine children. They chose a river-front site on a cul-de-sac at 2150 Pawnee Road, on the other side of the wooded valley from the Browns. Fineout designed their large ranch, completed in 1965 (plate 75). The 2,550-square-foot brick and wood house has

▶ **FIGURE 92.** Couchois House, Gordon Fineout, river side, Okemos. Photograph © 2020 Kim Kauffman.

five bedrooms and two baths on two levels and has since been expanded and renovated.[85] The entrance to the house is beyond the garage and kitchen on the right and a brick planter on the left. The double front doors surrounded by full glazing to the height of the angled roof, the visible beam ends, and sheltering deep overhang echo Scholz's Mark '58 and '60 designs.[86] Couchois undoubtedly admired this unusual feature in his partner's house and borrowed it.

The house is set parallel to the river on the west and off the north–south axis. It sits high up in the back and has a full basement accessed by stairs near the entrance. The large kitchen has a central L-shaped counter that separates the working area from the eating space. This open "family kitchen" combination was used in other Couchois and Miller houses as well as in the Mark '58 but had also appeared earlier in Ralph Herrick's 1950 house in Lansing. The two-sided fireplace and brick wall in the eating area is shared with the formal dining room with exposed beams on the other side. Here glass doors open onto a suspended deck that faces the river (figure 92). The living room and a large covered deck (now enclosed) project forward on the south, facing the expansive lawn leading to the river. Additionally, a narrow balcony wraps around to the east at this level. Most of the multiple roofs have glass in the upper triangles of the gables, providing visual interest and light. The lower level has bedrooms and a recreation room with a patterned cement wall. While Couchois and Fineout found inspiration in several different designs, the decks and unique balconies they added take full advantage of the beautiful site and its proximity to the Red Cedar River.

In the seemingly land-locked middle of the state, numerous houses like the ones discussed here reveled in their nearness to water. Privileged views and access to the water enhanced living in them. It is typical for a ranch house to respond to its setting, usually going from one story on the front to two in the back as the ground slopes away. It is also characteristic of ranch houses to redefine the outdoors as usable entertainment and recreational extensions of the livable space.[87] This is certainly the case with residences near water like the Couchois example.

Shaker Heights

Couchois-Miller Building Contracting and Development Company started out building modestly priced houses in new subdivisions, for example, Lakeview Heights and Hillbrook Park near Lake Lansing in the mid-1950s.[88] At the latter, by summer 1958, they erected larger five-bedroom houses with open plans, beamed and studio ceilings, and a "family kitchen" made its first appearance in their buildings.[89]

By the late 1960s, the builders graduated to singular designs, often provided by Fineout, at higher prices in more exclusive areas. They developed Shaker Heights in Okemos to the east of Tacoma Hills into one of distinction with larger houses in "an architecturally controlled area."[90] Their ads clearly expressed this: "A dash of luxury. A touch of elegance. Know the pride of saying I live in Shaker Heights. A completely planned community of imaginative and discriminating homes built just a little bit better."[91]

The most modern and atypical of these called "The Gallery" at 1834 Mirabeau Drive is a flat-roofed house that was featured in the October 1967 Parade of Homes (plate 84). It has a spectacular setting on a deep wooded lot on a cul-de-sac.[92] The following May, in "Stark Contemporary Design Covers Warm Interior," Susan Elder interviewed Mr. and Mrs. Edward Pratt, the owners. Mrs. Pratt explained that they saw the house on the Parade of Homes and that "each time we came back we saw something new" and they ended up purchasing it. They liked that "'the house is easy to keep, the rooms flow into each other for a relaxed feeling.' . . . The exterior façade is 'stark modern wood, stone and marble chips. The interior is warmly contemporary without being stark, and simple without being Spartan.'"[93]

On the exterior, the varying heights of the flat roofs emphasize the horizontal and the boxy design. From the entry, stairs ascend to the upper bedroom level. Two steps down at the entry lead to the lower level with a two-sided fireplace in the family and living room. The latter is up two steps and has story-and-a-half walls that add to the "restrained beauty of the entire formal area . . . and dining room." With skylights in the entry, many windows high in the walls, and clerestory windows in the family room "'even on the dreariest day, it's never dark here. Light comes in everywhere without intruding on our privacy,' Mrs. Pratt said."[94]

Because of the stark modernism of the house, Couchois and Miller took a gamble building it on speculation.[95] Others they built on this and adjoining streets, for example, 1824 Mirabeau (1968) and 4418 Calgary (1972, designed by Fineout) are all large and different in style from each other but not as strikingly contemporary.

Lantern Hill, Next Phase

R. B. Sloan Jr., the designer of the Arbaugh House, also designed two houses in East Lansing constructed during the second phase of the Lantern Hill project. The first phase comprising forty-one lots is discussed in chapter 6. They bordered Burcham Road on the south and encompassed Knoll Road on the east and

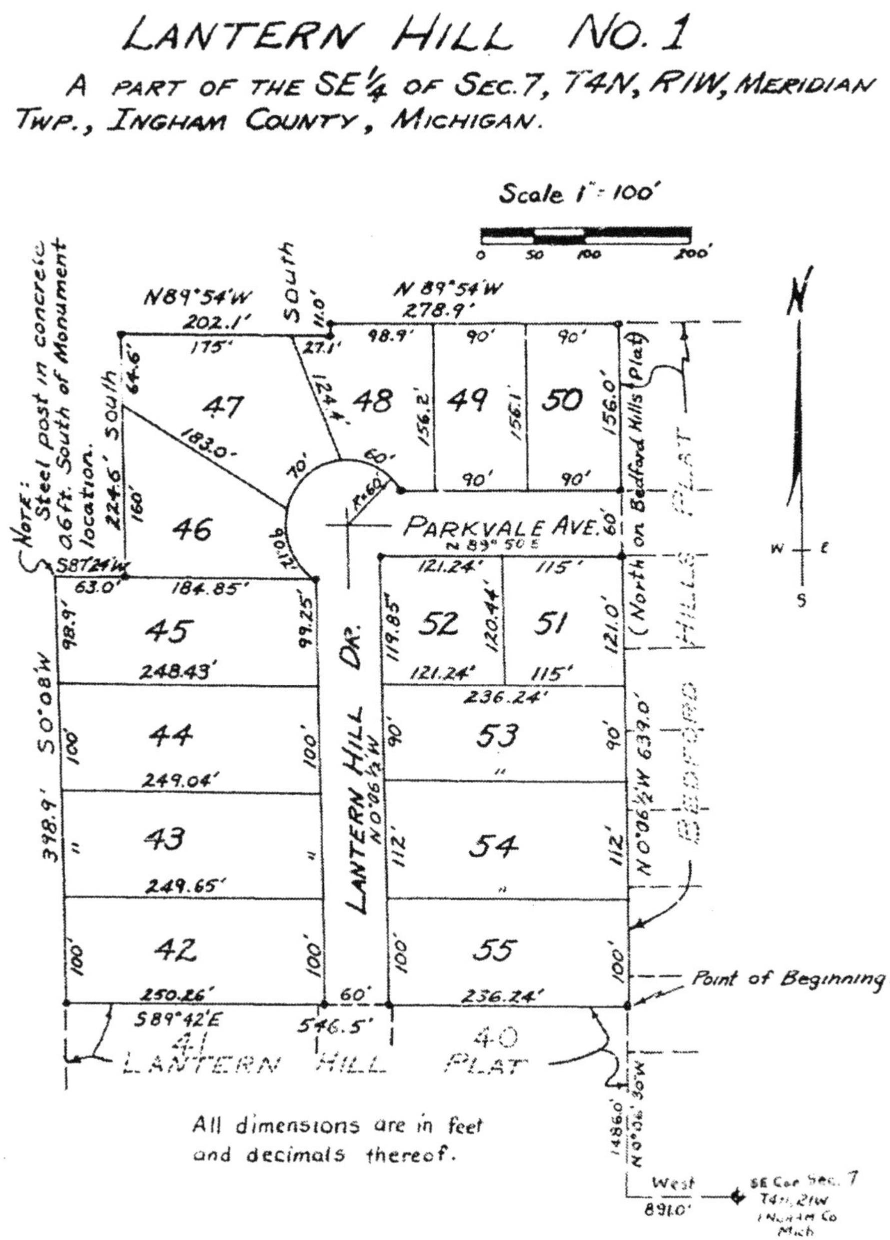

the curving section of Lantern Hill Drive on the west, stretching midway up this street to the north (figure 50). The Stubbins-designed houses were erected quickly between 1950 and 1952. The next phase extended Lantern Hill Drive to the north (figure 93). Three couples, all of whom had been involved in phase 1, purchased this farm land from the Willmarth family, subdivided it into fourteen lots (lots 42–55) similar in size to phase 1 (averaging 230 feet by 100 feet, with several smaller ones in the north end). They kept three (42, 54, 55) at the southern end for themselves and started selling the rest. While there were restrictions regarding the height of buildings and setbacks from the street, similar to the Lantern Hill covenants, there was no attempt to use the same architect nor to duplicate the communal approach of that phase. As a result, the houses in the new section vary in style, size, and material. Two in particular deserve mention: the Varner and Boger houses on the east side of the street, parcels 55 and 54. Both families hired the same architect to design large houses. In fact, both had built Stubbins designs on Knoll Road, but as their families expanded and their increasingly important appointments at the university grew their salaries, they sought bigger homes.

The house at 1006 Lantern Hill Drive was designed by R. B. Sloan Jr. in 1957 for Durward (Woody) (1917–1999) and Paula P. Varner (plate 42).[96] He received his bachelor's in agricultural economics from Texas A&M, and a master's in economics from the University of Chicago in 1949. He started his academic career at MSU in 1949 as an assistant professor and extension specialist in agricultural economics. In 1955, he was vice president for off-campus education, heading the continuing education and extension program. He became President John Hannah's point person in the conception of the new Oakland University near Detroit and was appointed its first chancellor in 1959. He then became president of the University of Nebraska in 1970 until he retired in 1977.

The Varners had lived in a Stubbins-designed house at 820 Knoll Road that was enveloped in 1978 into Tivador Balogh's nearly 4,000-square-foot design. The Varners new house at 1006 Lantern Hill Drive, a 3,424-square-foot bi-level, is significantly larger than their original house was. Unfortunately, the Varners had little time to enjoy it before he left for Oakland University in 1959.

This rectangular house has an asymmetrical roof with the shorter slope on the north side and the longer one dynamically extending towards the entrance where it intersects with a second gable roof that covers the two-car carport. Approaching the house from the south provides the most exciting view of the intersecting gabled roofs and the ridges and valleys and slopes. Triads of windows are used to unify the levels on this side. On the back, there are larger pairs of windows on the two levels, separated by a plywood panel above the door to the backyard.

The front exterior anticipates the multiple levels on the interior. The entrance is off center and leads into an ample foyer. From here, the large living room takes up the width of the house on the south and has a brick fireplace in the middle (figure 94). This space flows into the dining ell, which continues the wall of floor-to-ceiling windows facing the back. A family room with another fireplace is adjacent and opposite the open kitchen at the front of the house. Stairs lead up to the bedroom wing on the north. Stairs down access the lower level under the bedrooms where the plans indicated a large recreation space with fireplace and access to the back yard, a hobby and guest room, and fruit cupboards.

Details, such as built-in planters along the stairs, multiple fireplaces, a folding screen to close off the formal from informal dining areas, a grill beside the fireplace near the kitchen, are all indications of careful planning and an ample budget. Gable ceilings and an abundance of wood in the interior are included as well.[97]

The house at 988 Lantern Hill Drive was designed at the same time by R. B. Sloan Jr. for Lawrence L. (1923–2001) and Frances J. Boger (1923–2006) (plate 43).[98] He had degrees from Purdue (1947)

◀ **FIGURE 93.** Lantern Hill, phase 2 plot plan. Courtesy of Gary Shueren and Hans Schwab.

and MSU (master of science, 1948; doctorate, 1950). He rose through the ranks at MSU starting as a graduate assistant (1947), instructor (1948), assistant professor (1950), and associate professor (1952) in the Department of Agriculture, Food, and Resource Economics. He became chair of the department in 1954, dean of the College of Agriculture and Natural Resources (1969), acting provost (1975), and provost in 1975. He left MSU on June 15, 1977, to become president of Oklahoma State University in Stillwater, from which he retired in 1988.[99]

Boger had served as secretary for the Home Sites group and their Stubbins-designed basementless, 1,346-square-foot house was at 810 Knoll Road. In comparison, 988 Lantern Hill Drive has over 2,500 square feet with thirteen rooms, including a full basement with a small kitchen, bathroom, and additional rooms as well as a walkout to the backyard. The garage is closest to the street but turned away from it to shield the front door. Visual interest is provided by the roof treatment: multiple peaks, cut-out angles, the contrast of the flat garage roof and the long slope towards the north, and glass in the gables above the door. Broad eaves on the one-story front are continued on the back with the addition of another eave above the basement level. On this side, brick is the primarily material, and the large projecting chimney creates a strong vertical mass that is balanced by the

► **FIGURE 94.** Varner House, R. B. Sloan Jr., interior, East Lansing. Photograph © 2020 Kim Kauffman.

slopes of the roof (figure 95). The view of the back of the house from the gracious yard is as interesting as the front.

On the interior, the focus of the high-ceilinged living room is the large expanse of the brick wall (figure 96). Large windows on the north and south sides bring a lot of light into the room in contrast to the more controlled and warm atmosphere of adjoining formal wood-paneled dining room. The two spaces are delineated by the wood beam above. Uplighting and the separating screen were all carefully considered by the designer. The adjacent porch on the south was eventually enclosed, and the door that separated it from the dining room was removed. An informal dining and family room with another fireplace is adjacent to the dining room, as is the large, high-ceilinged kitchen. The bedroom wing is to the north of the entry, along a hallway.

While R. B. Sloan Jr.'s name is not on the plans for this house, stylistic similarities and common lore affirm the attribution.[100] Moreover, it is clear that the two houses were conceived of at the same time with attention paid to the connection between them. The driveways are close together to create a wide expanse of lawn across the two lots and the houses are placed as far as possible at the edge of their respective lots. The most interesting views of each are from different directions; coming from the south for the Varners'

◀ **FIGURE 95.** Boger House, R. B. Sloan Jr., exterior, East Lansing. Photograph © 2020 Kim Kauffman.

house, and coming from the north for the Bogers'. These two houses, together with the contemporaneous Arbaugh House, show R. B. Sloan Jr. to be a master of siting the building on the lot. All three designs have complex roof lines, peaks and horizontals, walls that project forward or are cut back from the basic rectangle. Interiors show R. B. Sloan Jr.'s interest in flow, expansiveness and intimacy, distinguishing formal and informal spaces and the long views across them.

The third couple in the triad was Leyton V. and Martha Nelson. Leyton (d. 1976) received his bachelor of science in agriculture and applied science in 1939, and his master of science in 1941 in farm crops, both from MSU. He served as a research assistant from 1941–1945, was an assistant professor in 1949, and associate professor in 1953.[101] He, too, was a founding member of Lantern Hills, but the 1951 house at 963 Lantern Hill on lot 39 was not a Stubbins design. His new lot (no. 42) was two to the north, where he built a 2,000-square-foot brick ranch in 1956 (now 987), most likely on speculation because his family continued to reside at 963 into the 1970s.[102]

◄ **FIGURE 96.** Boger House, R. B. Sloan Jr., interior, East Lansing. Photograph © 2020 Kim Kauffman.

Modernism on Daisy Lane

The mid-Michigan burgeoning suburbs embraced both modern and traditional ranch styles as did

communities all over the country. People appreciated the differentiation between a house's public and private façades, open plans, and new technology that allowed for large expanses of glazing. Brick, gabled roofs, and large eaves influenced by Wright's Prairie and Usonian styles were preferred in mid-Michigan creating a moderating modernist style. While several commercial structures reference European modernism and the International style, there are only a few local residential examples that do. One is at 1057 Daisy Lane in the Red Cedar River watershed. It stands out not only because of the flat roof and stark lines but also because of its location. This is the "Flower Pot" district of East Lansing to the west of the MSU campus, so called because the streets are named for flowers. Originally the Stephen Hicks farm, it began to be subdivided into small lots in the 1920s but saw increased building activity after World War II. Known for its diverse and racially integrated community, unlike the rest of East Lansing, it became filled with fairly modest nondescript houses. Placed close together, many are mail-order or tract houses built on speculation, symmetrical plans that conformed to the idea of a comfortable house. The house at 1057 Daisy Lane, built in 1958 for the William (Bill) Sylvester and Margaret Jeannette Gamble family, is an exception (plate 48). He (1912–2009) was a faculty member in the studio art department at MSU, hired in 1948 to teach design.[103] The family of five had been living in faculty

◀ **FIGURE 97.** Gamble House, "ACH," rear, East Lansing.
Photograph © 2020 Kim Kauffman.

housing when they engaged an architect to design their house.[104] Various drawings done between March and summer 1958 are initialed "ACH," who has yet to be identified, and there are slight variations between the plans and the house as executed.

The rectangular house has a flat roof and is set parallel to the street; the enclosed garage was added in 1970.[105] Unlike two-story houses that rise above the ground or organic architecture where the house fits into the natural contours of the site, here a deep excavation allowed the house to descend and become two stories of equal height and size (1,248 square feet). The main one is at street level and sits on top of a full above-grade cement block basement, which acts as a podium (figure 97).

The shape of the house changed from nearly square in the early plans to a rectangle, and the kitchen moved from the middle, to the front, and finally the back of the house. The kitchen was separated from the dining area by a floor-to-ceiling wood paneled wall (since removed) with an opening behind the refrigerator and a cut-out passthrough towards the windows (figure 98).[106] There are three small bedrooms and a bathroom on the east side of the house. The master bedroom and bath and the living room are on the other side. In the basement, designs called for two bedrooms and two full baths, a studio, recreation area, and shop, although little of this was executed until very recently.

The exterior has redwood siding and flat rectangular panels colored in Mondrian-like yellow, green, and orange (recently changed to gray). These flat walls divided into a grid with solid color panels and transparent windows reflect knowledge of *Arts and Architecture*'s Case Study House experiment in contemporary architecture, begun in 1945 and publicized in the magazine. In particular, it echoes the façade treatment although not the steel and metal construction of Charles and Ray Eames's Case Study House #8, 1949, erected in Los Angeles.

To counteract the lack of eaves, to protect the flat exterior walls, and provide some shade from the sun, brackets were installed above the windows on the south side and above the basement door on the east. These held pieces of corrugated plastic sunscreens visible in the photograph before the recent renovation. At the front entry, a flat, gridded, wood roof is supported by a slender column; on the back, a flat, solid roof covers the deck and from here a long staircase descends to the backyard.

Gamble's interests in modernism and Japan, which explain some of the features of the house, were fostered while he was a student at the University of Washington (UW) from which he received his bachelor of art (1939), normal diploma (1940), and master of fine arts (1946). A 1948 *Lansing State Journal* article about his hiring at MSU gives a clue to his interest

◀ **FIGURE 98.** Gamble House, "ACH," interior, East Lansing. Photograph courtesy of Melissa Evans Itsell.

in the former.[107] "Among his teachers at UW have been Professor Johannes Molzahn . . . and Amadeus Ozenfant, well known New York painter." Molzahn (1892–1965) was in the Arbeitsrat für Kunst in Berlin, many of whose members were founders of the Bauhaus, including Walter Gropius and Bruno Taut. A painter and graphic designer, he emigrated to the United States in 1938 and taught at UW until 1941.[108] Ozenfant (1886–1966), a Frenchman and collaborator with architect and theorist Le Corbusier, brought ideas of Purism and color theory to New York in 1936 and to his students at UW. Like Ozenfant's, Gamble's art, especially his printmaking specialty, was a mix of cubist fracturing and minimal details, but he never totally gave up the figure.[109] In addition, Alexander Archipenko (1887–1964), a Ukrainian American sculptor who applied cubist principles to the human form, taught at UW in the summers of 1935 and 1936 when Gamble was there. All of these teachers would have encouraged Gamble's exposure to international modernism.

At UW, Gamble's interest in Japan also deepened. There he met Asian American George Tsutakawa (1910–1997), who attended as a student, returned after World War II to obtain his master of fine arts in 1947, and was hired to teach, part-time at first, and eventually full-time. Tsutakawa did printmaking and sculpture and was associated with the Northwest School based in Seattle that included Mark Tobey and Morris Graves. Their art was characterized by the diffuse lighting and earthy colors of the natural surroundings as well as Asian aesthetics. In the 1960s and 1970s, Tsutakawa became known as a fountain designer.[110] He and Gamble retained a lifelong friendship and mutual admiration, and owned each other's artwork.[111]

From September 1964 through July 1965, Gamble spent a sabbatical travelling in Japan and Taiwan, with extended time in Tokyo and Kyoto.[112] A two-part exhibition he curated for the Kresge Art Gallery at MSU in 1983 to mark his retirement included over 115 pieces from his collection of Japanese art, lacquerware, distinctive ceramics from Okinawa, paintings, 1960s prints, and other works on paper. The second part featured his own art.[113]

In Japan, he also learned about Satori plaster, a traditional Japanese wall finish using a trowel to apply plaster by hand. The plaster is embedded with natural materials such as blades of grass, straw, or fibers. At some point, Gamble treated two walls in his house in Satori plaster; one was in the living room, the other nearby. These walls were textured with an all-over pattern of randomly placed bits of grass and straw. Another Japanese-influenced motif is the abundance of dark redwood trim including rectangular surrounds of plaster above door frames.[114] Given Gamble's background, it appears logical that he would choose a design that looked to Le Corbusier, the Bauhaus, Walter Gropius, and the Case Study houses rather than the Midwestern ranch. Closer to home, he also would have been aware of Mies van der Rohe's Lafayette Park steel and glass townhouses under construction at that time in Detroit. To these influences, Gamble added a subtle Asian flare.

This book starts with Goetsch and Winckler's Wright house that embodies the concept of organic architecture. With its low profile, open plan, natural materials, and merging of inside and outside, it is an iconic example of that style. The book ends with the Bill Gamble's house that fits a very different tradition of contemporary architecture from Europe by way of California, a house that rises up rather than settles into the ground, that uses new rather than natural materials. It is amusing to think that these three artists not only were colleagues at MSU in the same department but also shared a specialty in art education and would have been in constant contact with each other. What unites them further was a desire to live in a house that looked forward and reflected contemporary life rather than back to convention and tradition. But they came to solutions from different perspectives and ends of the spectrum; one looked to America and the Prairie, and the other to Europe and the International style.

The Goetsch-Winckler House is well published and well known; the Gamble House is not, but its predecessors are. Both styles are featured in histories of twentieth-century architecture. However, the majority of postwar houses not just in mid-Michigan but across the country falls in between these two poles, yet it has received much less attention. As Alan Hess argues, the ranch was the most ubiquitous design of all and was a truly democratic architecture that cut across the economic spectrum and could be infinitely adapted and varied based on size, location, and budget. The gable roof, asymmetric façades, multifunctional rooms, closed one-story on the front and full of windows on the back, and flexible plans had great appeal.[115] The history of the ranch, he expounds, "challenges the way we have understood and written about twentieth century architecture."[116] By exploring mid-Michigan and the local manifestations of modernist architecture, especially the ranch style, this study fills in gaps in that understanding, knowledge and appreciation of the broad middle swath of the architectural landscape. It brings to light local architectural talent and their stories that deserve to be remembered and celebrated.

Epilogue

I spent a good part of my professional life in the 1959 Kresge Art Center on the MSU campus (plate 50). Beyond the distinguishing features that have already been discussed, another modernist detail is worth mentioning since it is hidden to half of the population while it puzzles the other half. This is the "woman's urinal" in the first stall of each of the women's bathrooms on three of the four floors (figure 99). The one on the first floor was recently replaced. For years, as my daily routine led me to pay a visit, I would be struck by these oddly shaped toilets that lacked seats, and like all the other women, I preferred the typical toilets with seats in the adjacent stalls. Frequently I thought to myself that I should uncover the story behind this curiosity. Here, then, is a brief consideration of the indelicate but fascinating subject of women's urinals, the science and the myths behind them, and their popularity in the 1950s–60s. It is informed by the new multidisciplinary research area of "toilet studies" that has developed in the past two decades bringing together a broad range of academic fields including women's and critical race studies, anthropology, sociology, public health, literature, art, economics, law, architecture, and more recently, gender orientation.[1]

Women's urinals in public institutions first showed up in the west in late nineteenth-century Germany, and today, variations are used in Asia and by campers and hikers.[2] The Sanistand in the Kresge Art Center building, however, was a decidedly short-lived American solution made by American Standard from 1949 until 1973, when production was discontinued.[3] Competing designs were Crane's Hy-San Fixture and Kohler's Hygiea.[4] All three were specifically for public institutions rather than domestic settings.

There were several considerations that the women's urinal sought to address. One was to expedite the typical lines in women's restrooms at peak times by separating those who only needed urinals from the others, as in men's restrooms. A second was that research found that most women do not sit on the seat but hover over it so the seat could be eliminated.[5] For "convenience, protection and sanitation," instructions on how to use the Crane Hy-San Fixture "suggested" the following: "1. Back up . . . and straddle the fixture. 2. Assume a natural squatting position directly over the bowl . . . 3. Keep feet flat on the floor."[6] Advertisements for the Sanistand emphasized the "no-touch" aspect that not only appealed to a woman's sense of hygiene but also reduced the cost and time of restroom maintenance for the owners.[7] Fashion also played a part as these were developed when most women wore skirts. In time, the prevalence of pantyhose and tights as well as the predominance of slacks as women's favored attire made use of the urinal inconvenient and downright awkward.

In the 1950s and 1960s, women's urinals were installed in many public institutions such as state parks, bus terminals, train stations, department stores, colleges and universities, and some factories. They can still be found at Brooklyn College; the National Zoo in Washington, DC; Harvard Stadium; Grand Teton National Park; Texas A&M; and Long Beach City Hall, among others.[8] They reflected a modernist solution to an ongoing problem and attitudes towards gender differences, learned behaviors, and expectations. As with other unloved and underappreciated experiments from the time, such as in-the-wall vacuums popularized in middle-class homes in the 1960s, wall hanging refrigerator-freezers, and bomb shelters, these toilets installed in modernist buildings between the late 1940s and early 1970s are fast disappearing.[9]

Other significant modernist losses in mid-Michigan since the first publication of this book include the Arby's pictured in plate 78 that was demolished in 2020 and the Glencairn Elementary School (plate 28), which was part of a sweeping construction project begun in 2018 to replace and rebuild five East Lansing elementary schools built between 1948 and 1963. Given new technology in the classroom, twenty-first-century educational methodologies, and ADA and other updated safety requirements for public buildings, the schools could neither safely nor economically be upgraded. The future is also uncertain for Lansing City Hall (plate 39). In 2017, then mayor Virg Bernero was intent on demolishing it, but the end of his term halted the conversation.[10] Some of these losses are understandable and even justifiable in light of evolving construction techniques, environmental concerns, and changing lifestyles, yet it is my hope that shining a light of mid-Michigan's mid-century architecture will continue to expand our appreciation and understanding of the context and significance of what we have.

◀ **FIGURE 99.** Woman's urinal, Kresge Art Center, East Lansing. Photograph ©2020 Kim Kauffman.

Descriptions of Illustrated Buildings

The buildings illustrated in color are ordered chronologically by the year of the design or the year the building was completed.

PLATE 1. **Charles W. and Grace Bachman House**

929 Roxburgh Avenue, East Lansing

Alden B. Dow, 1937 (see text pp. 28–30)

Photo courtesy of the Michigan State Historic Preservation Office

Sited on a rise of the land, the asymmetrical cubic design has large expanses of windows that merge the interior and exterior. The only house in mid-Michigan to use the Unit Block system that Dow developed, these molded six-sided blocks give the house its distinctive appearance.

PLATE 2. **Mildred Hagberg Studio House**

2231 Hamilton Road, Okemos

Barn, 1923; Ralph Rapson design, 1940 (see text pp. 84–88)

© 2014 Kim Kauffman

Mildred Hagberg asked Ralph Rapson, whom she had met at Cranbrook, to modernize a 1923 barn she had purchased. He suggested inserting large windows, flattening the roof, and adding balconies. Because not all of the land came with the barn, the building had to be sawed in half and the part that was not on her property was moved and attached at the back.

PLATE 3. **Goetsch-Winckler House**

2410 Hulett Road, Okemos

Frank Lloyd Wright, 1940 (see text pp. 4–7)

© 2014 Kim Kauffman

Considered by Wright as the "perfect Usonian," this 1,350-square-foot two-bedroom house was built for Alma Goetsch and Kathrine Winckler, artists and art educators at Michigan State College. The short side with the carport is turned towards the road. This is a fine example of Wright's Usonian principles of modest cost, use of prefabricated materials, gravity heating, flat roof, and carport. The house was listed in the National Register of Historic Places in 1995.

PLATE 4. O. Lee and Genevieve Ricker House

716 Wildwood Drive, East Lansing

Donald Hedges, 1940 (see text p. 119)

Photo by Natasha Crljenica

Donald Hedges (1905–2003) was a University of Michigan–trained architect who practiced in New Hope, Pennsylvania. He provided "an ultra modern" house for O. Lee Ricker, a local dentist. Redwood was used on the exterior, the interior entrance, and living room walls. There are four bedrooms, a game room, custom-made doors, and several flourishes, including a decorative pattern in the linoleum on the exterior side of the front door, and a mural in the living room (now covered over). The living area is down several steps and has a large picture window facing the back.

PLATE 5. 164 Maplewood Drive, East Lansing

Architect Unknown, 1941, (see text p. 119)

Photo by Natasha Crljenica

The Art Moderne buildings on display at the 1933–1934 Chicago Century of Progress World's Fair led to the style's popularity in the 1930s. There are several examples in East Lansing: the Hays house, 605 Butterfield (1937); 753 Snyder (1939); and to a lesser degree, 412 Rosewood (1935). This 1941 house shares the typical streamlined characteristics: minimal ornamentation, flat roofs, small, often square windows with many panes, wraparound windows, smooth (frequently stucco) walls, asymmetry, and no eaves. As a stripped-down version of Art Deco, the ornamentation is in the curving walls, horizontal bands, and small paned windows. Additionally, the emphasis is on new materials: steel, glass, glass blocks, and concrete.

PLATE 6. John F. A. and Elizabeth Taylor House

4539 Nakoma Drive, Okemos (see text p. 8)

Architect unknown, 1946

Photo by Natasha Crljenica

Taylor was a distinguished philosopher who trained at Princeton University and received a Guggenheim Fellowship in 1963. Upon discharge from the army, 1942–46, he was hired as head of the Department of Literature and Fine Arts at MSC. His very elegant prose was put to good use in persuading the congregants of Edgewood Church to choose a modern style for their building. It is no surprise that he chose Streamline Moderne for his own house, which was equally out of the norm. He wrote and lectured frequently about design and aesthetics in the visual arts, including *Design and Expression in the Visual Arts* (Dover Publications, 1964).

PLATE 7. Hayworth House, drawing

Alden B. Dow, 1946 (see text pp. 30–31)

Courtesy of Alden B. Dow Archives

In this two-story residence that was to have been built in East Lansing, Dow emphasized horizontal planes and rhythmically alternated open and closed walls and windows. The elevation shows the garage, but the front door is hidden from view. Above (upper left), the main living spaces are dominated by the large L-shaped living room with windows on two sides. The bedrooms are along the other side of the house. Exterior stairs, built-in seating, and bookcases, plus an additional bedroom on the lower floor, are also included in the drawing.

PLATE 8. Donald and Betty Price House

417 Clarendon Road, East Lansing

Lee Black and Kenneth C. Black, Architects, 1946 (see text pp. 90–91)

Photo courtesy of the Michigan State Historic Preservation Office

As the purveyor of modern-design housewares and gift items at Liebermann's store in downtown Lansing (see George Nelson's later design, plate 77), Betty Price was a modern enthusiast. For the Prices' home, the Blacks incorporated many modern elements: integration with the site reinforced by a horizontal emphasis, an open plan, and a synthesis between indoor and outdoor space facilitated by a large window wall on the back side.

PLATE 9. 901 Rosewood Avenue (1947)

Adrian Langius (see text p. 117)

Photo by Natasha Crljenica

This is one of two adjacent residences known by locals as the "bookend houses." The address of the second, built in 1952, is 910 Roxburgh. Both were designed on speculation by Adrian (Gus) Langius, who was chief architect for the state at the time. They were mirror images: compact tri-levels with shed roofs and a carport. Both have been altered and expanded.

PLATE 10. Paul and Rosamunde Hammond House

1913 Tecumseh River Drive, Lansing

Edwin Johnson, 1947 (see text pp. 22–23)

By siting the short end of the house toward the street, architect Edwin Johnson created a long wall of windows facing the woods and the pond below. The public spaces of the house are aligned on this long side of the L-shape while the bedrooms are on the shorter side. The slope of the shed roof is at its highest point in the living room.

PLATE 11. Alexis and Lucie Panshin House

2515 Arrowhead Road, Okemos

Keck & Keck, 1947 (see text pp. 40–48)

The Panshins purchased this plot near where two Frank Lloyd Wright houses (#14 and #16) were under construction. They hired Keck & Keck, a Chicago firm well known for their passive solar and innovative ventilation systems, as seen in this house. The garage is separate from the house and functions as a privacy wall of brick facing the street. On the south side of the house, the large panes of glass afford a broad view of the landscape.

PLATE 12. Clarence W. and Mary Muehlberger House, front elevation

Frank Lloyd Wright, 1947 (see text pp. 20–21)

The Muehlbergers' unbuilt house had a variety of rooflines that added visual interest to the design. This view from above shows the sheltering overhang for the cars and entrance, the generous masonry mass alongside, and the bedroom wing. The solid walls are relieved with small, narrow windows and a high band of windows below the eaves. The drawing also hints at the dramatic slope of the roof towards the rear.

PLATE 13. Clarence W. and Mary Muehlberger House, rear elevation

Frank Lloyd Wright, 1947 (see text pp. 20–21)

The rear elevation makes obvious not only the L-shape of the building but also the proliferation of angles of the roofline and the slant of the walls of windows. Clerestory windows are used throughout on this side. This was to have been built on acres of rolling land. In keeping with the breadth of the acreage, Wright designed a house that spreads out horizontally.

PLATE 14. Erling and Katherine Brauner House

2527 Arrowhead Road, Okemos

Frank Lloyd Wright, 1949 (see text pp. 7–9)

The Brauners built their Frank Lloyd Wright–designed house on a cul-de-sac surrounded by woods and the Herron Creek. The house is distinctive in the use of concrete blocks with small glass panes inserted to allow light into the hallway behind and to add decoration to the design. The long sloping roof shelters the entrance and carport.

PLATE 15. Harold H. and Gladys Anderson House

340 Wildwood Drive, East Lansing

Alden B. Dow, 1949 (see text pp. 31–33)

Photo by Natasha Crljenica

Built for the head of the psychology department at Michigan State College, the house looks fairly modest from the street, where the large overhang of the roof protects the front door and the garage. At the rear, however, is a two-story wall of large windows. The three-bedroom house has a living room, dining area, and kitchen facing the backyard, and a balcony study area on the mezzanine level.

PLATE 16. James and Dolores Edwards House

2504 Arrowhead Road, Okemos

Frank Lloyd Wright, 1949–51; addition, Taliesin Associates, 1968 (see text pp. 8–11)

© 2014 Kim Kauffman

The James and Dolores Edwards house, made of brick and red tidewater cypress, is across from the Panshin (#11) and Brauner (#14) houses, and is hidden from the street, placed on a large plot of land that slopes to the west. A brick fireplace dominates the living room with its wraparound windows. The master bedroom suite designed by Taliesin Associates in 1968 was added to the south of the original seven-room structure.

PLATE 17. Greyhound Bus Terminal

511 South Washington Street, Lansing

William Strudwick Arrasmith, 1950 (see text pp. 161–62)

Vintage postcard

All Greyhound bus terminals designed by Arrasmith exhibit the same Streamline characteristics: asymmetry, a large entrance canopy, a signature round window. By 1950 when this was built, the typical curved edges of the style were straightened out and the building appears boxier than earlier examples. Nevertheless, it is recognizable and welcoming to the travelers who had come to expect a spacious waiting room as well as a restaurant. The building has since been repurposed.

PLATE 18. Dale and Beatrice O'Donnell House, drawing, rear elevation

Frank Lloyd Wright, 1950 (see text pp. 18–20)

The Frank Lloyd Wright Foundation Archives (The Museum of Modern Art | Avery Architectural & Fine Arts Library, Columbia University, New York). All rights reserved.

In this view from the southwest, Wright dramatically emphasized the slanted roof, expansive overhang, and wall of windows of the living space, while the bedroom wing is in the background on the left. The living area is perched on top of the terrace that rises above the sloping land. Unfortunately, the house was not built.

PLATE 19. Auto-Owners Insurance Company

303 West Kalamazoo Street, Lansing

Lee Black and Kenneth C. Black, Architects, 1951 (see text pp. 150–51)

Photo courtesy of Michigan State Historic Preservation Office

When this four-story building opened, it was hailed as "ultra modern" and a symbol of the financial stability of the company. The architects' holistic approach included the structure, gardens, and modern furnishings. The exterior is largely intact, although the interior has been substantially changed.

PLATE 20. Clarence H. and Marcella Rosa House

1430 Lindbergh Drive, Lansing, 1951

Clarence H. Rosa (see text pp. 65–68)

© 2014 Kim Kauffman

This north-facing house has an unobstructed view of the Red Cedar River across the street. The slanting wall of glass in the living room was an uncommon feature for the Lansing area but, according to the architect, made the room feel larger and gave visual interest to the interior.

PLATE 21. Talbert and Leota Fry Abrams House (Wingspan)

1310 Cambridge Road, Lansing

William H. Baugh with Grover M. Pratt, 1951 (see text pp. 92–95)

Photo courtesy of Jim Perkins

The design of this ranch house, according to Mr. Abrams, founder of the Abrams Instrument Corporation and Abrams Aerial Survey Corporation, was inspired by seeing the shadow of an airplane on the upper surface of a cloud bank as he and his wife were flying at 15,000 feet. The long and shorter wings intersect in the center, and each end of the house is curved.

PLATE 22. Malcolm and Harriet Williams House

550 Whitehills Drive, East Lansing

Malcolm Williams, 1951 (see text p. 65)

Photo courtesy of the Michigan State Historic Preservation Office

When it was built, there were no other houses in this area of East Lansing with flat roofs or a contemporary design. The gravity heat and carport were also atypical. The roof of this 2,600-square-foot home and long planes provide the horizontal emphasis.

PLATE 23. John G. and Marjorie Goodell House

414 Oxford Road, East Lansing

Architect unknown, 1951 (see text p. 120)

© 2014 Kim Kauffman

John G. Goodell (1918–2008) served as a pilot in the United States Army Air Force in the China-Burma-India Theater during World War II, and was president of the Lansing Insurance Agency. A *Lansing State Journal* article on March 11, 1951, pointed out that although the lot is shallow, the house has an unusually wide frontage because the property is one-and-a-half lots. A retaining wall on the east adds to the impression of width on the ground floor. The main living spaces are on the second floor (living room, kitchen, and one bedroom) facing the street, with a door that opens directly to the backyard at grade level.

PLATE 24. Lantern Hill Model A2, drawing, exterior

Hugh Stubbins Jr., 1950 (see text p. 124)

Courtesy of the Frances Loeb Library, Harvard University Graduate School of Design

Architect Hugh Stubbins Jr. provided six color presentation drawings for the Lantern Hill project. Each of the three models was illustrated by an exterior and an interior view. This bird's-eye view shows the rectangular shape of the house with detached carport. Wood fences provide a modicum of privacy to enjoy the outdoors.

PLATE 25. Lantern Hill Model A2, drawing, interior

Hugh Stubbins Jr., 1950 (see text p. 124)

Courtesy of the Frances Loeb Library, Harvard University Graduate School of Design

This interior view is from the back of the house looking towards the front, emphasizing the open plan. Instead of walls, the furniture, rug, and partitions separate it into living, eating, and study spaces. Hugh Stubbins Jr. included modernist furniture—tables on metal legs, a contemporary hanging lamp with pleated shade in the dining area, and low upholstered chairs and couch, and a cocktail table—as well as framed abstract art. The bright Mondrian-like colors of yellow, orange, white, and blue enliven the space, and the sleek curved red fireplace is especially modern.

PLATE 26. Walter and Pauline Adams House

928 Lantern Hill Drive

Lantern Hill Subdivision, East Lansing

Hugh Stubbins Jr., 1950–52 (see text p. 124)

© 2014 Kim Kauffman

Almost all of the families in the Lantern Hill project chose to build the same design by architect Hugh Stubbins Jr.: a rectangular single-story structure on a slab with a detached, flat-roofed, one-car garage. Small windows on the street side are replaced with larger ones facing the rear yard. Because these were modest homes for young faculty, over the years most have been expanded and altered. This example is close to the original plans except for the addition on the left.

PLATE 27. Dr. Mahlon Samuel and Mary Sharp House

950 Audubon Road, East Lansing

Laitala and Nuechterlein, 1952 (see text pp. 104–7)

Photo courtesy of the Michigan State Historic Preservation Office

Like many local examples, the shed roof and horizontal lines present a modest impression from the street and give no sense of the way the plot slopes downward so that the main floor is actually a story above the rear yard. The interior plan is open and pivots around a large brick fireplace. The clerestory windows and ventilation louvers were additional modernist characteristics.

PLATE 28. Glencairn Elementary School

939 Harrison Road, East Lansing

Laitala and Nuechterlein, 1952 (see text pp. 170–71)

Photo by Natasha Crljenica

Glencairn Elementary was planned to meet the pressing need for elementary schools in the early 1950s. While most of the schools built at this time were straightforward and functional, Glencairn had several features considered unusual, such as a bright color scheme, a lobby, and a fireplace. With these elements, the local firm of Laitala and Nuechterlein strove to make a warm and pleasant atmosphere for the children.

PLATE 29. Clarke E. and Dora Harris House

4681 Woodcraft Road, Okemos

Clarke E. Harris, 1952 (see text pp. 68–72)

Photo by Natasha Crljenica

This low-slung, shed-roofed wood building appears to be one story. However, the plot slopes to the Herron Creek behind, and the rear of the building is two stories with terraces. Small windows on the front give way to floor-to-ceiling glazing on the back.

PLATE 30. Jack and Evelyn Wolfram House

1341 Cambridge Road, Lansing

Lee Black and Kenneth C. Black, Architects, 1952 (see text pp. 91–92)

© 2014 Kim Kauffman

This sprawling light-tan brick ranch was designed for the general manager of General Motors Oldsmobile division in Lansing, Michigan. It faces the gently curving street on the front and the Country Club of Lansing's fairway at the back. This exclusive neighborhood was started in the 1920s and has a mix of revival-style homes and modernist structures like this one. The residence has been substantially expanded.

PLATE 31. Robin A. and Elizabeth Drews House

1410 Sherwood Avenue, East Lansing

Trade Secrets House, 1954 (see text pp. 130–36)

© 2014 Kim Kauffman

In 1952, *Life Magazine* asked the National Association of Home Builders to design a 1,340-square-foot house using the latest engineering and assembly-line techniques as well as quality materials, all for a cost of $15,000. MSC faculty member Robin Drews became enthusiastic when he read about the model homes in national magazines. This East Lansing example is one of the few Trade Secrets houses in Michigan.

PLATE 32. Merten Insurance Company Building

935 East Grand River Avenue, East Lansing

Lee Black and Kenneth C. Black, Architects, 1954 (see text p. 152)

Photo by Natasha Crljenica

The Prairie style of this small, stand-alone commercial building for the Merten Insurance Company is achieved by the horizontal planes of the roof, the large overhanging eaves, the band of small windows on the two street sides, as well as the use of light brick and built-in planters.

PLATE 33. Zion Evangelical Lutheran Church

4001 South Pennsylvania Avenue, Lansing

Laitala and Nuechterlein, 1954 (addition 2000) (see text pp. 182–86)

1954 image courtesy of Diane Sowash

This is a fine example of the ubiquitous A-frame construction used for churches throughout the United

States in the 1950s. To counteract the typical dark interiors, windows were inserted towards the lower ends of the sharply slanting roof. A large addition in 2,000 reoriented the entrance of the building from the north to the south and changed the stand-alone structure into a larger complex.

PLATE 34. **Kenneth and Cornelia Hagberg House**

2247 Hamilton Road, Okemos

Bernard J. Mayotte, 1955 (see text pp. 86–88)

This low-slung residence was designed by Bernard J. Mayotte based on Kenneth Hagberg's ideas. From the front, the shed roof of the house and the flat roof of the garage make the house seem almost buried. However, it is two stories on the rear facing the Red Cedar River.

PLATE 35. **Richard and Cheryl Maury House**

809 Harrison Road, East Lansing

Manson & Carver, 1955 (see text pp. 96–97)

Photo by Natasha Crljenica

From Harrison Road, this house appears modest and one story. It sits close to the road with a curved driveway. On the rear, it has two floors that take full advantage of the views of the rolling parkland. The ventilation system uses louvered windows that are visible in the clerestory.

PLATE 36. **Stanley and Monna Lee Hartman House**

Frank Lloyd Wright, 1955 (see text pp. 15–18)

For the Hartmans, Wright designed a house that is lengthened horizontally and spreads low to the ground. This rear view shows the windows that were used extensively, the horizontal planes of the roof and trellises, as well as the lower line of the bedroom wing and the raised roof above the living spaces. This design was the basis for the house that was built on the site ten years later (#62).

PLATE 37. **Gordon and Catherine Stow House**

3505 Tecumseh River Drive, Lansing

Gordon Stow, 1955 (see text p. 225)

Gordon Stow was a University of Michigan–educated architect who spent his career at Warren Holmes Company, rising to become its president by 1970. The design for his family's residence is a spacious brick ranch with wide eaves and pierced openings to allow light into the kitchen. On the front, it appears to be one story and settles easily on the lot. Behind, the land slopes down towards the river where the large windows of the dining room and sunken living room provide expansive views, and the lower-level basement at grade has access to the back.

PLATE 38. **George H. and Elizabeth Arbaugh House**

6 Locust Lane, Lansing

R. B. Sloan Jr., 1956 (see text pp. 216–18)

R. B. Sloan Jr.'s design for the Arbaughs takes full advantage of the setting at a point where the Grand River is on three sides of the house. This side facing inland is closed and private but texturally rich in the use of brick and stone. From this side the clerestory windows and the emphatic horizontality are clear.

PLATE 39. **Lansing City Hall**

124 West Michigan Avenue, Lansing, 1956–58

Lansing Police Headquarters, 1958–59

120 West Michigan Avenue, Lansing

Lee Black and Kenneth C. Black, Architects (see text pp. 138–41)

Photo courtesy of Michigan State Historic Preservation Office

City Hall is the closest that Lansing architecture comes to the International-style office building, characterized by an abundance of glazing, curtain wall construction, steel framing, and sleek design. The nine-story rectangular block fronts onto a plaza on the south side. The six-story Police Headquarters set at a right angle on the east was designed to complement City Hall. With its solid walls and small, square windows, it creates a foil to City Hall's transparency. Both reflect Mayor

Crego's efforts to project an image of the future-oriented city government.

PLATE 40. The Albert G. and Ethel Redmond House

820 Southlawn Avenue, East Lansing

Manson & Carver, 1956 (see text pp. 97–98)

Photo by Natasha Crljenica

This large one-story brick ranch is approached by the circular driveway that leads past a sunken garden. Bedroom suites are on the west, the more open public living spaces for entertaining in the center, and the maid's quarters and kitchen on the east.

PLATE 41. Herbert and Mildred Weisinger House

4351 Wausau Road, Okemos

Earl Vaive, 1957; tower addition, 1967 (see text p. 114)

Photo by Natasha Crljenica

Located on a cul-de sac, the original building has a shed roof and a three-story wall of glass windows on the back facing the Red Cedar River. Among the amenities were an indoor pool and a recreation room. When the next owners needed more space, they added the tower wing in 1967, expanding the house to six bedrooms and 2,900 square feet.

PLATE 42. Durward and Paula P. Varner House

1006 Lantern Hill Drive, East Lansing

R. B. Sloan Jr., 1957 (see text pp. 254–55)

© 2020 Kim Kauffman

The Varners participated in the Home Sites group and had built a Stubbins-designed house a short distance away. For this much larger house, they picked a local designer. The multi-levels on the interior are anticipated in the treatment of the exterior. The carport and center of the house are at one level. On the north, the upper bedrooms are above the basement, which is partially below grade. The long slope of the asymmetric roof meets the gable roof and dramatically ties the front together.

PLATE 43. Lawrence L. and Frances J. Boger

988 Lantern Hill Drive, East Lansing

R. B. Sloan Jr., 1957 (see text pp. 255–60)

© 2020 Kim Kauffman

The garage is closest to the street and shields the front and entry. The varied roof treatment—flat over the garage and broadly sloped on the rest of the house plus the large eaves—anchor the house to the site on this side. The Bogers were original members of the Home Sites group and moved to this spacious house from a smaller Stubbins-designed one nearby.

PLATE 44. Edgewood United Church

469 North Hagadorn Road, East Lansing

Laitala and Nuechterlein, 1957; sanctuary wing, Gordon Cornwell, 1966 (see text pp. 186–93)

Photo courtesy of the Michigan State Historic Preservation Office

Edgewood United Church was built in phases. The first (on the right) was comprised of the educational building and the auditorium designed by Laitala and Nuechterlein. The third phase added the sanctuary, atrium, chapel, and fireplace room on the left, designed by Gordon Cornwell. The congregation carefully studied the relation of architecture to worship and chose a circular plan for the sanctuary, although it is hexagonal on the exterior.

PLATE 45. Donald and Mary Lou Schaberg House

1155 Wrightwind Drive, Okemos

Frank Lloyd Wright, 1958; addition, Taliesin Associates, 1966 (see text pp. 11–15)

© 2014 Kim Kauffman

Donald and Mary Lou Schaberg worked with Frank Lloyd Wright for over ten years to build their residence. It was expanded in 1966, turning the L into a U-shaped house. The low-slung structure is evidence of Wright's ideas about organic architecture.

PLATE 46. Edward and Lisa Hertel House

1631 Walnut Heights Drive, East Lansing

Manson & Carver, 1958 (see text pp. 98–99)

This large brick L-shaped, quad-level house has both a carport and a two-car garage on the east, a one-story section in the center, and a two-story wing on the west that projects forward. The shed roof over the entrance provides a transition between the different levels.

PLATE 47. Gordon and Angela Fineout

2512 Delta River Drive, Lansing

Gordon Fineout, 1958 (see text p. 242)

Architectural designer Gordon Fineout trained in Los Angeles as an industrial designer. He brought a familiarity with California Contemporary architecture to Lansing and became a designer of choice for builders across the area. His own house pays homage to Frank Lloyd Wright's style in its emphasis on horizontality, flat roof, and large windows.

PLATE 48. William Sylvester and Margaret Jeannette Gamble House

1057 Daisy Lane, East Lansing

"ACH," 1958; garage addition, 1970 (see text pp. 262–66)

This rectangular house sits on a deeply excavated site so that the basement is at ground level. The house has a flat roof and lacks eaves. The flat walls are divided geometrically into panels that were originally bright green, orange, yellow ochre, and white, creating a colorful Mondrian gridlike pattern.

PLATE 49. Lloyd and Fern Marie Miller House

2019 Osage Drive, Okemos

Donald Scholz, 1958 (see text pp. 247–50)

Lloyd Miller was a partner with Frank Couchois in the building profession. For his own house, he picked a prefabricated design by Donald Scholz, whose factory in Toledo provided the materials for this house. The Mark '58 model had highly desired features, such as the spacious patio entry, the flush double doors, gabled ceilings inside, and glass inserted into the gable triangles. By extending the brick walls on either side of the house, a sense of privacy was ensured. The openness, in terms of the flow of space and the light, airy design, made this a very successful model, examples of which can be found all over the country.

PLATE 50. Kresge Art Center, rear

600 Auditorium Road, Michigan State University, East Lansing

Ralph Calder Associates, 1958; additions 1966, 1973 (see text pp. 168–69)

Photo courtesy of the Michigan State Historic Preservation Office

The Kresge Art Center is one of many buildings from the 1950s and 1960s on the MSU campus that illustrate Ralph Calder's International style. Features include curtain wall construction, glass and brick with aluminum trim, flat reflective surfaces, and the lack of ornament. The cantilevered balconies on Kresge's south side with colorful sunscreens on the upper level provide views of the Red Cedar River.

PLATE 51. Maynard and Betty Simmons House

4359 Wausau Road, Okemos

Gordon Fineout, 1959 (see text pp. 241–44)

Maynard Simmons, who worked at Standard Cement Supply, used this house as a demonstration of the range of its products. The perforated concrete blocks of the privacy wall, the poured concrete of the patios, and the dimensional blocks on inside walls are all examples. When the house was finished, it was opened to the public for one day. The design by Gordon Fineout takes full advantage of the proximity to the river with floor-to-ceiling windows on the back. On the front, the house is organically integrated into the wooded site, and the concrete wall allows only a glimpse of it behind.

PLATE 52. Carleton W. and Heluiz Washburne House

2248 Kent Street, Okemos

Alden B. Dow, 1960 (see text pp. 33–36)

© 2014 Kim Kauffman

The Washburnes' narrow one-story house is oriented east-west on a keyhole-shaped property that provides privacy from the road. Situated at the rise of the land, the flat roof and horizontal lines echo the terrain. The house is made of cement cinder blocks that are exposed outside and inside, with light wood, many built-ins, and large windows facing the back.

PLATE 53. Henry E. and Mary Crouse House

4400 Bittersweet Lane, Lansing

John E. Crouse, Mayotte-Webb, 1961 (see text pp. 219–23)

© 2020 Kim Kauffman

John E. Crouse designed this house for his parents at the start of his career. Many elements included here would reappear in his later work: the large overhangs, alternating solids and windows, multiple levels, and a careful attention to the site, which in this case, is a large waterfront lot.

PLATE 54. University United Methodist

1120 South Harrison, East Lansing

Earl Confer, Wesley Foundation, 1961; sanctuary, 1963 (see text pp. 211–12)

© 2014 Kim Kauffman

Within walking distance of the MSC campus, the Wesley Foundation education wing was built first, followed by the sanctuary a few years later. The education building has a flat roof, large windows, and low profile that contrasts with the brick of the distinctive church steeple.

PLATE 55. Michigan State Medical Society

129 West Saginaw Street, East Lansing

Minoru Yamasaki and Associates, 1961; addition 1979 (see text pp. 142–44)

© 2014 Kim Kauffman

This graceful building is set back from the busy traffic on Saginaw Street. The south and north elevations feature delicate two-story-high arches and floor-to-ceiling glazing. Inside, the quiet spaces and original Knoll and Herman Miller furniture still reflect architect Minoru Yamasaki's design ideas. This is one of Yamasaki's early examples of his rejection of the stark International style and the return to historical influences. The building was listed in the National Register of Historic Places in 2012.

PLATE 56. Eastminster Presbyterian Church

1315 Abbot Road, East Lansing

Alden B. Dow, 1961 (west side); addition, Manson, Jackson & Kane, 1969 (see text pp. 197–204)

Photo by Natasha Crljenica

The Eastminster congregation chose Alden B. Dow to design a large complex to be built in phases as money became available. In fact, only a small portion to the west reflects Dow's building, but he was responsible for siting it at the top of the sloping land. A decade later, Manson, Jackson & Kane extended the building's footprint to the east, providing a large sanctuary. Their design respects Dow's lines, materials, and ideas, seamlessly blending the old and new.

PLATE 57. Capitol Savings and Loan Association, Okemos Branch

2119 Hamilton Road, Okemos

J. Wesley Olds, 1961 (see text p. 155)

Photo by Natasha Crljenica

This one-story brick building sits to the east of the busy intersection of Okemos's "four corners." The large windows, flat roof, and clerestory with tinted plate glass reflect the Prairie School influence in American modernism.

PLATE 58. Erle Verdun and Mary Leichty House, rear

1864 Walnut Heights, East Lansing

Earl Vaive, 1961 (see text pp. 114–16)

This modified A-frame is turned so that the long sides of the house face the street and the backyard. The high-pitched roof allows for a second story over half of the space. On the interior, a balcony overlooks the two-story living room below. Bedrooms are on both levels.

PLATE 59. H. N. Hayes House

6292 Skyline Drive, East Lansing

Laitala and Nuechterlein, 1962 (see text pp. 106–13)

Landscape: Drew and Skidmore

The flat roof of the loggia leads past the carport to a large entry door. A detached "mother-in-law" guest house is on the west. Inside the house is expansive; the living and dining spaces face the Walnut Creek Golf fairway at the back.

PLATE 60. Lansing Teachers Credit Union (now Michigan Press Association)

827 North Washington Avenue, Lansing

Charles V. Opdyke, 1962 (see text p. 151)

This one-story building is a prime example of the sleek, spare International style. With steel posts supporting the canopy and large areas of glazing contrasting with the solid block of limestone, the building is functional, understated, and proportionately elegant.

PLATE 61. John and Marguerite Crouse House

1792 Walnut Heights Drive, East Lansing

John Crouse, 1962; addition 1964 (see text pp. 73–74)

Photo courtesy of the Michigan State Historic Preservation Office

John Crouse designed his own ranch-style residence with the long wall of the bedroom wing facing the street. Narrow vertical windows divide the wall, providing light to the interior hallway. The carport is at a right angle to the house. Several stairs lead to the front door and prepare the visitor for the elevation changes inside.

PLATE 62. Dixon Shaw and Madeline Wilson House

414 Ardson Road, East Lansing

Dixon Shaw Wilson, 1963 (see text pp. 74, 78)

In this design for his own house on a corner lot, the architect placed the driveway on Grand River Avenue and the garage on the lower level. This enabled him to face the house onto Ardson Road, a much quieter and less-trafficked street.

PLATE 63. East Lansing Public Library

950 Abbot Road, East Lansing

Manson, Jackson & Kane, Inc., 1963; addition 1975, renovation 1997 (see text pp. 173–77)

Photo by Natasha Crljenica

The East Lansing Public Library, located on the edge of what was Burcham Woods, is distinguished by modernist features such as the zigzag roofline and the large glazing on the front elevation protected by a metal sunscreen. The 1975 addition made the roof less visible and a 1997 renovation changed the interior.

PLATE 64. Dawn Donuts (now Bell's Pizza)

1135 East Grand River Avenue, East Lansing

Architect unknown, 1963 (see text p. 161)

Photo courtesy of Amanda Seeger

Almost all of the Dawn Donuts shops, which were ubiquitous in Michigan in the 1960s, had the same steeply pitched, sharp-angled roofline. This is one of the few remaining examples of the exuberant, unrestrained, optimistic architectural style referred to as "Googie." Rather than high design, this is a vernacular style whose function was to call attention to itself.

PLATE 65. Wallis M. and Norine Antuck House

3815 Waverly Hills, Lansing

William Kessler, 1963 (see text pp. 88–89)

© 2014 Kim Kauffman

This is an exact replica of the steel-and-glass house, listed in the National Register of Historic Places, that William Kessler built for himself and his family in Grosse Pointe Park, near Detroit. The sawtooth roof divides the house into three equal bays. The north and south sides are fully transparent with floor to ceiling glazing; from this south side, there is a view of the Grand River beyond.

PLATE 66. Lansing Public Library (Clarence H. Rosa Public Library)

401 South Capitol Avenue, Lansing

Kenneth C. Black Associates, 1964

Landscape design: D. Newton Glick, west garden (see text pp. 177–80)

Photo courtesy of Michigan State Historic Preservation Office

The most distinctive feature of this building is the treatment of the upper façade with repeating patterns of molded panels, with quartz aggregate that makes the surfaces shimmer in the sunlight. The sunken plaza on the west side of the building is balanced on the east side by a Japanese garden that is hidden from the street. All of these details are evidence of Black's interest in pattern and texture that moved beyond the unornamented modernist International style.

PLATE 67. Michigan Education Association

1216 Kendale Boulevard, East Lansing

The Warren Holmes Company, 1964 (see text pp. 144–50)

© 2014 Kim Kauffman

The Michigan Education Association building, designed by the Warren Holmes Company, is two stories raised above a lower plaza that surrounds it on three sides. This elevation faces Saginaw Street, a major thoroughfare in East Lansing. At the center, the sunscreen shades the board room behind. The building's central focus, however, is the two-story interior courtyard.

PLATE 68. Martin Luther Chapel

444 Abbot Road, East Lansing

Charles Stade, 1964; addition, Tim Mrozowski, 2001 (see text pp. 193–97)

Photo by Natasha Crljenica

This dramatic chapel is described in the church's literature as strong, masculine, and monumental, tied to the earth by the steeply pitched roof but also soaring into space to reflect Christian worship. The sanctuary is at the northeast corner of the property; the narthex, offices, and education spaces extend on a diagonal to the southwest.

PLATE 69. Kenneth C. and Marie Black House

1501 Cambridge Road

Kenneth C. Black, 1964 (see text pp. 74–80)

Landscape: D. Newton Glick

© 2014 Kim Kauffman

Kenneth Black's design for his own residence is an example of his sophisticated approach to modernism and his concern for the totality of architecture, art, and landscape design. The patterned cement blocks echo the ornamented approach he used on the Lansing Public Library building of the same year.

PLATE 70. Sanford Farness House

730 Grove Street, East Lansing

Sanford Farness, 1964 (see text pp. 117–18)

Photo by Natasha Crljenica

Sanford Farness, professor of urban planning, came to Michigan State College from California, which explains the California-bungalow style of his home. Beyond the three-car carport (now enclosed) is a private courtyard that leads to the large rambling house on several levels. Each change of height is marked by a change in roofline emphasized by large overhanging eaves.

PLATE 71. **Robert E. and B. Katherine Brown House**

2070 Lagoon Drive, Okemos

Earl Vaive, 1964 (see text pp. 244–47)

© 2020 Kim Kauffman

The Browns hired architect Earl Vaive to design their contemporary residence that has river access at the back and a view of the lagoon from the front. The house grows organically from the site. Sitting low on the street side at the ground's highest level, it appears to be one story. Coming around to the entrance on the south, as the land slopes down, the structure rises two stories in height. Large windows provide long vistas in three directions.

PLATE 72. **Dale and Hope Crites House**

4317 Tacoma Boulevard , Okemos

Laitala and Nuechterlein, 1964 (see text pp. 112–14)

Landscape: Drew and Skidmore

Photo by Natasha Crljenica

This large two-story house fronts on a bend in the road and backs onto the Red Cedar River. The flat lines of the carport and loggia announce the modernist approach of the interior. The house has an open plan on the main level and an open staircase leading to the bedrooms above.

PLATE 73. **Dr. Kent and Donna Hay House**

1234 White Oaks Drive, Okemos

John Crouse, Mayotte-Webb, 1964 (see text p. 102)

© 2014 Kim Kauffman

The front elevation of this light-colored brick house does not prepare the visitor for the dramatic way it sits up on large piers with open patio spaces beneath on the back side.

PLATE 74. **Stanley and Monna Lee Hartman House**

1185 Wrightwind Drive, Okemos

John Crouse, Mayotte-Webb, 1965 (see text pp. 99–100)

© 2014 Kim Kauffman

The Hartmans asked architect John Crouse to modify and build their Frank Lloyd Wright design (#34). This property is adjacent to the Schabergs' Wright-designed residence (#39). In keeping with the organic approach to architecture, this one-story building with its low slanting roof hugs the landscape.

PLATE 75. **Frank and Martha Couchois House**

2150 Pawnee Drive, Okemos

Gordon Fineout, 1965 (see text pp. 251–52)

© 2020 Kim Kauffman

Builder Frank Couchois picked an expansive site at the end of the street in Tacoma Hills to build his own home. Working with designer Gordon Fineout, he took full advantage of the slope of the land and the river paralleling the lot on the west. From the front, the house appears to be one story with a large gracious entry protected by the deep gable that has exposed beams.

PLATE 76. **John P. and Margaret A. Henderson House**

1744 Ridgewood Drive, East Lansing

Margaret A. Henderson design, 1965 (see text p. 120)

© 2014 Kim Kauffman

This 2,000-square-foot house was originally known by the neighbors as the "fishbowl" because of the placement on the corner lot (at Ridgewood and Woodside), the extensive use of glass, and lack of landscaping at the time. It has large eaves and covered porches on two sides. The interior pivots around the centrally placed kitchen.

PLATE 77. **Liebermann's**

113 South Washington Square, Lansing

George Nelson, 1966 (see text pp. 141–42)

Photo courtesy of Michigan State Historic Preservation Office

George Nelson designed a new store for Betty Price in downtown Lansing using the bare bones of an older building. The striking two-story building with a 22-foot-high glass front signals the new, modern design of the goods sold inside. The open, soaring space creates a unity between the interior and exterior, inviting the passersby into the store.

PLATE 78. Arby's (Bigby's Coffee)

270 West Grand River Avenue, East Lansing

Lester H. Weinberg, engineer, 1966; addition 1975 (see text p. 161)

Photo courtesy of Amanda Seeger

All Arby's restaurants used the same Googie design. The most distinctive feature is the curved roofline designed to resemble a Conestoga wagon from the old West. The flat-roofed section on the west is a later addition. The building is slated to be demolished to make way for a mixed-use development.

PLATE 79. Myles and Virginia Delano House

4600 Comanche Drive, Okemos

Alexander William Dempsey, 1966; addition above garage, 2007 (see text pp. 230–34)

© 2020 Kim Kauffman

On the exterior, the house appears to be two stories with two entrances: one at street level and the other, marked by an awning, is several steps below. This hints at the multi-levels of the interior. The wood exterior is also continued on the interior. Large windows are on the front, south end, and on the back, where the house sits high above the swale.

PLATE 80. Richard and Sharon Taber House

1190 Wrightwind Drive, Okemos

John Crouse, Mayotte-Webb, 1967 (see text pp. 100–102)

© 2014 Kim Kauffman

Set on three-and-a-half acres, this large 3,000-square-foot house has red brick and redwood trim on the interior and exterior. The large expanses of the mansard roof give the building a massive and masculine character.

PLATE 81. Michael and Rhea Dow House

1172 Wrightwind Drive, Okemos

Alden B. Dow, 1967 (see text p. 36)

© 2014 Kim Kauffman

Designed by Alden B. Dow for his son and daughter-in-law, Michael and Rhea, this is also one of the last houses by the architect. It is located on a large lot and the structure is equally expansive, with many built-ins as well as a swimming pool.

PLATE 82. Jens and Nancy Plum House, rear

4085 Van Atta Road, Okemos

Robert Hanamura, 1967 (see text p. 73)

Photograph courtesy of Nancy Plum

Born in 1923 in San Francisco, Robert Hanamura received a BA in architecture from the Miami University of Ohio. He arrived in the Detroit area after serving in World War II and came to know people associated with Cranbrook, such as Charles Eames, Saarinen, Alexander Gerard, as well as Minoru Yamasaki. He ran a gallery focused on design, and taught design at Wayne State University and the University of Michigan. His architectural output was small, primarily store interiors and additions to houses. Artists Jens and Nancy Plum had been students at Cranbrook, came to know Bob at his gallery, and admired his design work at the Hagopian Oriental Rug Store in Birmingham. He designed this contemporary space for them, taking full advantage of views of the Red Cedar River at the back.

PLATE 83. Harold and Wilma Good House

812 Applegate Lane, East Lansing

Alfred Browning Parker, 1967 (see text p. 120)

Photo courtesy of the Michigan State Historic Preservation Office

Alfred Browning Parker (1916–2011) established his architectural practice in South Florida in 1946. Harold Good, an Oldsmobile executive, and his wife, a Smucker's Jelly heiress, commissioned Parker to build their Florida home at the same time as this East Lansing home. Parker was inspired by the organic architecture of Frank Lloyd Wright. Three of his houses were published by *House Beautiful* in the 1950s. Here, the portico entrance is 28 feet long. The gables, repeated at different heights, are glazed to create light-filled spaces on the interior. A large fireplace dominates the living and dining area, and mahogany wood was used on many walls and for handcrafted trim and knobs.

PLATE 84. **Edward and Mrs. Pratt House**

1834 Mirabeau Drive, Okemos
Couchois and Miller Builders and Developers, 1967; addition behind garage, 2006 (see text p. 253)
© 2020 Kim Kauffman

Couchois and Miller built this very contemporary house on speculation in an upscale subdivision they created in the late 1960s. The design is a series of boxes of different heights, with skylights and clerestory and high windows. On the front side, privacy is paramount. On the back, large windows and sliding glass doors provide access to patios in the surrounding wooded area. Horizontal roofs and lines counteract the verticals of the walls. The portion behind the garage is a recent addition but in keeping with the overall design.

PLATE 85. **Dr. Carl W. and Mrs. West House**

4609 Comanche Drive, Okemos
Arai and Hummel Architects, 1967; dining area addition, 1997; Landscape: Jack A. Drew Associates (see text pp. 234–40)
© 2020 Kim Kauffman.

Arai and Hummel Architects, based in Suttons Bay, designed many houses in northern Michigan but only a few farther south. Like their up-north examples, this house is also on the water. It has multiple roof lines and staggered walls that project forward and then angle back to create an active presence and complexity.

PLATE 86. **Saint Thomas Aquinas**

955 Alton Road, East Lansing
Mayotte-Webb, 1968; education wing, Laitala and Nuechterlein, 1956 (see text pp. 207–12)
Photo by Natasha Crljenica

The large stained-glass window (60 × 50 feet) on the east side became the organizing feature for the rest of the building. To cover the expanse, a gambrel roof was used. The sanctuary, the school to the south, and offices and residences behind are set back from the road to create a campus atmosphere.

PLATE 87. **Shaarey Zedek Synagogue**

1924 Coolidge Road, East Lansing
Smith, Hinchman & Grylls, 1969 (see text pp. 213–14)
Photo courtesy of the Michigan State Historic Preservation Office

Constructed of brick, this sprawling complex is 32,000 square feet set on ten acres. It consists of the sanctuary and fellowship hall connected by a glass atrium to the classroom and office wing. A high, narrow band of windows in the sanctuary is one of the modernist features, as are the lack of ornamentation and the dramatic sweep of the tower. Whether it was a design flaw or deliberate, the ark in the sanctuary faces west rather than east towards Jerusalem, as is typical in most Western synagogues.

Biographies of Architects and Landscape Architects

Glenn Tsutomi Arai

Glenn Tsutomi Arai (1925–1998) was born in Los Angeles and spent his teens years between 1942 and 1945 in the Manzanar Relocation Center in California with his parents. He received a bachelor of arts in architecture from University of Illinois in 1947 and practiced in Chicago from 1950 to 1955. With Roger A. Hummel, he opened Arai and Hummel Architects in 1965 based in Suttons Bay, Michigan. The majority of their work was in Traverse City and the Leelanau Peninsula in northern Michigan. By using natural materials such as indigenous wood and stone, they sought to connect buildings to their settings. Fragmented or full views from one space into another and to the outside did this as well. In the 1970s, they also developed a patented flexible modular system that put together preformed box shapes to form a whole building.

Florence Dyer Baldwin

Florence Helen Dyer (1919–2011), known as Florence Dyer Baldwin after marrying in 1958, was born in Orange, New Jersey. She received her bachelor's in architecture in 1940 from the University of Michigan, attended New York University in 1943, and attended Michigan State College, 1948–1950. From 1943 until 1958, she was employed as an architectural engineer for the state in the Michigan Planning Division, working in the Lewis Cass Building in Lansing. In 1959, she was appointed project architect for the state. By 1970, she had retired and moved to California. She served as secretary of the Detroit Professional Chapter of the Association of Women in Architecture.

Lee Black and Kenneth C. Black, Architects/ Kenneth C. Black Associates, Inc.

Kenneth C. Black (1901–1991) joined his father, Lee Black (1877–1960), at his Lansing architecture firm in 1932, which was renamed Lee Black and Kenneth C. Black, Architects. Lee was educated as a draftsman and was first employed in Lansing by Thomas E. White and then started his own firm in 1913. Kenneth was educated at the University of Michigan and received the George G. Booth Traveling Fellowship in 1925–26, which enabled him to travel around the globe. Together the Blacks designed some of Lansing's most significant buildings, including the International-style City Hall and Police Headquarters complex (1956–58), and Auto-Owners Insurance Company (1952). After his father retired in 1958, Kenneth formed Kenneth C. Black Associates and designed the Lansing Public Library (1964). Kenneth was very active locally on numerous commissions and in the AIA Detroit chapter, and served as president of the Michigan Society of Architects (1943–45). In 1973, his firm merged with Warren Holmes Company, forming the Warren Holmes–Kenneth Black Company.

Bowd-Munson/O. J. Munson Architects

Orlie J. Munson (1891–1957) and Edwyn A. Bowd (1865–1940) formed a partnership in 1929 and became one of the most respected Lansing architectural firms for decades. Bowd was born and educated in England and immigrated to the United States in the 1880s, establishing his firm in Lansing in 1883. He designed numerous buildings on the Michigan State College campus in a variety of styles. Munson worked for Bowd from 1908 until 1912, when he left to work for the U.S. government. He returned to Lansing in 1922. Bowd-Munson designed the landmarked Knapp's building (1937–39) in a Streamline Moderne style in downtown Lansing and was responsible in the 1930s for numerous Collegiate Gothic buildings that characterize the oldest part of MSC's north campus. Following Bowd's death in 1940, O. J. Munson Architects continued work on the campus through the 1940s.

Ralph Calder Associates/Ralph Calder and Associates, Inc.

Ralph R. Calder (1900–1968) was educated at the University of Michigan and spent a year (1924–25) traveling in Europe on a Booth Traveling Fellowship in Architecture, followed by a year as staff architect for University of Michigan in Tunisia. When he returned, he worked for Eliel Saarinen (1925–26); Malcomson, Higginbotham and Trout (1926–35); then Malcomson, Calder and Hammond (1935–45), before opening his own Detroit firm in 1945. It was responsible for numerous buildings for Michigan's state universities, including Eastern Michigan, Western Michigan, Wayne State, and the University of Michigan. At MSU, he was the architect of many of the buildings of the 1950s and 1960s, including the Hannah Administration Building (1968), Kresge Art Center (1959), the MSU Library (1955), and several high-rise dormitories.

Gordon Cornwell

Gordon Cornwell (1917–2011) studied architecture at Syracuse University, earning degrees in 1939 and 1940. After serving in the navy during World War II, he settled in Traverse City and opened his practice in 1947. Cornwell Associates continues as a firm today, focusing on Northern Michigan.

John Crouse

John Emerson Crouse (1935–2009) received his BA in architecture from the University of Michigan in 1959. He joined Mayotte-Webb Architects of East Lansing in 1960, which became Mayotte, Crouse and D'Haene Architects in 1961. He was active in the mid-Michigan AIA chapter. The firm worked on many projects for MSU and in mid-Michigan. In 1962 Crouse designed his own ranch-style residence in East Lansing as well as several houses on Wrightwind Drive in Okemos.

Alexander William Dempsey

Alexander William Dempsey (1929–1989) graduated from the University of Michigan in 1956 and started out as a draftsman with Daverman Company in Grand

Rapids. In 1959, he joined Warren Holmes Company also as a draftsman and became self-employed towards the end of 1964. In 1973, he was admitted to the AIA. The 1966 Delano House is the earliest of his buildings that has been identified. Others date from the 1970s: the Myron Beal House at 4650 Sequoia Trail, 1975, in the same subdivision; the Holt Assembly of God Church, 1974; and the Pleasant Grove Church, 1977.

Alden B. Dow

Alden B. Dow (1904–1983) studied architecture at Columbia University and then apprenticed with Frank Lloyd Wright at Taliesin for a short time. He opened his Midland, Michigan, practice in 1934. Dow designed more than 350 structures in Michigan, including Eastminster Church and four residences in East Lansing and Okemos. His patented Unit Block system was used at 929 Roxburgh, East Lansing. His masterpiece is his landmarked home and studio in Midland, now open to the public. Dow's design philosophy is recorded in numerous writings and documents. Upon his retirement, James Howell succeeded Dow as chairman of the board of the company in 1974, and the name was changed to Dow, Howell, Gilmore Associates, Inc. (DHGA) after Dow's death.

Drew and Skidmore, Landscape Architects

Jack Drew (1925–1988) and Joseph E. Skidmore (1932–1993) were Lansing landscape architects in partnership through 1964. Drew studied horticulture and landscape architecture at MSU. Skidmore also was a graduate of MSU's College of Agriculture. As of 1965, Drew started his own firm, Jack A. Drew Associates, Inc., and then joined Warren Holmes in 1967. Drew was made an honorary associate member of the Mid-Michigan Chapter of the AIA in 1965. A *Lansing State Journal* article on November 7, 1965, noted that he was recognized for "his outstanding contributions to the practice of landscape architecture and his interest in and support of the chapter." Skidmore joined Robert's Landscaping by 1966.

Buckminster Fuller

Buckminster Fuller (1895–1983) was a visionary, inventor, and architect. Among his most celebrated designs were the Dymaxion house (first constructed in 1948) and Dymaxion car (1930s), neither of which went into production. His geodesic domes, however, caught on as lightweight structures that could be erected quickly and economically. They were seen at the New York World's Fair (1964) and Expo '67 in Montreal, and many continue to be used.

D. Newton Glick, Landscape Architect

MSU professor D. Newton Glick became chair of the Department of Landscape Studies when it expanded to a four-year undergraduate major in Urban Planning in 1946. When the department was transferred to the new College of Social Science in 1962, he became associate director of Landscape Architecture. In 1955 he authored a book on landscape planning for residential properties for the MSU Cooperative Extension Services.

Clarke E. Harris

Clarke E. Harris (1906–1993) graduated from the University of Michigan in 1929 and became associated with Warren Holmes in 1935 through 1942. For two years he worked for the Michigan State Building Division and then returned to Warren Holmes Company as a principal in 1944.

Bruce Miles Hartwick

Bruce Miles Hartwick (1919–1995) received his BA in architecture from the University of Michigan in 1943. After serving in the army, he moved to Lansing and joined with Stanley Gibson Simpson (1900–1961) to form the partnership Simpson and Hartwick in 1953, following the death of Simpson's original partner Ralph Herrick. Upon Simpson's death in 1961, Hartwick formed Hartwick & Associates.

Ralph B. Herrick

Ralph B. Herrick (ca. 1895–1952) was an architect with J. N. Churchill (1929), then Lee Black in Lansing, and formed Herrick and Simpson, a partnership with Stanley Gibson Simpson, in 1938 until his death.

The Warren Holmes Company

Warren Samuel Holmes (1889–1978) founded his firm in 1920 in Lansing. In 1944 he expanded it to a partnership that eventually became one of the largest in mid-Michigan. Holmes first designed educational buildings, as well as the Michigan Education Association building in East Lansing, and over time expanded to commercial office and municipal buildings. In 1973 the firm merged with another prominent Lansing firm, Kenneth C. Black Associates.

Roger A. Hummel

Upon graduating from the University of Michigan with a degree in architecture, Roger A. Hummel (b. 1931) moved to Traverse City and worked for several of the established firms. He joined with Glenn Tsutomi Arai to form Arai and Hummel Architects, based in Suttons Bay, Michigan, in 1965, and he was a member of the AIA from 1966 on. After Arai's death, Hummel became a solo practitioner and retired around 2014. He designed numerous lodges and residences in northern Michigan, including Pine Hollow, a 17,000-square-foot home in Elk Rapids, Michigan, that is now a nonprofit retreat center.

Edwin Johnson

Edwin Johnson (1903–1971) was educated at the Webb Institute of Naval Architecture. He joined with John Merrall Whitcomb in 1946 to organize Johnson and Whitcomb, with offices in Cambridge, Massachusetts. He also taught architectural design and was involved with education activities at Harvard University in 1951, and the Franklin Technological Institute, 1952–53.

Keck & Keck

The Keck brothers, George Fred (1895–1980), known as Fred, and William (1908–1995), formed their partnership in the 1920s in Chicago and came to prominence as a result of two houses they contributed to the Century of Progress Fair in 1933 (the House of Tomorrow) and in 1934 (the Crystal House). They worked primarily in the Midwest, designing numerous houses utilizing innovative ventilation and passive solar systems.

William Kessler

William Kessler (1924–2002) trained at Harvard University with Walter Gropius. He arrived in Michigan to work for Minoru Yamasaki (Leinweber, Yamasaki & Hellmuth) and eventually started his own firm, Meathe, Kessler and Associates in 1955; William Kessler and Associates in 1968; and Kessler Francis Cardoza Architects in 1999. The practice was based in the Detroit suburb of Grosse Pointe. In addition to designing the Detroit Receiving Hospital (1979), Detroit Science Center (now the Michigan Science Center) (1979), and the Kresge-Ford Building at the College for Creative Studies (1974), he designed the Michigan Historical Center in Lansing (1985–88).

Karl Frederick Krauss Jr.

Karl Frederick Krauss Jr. (1923–2008) studied at the University of Michigan and started as a draftsman for Warren Holmes Company in 1940. He worked for a variety of firms until he started his individual practice in 1953. The following year he opened Krauss and Farnsworth with an office in Lansing and then returned to a sole practice (Karl Krauss Jr., Architects) in 1957, the year he designed the Griswold house in East Lansing.He left Michigan for Wisconsin in 1964; by 1970 he was in Tucson, Arizona; he was in Illinois in 1971; and by 1979 he was in El Paso, Texas. He specialized in school and church designs.

Laitala and Nuechterlein

Walter Mathew Laitala (1917–1992) was educated at the University of Michigan from 1939 to 1943. He began as a draftsman with Lee and Kenneth Black, 1944–1948. He formed a partnership in 1948 with Wilmar (Nick)

Nuechterlein (1920–2009), also a graduate of the University of Michigan, 1939–43. He had an AIA traveling fellowship to Europe in 1940 and served in the navy for three years (1943–46). He, too, started as a draftsman with Lee and Kenneth Black, and then worked for Warren Holmes in 1947. Laitala and Nuechterlein were best known for designing churches and schools, many in mid-Michigan, including Edgewood Church and Glencairn Elementary School in East Lansing. They also designed numerous modern houses in the region. By 1966, their partnership dissolved. In 1972 Laitala merged with Freeman, Smith and Associates, begun in 1957, and the successor firm, Laitala, Freeman, Smith and Fowler, continued to work in mid-Michigan. Nuechterlein retired in 1983.

Adrian Langius

From 1939 until he retired in 1971, architect Adrian (Gus) Langius (1903–1991) was employed by the State of Michigan. As the state architect, he made an impact in preservation, planning, and construction codes. His modernist design approach is evident in two adjacent East Lansing houses.

Manson & Carver/Manson, Jackson & Kane, Inc.

The Lansing firm of Manson, Jackson & Kane, Inc. began as a solo practice founded in 1941 by Elmer J. Manson (1913–1991). He was educated in architecture at Cornell University and received awards and a travel grant to visit Europe. He started his career in Vermont, then worked in Syracuse and Utica, New York, before moving the practice to Lansing in 1946. With his college classmate William White Carver (1913–1987), he organized Manson & Carver in 1949. Carver was born in Ithaca, New York, and attended Cornell University, graduating in 1936. He began his career as a draftsman in Ithaca; moved to Funk, Molander & Johnson in Spokane, Washington; and was in the navy from 1942 to 1944. He joined Manson in Lansing in 1949. In 1960 he took a teaching position at the School of Architecture, Montana State College in Bozeman. After Carver left, Manson took on other partners: Edward Jackson, who was educated in Stuttgart, Germany, and joined Manson's group in 1950, becoming a partner in 1955; and William J. H. Kane, who attended the University of Notre Dame and began his career in Chicago. He joined Manson's firm and became a partner in 1959. The name Manson, Jackson & Kane was adopted in 1960. By 1965 the firm (then Manson, Mattern and Barker) had designed more than one hundred educational, commercial, and residential buildings in mid-Michigan, primarily in the Lansing metropolitan region. In addition to the East Lansing Public Library, it was responsible for many spacious ranches in the Whitehills and Walnut Heights areas of East Lansing during the 1950s and 1960s. Manson held numerous offices in the West Michigan chapter of the AIA as well as the Michigan Society of Architects.

Mayotte-Webb

Bernard Joseph Mayotte (1923–2006) graduated from the University of Notre Dame in 1950 and worked for Lee and Kenneth Black (1952–58). In 1958 he established Mayotte-Webb Architects in East Lansing with partner Wesley W. Webb (1918–2004). Nobyn H. D'Haene and John Crouse became principals in 1961 (Mayotte, Crouse and D'Haene Architects), and then it became Mayotte, D'Haene and Associates. In 1986 it merged with the Warren Holmes–Kenneth Black Company (renamed MBDS Architects) and relocated in 1988 to Delta Township. In 1996 the firm became MayotteJacob Architects, and in 2006, MAYOTTEgroup Architects. In 2014 it partnered with Keystone Design Group, another Lansing-based architectural firm, creating the largest firm in the Lansing area.

George Nelson

George Nelson (1908–1986) studied at the Yale School of Fine Arts and started as a writer for *Architectural Forum*, becoming managing editor in 1943. He opened his design firm in 1947 while serving as design director at Herman Miller, Inc., from 1946 until 1972. Many of his iconic furniture designs became well known and continue in production. Additionally, he did graphic design, buildings, and interiors.

J. Wesley Olds

J. Wesley Olds (1917–2010) graduated from the University of Michigan in 1942. He was an architect with C. William Palmer, based in Detroit. He then formed his solo practice in mid-Michigan, J. Wesley Olds, Architect (1955–58), and in 1961 joined with Morris Stein, an engineer, to form J. Wesley Olds–Morris Stein, based in Okemos. In 1970 he became an architectural analyst for the State of Michigan Bureau of Budget.

Charles Victor Opdyke

Charles Victor Opdyke (1918–1991) was a Lansing native. After returning home from service in the U.S. Army across Europe, he took a position as an architectural engineer for the state (1945–48), then worked with Clark R. Ackley (1948–51) and Warren Holmes Company (1951–53), and organized his solo practice in 1953. He later worked as an architect for Manson, Jackson & Kane.

Alfred Browning Parker

Inspired by the organic architecture of Frank Lloyd Wright, Alfred Browning Parker (1916–2011) established his practice in South Florida in 1946. Three of his houses were featured in *House Beautiful* in the 1950s, and in 2006, *Wall Paper* magazine selected a Parker residence for inclusion in the "Top 10 Houses in the World," the only North American house selected. He designed the Harold Good family homes in Florida and East Lansing (1967).

Anna R. Peters

Anna R. Peters (1907–2001) was born in Howell, Michigan. She attended Immaculata Seminary in Washington, DC (1920–1925); St. Mary of the Woods, Indiana (1926–1927); and the University of Michigan for her bachelor's in architecture (1927–1931). From 1940 to 1941 and in 1944, she was a draftsperson in Clark R. Ackley's architectural office. By 1947, she had her own practice with an office at 428 LaSalle Boulevard, Lansing, and became a registered architect with the AIA in 1949. She was active in the Detroit Professional Chapter of the Association of Women in Architecture.

Ralph Rapson

Ralph Rapson (1914–2008) studied architecture at the University of Michigan and Cranbrook Academy of Art. He began his teaching career at the New Bauhaus in Chicago in 1942, moved to the Massachusetts Institute of Technology in 1946, and then the University of Minnesota from 1954 until 1984. He designed numerous buildings all over the world, including embassies, performing arts centers and theaters, and residences, as well as furniture.

Clarence H. Rosa

Clarence H. Rosa (1912–1990) was a native Lansing architect, educated at Michigan State College and the University of Michigan. He served as deputy director of the Department of Administration Building Division for the State of Michigan from 1941, responsible for buildings designed and constructed for the state ranging from offices to hospitals, education and penal facilities. He held numerous offices in the West Michigan chapter of the AIA in the 1940s.

Stanley Gibson Simpson

Stanley Gibson Simpson (1900–1961) was educated at the University of Michigan, worked as a designer for Warren Holmes Company (1926–37), and then formed Herrick and Simpson (1937–1952). Following the death of Ralph Herrick, Simpson formed the partnership Simpson and Hartwick in 1953.

Smith, Hinchman & Grylls

Smith, Hinchman & Grylls was established in Detroit in 1853. Three generations of Smith architects benefited from the expansion of Detroit in the late nineteenth and early twentieth centuries. After weathering the Depression with a reduced staff, the company rebounded, especially after World War II. In the mid-1940s, the firm turned to contemporary design, assisted by its chief designer, Minoru Yamasaki. By this time, it had received commissions around the globe, including South Korea, and expanded its market to Washington, DC, Chicago, and Louisville. Now known as the SmithGroup, it is one of the country's oldest and largest firms and designs a variety of building types, from hospitals, medical laboratories, and factories to civic and educational buildings, as well as comprehensive planning. The firm designed the Shaarey Zedek Synagogue in East Lansing, built in 1969, and has worked on the MSU campus.

Jane L. Smith, Landscape Architect

Jane L. Smith was a well-known and respected landscape architect who returned to school after marrying and having children. She earned her degree at Michigan State University in 1957. She was one of very few landscape architects in mid-Michigan and was active in the profession, serving as president of the Michigan Association of Landscape Architects in 1959, among other roles. She and her husband Edwin E. formed Smith Tree Service in Lansing in 1948, which continues to this day.

Richard G. Snyder

Richard (Dick) G. Sn yder (1913–2012) started out at Warren Holmes Company as a draftsman (1935–1941) and field supervisor (1935–1938). He was a draftsman for the Detroit firm of Giffels and Vallet Inc. from 1941–1943 while attending University of Michigan. He received his undergraduate degree in architecture in 1943 and became a registered architect in 1944. He served in the U.S. Army's antiaircraft artillery battery in 1941–1946, and returned to Warren Holmes as an architect in 1950. He specialized in high school buildings.

Charles Edward Stade

Charles Edward Stade (1923–1993) received degrees in architecture from the University of Illinois (1946) and Princeton University (1948) and opened Charles Edward Stade & Associates in Park Ridge, Illinois, in 1951. He specialized in church architecture; was a member of the Church Architecture Guild, an affiliate of the American Institute of Architects started in 1958; and served as president of the American Society of Church Architecture. His masterpiece is the large Chapel of the Resurrection at Valparaiso University (1959). Many of his churches were A-frame designs with minimal ornamentation that relied on geometric stained-glass windows to illuminate the interiors. Stade had several different partners over the decades (Stade & Cooley; Stade, Dolan and Anderson; Stade, Dolan, Smith & Associates) until his retirement in 1981.

Gordon H. Stow

Gordon H. Stow (1913–2007) received his bachelor of science and masters of science in architecture in 1936 from the University of Michigan, took a year to travel in Europe, Egypt, and Iran, before starting as a draftsman and architectural engineer at Warren Holmes Company in 1937. Except for four years in the U.S. Army (1942–1947), his professional career was spent there, eventually becoming president of the company. He was very active in Lansing civic life and held numerous elected positions in the YMCA as well as president of the international YMCA.

Hugh Stubbins Jr.

Hugh Stubbins Jr. (1912–2006) studied architecture at Harvard University under renowned Bauhaus architect Walter Gropius, graduating in 1935. He returned to teach at Harvard and remained through 1972. In 1949, he formed Hugh Stubbins, Architect. He went on to become internationally known, designing buildings in Germany, Singapore, and Iran, as well as the United States. The Ronald Reagan Library (1991), Citycorp Center (1978), and Landmark Tower in Yokohama (1993) are among his best-known buildings. The successor firm, Stubbins Associates, merged with Kling, a Philadelphia-based firm, to form KlingStubbins in 2007.

Earl Vaive

Earl Vaive (1924–1999) was an architect for the State of Michigan for forty-one years before retiring in 1988.

Malcom Mills Williams

After receiving his architecture degree from Cornell University in 1935, Malcom (Mal) Williams (1912–1991) worked for Walter H. Whitlock, an architect in New York, until 1941. The next year Williams accepted a teaching position with the College of Engineering, MSC. Two years later he joined the Warren Holmes Company, and in 1946 was made a partner.

Dixon Shaw Wilson

Dixon Shaw Wilson (1923–2001) graduated from Ohio State University in 1949 and worked in Ohio and Michigan before joining Manson & Carver Associates in 1954. He was made partner in 1958 and started his own firm in 1960.

Frank Lloyd Wright

Over his long career, Frank Lloyd Wright (1867–1959) designed numerous residences and commercial buildings, primarily in the Midwest. After his early Prairie style in the Chicago area, and following the Great Depression, he sought to build moderate-cost homes for middle-income clients. Usonia 2, a project for MSC faculty, was unrealized, but one of the houses (for Alma Goetsch and Kathrine Winckler) was built in 1940. Later houses after the war were increasingly more expensive. His approach to organic architecture in which the setting in, and relationship to, nature is paramount was to influence many local architects who designed domestic and commercial structures.

Minoru Yamasaki and Associates

Minoru Yamasaki (1912–1986) earned an undergraduate degree in architecture from the University of Washington in 1934 and studied for a master's degree from New York University. He came to Detroit in 1945 to become chief of design for Smith, Hinchman & Grylls. In 1949 he cofounded Leinweber, Yamasaki & Hellmuth. He designed the Lambert–St. Louis Municipal Air Terminal (1956) along with several Michigan buildings before founding his own practice in Troy, Michigan, in 1959. The Michigan State Medical Society building represents one of his earliest forays into the New Formalism, a developing branch of modernism. In addition to his master plan for Wayne State University from 1954, several of his buildings on the campus with reflecting pools and arcades are among his masterpieces. He is best known for the World Trade Center (1971) in New York City.

Information for this section is from several sources, including *Michigan Modern: East Lansing Modern, Driving/Biking Tour*, by Susan J. Bandes; the State Historic Preservation Office's michiganmodern.org website; and *The AIA Historical Directory of American Architects*.

Notes

Introduction

1. Caroline Rob Zalewski, *Long Island Modernism* (New York: W.W. Norton, 2012); *California Design*, Los Angeles County Art Museum, October 1, 2011–June 3, 2012; *Michigan Modern: Design That Shaped America*, Cranbrook Art Museum, June 14–October 13, 2012, and Grand Rapids Art Museum, May 18–August 24, 2014. The Michigan Modern website (michiganmodern.org) contains a wealth of information. Another example is North Carolina Modernist Houses, Architecture You Love (ncmodernist.org).
2. Jim Weber, "Area Architects Talk Buildings," *Lansing State Journal*, May 19, 1974.
3. John Albright, "Architects Choices of Favorite Buildings Blend Styles," *Lansing State Journal*, February 23, 1988. He asked ten Lansing-area architects to point out their favorite buildings (excluding the Capitol). Several picked late nineteenth-century through the 1930s examples (Michigan National Tower, Bank of Lansing, Turner Dodge House, Ottawa Power Station) or ones from the 1980s (Michigan State University's Wharton Center, Michigan Library and Historical Center, Lansing Center). Of the modernist buildings, only the MSMS and Goetsch-Winckler remained on the list.
4. "Calls for Changing in Urban Planning," *New York Times*, June 8, 1947. I am grateful to Todd Walsh for alerting me to this article.
5. "Architecture Shelves the Rule Book; New Age Realizes Homes Are Built for People," *Lansing State Journal*, January 1, 1951.
6. Thomas Hubka, *Houses without Names: Architectural Nomenclature and the Classification of America's Common Houses* (Knoxville: University of Tennessee Press, 2013), 7. Of the 80 million houses in the United States, 80 percent are "common" houses that replicate a range of standard types and were designed and built

for unknown residents and clearly appealed to shared values; only 5 percent are unique owner-built houses that are individualized and usually architect-designed.

7. For example, the National Register of Historic Places, Lansing Downtown Historic District, Ingham County, Nomination, 2009. Architectural Records, a project of SHPO and the Saarinen Chapter of the Society of Architectural Historians, has as its goal the preservation of Michigan's architectural records, which is happening across the state.
8. Susan J. Bandes, ed., *Affordable Dreams: The Goetsch-Winckler House and Frank Lloyd Wright* (East Lansing: Michigan State University Kresge Art Museum, 1991).
9. Linda O. Stanford and C. Kurt Dewhurst, *MSU Campus, Buildings, Places, Spaces* (East Lansing: Michigan State University Press, 2002).
10. Even after he moved to other positions at the paper, the *Lansing State Journal* continued to introduce readers to significant buildings. For example, a series in late 1967 and early 1968 "intended to awaken a greater interest in the architecture and buildings of our city" (December 29, 1967). Articles covered the Lansing Public Library and the MEA building, with the headline "MEA Building Provides Stylish Education Image."

CHAPTER 1. Frank Lloyd Wright in Mid-Michigan

1. Susan J. Bandes, ed., *Affordable Dreams: The Goetsch-Winckler House and Frank Lloyd Wright* (East Lansing: Michigan State University Kresge Art Museum, 1991).
2. Anatole Senkevitch Jr., "Usonia II and the Goetsch-Winckler House: Manifestations of Wright's Early Vision of Broadacre City," in *Affordable Dreams*, ed. Bandes, 8–9.
3. Ibid., 64–65, plates 2, 3, 4.
4. Ibid., 9–13. See also here 226–28.
5. Ibid., 13.
6. Ibid.
7. Lucie Panshin to Frank Lloyd Wright, July 7, 1939, Frank Lloyd Wright Foundation Archives (New York: Museum of Modern Art | Avery Architectural & Fine Arts Library, Columbia University).
8. Senkevitch, "Usonia II and the Goetsch-Winckler House," 12, plate 4.
9. Alexis Panshin to Frank Lloyd Wright, August 3, 1939, five-page letter canceling the order for house plans, Frank Lloyd Wright Foundation Archives.
10. Ibid.; Senkevitch, "Usonia II and the Goetsch-Winckler House," 25, n. 47.
11. Lucie Panshin to Frank Lloyd Wright, August 12, 1939, Frank Lloyd Wright Foundation Archives.
12. Alexis Panshin to Frank Lloyd Wright, August 22, 1939, Frank Lloyd Wright Foundation Archives.
13. A two-page "idiosyncrasy letter" dated October 25, 1938, was written primarily by Winckler to outline their requirements and hopes. In the short postscript, Goetsch writes that she is only 5′2″ and is worried about living in the country, and she asks Wright to make her feel secure. Bandes, *Affordable Dreams*, xxiv–xxv. See also the National Register of Historic Places Registration Form.
14. Ibid., plate 30.
15. Ibid., plates 29 (front elevation) and 30 (site plan) for Goetsch-Winckler II, plus 71–72. A drawing of the rear elevation was published in Bruce Brooks Pfeiffer, Frank Lloyd Wright, and Donald D. Walker, *Frank Lloyd Wright Treasures of Taliesin: Seventy-Six Unbuilt Designs* (Fresno: The Press at California State University, 1985), 50.
16. Diane Tepfer, "From Frank Lloyd Wright to E. Fay Jones: Alma Goetsch and Kathrine Winckler, Ordinary Extraordinary Architectural Patrons," in *Affordable Dreams*, ed. Bandes, 37–38.
17. Ibid., 39–43.
18. Erling Brauner to Frank Lloyd Wright, November 17, 1946, Frank Lloyd Wright Foundation Archives.
19. Frank Lloyd Wright to Erling Brauner, December 10, 1946, Frank Lloyd Wright Foundation Archives.
20. Erling Brauner to Frank Lloyd Wright, April 14, 1947, through September 1947, Frank Lloyd Wright Foundation Archives.
21. Erling Brauner to Frank Lloyd Wright, October 10, 1948, Frank Lloyd Wright Foundation Archives.
22. Erling Brauner to Frank Lloyd Wright, November 3, 1948, Frank Lloyd Wright Foundation Archives.
23. Frank Lloyd Wright to Erling Brauner, November 22, 1948, Frank Lloyd Wright Foundation Archives.

24. Frank Lloyd Wright to Erling Brauner, March 14, 1949, Frank Lloyd Wright Foundation Archives.
25. Form completed by Erling Brauner for Taliesin with facts about the house, July 3, 1967, with handwritten note on the verso, Frank Lloyd Wright Foundation Archives.
26. James Edwards to Frank Lloyd Wright, August 2, 1948, Frank Lloyd Wright Foundation Archives.
27. Ibid.
28. James Edwards to Frank Lloyd Wright, October 5, 1948, Frank Lloyd Wright Foundation Archives.
29. Frank Lloyd Wright to James Edwards, October 16, 1948, Frank Lloyd Wright Foundation Archives.
30. James Edwards to Frank Lloyd Wright, March 1, 1952, Frank Lloyd Wright Foundation Archives.
31. James Edwards to Frank Lloyd Wright, November 12, 1948, Frank Lloyd Wright Foundation Archives.
32. Dolores Edwards to Frank Lloyd Wright, July 25, 1951, Frank Lloyd Wright Foundation Archives.
33. Donald Schaberg to Frank Lloyd Wright, May 19, 1949, Frank Lloyd Wright Foundation Archives.
34. Letters from Donald Schaberg to Frank Lloyd Wright on September 9, October 2, and November 1, 1949, and January 23 (telegram) and March 19, 1950, Frank Lloyd Wright Foundation Archives.
35. Donald Schaberg to Eugene Masselink, May 8, 1950, Frank Lloyd Wright Foundation Archives.
36. Frank Lloyd Wright to Donald and Mary Lou Schaberg, May 28, 1950, Frank Lloyd Wright Foundation Archives.
37. "Contemporary Home Planning Ideas Gain Acceptance," *Lansing State Journal*, November 25, 1951.
38. Donald Schaberg to Frank Lloyd Wright, January 6, 1954, Frank Lloyd Wright Foundation Archives.
39. Donald Schaberg to Frank Lloyd Wright, April 22, 1955, Frank Lloyd Wright Foundation Archives.
40. Donald Schaberg to Eugene Masselink, January 4, 1956, Frank Lloyd Wright Foundation Archives.
41. Alan Weintraub, Alan Hess, John Zukowsky, and Monica Ramirez-Montagut, *Frank Lloyd Wright Mid-Century Modern* (New York: Rizzoli, 2007), illustrations on 170–73. Donald Schaberg privately published *Accolades* (Lansing, MI: 1996), a book of his poems, among them seven on architecture (19–28). Several express appreciation for Wright's unique design, the changing seasons witnessed from the windows of the house, and the myriad of sensations evoked by experiencing different parts of the house. For example, in the poem, "Our Adventure," 19, Schaberg wrote "It is a fortress within nature, and with its flowing freedom welcomes all new discoveries as one makes them."
42. Stanley and Monna Lee Hartman to Frank Lloyd Wright, August 24, 1955, Frank Lloyd Wright Foundation Archives.
43. Stanley Hartman to Frank Lloyd Wright, October 16, 1955, Frank Lloyd Wright Foundation Archives.
44. Stanley and Monna Lee Hartman to Frank Lloyd Wright, December 19, 1956, Frank Lloyd Wright Foundation Archives.
45. Stanley Hartman to Frank Lloyd Wright, January 21, 1957, Frank Lloyd Wright Foundation Archives.
46. Stanley Hartman to Frank Lloyd Wright, February 17, 1957, Frank Lloyd Wright Foundation Archives.
47. Stanley Hartman to Frank Lloyd Wright, March 17, 1957, Frank Lloyd Wright Foundation Archives.
48. Stanley Hartman to Frank Lloyd Wright, June 26, 1957, Frank Lloyd Wright Foundation Archives.
49. Monna Lee Hartman to Frank Lloyd Wright, August 24, 1958, Frank Lloyd Wright Foundation Archives.
50. Ibid.
51. Pat Hartman, conversation with author, August 18, 2015.
52. Dale and Beatrice O'Donnell to Eugene Masselink, August 1, 1949, referenced Masselink's letter of December 27, 1948, Frank Lloyd Wright Foundation Archives.
53. Michigan State University Archives, folder 30, box 1538, Coll VA 8.1.1. Beatrice received her PhD from MSU in 1954 and was promoted to associate professor in 1957. Dale and Beatrice lived in a faculty apartment while planning the new house.
54. Dale and Beatrice O'Donnell to Eugene Masselink, August 1, 1949, Frank Lloyd Wright Foundation Archives.
55. Dale O'Donnell to Frank Lloyd Wright, January 1, 1950, Frank Lloyd Wright Foundation Archives.
56. Frank Lloyd Wright to Dale O'Donnell, January 25, 1950, Frank Lloyd Wright Foundation Archives.
57. Dale O'Donnell to Frank Lloyd Wright, no date, Frank Lloyd Wright Foundation Archives.

58. Eugene Masselink to Dale O'Donnell, May 27, 1952, Frank Lloyd Wright Foundation Archives.
59. Dale O'Donnell to Frank Lloyd Wright, October 4, 1955, Frank Lloyd Wright Foundation Archives.
60. Frank Lloyd Wright to Dale and Beatrice O'Donnell, October 15, 1955, Frank Lloyd Wright Foundation Archives.
61. Biographical information from Fred E. Inbau, "Clarence W. Muehlberger, 1896–1966," *Journal of Criminal Law and Criminology* 57 (1966): 517.
62. Mary Muehlberger to Frank Lloyd Wright, June 18, 1946, Frank Lloyd Wright Foundation Archives.
63. Mary Muehlberger to Frank Lloyd Wright, September 8, 1947, Frank Lloyd Wright Foundation Archives.
64. Clarence W. Muehlberger to Frank Lloyd Wright, November 14, 1948, Frank Lloyd Wright Foundation Archives.
65. Frank Lloyd Wright to Clarence W. Muehlberger, November 22, 1948, Frank Lloyd Wright Foundation Archives.
66. Clarence W. Muehlberger to Frank Lloyd Wright, November 25, 1948, Frank Lloyd Wright Foundation Archives.
67. Clarence W. Muehlberger to Frank Lloyd Wright, January 3, 1949, Frank Lloyd Wright Foundation Archives.
68. Eugene Masselink to Clarence W. Muehlberger, June 30, 1951, Frank Lloyd Wright Foundation Archives.
69. The Panshins hired Keck & Keck to build their house (discussed here in chapter 3). Lucie Panshin to George Keck, September 30, 1947, George Fred and William Keck Papers, 1903–1995, Wisconsin Historical Society, Madison.
70. The aerial view (4820.15), general plan (4820.08), and elevations (4820.09) were reproduced in Yukio Futagawa and Bruce Brooks Pfeiffer, *Frank Lloyd Wright Monograph, 1942–1950*, vol. 7 (Tokyo: A.d.A. Edita, 1988), figs. 307–9.
71. Wright Chat, "R. Joseph Fabris," April 10, 2013, at Frank Lloyd Wright Building Conservancy, Save Wright, http://www.savewright.org/wright_chat/viewtopic.php?t=7004&sid=541ff58a6cdb2fa281408edb58e9c38f.
72. The Theodore van Fossen papers in the Northwest Architectural Archives, Manuscripts Division, University of Minnesota, list two relevant houses. The Dike house, Okemos, 1966, and the Skipper house in East Lansing, 1956, 1958, 1968. The Skipper House is called "Red Cedar River Job 116," Allen "Al" J. Leweke building. For the Dike House, "Development of Residence," there is a reference to Mr. and Mrs. Skipper. One explanation is that the house was planned and built for the Skippers and completed or expanded for the Dikes. See "Lost and Found; Obscurity Behind It," *New York Times*, June 14, 2004, on van Fossen and Rush Creek.
73. Biographical data in *The AIA Historical Directory of American Architects* (ahd1022235) does not list either education or experience with Frank Lloyd Wright.
74. Emily Tabuteau, discussion with author, May 3, 2014.
75. The windows were replaced by the current owner but follow the original design.
76. Obituary, *Lansing State Journal*, November 2, 2008. She also was author of *Weaving Solutions: Shortcuts, Tips and Ideas for the Hand Weaver* (Milan, MI: A & G Publications, 2000).
77. *The AIA Historical Directory of American Architects* (ahd1024842). His own 1,646-square-foot house at 2625 Arlington Road from 1960, on the west side of Lansing, has a similar design. He also designed 1776 Hitching Post, East Lansing, 1961, for James Hayhoe of Capitol City Lumber Co., according to the second owner's family, the Lee Winders (related by Laurie Sommers to author, e-mail October 27, 2020). The distinguishing modernist features are a stepped-down living room and narrow windows.
78. On the west side of Lansing on Delta River Drive and River Ridge Road, there are several Wrightian houses from the 1950s that deserve to be researched further: for example, 4910 Delta River Drive, 1952, a large Prairie-style, two-story wood house on 9 acres, for the Raymond J. Wilcox family, designed by Lawrence Powell ("They Can Dream Again about Their Dream House," *Lansing State Journal*, October 21, 1956, 60).
79. Ancestry.com, 1940 United States Federal Census, Michigan, Ingham, Meridian, Sheet 13 B. The professions listed in the 1940s U.S. Census are indecipherable.

80. See the John Geiger, "Directory of Frank Lloyd Wright Associates: Apprentices 1929–1959" at Frank Lloyd Wright Building Conservancy, Save Wright, http://www.savewright.org/wright_chat/viewtopic.php?t=5426&sid=be1606f93a8098a02af0b2b0fef31ec7.

CHAPTER 2. Alden B. Dow, Built and Unbuilt Houses

1. Diane Maddex, *Alden B. Dow: Midwestern Modern* (Midland, MI: Alden B. Dow Home and Studio, 2007). Also Sidney K. Robinson, *The Architecture of Alden B. Dow* (Detroit: Wayne State University Press, 1983). A comprehensive website of Dow's structures is available at "Alden Ball Dow, FAIA (1904–1983)" in the Masters Gallery on the North Carolina Modernist Houses website (http://www.ncmodernist.org/dow.htm).
2. "Unit Blocks" on the Alden B. Dow Home and Studio website (http://www.abdow.org/history/innovator/unit-blocks). Another innovative feature of the block was the use of cinder waste from the Dow Chemical Company furnaces.
3. 929 Roxburgh, February 16, 1965, asking price $43,500; Stebbins Realty records, Capital Area District Library, Main Branch, Local History division.
4. When completed, the house cost $13,093.95, a large sum at the time.
5. Warren Brintnall, "East Lansing Residence Lives Up to Dow's Reputation," *Lansing State Journal*, December 11, 1949.
6. Alden B. Dow to Harold Anderson, July 15, 1948, Dow Archives.
7. Harold Anderson to Alden B. Dow, July 24, 1949, Dow Archives.
8. Gladys Anderson to Alden B. Dow, August 7, 1949, Dow Archives.
9. Brintnall, "East Lansing Residence Lives Up to Dow's Reputation."
10. Harold Anderson to Alden B. Dow, October 12, 1950, Dow Archives, regarding gaps in the insulation because of the way the lighting fixtures had been installed, and water seepage. Dow responded on October 13 that "I do not think there is any use of fooling around anymore with Mr. Tomlinson," (who was the contractor) and his own person would see to the repairs.
11. David Thomas, "The Mid-Michigan Architecture of Alden B. Dow," *Lansing City Magazine*, April 1992, 27–33.
12. Joel and Marilyn Aronoff, former owners, e-mail to author, March 17, 2010.
13. Carleton Washburne to Alden B. Dow, November 22, 1959, Dow Archives.
14. Carleton Washburne to Meridian Township Zoning Board, April 11, 1960, requesting a variance to build on the property. It was eventually granted.
15. John Bonarenko, contractor, Dow Archives, box 101, folders 4, 5.
16. Carleton Washburne to Alden B. Dow, March 20, 1961, Dow Archives.
17. A bedroom addition as planned by Dow was added by the second owners, the Washburnes' daughter and her husband, Margaret and James Plagge. This enlarged the house to 1,885 square feet.
18. Carleton Washburne to Alden B. Dow, March 27, 1960, Dow Archives.
19. Correspondence from March 20, 1961, and August 7 and 30, 1961 concerns the initial expectation of $50 plus $15 for installation, but instead the bill was $261.31, and was finally settled at $100.
20. Carleton Washburne to Alden B. Dow, April 29, 1961, Dow Archives.
21. Dow Archives, box 193, folder 1.
22. Dow Archives, box 193, folder 2 contains several invoices from Herman Miller listing chairs and specific Knoll pieces, December 1968.
23. Dow Archives, four files of drawings, four files of contracts and correspondence. Due to illness, Alden Dow had little to do with this design.
24. "A Way of Life," in Maddex, *Alden B. Dow*, 66–69; also "Philosopher" on the Alden B. Dow Home and Studio website (http://www.abdow.org/history/philosopher).
25. "A Way of Life," in Maddex, *Alden B. Dow*, 68–69.

CHAPTER 3. Keck & Keck, Realized and Unrealized Houses

1. Narciso G. Menocal, *Keck & Keck, Architects* (Madison, WI: Elvehjem Museum of Art, University

of Wisconsin-Madison, 1980), for a brief history and background on the Keck & Keck firm.

2. Lisa D. Shrenk, *Building a Century of Progress: The Architecture of Chicago's World's Fair* (Minneapolis: University of Minnesota Press, 2007), 157–86.
3. After the fair, Chicago developer Robert Bartlett purchased this and fourteen other homes that he moved by barge down Lake Michigan to the Indiana Dunes, where he intended to re-erect them in a new subdivision. While this did not happen, five were re-erected and are now being preserved by the National Park Service. As of summer 2015, the House of Tomorrow had not been leased and is awaiting restoration. See Robin A. Carlascio and Theresa K. Badovich, *Saving a Century of Progress* (Crown Point, IN: Amalfi Publishing, 2014).
4. Menocal, *Keck & Keck*, 36.
5. Ibid., 37.
6. Ibid., 19. The exterior blinds proved difficult to manufacture and maintain, and in the 1940s were discontinued. Subsequently blinds were installed on the interior of their houses.
7. Christine A. Bernick, "Preservation of Keck and Keck's Passive-Solar Subdivisions of the 1940s and 50s" (master's thesis, School of the Art Institute of Chicago, 2010).
8. Ibid., 31.
9. Menocal, *Keck & Keck*, 60.
10. Bernick, "Preservation of Keck and Keck's," 68.
11. Menocal, *Keck & Keck*, 68.
12. The correspondence is preserved in the George Fred and William Keck Papers, 1903–1995, Wisconsin Historical Society, Madison (hereafter Keck Papers). Lucie Panshin to George Keck, January 12, 1947; Stevens did not follow up.
13. Lucie Panshin to George Keck, March 3, 1947, Keck Papers.
14. Susan J. Bandes, ed., *Affordable Dreams: The Goetsch-Winckler House and Frank Lloyd Wright* (East Lansing: Michigan State University Kresge Art Museum, 1991), xiv.
15. Ibid., 37.
16. Lucie Panshin to George Keck, March 20,, 1947, Keck Papers.
17. George Keck to Lucie Panshin, March 29, 1947, Keck Papers.
18. Lucie Panshin to George Keck, March 31, 1947, Keck Papers.
19. George Keck to Lucie Panshin, April 8, 1947, Keck Papers.
20. George Keck to Thomas Padget (Lucie's brother), May 19, 1947, Keck Papers.
21. Lucie Panshin to George Keck, September 30, 1947, Keck Papers.
22. Lucie Panshin to George Keck, Christmas 1947, Keck Papers.
23. *Keck & Keck Architects*, two-part video (Michigan City, IN: Hall Associates, 1993), part 2, interview with Fred Keck. Their first use of a detached garage linked by a light roof plane was at the Bennett House in Chicago prior to World War II.
24. Information from the Michigan State University Archives, Hayworth file.
25. "Hayworth, Donald," *Biographical Directory of the United States Congress, 1774 to the Present*, http://bioguide.congress.gov/scripts/biodisplay.pl?index=H000412.
26. Donald Hayworth to George Keck, August 9, 1946, Keck Papers.
27. This letterhead was used for all correspondence now in the Keck Papers.
28. Glen Cairn brochure, Keck Papers.
29. Donald Hayworth to George Keck, August 9, 1946, Keck Papers.
30. Ibid.
31. Donald Hayworth to George Keck, September 9, 1946, Keck Papers.
32. George Keck to Donald Hayworth, September 13, 1946, Keck Papers.
33. Ibid.
34. Donald Hayworth to George Keck, September 14, 1947, Keck Papers.
35. Donald Hayworth to George Keck, December 15, 1947, Keck Papers.
36. Donald Hayworth to George Keck, August 16, 1948, Keck Papers; he wrote that with several veterans, he was beginning to build a small, conventional Cape Cod to sell later in the fall. Although he was doing this for the experience of building, he also expected to make some money on the deal.

37. Donald Hayworth to Mr. Keck, February 1, 1949, Keck Papers.
38. Donald Hayworth to Mr. Keck, May 1, 1949, Keck Papers.
39. Donald Hayworth to Mr. Keck, July 17, 1949, Keck Papers.
40. George Keck to Donald Hayworth, October 12, 1949, Keck Papers.
41. Donald Hayworth to George Keck, 1949, Keck Papers.
42. *Lansing Suburban City Directory (Ingham County, Michigan)* (Taylor, MI: R. L. Polk & Co., 1957).
43. Thomas Padget to "Fred" Keck, October 7, 1947, Keck Papers.
44. *Lansing State Journal*, August 13, 1950, described as "brand-new house."

CHAPTER 4. When Architects Design Their Own

1. H. I. Brock, "When the Architect Builds His Own Home," *New York Times*, August 2, 1931. I thank Todd Walsh for bringing this to my attention.
2. Dow's house was listed in 1989. In 2013, the State Historic Preservation Office nominated a group of seven to exemplify Michigan's modernist architecture. They include Yamasaki, William Kessler, Louis Redstone (District), William Muschenheim, Robert Metcalf, Tivadar Balogh, and Robert Schwartz.
3. See Kathryn Bishop Eckert, *Buildings of Michigan* (New York: Oxford University Press, 1993), 298. On Moon, see Faith Rich, "Moon Remembered," 1997, http://www.angelfire.com/mi/shockweb/MoonText.html. Largely self-taught, Moon designed over 250 structures between 1890 and 1920, most of which, including the large residence for Ransom E. Olds, have been demolished. Moon's own house was spared when it was moved from Logan Street to 216 Huron Street in 1979. See Lawrence Cosentino, "Phantom Moon Over Lansing," *City Pulse*, November 16, 2005.
4. There are at least two architect-designed homes from the 1930s. Howard E. Hunter (1906–2008), a professional engineer, started working for the Warren Holmes Company in 1929, becoming a partner in 1946 and director of field supervision (information is from the Warren Holmes Company prospectus, ca. 1970s). His own home at 7312 Old River Trail, Delta Township, built in 1937, is white clapboard, 1,500 square feet, and part of a complex with a barn and orchard on approximately thirty acres on the Grand River. State architect Adrian Langius designed his home at 923 Westlawn Avenue, East Lansing, built in 1936.
5. National Register of Historic Places, Ottawa Street Station, Registration Form, 2008. On Bowd-Munson, 15.
6. Flint Faience, a subsidiary of AC Spark Plug, existed from 1921 through 1933. See Margaret Carney and Ken Galvas, *Flint Faience Tiles A to Z* (Atglen, PA: Schiffer Publishing, 2004). The decorative tiles they produced enhanced several of Lansing's most luxurious houses of the late 1920s (the Potter house at 1348 Cambridge, 1927, and the Harper house, 1408 Cambridge, 1929). Munson must have used tiles that he had available, since his house dates after the company went out of business. Using earlier materials reinforces the architect's traditional rather than innovative design.
7. See Eckert, *Buildings of Michigan*, rev. ed. (Charlottesville: University of Virginia, 2012), 292–94. Both are on the National Historic Register. The J. W. Knapp Company Building is described in detail in the fourteen-page report of the Knapp Building Historic District Committee, Lansing, Michigan, July 2011. Munson also designed the modernist Michigan Hospital Association building, 2213 E. Michigan, Lansing.
8. Simpson-Hartwick Architects formed in 1952. After Simpson's death, Hartwick formed his own firm, Hartwick and Associates, in 1961. *The AIA Historical Directory of American Architects* (ahd1018669). He also designed the early Wrightian John Knecht House, 2237 Raby Rd, Haslett, 1947, pictured in Warren Brintnall, "Contemporary Home Planning Ideas Gain Acceptance," *Lansing State Journal*, November 25, 1951, 49.
9. "Architect Has Reasons for Design Features in His Home," *Lansing State Journal*, July 15, 1951.
10. Another example by Herrick is the Bertrand L. and Mildred Hewett house at 901 N. Harrison Road, East Lansing. Hewett was the first vice president of Michigan Millers Association Insurance Company. Warren Brintnall, in "East Lansing Ranch Type Home Is Colonial Indoors," *Lansing State Journal*, January 23, 1953, remarked on

the flexible plan, easy traffic flow, and casual entertaining in the family room; but most striking of all was the comfortable Colonial atmosphere that was a result of the furnishings.

11. *The AIA Historical Directory of American Architects*, s.v. "Ralph B. Herrick" (ahd1019498).
12. Warren Brintnall, "Modern Design Calls for New Appraisal Rules," *Lansing State Journal*, June 3, 1951.
13. Malcolm Williams, interview by Anne Green, July 8, 1975, transcript, Sesquicentennial Oral History Project, City of East Lansing, East Lansing Public Library, 4.
14. "Work of Local Architects Wins Awards," *Lansing State Journal*, April 26, 1953.
15. As president of the Lansing Board of Education, he was instrumental in securing funding for the new library, designed by Kenneth Black, that opened in 1964, which was subsequently dedicated to Rosa. See chapter 9. Marcella Rosa, a University of Michigan graduate in interior design, married Clarence in 1937. According to the *Lansing State Journal*, February 17, 1957, 47, she became highly successful as an interior designer using the professional name "M. Vonda Orr Rosa."
16. "Here's New Slant on Picture Windows," *Lansing State Journal*, April 8, 1951. Perhaps Rosa also read the article "A Store Front Designed to Reduce Ceiling Glare," *Architectural Record*, October 1949, about Siegel's in Grand Rapids, or earlier ones (July 1946) that discuss specific advantages of slanting storefront windows.
17. Ibid.
18. The house number given in the article is in error; it should be 1535 Roseland, east of Hagadorn.
19. The Warren Holmes Company, *Warren Holmes Company Architects*, prospectus (Lansing, MI: ca. 1970s), Library of Michigan. The Lansing City Directory lists him as working for Clark R. Ackley in 1964. He designed a number of houses in the area, including one set up on a hill on Myers Road, Dewitt, 1977, for John Richard Mitchell and his wife.
20. Clarke E. Harris graduated from the University of Michigan in 1929, became associated with Warren Holmes in 1935, and made principal in 1944. Information from Warren Holmes Company prospectus. Warren Brintnall described the house in "Harris Home Is Modern—but in Moderation," *Lansing State Journal*, August 23, 1953.
21. Information from Laitala's daughter Diane Sowash, interview with author, January 13, 2013.
22. Diane Sowash, e-mail to author, February 1, 2013.
23. Among these is Riccardo Anselmo's (1929–2015) 1964 home at 1024 North Magnolia Street, Lansing. Sandwiched between smaller comfortable houses on the block, this two-story, 2,517-square-foot structure has a flat-roofed garage.
24. Building permit filed by Crouse as contractor, Code and Enforcement Office, East Lansing City Hall. Richard Maury, the owner in 1980, added the attached deck.
25. In 1957, his biography was included in the Manson-Carver business prospectus submitted by the firm for the Eastminster Church project (Eastminster Archives). Additional information is from the *The AIA Historical Directory of American Architects* (ahd1048873).
26. Kenneth C. Black Associates, *Kenneth C. Black Associates, Inc.: Architects and Engineers* (Lansing, MI: Kenneth C. Black Associates, 1970). Copy in the Library of Michigan, Lansing.
27. Leavenworth Archive, Kenneth Black files, 97.3, box 4, Archives of Michigan, Lansing. Interiors dated April 7, 1966, 66–1563–65, 66–155–56. Exteriors dated December 28, 1966, 66–1755–56, 66–1820, 66–1841–42.
28. In the 1970s, a group of younger architects designed their own homes. A partial list includes (all in East Lansing): Dimitrios Economides's 2,670-square-foot home at 605 Burcham Drive, 1976 (he had worked for Manson, Jackson & Kane in the 1960s); B. Chadwick Walter II (who also worked for that firm), a solar house at 925 Whittier Drive, 1976; Bert Seyfarth at 340 Northlawn Street, 1977, a large one-story that has been remodeled and expanded; Isaac Green at 1126 Southlawn Avenue, a 2,700-square-foot house in 1984. In Okemos: Alton Wehr, 4215 Red Cedar Road in 1976 (whose New England heritage influenced his "contemporary saltbox" design). In Lansing: Barry D. Wood, of the Keystone Design Group, built a white cement, flat-roofed house at 2222 Moores River Drive, in 2006, on a beautiful site along the Grand River.

CHAPTER 5. When Architects Design for Clients

1. On Rapson, see Rip Rapson, Jane King Hession, and Bruce N. Wright, *Ralph Rapson: Sixty Years of Modern Design* (Afton, MN: Afton Historical Society Press, 1999).
2. Maynard Hill, "Determination, Coupled with a Goal, Okemos Woman with a Full Life," *Lansing State Journal*, January 25, 1948.
3. Ralph Rapson, *Ralph Rapson: Sketches and Drawings from around the World* (Afton, MN: Afton Historical Society Press, 2002), 114.
4. I appreciate Cranbrook archivist Leslie Edwards's assistance with these drawings.
5. Betty Hagberg (Kenneth's second wife), interview with author, May 3, 2014. The white house was demolished in the 1970s.
6. Rapson, Hession, and Wright, *Ralph Rapson*, illustrated on 29, discussion on 28–29. The caption indicates that the house illustrated was built, however it is not the one that was constructed years later.
7. See Kathryn Bishop Eckert, *Buildings of Michigan*, rev. ed. (Charlottesville: University of Virginia, 2012), 289.
8. Ibid., 303.
9. From his obituary, "William Kessler," *Grosse Pointe News*, November 16, 2002.
10. Michigan Modern, William and Margot Kessler House, http://www.michiganmodern.org/buildings/william-and-margot-kessler-house. See also National Register of Historic Places Nomination, 2013.
11. On Kessler, National Register of Historic Places Nomination, 9-11. On his own house, William Kessler House," Grosse Pointe Modernism, March 19, 2013, http://grossepointemodernism.blogspot.com/2013/03/william-kessler-house.html.
12. Michigan Modern, Jack and Faye Beckwith House, http://www.michiganmodern.org/buildings/jack-and-faye-beckwith-house.
13. Edward Francis, Resendes Design Group, Detroit, conversation with the author, June 29, 2015. Francis had worked for Kessler Associates starting in 1959 and related the word-of-mouth story that Kessler sold the plans for $500, but that he was not usually involved in the actual building.
14. Sarah Firshein, "The *Other* Glass House, Built by a Noted Michigan Architect," *Curbed*, December 27, 2011, http://curbed.com/tags/william-kessler.
15. Plans by Lee and Kenneth Black for several East Lansing houses are in the Archives of Michigan, MS 2009–5: S. F. Sexton Residence, 1936; McGillicuddy Residence, 1940; Stringer Residence, ca. 1940; R. B. Harvey Residence, 1947–50; Stoddard Residence, 1945–46.
16. Stebbins Real Estate Collection, Special Collections, Capital Area District Library, Lansing. Williams was governor from 1963 to 1969. It was not until 1969 that a home for the governor was donated to the state by Howard and Letha Sober. The over 10,000-square-foot ranch at 2520 Oxford Road, Lansing, was designed by Wallace Frost, 1959. Eckert, *Buildings of Michigan*, 295.
17. Sandra Seaton, "Betty Price and George Nelson, Spreading the Word about Modern Design," *Modernism* (Fall 2011): 38.
18. Kenneth C. Black, "Architecture Shelves the Rule Book," *Lansing State Journal*, January 1, 1951.
19. Camala Riessinger, former owner, conversation with author, August 14, 2015.
20. On the J. H. Moores and Riverside Homes Subdivisions, see Eckert, *Buildings of Michigan*, 294.
21. Leavenworth photographs, Kenneth Black collection, Archives of Michigan, box 5, twenty-four black-and-white photographs showing the exterior (#3813.1–6) and interior (#4760–71), dated December 10, 1953.
22. Eckert, *Buildings of Michigan*, 295.
23. James Perkins, current owner, e-mail to author, July 4, 2014.
24. Ibid.
25. Warren Brintnall, "Abrams Home Influenced by Owners' Air Mindedness," *Lansing State Journal*, January 6, 1952.
26. "Many New City Homes Costing in Five Figures," *Lansing State Journal*, August 13, 1950. Rebecca Binno, "The Airplane House," *The Modern* 14, no. 1 (Spring 2000).
27. The firm was founded in 1941 by Elmer J. Manson.
28. Nancy McRay, former owner, interview with Nicholas Junemann, November 11, 2012.
29. Other examples are the Alan and Beverly Suits House,

609 Belmonte Circle, designed in 1966 by Manson, Mattern and Barber, Inc.; 1108 Southlawn for Dr. Harry and Mrs. Mary L. LeVett, 1958; and at 5020 River Ridge, Lansing, 1964, the firm "assisted" Mr. and Mrs. Harold Hicks with their design (*Lansing State Journal*, 1968, 40).

30. Pat Hartman, conversation with author, August 18, 2015.
31. See also the early house he designed for his parents on Bittersweet Lane, 1961, plate 53.
32. Diane Sowash, interview with author, January 13, 2013.
33. "Garrisons Call Their Home Michigan Modern," *Lansing State Journal*, May 25, 1952.
34. A sculpture in her honor placed in front of the East Lansing City Hall was dedicated in summer 2013. "Sharp Art, East Lansing Raising Funds for Sculpture to Honor City Icon," *City Pulse*, March 15, 2013. Also, "Mary Potter Sharp, An East Lansing trailblazer who advocated for equality and civil rights," City of East Lansing, Arts Commission, Mary Sharp sculpture.
35. See Bill Castinier, "A House Divided," *City Pulse*, February 25, 2015.
36. The John D. and Marguerite Cruise House at 849 Audubon, 1951, was designed by Alfred C. Roth (1907–90), who was chief planning engineer for the Michigan State Highway Department. The brick structure has flat roofs over the garage and bedrooms, and a shed roof over the center portion with clerestory windows below. Roth also designed his own home in East Lansing.
37. Laitala and Nuechterlein bid book, lent to me by the current owners, Bill and Chris Triola.
38. Another Laitala and Neuchterlerin bi-level design is at 1107 Burcham Road, 1963, for Harold and Gert Sadoff. There are additional modern residences in this area that would be fruitful to research, both on Skyline Drive and Dawn Avenue on the opposite side of the golf course.
39. "Vaive, Earl A.," obituary, *Lansing State Journal*, March 22, 1999.
40. Michael L. Moore, owner until 1998, interview with author, October 17, 2013.
41. When they sold the house in 1973, the lot behind was separated and sold as well. A house was subsequently built on it.
42. Pauline Sondag, current owner, interview with author, December 2, 2013.
43. Chad Randl, *A-Frame* (New York: Princeton Architectural Press, 2004).
44. Paul Strassmann, owner, interview with author, April 29, 2013.
45. "Langius, Adrian Nelson 'Gus,'" obituary, *Lansing State Journal*, July 2, 1991.
46. As director of the state building division, Langius was directly involved in plans to construct a new capitol complex in Lansing in the 1950s, In the 1960s, he strongly advocated tearing the old capitol down and starting anew with a design by Smith, Hinchman and Grylls. By 1971 the state's economic slowdown and general lack of support for the design ended the project. A file of clippings is maintained by the Library of Michigan; I am grateful to Kerry Chartkoff for pointing this out and providing me with information.
47. Barbara and Tom Astley, former owners of #910, interview with author, April 12, 2014.
48. One of his former students, architect Elizabeth Harrow remembers him saying that he designed the house. Elizabeth Harrow, e-mail to author, April 28, 2014. I have not yet been able to confirm the attribution to Pond (1926–present), who practiced in Ann Arbor (1950–55) and became a design architect at Indiana University. One example of his house design is included in *Michigan Modern: Ann Arbor Modern, Ann Arbor Hills Tour*, Washtenaw County and Michigan State Historic Preservation Office, http://www.michiganmodern.org/tours. About another of his later designs, see p. 318 n. 64.
49. Sally Davidson, conversation with author, July 25, 2015. A *Lansing State Journal* article, "Davidson Home Design Unique," tanuary 17, 1965, reported briefly on the house's progress.
50. Kia Klaassen, one of the Davidson daughters, suggested that although her father did not attend the fair, he would have known the building through publicity. See "Groundbreaking at the New York World's Fair 1964–1965; The Eastman Kodak Company, August 21, 1962" (Flushing, NY: New York World's Fair 1964–1965 Corporation, 1962).

51. The story of the house was recounted by Sally Davidson in conversations with author, July 23 and 25, 2015.
52. Jim Perkins, e-mail to author, March 25, 2013.
53. Delta Township Assessment information dates the house to 1984.
54. Kirk Domer, current owner, conversation with author, January 13, 2016. This information was related to him by the Hendersons's daughter.
55. Additional architect-designed houses that are later than the years considered in this book include Plymouth, Michigan–based Tivadar Balogh (1926–2006), who taught at the University of Michigan and had his own firm. He designed the Erikos and Manya Constant house (1974), Emerald Lake residences (1987), Saper Galleries (1985), and the Martin and Thelma Saper house (1992), among others. Irving Tobochman, the Birmingham, Michigan–based architect, designed the Larry and Faylene Owen house (1988) with characteristic white bricks, a flat roof, and large windows.

CHAPTER 6. Hugh Stubbins Jr. and Lantern Hill, an East Lansing Community

1. Alan Grimes, "Remembering Lantern Hill, 1950–1952" (self-published manuscript, 1999). Copies are available at MSU Archives, Special Collections, Archives of Michigan and from the homeowners. Copies are provided to new Lantern Hill buyers.
2. Pauline Adams, original owner, conversation with author, October 5, 2015.
3. Warren Brintnall, "Lantern Hill Is a Cooperative Neighborhood," *Lansing State Journal*, January 28, 1951.
4. Dianne M. Ludman, *Hugh Stubbins and His Associates: The First Fifty Years* (Cambridge, MA: Stubbins Associates, 1986). His papers are in the Special Collections, Harvard University, Graduate School of Design.
5. Architecture Week, Great Buildings Collection, Hugh Stubbins, http://www.greatbuildings.com/architects/Hugh_Stubbins.html.
6. Rachel Strutt, "Was Six Moon Hill a Success?" *Boston Globe*, October 31, 2004.
7. Build LCC, "Mid-Century Modern Communities," January 18, 2010, http://blog.buildllc.com/2010/01/mid-century-modern-communities, discusses five such communities, and blog posts add many more, including Parkwyn Village in Kalamazoo, designed by Frank Lloyd Wright starting in 1947.
8. Catherine Larson, "Ingersoll Village," Kalamazoo Public Library, 2007, http://www.kpl.gov/local-history/houses-buildings/ingersoll-village.aspx. He also designed eighty-five square two-bedroom units for the FWA Division of Defense Housing, 1942, built at Windsor Locks, Connecticut. Elizabeth Mock, ed., *Built in USA, 1932–1944* (New York: Museum of Modern Art, 1944), 64–65.
9. Paul Heyer, *Architects on Architecture* (New York: Walker and Company, 1966), 300–301.
10. Copies of the blueprints are available at the MSU Archives and MSU Special Collections, among other resources.
11. Stubbins papers, Frances Loeb Library, Harvard University, Graduate School of Design, C142.01-04. The drawings are dated June 18 through 21, 1950.
12. Mary and Russel Wright's very popular *Guide to Easier Living* (New York: Simon and Schuster, 1950) contains line drawings and bird's-eye views of open plan interiors and furniture similar to Stubbins's as well as instructions about living in a "servantless" household that helped people understand the new informal lifestyle.
13. Roger Funk, former Lantern Hill homeowner, e-mail to author, September 23, 2013.
14. Grimes, "Remembering Lantern Hill, 1950–1952," 10.
15. The Home-Sites, Inc., Articles of Incorporation and Protective Covenants, December 27, 1950. Copies of the Articles are available in the Archives of Michigan, and the Protective Covenants are in the MSU Archives.
16. Strutt discusses these tendencies and the sense of community in various collaborative projects in "Was Six Moon Hill a Success?."
17. The contents of this chapter are published in Susan J. Bandes, "Mid-Michigan Modern: Frank Lloyd Wright and Hugh Stubbins Jr.," in *Proceedings of the Creating-Making Forum* (Norman: University of Oklahoma, Division of Architecture, 2015), 122–27.

18. Pauline Adams, phone conversation with author, July 9, 2014; Adams, interview with author, July 11, 2014.

CHAPTER 7. Trade Secrets Revealed

1. "Factory-built Houses Unknown Back in 1900," *Lansing State Journal*, January 1, 1950.
2. On the heavily subsidized Lustron houses—2,000 units of which were sold before the corporation folded—see Thomas T. Fetters, *The Lustron Home: The History of a Postwar Prefabricated Housing Experiment* (Jefferson, NC: McFarland & Company, Inc., 2006). There are none in the Lansing area.
3. The article "Firm Cuts Cash Sum: Three-Bedroom Dwelling Will Open to Public Sunday Afternoon," *Lansing State Journal*, January 22, 1950, reported on the new North American Homes three-bedroom model produced at the National Home Corp. plant in Lafayette and erected at 2014 Marion Avenue, Lansing. It could be purchased for $325 down with an FHA loan.
4. For example, Thyer Manufacturing Corporation, *Pollman Homes: Let's Talk about a Home for You* (Toledo, OH: The Thyer Manufacturing Corporation, ca. 1950). From the 1950s through the 1970s architect Richard Pollman also published dozens of popular low-cost books containing a variety of house designs of different sizes, styles, and costs.
5. "Watch This House Go Up: Part I, Meet the Plan and the Man," *Changing Times*, May 1953, 29.
6. I would like to express my thanks to the current home owners, Jan and Bill Simpson, who shared their extensive knowledge of the project and opened their home to me.
7. "Watch This House Go Up," 30.
8. "$15,000 'Trade Secrets' House," *Life Magazine*, January 5, 1953, 8–14. A follow-up article, "Crowds Beat Path to Trade Secrets House," appeared in the March 9, 1953, issue, 111–114.
9. "Watch This House Go Up," 32–33. These were listed by city and builder. The East Lansing builder was Ruppert Gaybrick Lumber Co.
10. "Part 3: Is the Price Too High?" *Changing Times*, July 1953, 38.
11. Ibid.
12. Ibid., 39.
13. "Part 4: What Do the Customers Think of It?," *Changing Times*, August 1953, 7–8, 23.
14. Ibid., 8.
15. Ibid., 23.
16. "Part 5: How the Buyers Fit It into Their Budget," *Changing Times*, September 1953, 10.
17. MSU Archives, folder 23, box 1519 Coll. VA8.1. He passed away in 1997.
18. *Lansing State Journal*, January 15, 1950, caption of illustration.
19. "Suburban Neighbors," *Lansing State Journal*, September 2, 1951.
20. Current owner, Kriss Ostrom, e-mail to author, May 14, 2013.

CHAPTER 8. City Hall, Associations, and Commercial Buildings

1. Leavenworth photographs, Kenneth Black collection, Archives of Michigan, box 2, #34503 and 34559, photographs of model, dated November 6, 1945; #34404–7, dated September 28, 1946; another, #36353, dated November 11, 1946.
2. National Register of Historic Places, Lansing Downtown Historic District, Ingham County, Nomination, 2009, Section 7, 19–20; Section 8, 31–32. See also Section 8, 33–35 on mid-century architecture in the downtown district.
3. Kathryn Bishop Eckert, *Buildings of Michigan*, rev. ed. (Charlottesville: University of Virginia Press, 2012), 289–91.
4. Reproduced in Larry Cosentino, "The Chair, the Babies and the Mayor's Ties," *City Pulse*, January 29, 2014, 10. It is illustrated here courtesy of Jim Perkins and the Greater Lansing Historical Society. She signed the painting "Barden Durst," omitting her first name as a way to prevent gender bias.
5. While there are additional steel-frame-and-glaze office buildings in the area, such as the Alcoa Building at 1293 Kendale Boulevard in East Lansing, from 1970, they lack the finesse of City Hall. Nevertheless, there are

several more adept examples such as Kenneth C. Black Associates' design for the Stoddard building, now the Billie S. Farnum Building, 1959–60, at 125 West Allegan. When completed, this eleven-story, square steel-frame building, originally constructed for Michigan National Bank, was considered modern because of the air conditioning, high-speed elevators, and Thermopane windows. It used curtain wall construction with glass, aluminum, and black granite. See National Register of Historic Places, Section 7, 8. Another fine example is the multi-story medical center building from 1965 designed by Mayotte-Webb at the intersection of West Saginaw Street and Martin Luther King Boulevard, Lansing, to house doctors' suites near St. Lawrence Hospital.

6. Eckert, *Buildings of Michigan* (2012), 60.
7. Ibid., 244.
8. Sandra Seaton, "Betty Price and George Nelson, Spreading the World about Modern Design," *Modernism* (Fall 2011): 38–45, esp. 44. The oral histories upon which this article is based are now in the Vincent Voice Library, MSU.
9. See Michigan Modern, Liebermann's, Lansing, George Nelson, http://www.michiganmodern.org/buildings/leibermann-s.
10. National Register of Historic Places, Section 7, 26; Section 8, 35.
11. Seaton, "Betty Price and George Nelson," 45.
12. Ibid., 41–42.
13. Michigan Modern, Liebermann's, Lansing, George Nelson, http://www.michiganmodern.org/buildings/leibermann-s.
14. Michigan Modern, Michigan State Medical Society Building, East Lansing, Minoru Yamaski, http://michiganmodern.org/buildings/michigan-state-medical-society-building; also Nathaniel H. Nietering, Michigan State Medical Society Building, National Register of Historic Places Registration Form, Lansing, MI, 2011.
15. Michigan State Medical Society, https://www.msms.org/AboutMSMS.aspx.
16. Nietering, National Register of Historic Places Registration Form, 6. Yamasaki and Associates designed a two-story addition (the Cyrus M. Stockwell Wing), built in 1979, that connects to the original building at right angles on the west, but it is hidden by the landscaping and defers to that structure.
17. Minoru Yamasaki, *A Life in Architecture* (New York: Weatherhill, 1979).
18. Michigan Modern, Wayne State University McGregor Memorial Conference Center, Detroit, Minoru Yamasaki, http://www.michiganmodern.org/buildings/wayne-state-university-mcgregor-memorial-conference-center.
19. *The New Headquarters of the Michigan Education Association* (East Lansing, MI: MEA Press, September 1964).
20. Ibid.
21. Several smaller buildings in the Lansing area have elevations similar to the MEA's—for example, the 1966 University Branch of the Michigan National Bank at 2731 West Grand River Ave. in Meridian Township (architect unknown). This freestanding building has dark stone on the first level that serves as the base for the upper level, where light marble panels placed in vertical channels alternate with smaller dark vertical elements. Additionally, other professional associations built smaller modernist structures, such as Michigan Congress of Parents and Teachers State Headquarters, 1011 N. Washington Ave., by Manson, Jackson & Kane.
22. *Lansing State Journal*, June 5, 1964.
23. See National Register of Historic Places, Lansing Downtown Historic District, Section 7, 15–16. Although south of the district, Kenneth and Lee Black's 1954 design of the Seventh Day Adventist Headquarters at 320 West St. Joseph Highway used decorative concrete, steel and glass.
24. Amanda Harrell Seyburn, "Eye Candy of the Week," *City Pulse*, February 2, 2012, 5.
25. Daniel E. Bollman, "Eye Candy of the Week," *City Pulse*, February 19, 2014. He points out that originally smaller glass panes on the façade would have emphasized the horizontal even more.
26. "Architects Relocated, Warren Holmes Company in Washington Avenue Office Building," *Lansing State Journal*, March 15, 1959.
27. "Projects Underway at Okemos," *Lansing State Journal*,

February 9, 1962.

28. Leavenworth Photographs, Kenneth Black collection, Archives of Michigan, box 2, #40025–28, photographs dated December 18, 1950, of the model.
29. Ibid., box 5, photographs dated March 8, 1966, of model, #66484–97. One of his American State Bank and Trust buildings on East Michigan Avenue opened in January 1965, across from where there had been a branch since 1946. It featured the bank building plus a separate drive-in structure at the end of the parking lot.
30. The building was started by City National Bank, but when it failed in the Depression, the Bank of Lansing took over and completed the structure. National Register of Historic Places, Nomination, Section 7, 22.
31. On the history of bank architecture, see *Money Matters: A Critical Look at Bank Architecture* (New York: McGraw-Hill, 1990), esp. 249–52.
32. Ibid., 259.
33. Leavenworth Photographs, Kenneth Black collection, box 4, photograph dated August 21, 1961, of a model with the accordion roof, 58082, 58091–94, 58125–28.
34. These are included in Roadside Architecture.com, Michigan Mid-Century Modern Buildings, Michigan Banks, http://www.agilitynut.com/modarch/mibank.html.
35. I am grateful to Richard J. Hathaway for sharing his research with me. Hathaway, e-mail to author, July 29, 2014.
36. The general contractor was Vandenburg Construction.
37. The other stores only had the name of the supermarket, as seen in ads in the *Lansing State Journal* in January 1958.
38. Roadside Architecture, Michigan Signs, http://www.roadarch.com/signs/mi.html, page 3.
39. One example is the Bowling Alley (now called Thunder Bowl Arena) in Allen Park, MI (see Roadside Architecture, Michigan Midcentury Roofs and Canopies, http://www.agilitynut.com/modarch/miroof.html), built in 1962 with a total of 70 lanes. Trussless buildings were not unknown in Lansing. For example, Jack's Wonder Bar at 5008 S. Logan, built in 1955, had a barrel vault 66 feet long and 50 feet wide, a "Quonset-hut-like building so that passersby would wonder about the interior of the place and drop in for a look"; Warren Brintnall, "Trussless Building Is Like Part of Huge Barrel," *Lansing State Journal*, January 16, 1955. This was a steel structure erected with a patented "Trussless" system from Wonder Buildings of Western Michigan, more typically used on farms.
40. The Oldsmobile showroom on Michigan Avenue visibly retained its Googie characteristics until the early twenty-first century. The zigzag roof, however, existed under the new façade until its demolition in 2016.
41. Dawn Food Products, Inc., "About Us, History," http://www.dawnfoods.com/public/managed/about_us/history/index.asp. On Googie architecture, see Chris Jepsen, "Googie Architecture Online," http://www.spaceagecity.com/googie/.
42. Alan Hess, *Googie: Fifties Coffee Shop Architecture* (San Francisco: Chronicle Books, 1986). Also Todd Walsh, "Googie Architecture," *Seeking Michigan*, Modern Architecture Uninhibited, May 24, 2011, http://seekingmichigan.org/look/2011/05/24/googie. The Dawn Donuts in Bangor Township and in Flint, Michigan, were demolished in 2012 and 2013.
43. Anne Norcross, daughter of the original owners, e-mails to author, April 30, 2013; May 3, 2013. The addition on the west is from 1975.
44. Frank E Wrenick, *The Streamline Era Greyhound Terminals: The Architecture of W.S. Arrasmith* (Jefferson, NC: McFarland, 2007), esp. 163–64 on the Lansing building. See also "Michigan Greyhound Bus Stations," RoadsideArchitecture.com.
45. Wrenick, *The Streamline Era Greyhound Terminals*, 164.
46. K. Michael Hays and Dana A. Miller, *Buckminster Fuller: Starting with the Universe* (New Haven, CT: Yale University Press, 2008), 194. The companies were Synergetics, Inc. and Geodesics Inc.
47. Buckminster Fuller: The Estate of Buckminster Fuller, http://buckminsterfuller.net/aboutus.html.
48. The Buckminster Fuller Virtual Index contains a very extensive list of geodesic dome manufacturers at http://www.buckminster.info/Index/D/Domes-Manuf-G.htm. However, the list for Michigan (http://www.buckminster.info/Index/D/Domes-Michigan-A-L.html) does not

include the Davison company nor any domes in mid-Michigan.

49. Tom Young, interview by author, June 24, 2014.
50. There is a large body of literature on Fuller in addition to the Buckminster Fuller Institute website, www.bfi.org, and the collection of his papers at Stanford University.

CHAPTER 9. **Academic Buildings, Schools, and Libraries**

1. Michigan State University, Office of the Registrar, Historical Enrollment and Term End Reports.
2. The history of campus architecture and landscape design has been explored extensively by Linda O. Stanford and C. Kurt Dewhurst, *MSU Campus: Buildings, Places, Spaces* (East Lansing: Michigan State University Press, 2002), 16–18. The Olmsted brothers were nationally known and planned numerous college and university campuses as well as parks.
3. Ibid., 29.
4. Wayne State University and Michigan State Historic Preservation Office, *Michigan Modern, Detroit Modern, Wayne State University Tour*, no date.
5. Stanford and Dewhurst, *MSU Campus: Buildings, Places, Spaces*, 94.
6. Ibid., 16.
7. Ibid., 83.
8. Ibid., 77.
9. Ibid., 137, 150.
10. Ibid., 41; see also the list of architects who worked on the campus, 193.
11. On public school building in Michigan in general, see Roy Strickland, *An Honor and an Ornament: Public School Buildings in Michigan* (Lansing, MI: Michigan Department of History, Arts, and Libraries, 2003).
12. Listing of projects in the Glencairn dedication brochure, 1952. In 1952 the East Lansing planning board hired Laitala and Nuechterlein, with Eberle M. Smith, Detroit school architects, to draw up plans for a new high school to accommodate 1,200 students, grades 9–12. In anticipation, a fifty-acre site of the former historic Burcham Woods was purchased and annexed to the city. "East Lansing High School, Architects Are Hired," *Lansing State Journal*, September 9, 1952.
13. "Superintendent Requests More School Taxes," *Lansing State Journal*, October 14, 1952, reported that unprecedented enrollment gains resulted in crowded elementary buildings, and without increased funding, classes would have to be cut back to half-days. In the same issue, "High School Project at E. Lansing Studied" considered that high school enrollment would necessitate a new building in five years.
14. Jeannette Sloan and Carolyn Lee, interview by Edna Anderson, October 17, 1975, transcript, Sesquicentennial Oral History Project, City of East Lansing, East Lansing Public Library.
15. Ibid., 2.
16. Ibid., 3.
17. I thank Randy A. Bell, who sent me this ad. Bell, e-mail to author, May 1, 2013; *School Board Journal*, April 1954, 21.
18. I express appreciation to Diane Sowash, Laitala's daughter, for sharing this material with me.
19. Headlines like "Little School Concept Designed for Student-Centered Curriculum" explained that "The concept of school-within-a-school . . . originated with educators who wanted a school plant that was designed around a student-centered rather than a subject-centered curriculum"; *Meridian*, January 18, 1961.
20. Ibid., 8.
21. Madison Kuhn, *Michigan State: The First Hundred Years, 1850–1965* (East Lansing: Michigan State University Press, 1955), 452.
22. David A. Thomas, *Michigan State College: John Hannah and the Creation of a World University, 1926–1969* (East Lansing: Michigan State University Press, 2008), esp. 137–39, 142.
23. Stanford and Dewhurst, *MSU Campus: Buildings, Places, Spaces*, 51.
24. "East Lansing to Vote on Civic Building Projects," *Lansing State Journal*, March 25, 1951.
25. Ibid.; also "East Lansing Looks Forward to Its Long-awaited New Public Library," *Lansing State Journal*, January 1, 1951.
26. Ibid.
27. "Building Issue Stirs East Lansing Voters," *Lansing State*

Journal, April 1, 1951.

28. East Lansing Public Library, *History of East Lansing Public Library from 1923–1968*, 1968, 3, http://www.elpl.org/forms/library_history_ELPL.pdf.
29. Manson, Jackson & Kane, *Manson, Jackson & Kane, Inc. Architects* (Lansing, MI: Manson, Jackson & Kane, 1965).
30. Now known as the Downtown Library of the Capital Area District Library.
31. It was one of only three Lansing buildings included in the *Michigan Modern: Design That Shaped America* exhibition at Cranbrook Art Museum, Bloomfield Hills, Michigan, summer 2013.
32. Kenneth Black prospectus; D. Newton Glick, landscape designer of the west garden, 1964, Capital Area District Library.
33. "Library's Exterior Appears Backless," *Lansing State Journal*, December 29, 1967.
34. The building is included in the National Register of Historic Places, Lansing Downtown Historic District Nomination report, 2009, Section 7, 11; Section 8, 23.
35. Ibid. It was a gift of the Ransom Fidelity Company in memory of its founder, R. E. Olds.
36. *Lansing [School District] Libraries, Central Building*, Lansing, Michigan (Lansing, MI: 1964), no pagination; dedication brochure, description of ground floor.

CHAPTER 10. **Sacred Spaces**

1. Each January 1st, the *Lansing State Journal* provided a roundup of church construction for the previous year. Thelma Harnett, "Churches Built, Expanded," *Lansing State Journal*, February 9, 1969, noticed this tapering off.
2. Jay M. Price, *Temples for a Modern God: Religious Architecture in Postwar America* (New York: Oxford University Press, 2013), 111.
3. "The Tent Form—a Village Gothic for Today," *Architectural Forum* 101, no. 6 (1954): 128–31. The article is illustrated with a thirteenth-century Lutheran church in Finland.
4. Ibid., 128.
5. Gretchen Buggeln, "The Rise and Fall of the Postwar A-Frame Church," video of lecture, April 1, 2013, University of Minnesota. See also Gretchen Buggeln, *The Suburban Church: Modernism and Community in Postwar America* (Minneapolis: University of Minnesota Press, 2015), 85-123, on A-frame churches and their symbolism as well as the development of the modern church movement in general.
6. Albert Christ-Janer and Mary Mix Foley, *Modern Church Architecture: A Guide to the Form and Spirit of 20th Century Religious Buildings* (New York: McGraw-Hill, 1962), 272–79, 308–19. Also Mark A. Torgeson, *An Architecture of Immanence: Architecture for Worship and Ministry Today* (Grand Rapids, MI: Eerdmans, 2007), 131n10, on the importance of the Kramer Chapel as a model.
7. Zion dedication brochure, November 7, 1954, provided by Diane Sowash, Laitala's daughter, to the author.
8. Price, *Temples for a Modern God*, 58–59, discusses that as churches moved to more residential areas, the result was a change in the orientation of the entrance and the increasing importance of landscaping.
9. For example, St. Katherine's Episcopal, 4650 Meridian Road, Williamston, MI. The original nineteenth-century family chapel remains. Laitala and Nuechterlein designed an educational wing, begun in 1962, and Clark R. Ackley designed the A-frame church. River Terrace Church, 1509 River Terrace Drive, East Lansing, 1969, by Dan Vos of Ada, Michigan, is a late example.
10. Jason John Paul Haskins, Locus Iste: Church Architecture: Research + Design, "An Uplifting Mid-Century Chapel for the Children," September 8, 2013.
11. Information and documents are from the Edgewood Church archives. Originally known as Edgewood Peoples Church, it was spun off from Peoples Church to serve those living on East Lansing's east side, around Marble School, where they started holding services in June 1953. They signed a charter in 1954. The early history of the church and the first unit are described in detail in "The Story of a Community That Finally Realized Its Dream of a Cooperative Adventure in Religion under Full Time Leadership," as recorded by Mr. and Mrs. Coggen, appointed historians, chapters 6 ("The Churches Unite to Finance a Building Program") and 10 ("The Building Study Committee and the Building Committee"), typed manuscript.

12. Sutherland Frame, "Building the Edgewood United Church Sanctuary," *The Sanctuary of Edgewood Church*, n.d. (after 1981), 2, Edgewood Archives. Frame was chairman of the Sanctuary Committee. An undated color sketch by Laitala and Nuechterlein in the church archive for the "Proposed Edgewood Peoples Church" shows a large window wall that was not executed. Vandenburg Construction Company was the general contractor.
13. Price, *Temples for a Modern God*, 76–77.
14. For example, Truman A. Morrison, "The Plumb-line and the Dream" (a church anniversary sermon, April 10, 1994, typed script), 4, Edgewood Archives, recounts the "lengthy Sanctuary Building committee meetings over many, many months."
15. Frame, "Building the Edgewood United Church Sanctuary," 3–4, lists lectures they heard and sources they read, including a paper on Edward Sovik, an influential contemporary ecclesiastical architect who argued for simplicity and central planning.
16. Schwarz's book was published in Germany in 1938, but its widespread influence came after the war; Edwin Heathcote and Laura Moffatt, *Contemporary Church Architecture* (Hoboken, NJ: Wiley-Academy, 2007), 36. Schwarz was quoted in "Edgewood United Church, Completion Canvass," 1963, the fundraising literature used in the sanctuary campaign.
17. Price, *Temples for a Modern God*, 148–50.
18. From the typed script of Rev. Truman A. Morrison's benediction for the groundbreaking ceremony for the sanctuary, Edgewood Archives. Also "New Power in the Local Church: The Culture of a Congregation," *Register* 62, no. 3 (April 1973), a publication of the Chicago Theological Seminary; this entire issue is on Edgewood, with chapters on its ministry, culture, architecture, and symbolism of the church.
19. John F. A. Taylor, "Architecture and Communion" (address, Congregation of Edgewood United Church, East Lansing, MI, May 15, 1966), copy in Eastminster Archives, Building file. Taylor's interest in architecture had already been seen in his Streamline Moderne house of 1945, plate 6.
20. Frame, "Building the Edgewood United Church Sanctuary," 5.
21. Ibid., 7. The cost of the sanctuary addition was $270,000 (the architect's fee was 8.45 percent). It was built on the southeastern portion of the property. Granger Brothers was the general contractor. In the 1980s a rental house on the property was demolished, expanding the green space around the sanctuary and making it much more visible.
22. Ibid., 8, 9. Ten large stained-glass windows for the sanctuary and others for the atrium and the small chapel were designed by Helen Rother, a French artist from Detroit, and fabricated in France. The decision to omit human figures was deliberate.
23. Notebooks with finance reports, Minutes of March 12, 1962, meeting, Martin Luther Chapel Archive. I would like to thank Reverend Dressler for sharing his knowledge and allowing me access to the records. The development and role of Protestant building committees and consultants is explored in Price, *Temples for a Modern God*, 23–28. Briefly, national committees developed in the nineteenth century primarily as a way for national church organizations to help finance new congregations as America moved west, and to gain a foothold in poorer areas that could not build a church on their own. By the 1920s various mission councils developed architectural offices that published guides to church building. By the early 1960s, architects specializing in religious structures formed several national organizations, held conferences, and published journals.
24. Gretchen Buggeln, "The Shape of a New Era: Valparaiso's Chapel of the Resurrection in Historical Context," *Cresset* 73, no. 3 (2010), 6–14, esp. 9.
25. Kenan Heise, "Charles Stade, Award Winning Designer," *Chicago Tribune*, February 1, 1993. See also A Chicago Sojourn, A Journey through the architecture and urban landscape of Chicago, "Charles Stade," May 2010, http://achicagosojourn.wordpress.com/2010/05/24/charles-e-stade-architect. There are no specific details of the architecture selection process in the Martin Luther Chapel archive.
26. "The Chancel Furnishings, the Symbols, the Works of Religious Art," handout, no date (ca. 1960s), Martin Luther Chapel archive.

27. Dedication brochure, October 18, 1964, Martin Luther Chapel archive.
28. Letter sent by Chaplain Bundenthal to MSC parents, March 29, 1964, states that "our architecture is age old 9th century Scandinavian and yet today modern and functional." Martin Luther Chapel archive.
29. Buggeln, "The Shape of a New Era," 2.
30. Eero Saarinen and Aline B. Saarinen, *Eero Saarinen on His Work: A Selection of Buildings Dating from 1947 to 1964* (New Haven: Yale University Press, 1968) 96.
31. Buggeln, "The Shape of a New Era," 4–6. Buggeln, *The Suburban Church*, considers many of Stade's churches, most of which were A-frame designs, as well as Wright's and Dow's influences on his approach. Appendix C (268–201) lists nearly one hundred of his church commissions, including the Martin Luther Chapel, one of his later works (271). But its central plan and appearance is atypical of the rest of his buildings.
32. "Chapel, Center Are Unique," *(MSU) State News*, September 1964.
33. Ibid.
34. See A Chicago Sojourn, A Journey through the architecture and urban landscape of Chicago, May 2010, http://achicagosojourn.wordpress.com/2010/05/24/charles-e-stade-architect/ for seven examples.
35. Buggeln, "The Shape of a New Era," 4.
36. Janer and Foley, *Modern Church Architecture*, on what constitutes successful contemporary church design in Catholic and Protestant architecture.
37. *The Voice of Eastminster*, March 16, 1959, Early History file, Eastminster Archives. Rev. Margie Osborn was most helpful in answering my questions and giving me access to the archive.
38. Copies in Architects Correspondence file, 1958–61, Building History files. "The Developing Years, 1958–59," newsletter, June 1982 (second in series on the church's history on its twenty-fifth anniversary), Early History file, Eastminster Archives.
39. Handwritten notes from workshop, Architects Correspondence file, 1958–61, Eastminster Archives.
40. Pamphlet on the history of the church, no date, Early History file, Building Archives, April 30, 1958; credentials sent, Architects Correspondence, 1958–61, Eastminster Archives.
41. Alden B. Dow to Erskine Morse, April 23, 1958, Dow Archives, Midland, MI. Dow had already designed several churches in Midland, including First United Methodist Church, 1950; St. John's Lutheran, 1952; and St. John's Episcopal, 1950.
42. Building Committee Report, January 23, 1960, Eastminster Archives.
43. T. C. Cobb to Alden B. Dow, April 2, 1960, Eastminster Archives.
44. T. C. Cobb to Alden B. Dow, April 13, 1960, Eastminster Archives.
45. Alden B. Dow to T. C. Cobb, March 22, 1960; estimates based on August 24, 1959, sketches, Eastminster Archives.
46. Anat Geva, *Frank Lloyd Wright's Sacred Architecture* (New York: Routledge, 2012), esp. 66–68, 106–13.
47. Drawings of the first and lower floors in the Eastminster Archive show this version, no date.
48. Building Committee Minutes, June 5, 1967, Building files, Eastminster Archives.
49. Building Committee Minutes, July 19, 1967, Building files, Eastminster Archives.
50. See Diane Maddex, *Alden B. Dow: Midwestern Modern* (Midland, MI: Alden B. Dow Home and Studio, 2007), 62–65.
51. One-page sheet, no date, summary of changes in preliminary plan, Building files, Eastminster Archives.
52. Douglas R. Hoffman, *Seeking the Sacred in Contemporary Religious Architecture* (Kent, OH: Kent State University Press, 2010), 69–72, discusses the importance of pathway and gate in the progressive experience of sacred space.
53. Dow had retired by this time, and James Howell succeeded him as chairman of the board in 1974.
54. Evelyn King Eschbach, ed., *Under the Mustard Tree: The Plymouth Story: 1864–1989* (Lansing, MI: Plymouth Congregational Church, 1989).
55. Okemos Methodist Church, historical marker on the premises; "Major Building Program Highlights Church Activities," *Lansing State Journal*, January 1, 1957.

56. "Kaleidoscope of Faith, an Oral History of the Diocese of Lansing," Bernard Mayotte, interview by Father George C. Michalek, July 12, 1989, East Lansing, MI. Transcript in Catholic Diocese of Lansing Archives, 326 W. Ionia St., Lansing. I appreciate the assistance I received from Msgr. George C. Michalek, the archivist.
57. St. Gerard Parish at 4437 W. Willow Highway, Lansing, was established in 1958; an educational wing was constructed in 1959 and the permanent sanctuary was erected in 1974–75. More recent additions have engulfed the original Mayotte-Webb structure.
58. "Kaleidoscope of Faith," 6.
59. Torgeson, *An Architecture of Immanence*, 131–32.
60. The iconography is fully described in the Dedication brochure, New Building file, Diocese of Lansing Archives, April 3, 1968.
61. Conrad Pickel, a specialist in glass art, was chosen from among six submissions; dedication brochure, April 3, 1968, New Building file, Diocese of Lansing Archives.
62. Heathcote and Moffatt, *Contemporary Church Architecture*, 36–37, 44 and on American architecture, 56-61.
63. Dedication brochure, New Building file, Diocese of Lansing Archives, April 3, 1968.
64. "Tradition, Aggiornamento Mingle in New St. Thomas Aquinas Church," *Catholic Weekly*, April 5, 1963, 2.
65. "Kaleidoscope of Faith," 12–13.
66. George R. Price to Bishop Zaleski, March 28, 1966, New Building file, Diocese of Lansing Archives.
67. Bishop Zaleski to George R. Price, New Building file, Diocese of Lansing Archives, April 5, 1966.
68. Hoffman, *Seeking the Sacred*, esp. 69–77.
69. According to his listing in *The AIA Historical Directory of American Architects* (ahd1008527), he started his own firm in 1929. Another example of his work is St. Paul Lutheran Church and School in Flint, 1958.
70. *University United Methodist Church, 1957–2007, Celebrating Fifty Years of Ministry to East Lansing, Michigan and Michigan State University* (East Lansing, MI: University United Methodist, 2007), 27. This 42-page publication was distributed by the church. In 2002 18,000 square feet, including a greeting space and sanctuary balcony were added.
71. Thelma Harnett, "$3 Million in Church Construction in Lansing in '57," *Lansing State Journal*, January 1, 1958.
72. Thelma Harnett, "Greater Lansing Churches Expanding Again," *Lansing State Journal*, January 1, 1961. These include a $100,000 convent for Immaculate Heart of Mary church, designed by Mayotte-Webb, at 3815 S. Cedar; Dow's Eastminster educational wing; First Pilgrims Holiness Church; St. Michael's Episcopal Mission; addition to University Lutheran church and student center; and St. Stephens's Lutheran Church.
73. Other examples could be given, such as St. Stephen's Evangelical Lutheran Church, 3838 Delta River Drive, at Waverly Road, Lansing, by Laitala and Nuechterlein, 1960. Several architecturally striking churches were built after 1970: Laitala, Fowler, Freeman & Smith designed the contemporary Holy Trinity Greek Orthodox Church, 1701 East Saginaw Street, after 1972; University Lutheran Church, 1020 South Harrison, East Lansing, was designed by Saginaw architect Daniel W. Toshach in 1970, completed in 1972. Toshach (1928–1992), a Yale-trained architect, worked for Alden B. Dow (1953–1954) and Glenn M. Beach (1954–1957), before starting his own firm, Prine, Toshach, Spears Architect and Engineers, in 1957 in Saginaw. Although there were various name changes, he remained a principal. *AIA Historical Directory*, ahd1045272.
74. Fay L. Hendry, *Outdoor Sculpture in Lansing* (Okemos, MI: Iota Press, 1980), 124–25.
75. For the Islamic Center, see Kathryn Bishop Eckert, *Buildings of Michigan*, rev. ed. (Charlottesville: University of Virginia, 2012), 299.

CHAPTER 11. Life Along the Water

1. Virginia Redfern, "Picturesque Homes Line Winding River," *Lansing State Journal*, September 20, 1964, 59.
2. National Register of Historic Places, Arbaugh's Department Store Building, Ingham County, Michigan, Nomination, 2007, Section 8, 1–3.
3. *Polk's Lansing City Directory (Ingham County, Michigan)* (Detroit: R. L. Polk & Co., 1960), 169.
4. Rachel Greco, "Historic Arbaugh Estate Along Grand

River in Lansing Is on the Market," *Lansing State Journal*, July 10, 2018, https://www.lansingstatejournal.com/story/news/local/2018/07/10/cool-spaces-arbaugh-estate-grand-river-market/752954002/.

5. Blueprints courtesy of Bruce Bower and Christine Altese, current owners. Laverne J. Hendryx is listed as engineer and surveyor.
6. Early undated photographs of the house courtesy of Bower and Altese.
7. Virginia Redfern, "Wives of Chiefs-of-Staff Busy on Charity Ball Benefit," *Lansing State Journal*, November 9, 1958, 32.
8. Ibid.
9. *Bresser's Cross-Index Directory for Lansing and East Lansing* (Detroit: Walter Bresser and Sons, 1968), 262, lists the Harrold's address at 2812 Waverly Road, which is the closest major intersecting street. "Pinetree" was likely named and distinguished from it at a later date. Likewise, other rural and less developed areas often had "rural road" addresses at this time, making exact determinations of addresses problematic.
10. Manson, Jackson & Kane, Inc., Architects, *Manson, Jackson & Kane* (Lansing, MI: Manson Jackson & Kane, 1965), no pagination.
11. Redfern, "Wives of Chiefs-of-Staff Busy on Charity Ball Benefit," 32. Their house at 8 Waverly Road was one of six on the "Cook's Kitchen Tour" on the Grand River briefly described in the *Lansing State Journal*, September 26, 1954, 25. The Delta Township assessing record gives 1940 as the date, a discrepancy to be researched.
12. Redfern, "Picturesque Homes," 59.
13. "Crouse Has Important Role in Community Betterment," *Lansing State Journal*, April 19, 1964, 27.
14. "Fashionable Benefit Dance Sponsored by Edward W. Sparrow Hospital Guild," *Lansing State Journal*, October 27, 1957, 46. "Governor's Residence Perfect for 'Home Away from Home,'" *Lansing State Journal*, February 24, 1963, 42.
15. "'It's a Happy House,' Says Mrs. Crouse Describing Her Handsome New Home," *Lansing State Journal*, April 2, 1961, 37, 45. "Mayotte-Webb" is the name on the blueprints, courtesy of Yvonne Caamal Canul and Victor Caamal Canul, current owners.
16. Ibid., 37.
17. The house bears similarities in style to the Bittersweet Lane house. Edward and Patricia Crouse are listed at this address in *Bresser's* 1968, a year after it was built. Edward took over Heatherwood Farms from their father.
18. Virginia Redfern, "'Dream House' Coming True," *Lansing State Journal*, February 24, 1970, 22.
19. Plans courtesy of the current owners.
20. Photo caption, "New Home . . . Mrs. Wilson, who designed her home, is standing by the family's pontoon boat, scene of many social outings," in Redfern, "Picturesque Homes," 59.
21. In "Patio Dinner Party," *Lansing State Journal*, August 6, 1963, 14, the Victor Andersons, who bought the Ochsner's Cambridge Road house, are reported to be "remodeling and redecorating" it. The Ochsner's likely sold it then in anticipation of moving to this new house where they subsequently are recorded in *Bresser's*.
22. It was described as "picturesque" in "Local Architects, Families Enjoy Varied Community, Home Activities," *Lansing State Journal*, February 17, 1957, 47.
23. *The AIA Historical Directory of American Architects*, ahd1042129.
24. *The AIA Historical Directory of American Architects*, ahd1043443.
25. Another Warren Holmes architect, Delphin (Bud) Budzyinski Jr. (1925–1992), built his family's house at 1450 Biscayne Way in Haslett. Designed in 1954, he substantially expanded it in three phases as the family grew, adding bedrooms and decks, and converting the carport into a two-car garage. The landscape design was by Jack Drew. Virginia Redfern, "Homes on Oct. 9 Tour," *Lansing State Journal*, June 14, 1979, 30; also Virginia Redfern, "Mixing Tradition, Modern: a Reflection of Lifestyles," *Lansing State Journal*, September 30, 1979, 49. Bud worked his way up at Warren Holmes from draftsman in 1953, to architect in 1959, and president when the firm merged with Kenneth Black Associate Architects in 1976.
26. Tecumseh River Drive ends at Waverly Road, but the

river continues west into a hilly rural area. Several custom houses were built in the 1950s and later on Delta River Drive closer to the road than the water. Of note are 4205 in 1956, 4713 in 1960, and a large sprawling compound on the north side of the road at 4910 in 1952.

27. The first complaint was filed in February 1949. Carlisle Carver, "Landowners Declare War on Meridian Pig Farm," *Lansing State Journal*, March 10, 1951, 2.
28. John Sergeant, *Frank Lloyd Wright's Usonian Houses: The Case for Organic Architecture* (New York: Whitney Library of Design, 1984), 118. Turner traveled the country for Wright and ended up in Michigan working for Wright but also building Wrightian designs including his own Usonian-style house in southeast Michigan in 1950 as well as about fifty-five others throughout the state.
29. See Susan J. Bandes, ed., *Affordable Dreams: The Goetsch-Winckler House and Frank Lloyd Wright* (East Lansing: Michigan State University Kresge Art Museum, 1991).
30. Frank Lloyd Wright to Sidney H. Newman, undated letter [April 1940?], 2, Frank Lloyd Wright Foundation Archives (New York: Museum of Modern Art | Avery Architectural & Fine Arts Library, Columbia University). See also Anatole Senkevitch Jr., "Usonia II and the Goetsch-Winckler House: Manifestations of Wright's Early Vision of Broadacre City," in *Affordable Dreams* 11, no. 40.
31. Frank Lloyd Wright to Sidney H. Newman, April 18, 1940 (telegram), Frank Lloyd Wright Foundation Archives.
32. Sidney H. Newman to Frank Lloyd Wright, May 24, 1940, 2, Frank Lloyd Wright Foundation Archives.
33. V. D. Thompson and H. P. David, "Sidney H. Newman (1912–1989): Obituary," *American Psychologist*, 45, no. 10, 1169, https://doi.org/10.1037/h0090810.
34. Carver, "Landowners Declare War on Meridian Pig Farm," 2. Meridien Township assessing record, sale by Denny recorded on July 6, 2001.
35. Senkevitch, "Usonia II and the Goetsch-Winckler House," 11. There is scant information in Newman's file in the MSU Archives. Denny's file contains two forms with conflicting address information. On one, he is listed at 637 Cherry Lane in 1945 when his first son was born. On the other, he gave "R#2, Lansing" as his address when both his first and second child were born, the latter in 1948. The form has updates from 1957. "R#2" could be the Hawthorne House before the house number and street name were assigned. If so, the Dennys could have purchased the house in 1948 or perhaps earlier. Forms, M. Ray Denny, n.d., Media Communication Papers, UA 8.1.1, Michigan State University Archives and Historical Collections. My appreciation to MSU archivist Tim McRoberts for his help.
36. Information from Monte Pride, owner of two Hinman houses, e-mail to author, November 11, 2020. Both Hinmans were members of the Michigan Association of Home Builders, Lansing chapter, and both served as president.
37. "Indian Hills Opens Today," *Lansing State Journal*, June 22, 1929, 11.
38. "Indian Hills Area Booms," *Lansing State Journal*, September 16, 1951, 70.
39. "On Hospital Fund Team," *Lansing State Journal*, April 19, 1954, 14; an East Lansing native, Richard Bailey attended Michigan State College and the University of Michigan dental school before starting in practice in 1951 with his father, Dr. Wilber E. Bailey. Richard and his wife moved from 2244 Raby Road, a 1954 Cape Cod. Stebbins Realty Records, Capital Area District Library, Main Branch, Local History Division, card dated 1960.
40. "4702 Huron Hill Dr.," Realtor.com, https://www.realtor.com/realestateandhomes-detail/4702-Huron-Hill-Dr_Okemos_MI_48864_M47660-47999.
41. Deed restrictions, Section 1, Liber 880, 610, October 1, 1964; Indian Lakes Estates Homeowners Association, Bylaws and Deed Restrictions, https://www.ileha.org/documents/bylaws-and-deed-restrictions/.
42. Among the many custom houses is the tri-level at 4587 Sequoia Trail that Robert (Bob) A. Britsch, who was in construction, and his wife Jeannette designed themselves. The unusual façade consists of the unbroken horizontal bands of boarding of the upper and lower roofs creating a parallel rhythm that stretches across the structure and rises to a peak above the entry.
43. The family moved from another large, modern home in Chippewa Hills, south of Mount Hope Avenue at 4401

Apache Drive, built in 1954. Virginia Redfern, "Make Theirs Country Style, but Keep the City Nearby," *Lansing State Journal*, May 15, 1955, 43. The caption for an interior view describes it as "a big, modern, wood and stone home that blends in with the wooded hills on which it is situated."

44. "Harold Jack Begrow," Michigan Modern, http://www.michiganmodern.org/designers/harold-jack-begrow. He was credited with reshaping the town of Charlevoix. "H. Jack Begrow, Obituary," *Northern Michigan Review*, November 15, 2019, https://www.petoskeynews.com/charlevoix/obituaries/h-jack-begrow-88/article_8e314b4c-f211-5a81-a72d-93477e017958.html.
45. Her name is recorded in the Stebbins Realty Records, Capital Area District Library, Main Branch, Local History Division, 1966, card dated 1968.
46. "Lansing Woman to Judge Show," *Lansing State Journal*, February 8, 1959, 11. She is one of two landscape architects in the 1959 *Lansing Directory*, 232. Several MSU landscape architecture faculty members such as Myles Boylan, Carl S. Gerlach, and D. Newton Glick occasionally worked for private clients at this time.
47. Virginia Delano, Untitled and undated document, seven typed pages. Courtesy of Barbara Stynes, current owner.
48. This and additional plans courtesy of Barbara Stynes, current owner.
49. There are two additional two-page lists of questions and comments on the plans and specifications, undated. One ends with comment #15: "I still can't figure out where to store card tables." Courtesy of Stynes.
50. "Specifications for Residence for Mr. and Mrs. Myles Delano," twenty-four typed pages, designed by A. William Dempsey, April 1, 1966, courtesy of Stynes.
51. *AIA Historical Directory of American Architects*, ahd1010672. He was affiliated with the AIA from 1973 on, but detailed information is lacking in the entry.
52. Pictured in the ad in the *Lansing State Journal*, September 19, 1965, 112.
53. Plans courtesy of Birgit Puschner and Charles Laub, current owners. This house is on the list of Arai's commissions put together by his daughter, Grace Arai, email to author, January 28, 2021; the address for the Wests on the list is 2404 Shawnee Trail, a 1955 house where they were living, rather than the site of the future building.
54. Undated plans, courtesy of Puschner and Laub.
55. A 20-foot by 12-foot addition in 1997 changed the proportions of the dining area; Meridian Township Assessing, building permit. The porch outside the kitchen was also enclosed.
56. Framing plans, F1-3, courtesy of Puschner and Laub.
57. Jacqueline Shinners, Traverse City Architecture: Mid-Century Modern Driving Tour, https://tcdrivingtourwebsi.wixsite.com/tour. *The AIA Historical Directory of American Architects*, ahd1001139.
58. *The AIA Historical Directory of American Architects*, ahd1021073; listed in 1970. After Arai's death, Hummel practiced on his own. His largest and most complex building is Pine Hollow in Elk Rapids. See Dani Knoph, "Inside Pine Hollow: A Thousand Years Onward," *My North*, August 18,2014, https://mynorth.com/2014/08/inside-pine-hollow-a-thousand-years-onward/.
59. Diane Kolak, "Inside Modern Old Mission Peninsula Home Designed by Architect Glenn Arai," *My North*, December 1, 2016, https://mynorth.com/2016/12/inside-modern-home-designed-architect-glenn-arai/.
60. Roger A. Hummel, "Modular Building Construction," U.S. Patent 3964216, filed October 31, 1974, issued June 22, 1976, https://www.freepatentsonline.com/3964216.html.
61. Information from Pia Banzhaf current owner, e-mail to author, October 5, 2020. The Sheathelms sold the house in 1989.
62. The builder was Bill Luginsland (d. 1979), well-enough known for his high-quality buildings that his name was often included in ads. For example, "Builder of Better Home," *Lansing State Journal*, April 9, 1961, 69, ad for 2306 Belaire Drive.
63. Virginia Redfern, "Kresge tour is Oct. 11," *Lansing State Journal*, October 2, 1977, 42.
64. Although most of the large houses in this 1970s subdivision are traditional, the Nathan E. Tolberts hired architect Robert Pond to design their Wrightian house at 350 Winterberry Lane. This 1977 Y-shaped house is designed on a diamond-shape module resulting in

numerous angled walls. It has extensive wood paneling and glazing in the gables and takes full advantage of water views.

65. "Luxurious Home Fits Subdivision," *Lansing State Journal*, September 16, 1956, 40.
66. He had previously built a brick house at 4759 Ottawa Drive in Indian Hills, featured in the *Lansing State Journal*, August 15, 1954, 27, as one of three new homes recently completed. It was on the market in May 1955, *Lansing State Journal*, 103, as an "unusual" house.
67. "Open House Showroom: Standard Block & Supply Presents Products in Display Model," *Lansing State Journal*, August 18, 1957, 49.
68. Dale Allen Gyure, *Minoru Yamasaki: Humanist Architecture for a Modernist World* (New Haven, CT: Yale University Press, 2017), 107.
69. Ibid., 107–12.
70. Obituary, *Lansing State Journal*, April 22, 2010; also "Modernizing Value Shown by Designer," *Lansing State Journal*, April 22, 1956, 38.
71. "New Type Walls on Display Today at Okemos House," *Lansing State Journal*, October 4, 1959, 30.
72. Warren Brintnall, "Old Saying Challenged: Home Suits Family Well," *Lansing State Journal*, November 11, 1962, 25. The old saying referenced in the article's title is "success on fourth try," which refers to the fact that this was the fourth house that was custom built for the family.
73. "New Type Walls" calls these "shadow blocks." It also explains that the walls are of light aggregate concrete blocks with cores that were filled with Zonolite insulation, left in their natural gray color on the exterior and painted on the interior.
74. Information from the second owners, Drs. Fedon and Elizabeth Mavromatis, who purchased it in 1964; interview with author, September 7, 2020.
75. Fineout worked with Standard Block and Supply on several model homes. The building at 2803 Woodview Drive, Lansing (now 2705), was described as "different in design" and "highly unconventional" with "an unusual floor plan" in "Open House Different in Design," *Lansing State Journal*, August 20, 1961, 44. The patterned cement-block wall of the garage is very visible from the street. The house at 2214 Belaire Road was another Fineout design with Standard Block material including a concrete screen wall. *Lansing State Journal*, March 12, 1961, 50. An earlier "L for Living" model is at 2710 Northwest Street, 1955.
76. MSU Archives, Robert E. Brown papers. He received a bachelor of arts degree from the University of Washington and PhD from the University of Wisconsin.
77. Helen Clegg, "MSU Pair Probes Past, Revolution Revamped," *Lansing State Journal*, August 21, 1967, 2. They are pictured in the living room with the caption "The Browns at Work in Their Okemos Home, 2070 Lagoon Drive." Sample real estate advertisements in *Lansing State Journal*, September 12, 1976, 80; and *Lansing State Journal*, January 30, 1977, 69.
78. Plans dated September 3, 1964, courtesy of Andrew and Sarah Finley, current owners. The dumbwaiter from the kitchen to the basement shown in the plan was omitted.
79. Mark Nixon, "Humane Tide Follows Flood," *Lansing State Journal*, April 23, 1975, 21.
80. "Donald J. Scholz," *NC Modernist*, https://ncmodernist.org/scholz.htm.
81. Warren Brintnall, "Scholz Mark '58 Home Makes Forest Hills Debut," *Lansing State Journal*, May 25, 1958, 59. The other Michigan cities with models were Benton Harbor, Detroit, Kalamazoo, Saginaw, and Sturgis. "State Showings," *Lansing State Journal*, May 25, 1958, 59. The ad in the June 23, 1958, issue of *Life Magazine*, 100–101, included several views and a plan of a Mark '58 house as well as a list of the seventy-five houses. Oddly, the Okemos address (4434 Oakwood Drive) is wrong.
82. Scholz Homes, *The Famed Scholz Design Collection* (Toledo, OH: Scholz Homes, 1966), brochure; "The Contemporary California, Mark '58" plans from Scholz dated March 20, 1958, includes variations for the different models as well as optional components. These were used by Lansing designer A. L. Sargent to create blueprints, including a site plan, for Couchois and Miller, dated April 23, 1959. The most significant difference is the basement. Only Scholz's hillside variation had a full basement but Sargent replaced the crawl spaces with a full below-grade basement, including a recreation room

with a fireplace. Plans and blueprints courtesy of Erica Murdock and Michael Smokevitch, current owners.

83. Maryland Historical Trust, Inventory of Historic Properties Form for the Lang House, Scholz Mark '64, https://www.mncppc.org/DocumentCenter/View/5582/80-058-Scholz-Mark-64-Lang-House-MIHP-PDF, 12–17. The deliberate use of the word "Mark" brings to mind Detroit's automobile industry and connections to Ford's 1955 Continental Mark II, a hand-built, exclusive, and expensive car (14).

84. *The Famed Scholz Design Collection*; the Mark '58, living room view, unpaginated. The Mark '62 and '65 even came in French provincial and colonial variations. "An exact duplicate of the famous Mark "59" under the title of "L for Living" was advertised in Holly Park, *Lansing State Journal*, September 27, 1959, 88.

85. Plans courtesy of Jamie and Lisa Beardslee, current owners.

86. Maryland Historical Trust, 17, new designs were issued each year through 1965 and designated by the last two digits of the year. Annual changes of the Mark design are described on 17.

87. Alan Hess, *Ranch House* (New York: Harry N. Abrams, 2004), 74.

88. "3 Houses Held Open," *Lansing State Journal*, April 20, 1958, 18. While the mile-wide Lake Lansing is the largest body of water in mid Michigan, the (now) year-round residencies that replaced or expanded smaller 1930s cottages tend to be conservative in style. On the history of the lake, see Wilma Porter, "Lansing Society Finds Lake Lansing Ideal Spot for Summer," *Lansing State Journal*, August 7, 1938, 9. Evelyn Huber Raphael, *A History of the Haslett–Lake Lansing Area, Meridian Township*, sesquicentennial edition (Mason, MI: INCO, 1992), recounts its history and the renewal effort begun in 1978. Park Lake in Bath Township to the north is the next largest lake. Most houses are modest, built in the 1930s and '40s, and many are separated from the waterfront by a road.

89. "5-Bedroom Unit Shows," *Lansing State Journal*, July 13, 1958, 30; Warren Brintnall, "Eight Models Presented in Open House," *Lansing State Journal*, June 28, 1959, 22.

90. For example, "Parade of Homes, Shaker Heights," *Lansing State Journal*, October 11, 1967, 78.

91. "Move Up to Exclusive Shaker Heights," *Lansing State Journal*, on October 27, 1968, 98.

92. *Lansing State Journal*, October 8, 1967, Section D, 29–44. The Gallery is featured several times on pages 35, 37, 39.

93. Susan Elder, "Stark Contemporary Design Covers Warm Interior," *Lansing State Journal*, May 5, 1968, 38, 40.

94. Ibid.

95. A bedroom addition was added in 2006, at the west end of the house and north of the garage. Meridian Township Assessing record.

96. The plans are signed by the architect but not dated. Courtesy of Gary Scheuren and Hans Schwab, current owners.

97. Landscape architect Carl S. Gerlach drew up a plan for a screen fence, dated May 1961, for the owners Dr. and Mrs. Harry George. However, instead of erecting it, a pierced brick wall for the carport was installed based on plans dated October 30, 1963. Courtesy of Scheuren and Schwab.

98. Plans courtesy of Barbara Coey, current owner.

99. Forms, Lawrence L. Boger, Media Communication Papers, Michigan State University Archives and Historical Collections; also "Lawrence L. Boger," College of Agriculture & Natural Resources, Michigan State University, https://www.canr.msu.edu/people/boger_lawerence.

100. Art Teglund (1893–1988) is listed as the contractor on the 1006 plans. He had emigrated with his family from Sweden and ended up in the Lansing area by 1928.

101. Forms, Leyton V. Nelson, Media Communication Papers, Michigan State University Archives and Historical Collections.

102. Gary Scheuren, e-mail to author, November 13, 2020. At some time, probably in the 1960s, some house numbers on this street were changed. On August 1, 1958, "Legal Notice," *Lansing State Journal*, Nelson requested that curbs and gutters be installed in front of 1033 and 1039 Lantern Hill Drive. He gives his address as 1033, which does not exist. Number 1039 was built in 1958.

103. MSU Archives, William S. Gamble papers.
104. At 627 Cherry Lane, *Lansing Directory*, 1959; and 901 Cherry Lane, 1949. Plans and drawings courtesy of Anna Cardona, current owner.
105. The building permit was found in the garage when the second owner Melissa Evans Itsell purchased the house. Itsell, phone conversation with author, September 16, 2020.
106. This wall was removed in the 2020 renovations.
107. "Doctor Soria, Professor Gamble join Michigan State Art Staff," *Lansing State Journal*, September 26, 1948, 27. While at MSU, he earned a doctorate in art education from Teachers College, Columbia University, in 1961, and later established a program for inmates at Jackson State Prison.
108. Deborah A. Barnstone, *Beyond the Bauhaus: Cultural Modernity in Breslau, 1918–33* (Ann Arbor: University of Michigan Press, 2016), 203–4. He taught at the progressive Breslau Academy of Fine and Applied Arts with Otto Mueller and Oskar Schlemmer, 82–83.
109. Obituary, *Lansing State Journal*, February 12, 2009.
110. Mayumi Tsutakawa, "Tsutakawa, George (1910–1997)," History Link, 2001, https://www.historylink.org/File/3088.
111. William S. Gamble, *William S. Gamble: Artist/Collector*, February 6–March 6, 1983, typed catalogue of his Kresge Art Museum exhibition, Broad Art Museum artist file. "Establishing a Track" checklist, 4–6. It included one of his paintings and four of his prints borrowed from George and Ayame Tsutakawa, and Mayumi Tsutakawa and Glenn Chinn. A large image of Mount Fuji by Tsutakawa was framed and hung prominently in Gamble's house; Itsell, communication to author.
112. Gamble, "Adventure in Collecting," in *William S. Gamble*, 1.
113. Gamble, "Establishing a Track," in *William S. Gamble*, 4–6.
114. While many original features were retained in the 2020 renovation, such as the wood banister, the open mesh grate of the stairs to the basement level, and the folding rattan closet doors, the original color palette of green and orange-ochre on the exterior was changed. Three houses to the east, at 1037 Daisy Lane, is another flat roofed house from 1947 that was owned by D. Newton Glick, MSU professor of landscape architecture. Its detached garage and rectangular shape are the mirror opposite of the Gamble house. Although it is two stories on the back, its placement on the site relates to the slope of the terrain, rather than being deeply excavated.
115. Hess, *Ranch House*, especially 27–79.
116. Ibid., 128.

EPILOGUE

1. One example is Olga Gershenson and Barbara Penner, ed., *Ladies and Gents: Public Toilets and Gender* (Philadelphia: Temple University Press, 2009).
2. Ibid.; various chapters consider toilet histories, research and approaches across the globe including in Australia, Africa, Europe, and America.
3. Barbara Penner, "(Re)Designing the 'Unmentionable': Female Toilets in the Twentieth Century," in *Ladies and Gents*, ed. Gershenson and Penner, 141–50, esp. 145–46. See also Barbara Penner, "Leftovers / A Revolutionary Aim?," *Cabinet*, Fall 2005, 19, https://www.cabinetmagazine.org/issues/19/penner.php.
4. For more on the Kohler Hygeia removed from the women's bathroom and put into the collection, see Erin Brasell, "When Nature Calls, Accession It," Oregon Historical Society, blog, July 23, 2019, https://ohs.org/blog/when-nature-calls-accession-it.cfm.
5. Dimi Kyriakou and Jonathan Jackson, "We Know Squat about Female Urinals," *Plumbing Connection*, Autumn 2011, 56.
6. Ibid.
7. "Product News from American Standard, Sanistand Fixture," reproduced by Lisa Wade, in "Urinals for Women: An Alternative Reality," Sociological Images, February 11, 2012, https://thesocietypages.org/socimages/2012/02/11/urinals-for-women-an-alternative-reality/.
8. "Women's Urinal Installations," Urinal.net, http://www.urinal.net/archive/Womens.html. This website is a crowdsourced listing of these urinals.
9. My own 1956 brick ranch still had a 1955 petal pink

hanging GE refrigerator and freezer when I bought it in the late 1990s. Unfortunately, it barely worked and was inefficient so it no longer exists. For a brief history of kitchen appliances like these, see Sarah Archer, *The Midcentury Kitchen* (New York: Countryman Press, 2019).

10. Lawrence Cosentino, "Tales from the Dripping Slab," *City Pulse*, April 26, 2018, https://www.lansingcitypulse.com/stories/tales-from-the-dripping-slab,1091. This article explains the current state of the building.

Bibliography

Abercrombie, Stanley. *George Nelson: The Design of Modern Design*. Cambridge, MA: MIT Press, 1995.

AIA Historical Directory of American Architects, The.

American Institute of Architects. *A Guide to Lansing Architecture*. AIA Mid-Michigan, n.d.

Andrews, Wayne. *Architecture in Michigan*. Detroit: Wayne State University Press, 1967.

Bandes, Susan J., ed. *Affordable Dreams: The Goetsch-Winckler House and Frank Lloyd Wright*. East Lansing: Michigan State University Kresge Art Museum, 1991.

Belfour, Charles. *Monuments to Money: The Architecture of American Banks*. Jefferson, NC: McFarland & Co, Inc., 2005.

Bresser's Cross Index Directory of Lansing East Lansing and Suburban Communities. Detroit: Walter Bresser & Sons, 1968–69, 1972–75.

Buggeln, Gretchen. "The Rise and Fall of the Postwar A-Frame Church." Video of lecture, University of Minnesota, April 1, 2013. Http://ias.umn.edu/2013/03/07/buggeln-gretchen/.

——. *The Suburban Church: Modernism and Community in Postwar America*. Minneapolis: University of Minnesota Press, 2015.

Cheek, Richard. *Selling the Dwelling: The Books That Built America's Houses, 1775–2000*. New York: Grolier Club, 2013.

Christ-Janer, Albert, and Mary Mix Foley. *Modern Church Architecture: A Guide to the Form and Spirit of 20th Century Buildings*. New York: Dodge Book Dept., McGraw-Hill, 1962.

Design for Modern Merchandising: Stores, Shipping Centers, Showrooms. New York: F. W. Dodge Corp., 1954.

Eaton, Leonard K. *Two Chicago Architects and Their Clients: Frank Lloyd Wright and Howard Van Doren Shaw*. Cambridge, MA: MIT Press, 1969.

Eckert, Kathryn Bishop. *Buildings of Michigan*. New York:

Oxford University Press, 1993.

——. *Buildings of Michigan*, rev. ed. Charlottesville: University of Virginia Press, 2012.

Fuller, R. B., K. M. Hays, and Dana A. Miller. *Buckminster Fuller: Starting with the Universe*. New Haven, CT: Yale University Press, 2008.

Gamble, William S. *William S. Gamble: Artist/Collector, February 6–March 6, 1983*. East Lansing: Kresge Art Museum, 1983, typed manuscript.

Gershenson, Olga, and Barbara Penner, eds. *Ladies and Gents: Public Toilets and Gender*. Philadelphia: Temple University Press, 2009.

Grimes, Alan. "Remembering Lantern Hill, 1950–1952." Typed manuscript, 1999. MSU Archives, Special Collections, Archives of Michigan.

Guggenheimer, Tobias S. *A Taliesin Legacy: The Architecture of Frank Lloyd Wright's Apprentices*. New York: Van Nostrand Reinhold, 1995.

Gyure, Dale Allen. *Minoru Yamasaki: Humanist Architecture for a Modernist World*. New Haven, CT: Yale University Press, 2017.

Hess, Alan. *Googie: Fifties Coffee Shop Architecture*. San Francisco: Chronicle Books, 1986.

——. *Googie Redux: Ultramodern Roadside Architecture*. San Francisco: Chronicle Books, 2004.

——. *The Ranch House*. New York: Harry N. Abrams, 2004.

Hess, Alan, Alan Weintraub, John Zukowsky and Mónica Ramírez-Montagut. *Frank Lloyd Wright: Mid-Century Modern*. New York: Rizzoli, 2007.

Hoffman, Douglas R. *Seeking the Sacred in Contemporary Religious Architecture*. Kent, OH: Kent State University Press, 2010.

Holleman, Thomas J., and James P. Gallagher. *Smith, Hinchman & Grylls: 125 Years of Architecture and Engineering, 1853–1978*. Detroit: Wayne State University Press, 1978.

Hubka, Thomas C. *Houses without Names: Architectural Nomenclature and the Classification of America's Common Houses*. Knoxville: University of Tennessee Press, 2013.

Kenneth C. Black Associates. *Kenneth C. Black Associates, Inc.: Architects and Engineers*. Lansing, MI: Kenneth C. Black Associates, 1970.

Kestenbaum, Justin L. *At the Campus Gate: A History of East Lansing*. East Lansing, MI: East Lansing Bicentennial Committee, 1976.

——. *Out of a Wilderness: An Illustrated History of Greater Lansing*. Woodland Hills, CA: Windsor Publications, 1981.

Ludman, Dianne M. *Hugh Stubbins and His Associates: The First Fifty Years*. Cambridge, MA: Stubbins Associates, 1966.

Maddex, Diane. *Alden B. Dow: Midwestern Modern*. Midland, MI: Alden B. Dow Home and Studio, 2007.

Manson, Jackson & Kane, Inc., Architects. *Manson, Jackson & Kane*. Lansing, MI: Manson, Jackson & Kane, 1965.

Menocal, Narcisco G. *Keck and Keck, Architects*. Madison, WI: Elvehjem Museum of Art, University of Wisconsin–Madison, 1980.

Mock, Elizabeth, ed. *Built in USA, 1932–1944*. New York: Museum of Modern Art, 1944.

Parnassus Foundation and the Museum of Fine Arts, Houston. *Money Matters: A Critical Look at Bank Architecture*. New York: McGraw-Hill, 1990.

Polk's Lansing City Directory (Ingham County, Michigan). Detroit: R. L. Polk & Co., various years.

National Register of Historic Places Report. Lansing Downtown Historic District, Ingham County Nomination, 2009.

Pearson, Clifford A., and Thomas Hine. *Modern American Houses: 50 Years of Design in Architectural Record*. New York: Harry N. Abrams, 1996.

Price, Jay M. *Temples for a Modern God: Religious Architecture in Postwar America*. Oxford: Oxford University Press, 2013.

Randl, Chad. *A-Frame*. New York: Princeton Architectural Press, 2004.

Rapson, Ralph. *Ralph Rapson: Sketches and Drawings from around the World*. Afton, MN: Afton Historical Society Press, 2002.

Rapson, Rip, Jane King Hession, and Bruce N. Wright. *Ralph Rapson: Sixty Years of Modern Design*. Afton, MN: Afton Historical Society Press, 1999.

Reiff, Daniel D. *Houses from Books: Treatises, Pattern Books, and Catalogs in American Architecture, 1738–1950: A History and Guide*. University Park, PA: Pennsylvania State University Press, 2000.

Robinson, Sidney K. *The Architecture of Alden B. Dow*. Detroit:

Wayne State University Press, 1983.

Schneider, Robert, and Laurie Summers. *Final Report for a Reconnaissance Level Survey of Historical Architecture Resources in Lansing Center Neighborhoods*. Lansing, MI: City of Lansing, 1986.

Scholz Homes. *The Famed Scholz Design Collection*. Toledo, OH: Scholz Homes, 1966.

Seaton, Sandra. "Betty Price and George Nelson, Spreading the Word about Modern Design." *Modernism* (Fall 2011): 38–45.

Shrenck, Lisa D. *Building a Century of Progress: The Architecture of Chicago's 1933–34 World's Fair*. Minneapolis: University of Minnesota Press, 2007.

Simon, Katherine Ann. *Ranch House Style*. New York: Clarkson Potter/Publishers, 2003.

Stanford, Linda O., and C. K. Dewhurst. *MSU Campus: Buildings, Places, Spaces: Architecture and the Campus Park of Michigan State University*. East Lansing: Michigan State University Press, 2002.

Torgeson, Mark A. *An Architecture of Immanence: Architecture for Worship and Ministry Today*. Grand Rapids, MI: Eerdmans, 2007.

Zaleski, Caroline Rob. *Long Island Modernism: 1930–1980*. New York: W.W. Norton & Co., 2012.

Index

Page numbers in **boldface** refer to black-and-white illustrations in the text; color plates follow.

D

H

I

J

K

L

M

N

R

S

T

U

V

Y

Z